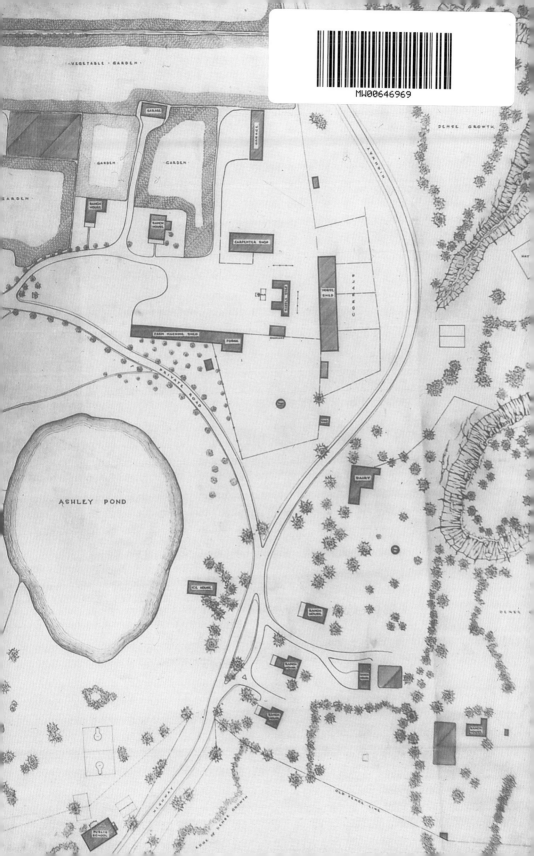

MW00646969

Los Alamos
THE RANCH SCHOOL YEARS
1917–1943

For Jacque whose reading
and guidance on this book
John so greatly appreciated.

Love from Nancy
Christmas, 2003

Los Alamos

THE RANCH SCHOOL YEARS
1917–1943

John D. Wirth
and Linda Harvey Aldrich

University of New Mexico Press | Albuquerque

In memory of:
Albert James Connell "A. J." (1882–1944)
Director of the School

Lawrence Sill Hitchcock "Hitch" (1898–1983)
Headmaster

Cecil W. Wirth "Cec" (1907–1943)
Master and Summer Camp Director

Hio, we sing of the mountains

© 2003 by the University of New Mexico Press
All rights reserved.
First Edition

Library of Congress Cataloging-in-Publication Data

Wirth, John D.
Los Alamos—the Ranch School years, 1917-1943 /
John D. Wirth and Linda Harvey Aldrich.— 1st ed.
p. cm.
Includes bibliographical references and index.
ISBN 0-8263-2883-0 (cloth : alk. paper)
1. Los Alamos Ranch School—History.
I. Aldrich, Linda K. (Linda Kathleen), 1944–
II. Title.
LD7501.L7298W57 2003
371.02'09789'58—dc21
2003007243

Design: Melissa Tandysh

Contents

PART II

FAMILIES AT LOS ALAMOS RANCH

Preface

These chapters tell of a place with well-tended gardens and vistas of surpassing splendor—Shangri-La, as some recalled it, another Rivendell, if you will—of a place, once remote, in rural New Mexico that was, and isn't. In the centuries-long human occupation of the Pajarito Plateau in the Jemez Mountains of northern New Mexico, the Ranch School years from 1917 to 1943 spanned but a generation. But in those short years a vibrant community of a few hundred people flourished on Los Alamos mesa, some thirty-five miles from Santa Fe, some of it via single-track dirt road replete with arroyos and precarious switchbacks. There, families from the original Spanish-American homesteaders and Indians from nearby San Ildefonso and Santa Clara pueblos joined with Anglo families, the school staff, school masters, and students to create a truly unique place. The Ranch School was small, a boarding school for boys twelve to eighteen, by design never numbering more than forty-eight students at a time. But with its college preparatory course and a vigorous outdoor program centering on horses, sports, and community work, Los Alamos Ranch School (LARS) achieved a national reputation. In combination, the magnificent setting on the edge of wilderness and the Valle Grande, the community where everyone knew each other, and the school with its well-to-do clientele created a strong sense of place.

The mystique lingers still, made poignant by the sudden ending when in 1943 the ranch was expropriated for military purposes. After an accelerated course of study, the last LARS class was graduated in January, and soon army bulldozers were ripping up the lawns and flowerbeds from which only a few short months before prize winning gladioli, zinnias, and delphiniums from

Adolfo Montoya's gardens had been entered at the New Mexico State Fair. It happened that hundreds of schools, parks, and private lands were taken for the war effort, so that Los Alamos Ranch was not unique. What is extraordinary to those who lived at the ranch, of course, are the improbable contingencies that led J. Robert Oppenheimer, who had a vacation ranch at Cowles, near the Pecos Wilderness northeast of Santa Fe, and General Leslie Groves, who ran the wartime Manhattan Project, to choose the remote mesa with poor communications and little water, for the industrial site to design and build the atomic bomb.

Are there regrets? Of course, and as Oppenheimer himself remarked to a former Los Alamos master after the war: "I am responsible for ruining a beautiful place."[1] This is not to gainsay the extraordinary national effort and the brilliant team he led; or the major contributions that the Los Alamos Laboratory has made to science and the national defense ever since; or the infusion of jobs and purchasing power into northern New Mexico. With the Cold War over, it is now possible to tell this story, not as prologue to the bomb, but as a stand-alone history of a vibrant community of families, teachers, and students who collectively left a legacy to American secondary education and New Mexico. The events herein described are recent enough to evoke rich recollections based on living memory, but remote enough to be seen objectively, especially now that the passage of time has for the most part healed the hurt of the school's dissolution. Yet the writing of this book has been complicated by the fundamental fact that the Los Alamos under review is the one few people know, whereas the Los Alamos after 1943 is the one that everyone knows at least something about, and *it* changed the world. How these themes intersect in the context of place is discussed in the conclusion. What follows are chapter-essays by historians and participants, all of whom seek to fix and hold that earlier sense of place at "the ranch," as those who lived there called it, while it is still part of living memory.

The book is divided into two sections. The first section explains LARS as an institution—its leadership, faculty, staff, organization, and mission—and where this particular school fits in the history of American boarding schools. Drawing on extensive archival research, interviews, and personal knowledge, we historians locate LARS in the social history of New Mexico in the inter-war years. We touch on such themes as student life, the role of Scouting, the key relationship of the school's director, A. J. Connell, and its headmaster, Lawrence S. Hitchcock, the outdoors program, and the summer camp. We also reflect on the central purpose of the Ranch School, which was to provide a rugged western experience for boys, some of whom had health problems, and to prepare them for college while (above all) turning them into responsible, self-confident young men.

The second section deals with the ranch as a community, focusing especially on the experiences of families and children in their growing-up years. Historian and bibliographer Theresa Strottman writes on the Hispanic homesteaders and families who made the ranch go, a fundamental part of the Los Alamos story that has not been told before. Then Richard Womelsduff, the ranch foreman's son, reflects upon the community from the perspective of his Anglo family working there. This second section concludes with reflections on John's boyhood at the ranch, where his father, Cecil Wirth, was a longtime master, from the faculty family point of view.

In keeping with our emphasis on people and their stories, the book is abundantly illustrated with photographs, many of them published here for the first time, including several portraits in black and white of leading individuals at the ranch. Kodachrome slides of the summer camp by Bill Carson, made when he was only twelve, and others by Charles Ripley, 1938, are the best ever taken of the camp and its fabled pack trips. Also included are images by Laura Gilpin and T. Harmon Parkhurst, the school's official photographers.

In the face of interest in, even fascination with (but little knowledge about) LARS and the ranch itself, we have been eager to sum things up— Linda as a longtime current resident of Los Alamos who has lectured on LARS, and John who was privileged to be a part of the place as it was and now divides his time between Santa Fe and Stanford. Each of us is familiar with the history and unique characteristics of independent boarding schools. In fact, Linda graduated from a small Episcopal school and her husband is a graduate of Williston Academy in Massachusetts, which was Lawrence Hitchcock's school. John has been, in turn, student, teacher, three times parent, and Chair of the Board of the Putney School in Vermont.[2] In the division of labor, Linda drafted the prologue and the first three chapters about LARS; and John the next three, his own memoir, and the conclusion; the end product is a truly collaborative book. Theresa Strottman and Richard Womelsduff contributed chapters as noted on the contents page.

For the enthusiastic and heartfelt support of former students, masters, staff, and families who shared their thoughts, memories, and documents with us we are most grateful.

Several individuals read parts of this manuscript and helped us to make it a better book: Jim Anderson, 1938; Carol Burnes; Bill Carson; Dora B. Harvey; Barbara Hitchcock; Jacqueline Hoefer; Dave Hughes, 1937; Ransom V. Lynch; Rogers Scudder, 1930; Theresa Strottman; Harry Walen; and Timothy E. Wirth. Dr. Sandra Jaramillo, director of the New Mexico State Archives, and her staff assisted our research in many ways, as did the staff at UNM's Southwest Research Center, and Janet Johnson of the New Mexico Medical

History Program and Health Sciences Center Archives. Ashley Pond IV, Mary Jane Aldrich-Moodie, Sharon Snyder (who is writing a biography of Peggy Pond Church), and Bill Erickson also provided valuable assistance.

Our book is published in collaboration with the Los Alamos Historical Society, whose Publications Committee encouraged us. We wish to thank Hedy Dunn and her colleagues at the Los Alamos Historical Society and Museum—who have done so much to document and preserve the histories of Los Alamos—for their always forthcoming research assistance for this book project on the Ranch School years. It was they who staffed the September 1991 Los Alamos Ranch School Reunion, organized by Bob Carter, 1942, and Peter Dechert, 1941. The Society also staffed the Los Alamos Ranch Reunion in September 1997, when Severo Gonzales, Margaret Montoya Caperton, and John Wirth invited all those who had lived and worked at the ranch—Hispanics, Indians, and Anglos—and their families and descendants to reconvene at Fuller Lodge, focal point of the place where the three were children.

John D. Wirth and *Linda Harvey Aldrich*

With John Wirth's untimely death in June 2002, this book stands not only as the tribute he intended to his father, but as a tribute to John, a westerner of great intelligence and vision. His absence is keenly felt. Although the thrust of his recent work was to bring about understanding and cooperation among the three North American nations, this history of LARS was dear to his heart. The sudden severing of his Ranch School roots when he was a boy shaped the man, leading him to a search for understanding and meaning in history. Our manuscript was completed before his death and his voice echoes strongly from the text.

Linda Harvey Aldrich

Fig. Preface 1
Severo Gonzales, Margaret Montoya Caperton,
and John Wirth, 1997. Wirth private collection.

Preface Map, overleaf

Los Alamos Ranch School map, 1937. Office of John Gaw Meem,
architect. Courtesy of Hugh and Kathleen Church.

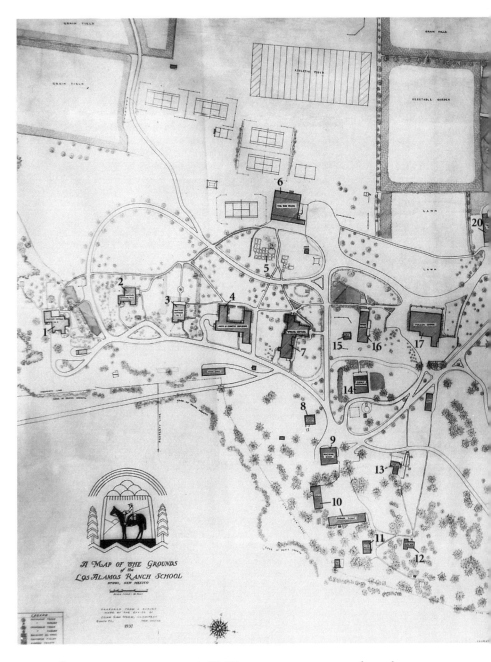

A MAP OF THE GROUNDS
of the
LOS ALAMOS RANCH SCHOOL
OTOWI, NEW MEXICO

Key

1-3. masters' cottages
4. Arts and Crafts Building
5. Indian ruin
6. Big House
7. Spruce Cottage
8. power house
9. machine shop
10. garages
11. club house
12. house boys
13. chef's house
14. chief mechanic's house
15. pack house
16. Guest Cottage

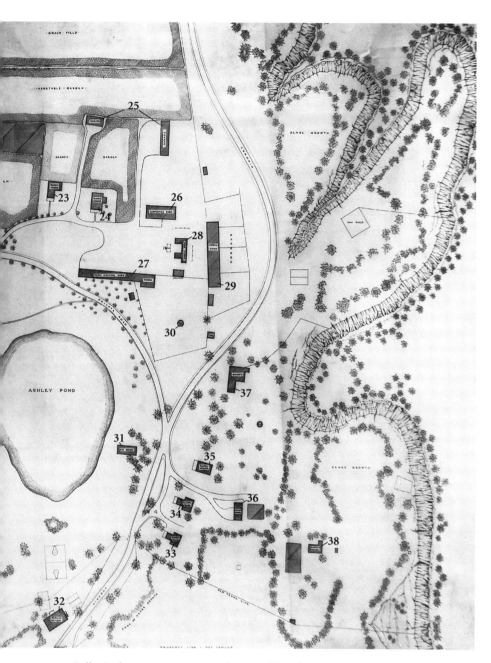

I was deeply influenced by Los Alamos School and think that in many ways it was really unique. It did what it did, honestly and without pretense.

The principles the school got across in everything it did, particularly outside the classroom, were of importance: 1) doing things right, 2) having and maintaining good equipment, 3) impeccable planning and organization. To my mind, that's a lot. What is more, little was said about these three principles, but everyone from the gardener and Ted Mather to Connell himself lived and practiced them 24 hours a day. The message was a powerful one.

Edward T. Hall
Los Alamos Ranch School student and camper

PART I

THE LOS ALAMOS RANCH SCHOOL

Prologue

Pathways to Pajarito

On a late February day in 1918 a small towheaded boy, frail and racked with coughing, arrived in Santa Fe with his mother, his nurse, and his younger brother. They came by train from Kingman, Arizona, where they had been for several months, hoping in vain that the desert climate would improve the boy's fragile health. As they disembarked, they were approached by a tall, slender man in his mid-thirties, dressed in olive drab, wearing puttees, and a high-crowned Stetson hat. His blue eyes were set in a ruddy complexion, and pale thinning hair was barely visible under the large Stetson. The man's narrow face was coldly formal, but a hint of warmth flickered as he greeted them.

The man was Albert James Connell, director of the nine-month-old Los Alamos Ranch School, who had come the thirty miles from the ranch to welcome this new student, Lancellot Inglesby Pelly, and to assure Elizabeth Pelly that her son would be well taken care of at Los Alamos.

At the Santa Fe hotel that night, Lance was restless, recalling other family trips in search of a place where he would not be ill. In his eleven years he had attended school for only a few months. Most of his life had been spent in bed recovering from bronchitis, whooping cough, pneumonia or influenza—one illness after another. Some years he had a tutor, but studying tired him out, and then he would be sick and the tutor would be let go. He desperately wanted to run and play like other boys but, apart from his brothers, his only companions had been adults. Friends had suggested Los Alamos to his parents; they had heard it was designed to help just such boys as Lance.[1]

The "outdoor school," as Los Alamos called itself, had opened the previous

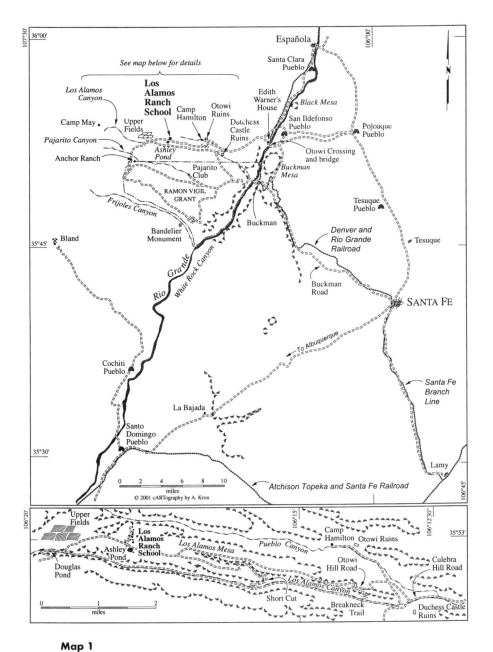

Map 1

Map of the Los Alamos Ranch School and Santa Fe area, 1920s.
Cartography by Andrea Kron.

May with no classrooms or teachers, as envisioned by its founder, Ashley Pond Jr. He intended it to be a place where boys, rather than sitting at desks poring over textbooks, explored the countryside and helped run the ranch, with the area's archaeologists and forest rangers providing occasional informal instruction. In this manner, Pond believed sickly boys would gain health, strength, and self-confidence and in a few short months return to their regular schools. The school was slow in catching on, however, and Lance was one of the first to enroll on a full-time basis.

The Pellys were met the next morning by Director Connell and an older boy, Bill Rose, a member of Connell's Santa Fe Boy Scout troop who planned to enroll at Los Alamos the next fall. In the meantime, as a Scout who knew the ropes, Bill came to the ranch whenever he could to help new boys adjust to western life.[2]

Their drive to the ranch that February took almost four hours over a rough dirt track called the Buckman Road, which led northwest from Santa Fe through steep arroyos and low-growing juniper and piñon trees, a few small brown adobe houses the only habitations. Dark evergreen-clad mountains capped with snow lined the eastern and western horizons, rising a mile above the dusty brown valley floor. It was strange country to Lance, accustomed as he was to the leafy green of Seattle, where his father Bernard was the British consul. Most unnerving was the descent into White Rock Canyon, where black basalt cliffs and boulder-covered slopes towered above the muddy Rio Grande and the railroad tracks running alongside it. They passed through Buckman, no more than a few ramshackle buildings and corrals beside the railroad, and crossed the river on a flimsy wooden span with no guardrails. On the other side, the road switch-backed steeply out of the canyon up what was called the Buckman Hill—a real "bugbear," Connell said when they stopped to let the radiator cool.

On the lower reaches of the Pajarito Plateau above the canyon, the piñon and juniper grew more thickly, interspersed with tall ponderosa pines. Turning north, they passed through broad canyons formed in volcanic tuff, the pale pink cliffs pocked with holes, some tiny, others enlarged by early Indian residents. When Mr. Connell talked about boys climbing cliffs and exploring the caves, the thought intrigued Lance but at the same time made him queasy. He had an unsettling mixture of happy anticipation and fear about this new place to which he was going.[3]

Turning west up Los Alamos Canyon, the road ran along a small icy stream amid pine and fir, with snow deepening where the canyon narrowed. At a small garage and hay shed they parked the truck and climbed into a buckboard wagon, which Bill and Mr. Connell hitched to a horse. A steeply angled trail in a rocky side canyon soon brought them out on the upper level of the plateau.[4] To the west a large barn and scattering of log buildings were visible amid the tall pines, and beyond these a mile or so the Jemez Mountains rose, their tops streaked with snow. To the north cattle grazed in wide fields. East toward Santa Fe they could see fields and low trees and then nothing at all, a vast emptiness and space where the plateau abruptly ended high above the river. Across the valley were the Sangre de Cristo Mountains, seeming almost close enough to touch, a dark blue wall against the eastern sky.

The horse stopped in front of a large two-story building of vertical logs, the main school building. Called the Big House, its broad façade was fronted on the east by a full-length portal where rocking chairs invited travelers to admire the magnificent view. They entered a large room whose softly glowing log walls were hung with patterned rugs and in the center of which stood a great free-standing stone fireplace. Before Lance could look around the room, however, Bill escorted them to the nearby guest cottage.

Like the other ranch buildings, the guest cottage was made of logs, its two small rooms furnished simply with iron bedsteads, rustic wooden furniture, wrought-iron fixtures, and Indian and Hispanic pottery and weavings. A welcoming fire blazed on the hearth, and late winter sun streamed through the windows. Shortly, a houseboy appeared with a tray of tea, milk, and cookies and in melodically accented English invited them to the Big House in an hour for midday dinner. The tense knot inside Lance's chest began to loosen a bit.

After his mother left, Lance moved into the Big House where, like the few other boys, he at first found the nights difficult, unaccustomed as he was to sleeping the year around in cold mountain air on a screened porch. The star-studded darkness seemed immense, and the nighttime silence made the boys uneasy. Nocturnal sounds sent shivers down their backs: the hooting of owls, the high-pitched yipping of coyotes, the eerie cries of mountain lions, and haunting howls of wolves. When the moon was full it washed the land in a ghostly silver light.

By day the high vault of deep azure sky that dominated the land held such clear air that it seemed one could see forever: north to where the mountains of southern Colorado spiked the horizon more than eighty miles away; south to the humped turtle shape of Sandia Mountain bordering Albuquerque; east to the Sangre de Cristos thirty miles away; west to where it seemed one could pick out individual trees on the Jemez ridges behind the ranch. In summer the mountains spawned towering dark thunderheads that announced their presence with loud alarums and blinding flashes. Rain sometimes came in great flooding downpours that filled arroyos with walls of brown water; at other times it sifted out of clouds in long gray streamers that evaporated before they reached the ground. Ashley Pond's daughter Peggy, an accomplished poet, captured well the dramatic views.

> It was a vista that clutched at one's senses . . . the way great music does. There was always movement going on in it—crescendos and diminuendos of wind, fugues of light and shadow, the poise of a bird balancing on invisible columns of air, the unfolding energy of clouds, banners of rain that seemed to be carried through the valley in ritual procession.[5]

Winter's deep powdery snows were followed by skies of intense blue. Still autumn days glowed like amber and painted golden patches on the mountains and along the watercourses. In spring, strong winds scoured the land and filled the air with stinging dust. A more dramatic setting for school life could scarcely be imagined. This expansive world enveloped teenage boys accustomed to horizons enclosed by buildings and smoky gray skies or to expanses of flat green fields and tamer landscapes.

New Mexico was an exotic world for the schoolboys, but they gradually came to know its ancient and historic landscapes. Spanish settlers arriving in

Fig. Prologue 1

Side view of the Big House, early 1918.
Courtesy Los Alamos Historical Museum Archives.

the 1600s had placed their towns and farms along the Rio Grande and its tributaries, but the Jemez Mountains, lower and drier than the Sangres to the east, attracted few settlers. West from the river that runs at the base of the Pajarito Plateau, one passes from graveled canyon reaches of cottonwood and sagebrush to progressively higher and cooler levels and finally onto the Jemez slopes, where the tallest peak, sacred to the Indians, is Chicoma (or Tschicoma), 11,561 feet high.

The microclimates of the plateau and Jemez fostered layers of use and provided habitat for black bear, mountain lion, wolf, deer, coyote, porcupine, badger, and raccoon, whose tracks still threaded the slopes and canyons.[6] Indians from nearby pueblos used the area's resources as they had for centuries, and descendants of Spanish settlers hunted and farmed on the plateau. The nearest town of any size was Española, twenty miles north beside the railroad tracks. On the plateau a dozen or more homesteads were worked by mostly Hispanic families, who grew corn and beans, grazed sheep and cattle, and periodically worked for the Los Alamos Ranch, the Forest Service, or the area mines, patching together a hard living from the land and a variety of seasonal jobs.

New Mexico's climate drew thousands of people who believed in the health-giving qualities of high, dry air, especially for curing the scourge of tuberculosis. Santa Fe had two sanatoriums: St. Vincent's, the oldest in New Mexico, and Sunmount, an attractive facility developed in 1906 by Dr. Frank Mera that drew people from around the country and was a center of cultural life in Santa Fe. Like these health-seekers, Lance and the other boys thrived on the plateau, just as Ashley Pond intended, roaming the mesas and mountain slopes on horseback.

The Santa Fe area was increasingly popular not only with health-seekers but tourists as well, and was enthusiastically promoted by city fathers intent on developing the city's unique blend of Hispanic and Pueblo culture.[7] Visitors sought the romance of the West in New Mexico's ranches and cowboys, its Pueblo Indian villages and the vestiges of their abandoned sites, and in its spectacular mountain and high desert scenery. At least half a dozen resorts and ranches took in guests within a fifty-mile radius of Santa Fe, among them the Pajarito Plateau's Ten Alders Ranch south of the school in Frijoles Canyon.[8] In the 1880s archaeologists had begun exploring the plateau's Indian ruins, called the "Cliff Cities" in tourist brochures, and as word of their findings spread, hardy visitors began to make their way to the area. In 1916 Bandelier National Monument was established on land surrounding ancient ruins in Frijoles Canyon. Later that same year Connell and his Santa Fe Scout troop appeared in a promotional film, part of Park Service Director Stephen

Fig. Prologue 2

Lance Pelly at left in back, Bill Rose next to him,
A. J. Connell at center front, on the Big House porch, 1918.
Courtesy Los Alamos Historical Museum Archives.

Mather's campaign to "See America First."[9] The cameramen returned in the fall to film ruins on the Pajarito.

Railroads vigorously promoted tourism in the Southwest, and families came by train or, increasingly, by automobile and stayed for weeks or months at a time. The success of tourism depended on good roads and easy access. By then the automobile's conquest of American life was well advanced, and New Mexico, along with other states, had a Good Roads Commission that worked closely with local chambers of commerce. In 1916 Congress committed the federal government to paying 50 percent of the cost of certain state highways, an act greeted with much enthusiasm in Santa Fe. In the rural Southwest the lack of roads suitable for automobile travel impeded development of business and tourism as well as improvements in medical care and other social services.[10]

When Lance arrived in 1918, much of northern New Mexico seemed a remote corner of America. Trails and wagon tracks crossed the plateau, some leading into the mountains, where a few guest ranches and hot-springs spas operated periodically, but the best of these tracks were similar to the Buckman

Road, hardly encouraging for travelers. Not surprisingly, the future of Los Alamos Ranch School depended on safer and more convenient access, and three years after Lance arrived the plateau became easier to reach. In 1921, the Culebra Hill road was built from the railroad crossing on the Rio Grande at Otowi to where the old road turned up Los Alamos Canyon, thus eliminating the bad stretch of road up Buckman Hill. To connect with this road, the school built a new section that switch-backed down Otowi Hill on the precipitous south face of Pueblo Canyon. While these new roads still twisted up steep grades and cliffs, causing many parents to be faint-hearted about visiting the school—more than one mother lay on the back seat with eyes tightly shut when transiting these sections—no longer was it necessary to use horse and wagon to reach the school in winter.[11]

For all its isolation, however, the plateau was impacted by events in the larger world. For Pond and Connell, seeking to enroll boys from well-to-do urban families, the times were not auspicious. When unrest in Mexico spilled over the border in early 1916, the New Mexico National Guard was called up and American troops under General Pershing pursued Pancho Villa into Mexico. Easterners especially, knowing little about New Mexico, associated it with danger and violence. Then, in April 1917, the United States entered the Great War, and war fervor swept the nation. Before the conflict's end an influenza pandemic swept the world, killing hundreds of thousands in the United States, over five thousand in New Mexico alone. Given the national turmoil, it is not surprising that at first parents were slow to enroll their sons. The stream of visitors to New Mexico only temporarily slowed, however, and within a few years Los Alamos was fully subscribed.

It was both in spite of its isolation on the Pajarito Plateau and because of it that the Los Alamos Ranch School (LARS) thrived for twenty-five years. Set in beautiful and rugged country far from urban distractions, it was nevertheless a cosmopolitan community with strong ties to the nation's great urban centers. Its roots lay in the world of eastern boarding schools, in Progressive-era concerns about children and health, and in the intersecting paths of its founder, Ashley Pond Jr., and director, Albert J. Connell, on the Pajarito Plateau. Their roles in founding and shaping Los Alamos provide the essential threads from which the school's story is woven.

A School with Nature as a Textbook

Beginnings

Unlike most boarding schools in the East, the Los Alàmos Ranch School did not have a religious foundation nor was there an initial group of wealthy backers and contributors to the school. It was the inspiration of one man, Ashley Pond Jr., acting alone in response to the ill health he experienced in his childhood and young adult years. Albert Connell, as the school's only director, provided dedicated leadership and creative vision in the critical early years and developed the school's program. But the initial vision was Pond's: to combine the restorative powers of outdoor life in the New Mexico mountains with a loosely structured program of experiential learning in the Progressive mold then in vogue among American educators. It was, as an article in a Boston newspaper described it, a "school with Nature as a textbook."[1]

The only surviving son of Ashley and Harriet Pond, Ashley Junior was born in Detroit in 1872, a child of wealth and privilege. His lawyer father was a director of the Michigan Central Railroad and chief midwestern counsel for Cornelius Vanderbilt. Prominent and highly respected, Ashley Sr. was reserved and noncommunicative, with little interest in matters outside the law. The son, by contrast, was gregarious and unfocused, a lover of sports frequently sidelined by illness. Young Ashley spent much time recuperating at the family cabin at the Huron Mountain Club, a private hunting and fishing retreat on the Pine River near Marquette, where prominent Detroit men and their families could relax from the rigors of business. When the boy was well enough he roamed Club lands with friends such as Roy Chapin and Henry Joy. Later, as chief executive officers of automobile companies, these men were Pond's partners in establishing on the Pajarito Plateau a club modeled on the Huron Mountain Club.[2]

At fifteen Ashley was sent to St. Paul's School in New Hampshire, where Headmaster Henry Coit, like many of his colleagues in the galaxy of elite boarding schools, maintained tight control and discipline over his charges, striving to inculcate "personal integrity, honor and justice"— to build men of character. Ashley's years at St. Paul's apparently fostered a lifelong expectation that honor, justice, and integrity would prevail in his dealings with others — a belief that at times made him vulnerable to opportunists and the unscrupulous. Discipline, self-control, and self-denial, essential in the views of Coit and other heads of school to the development of moral character, remained alien to Pond's enthusiastic and impulsive nature.[3]

Ashley was dogged by illness and spent weeks at a time in bed at St Paul's and at home, frustrating for the restless sports-loving teenager. Certainly these illnesses affected his schooling. In 1891 he entered Yale's Sheffield College but, after five years, left the university without a degree, apparently because of his poor health.[4] When the United States declared war on Spain in 1898, he joined Roosevelt's Rough Riders but to his chagrin was given charge of the unit's horses in Tampa and never made it to Cuba. Within a few months he was deathly ill with typhoid fever, his passion for action and adventure once again thwarted by illness.

The defining moment of his life came a short time later when his father sent him to a ranch near the tiny logging town of Catskill in northeastern New Mexico Territory. Here at long last, like his hero Teddy Roosevelt and countless others, he wrested a robust health from the high desert climate and active life of the West, banishing the haunting presence of illness from his life. He fell in love with the open spaces, landscapes, and unrestricted life of New Mexico's mountains and high desert. In 1900 he purchased three small ranches near Watrous, on the plains east of the Sangre de Cristo Mountains, and took up the life of a rancher, making New Mexico home for most of the rest of his life.

In early 1903, at the age of thirty, he married Hazel Hallett, the seventeen-year-old granddaughter of a neighboring rancher, and that December the first of their three children, Margaret (called Peggy), was born. In the meantime Pond had taken in several boys recovering from tuberculosis and, although they were gone by the time Peggy was born, the idea of starting a health school for boys had captured his imagination. Pond began planning a school on one of the Watrous ranches, but just before it was to open in September 1904 a disastrous flood on the Mora River destroyed most of the buildings. The family escaped in their nightclothes, but Ashley's plans were swept away. Within a year the New

Mexico ranches were sold, and the Ponds returned to the Detroit area where Ashley became vice-president of the Auto Commercial Company of Pontiac.[5]

Impractical and lacking any sense of money or how to manage it, Pond was clearly no businessman. Years later his eulogist stated that for Ashley Jr., "Simplicity of mind and habit of thought made difficult . . . any satisfying explanation of the subtleties of business, of politics and of social problems. To his way of thinking everything should be reduced to obvious standards of right and wrong conduct."[6] That Ashley Sr. recognized his son's shortcomings seems evident when, upon the father's death in early 1910, his will stated that Ashley, now almost forty and a married man with three children, was not to receive his full inheritance for five years.[7] Ashley Jr. was champing at the bit in the confines of Detroit, however, and two years after his father's death he was back in New Mexico.

Lured by ads for irrigated farmland and artesian wells, he brought his family to forty acres outside of Roswell, a small farming community on the dry south-central plains of New Mexico, worlds away from sophisticated Detroit society. On his land he first built a cement-floored garage, whose original purpose was not to house his vehicle but rather his family. Hazel tried her best to arrange the family antiques and oriental rugs in this unpromising space, but she was understandably miserable and in 1913 she and the children went to live near her mother and grandfather in Los Angeles. Life with Ashley Pond, an incorrigible dreamer, was never easy. Most of his ventures collapsed from impracticality or unprofitability, but he was forever seeing new possibilities. One appeared on the horizon in the fall of 1913, when he learned that the Ramón Vigil Land Grant on the Pajarito Plateau was for sale.

This eighteenth-century Spanish land grant of approximately thirty thousand acres, located north of present-day Bandelier National Monument and south of the modern town of Los Alamos, had been purchased by midwestern investors in the early 1880s and was overgrazed and heavily timbered by the time Pond became interested in it.[8] The Denver & Rio Grande Railroad (D&RG) was the first to cut the plateau timber, followed by an Oregon lumberman, Harry S. Buckman, who logged the grant around 1900, establishing as a shipping point for his timber the town in White Rock Canyon that bore his name. He was gone by 1903, leaving behind large swaths of tree stumps. Several years later Harold H. Brook, a plateau homesteader, and two partners purchased the grant and formed the Ramon Land and Lumber Company with plans to cut more timber. However, this business soon failed, and the grant was in the hands of a Santa Fe bank when Ashley first heard of it.[9]

In October of 1913 Pond took an option on the Vigil Grant and persuaded his boyhood friends Roy Chapin and Henry Joy, now respectively the heads of the Hudson and Packard Motor companies, along with Detroit bankers Paul and David Gray, to purchase the land with him. They formed the Pajarito Land Corporation, with Pond's portion of the eighty-thousand-dollar purchase price set at eight thousand dollars. Although the sale was not finally complete until mid-1914, Pond leapt into the venture with typical enthusiasm.[10]

Correspondence between the partners indicates they first envisioned it as a place where something like the Huron Mountain Club could be established, a rustic retreat for wealthy men and their families where, away from the cut-throat world of business, they could relax amid nature's restorative powers, hunt mountain lion, and explore the Indian ruins that abounded on the grant. Apparently no business plan was developed and little thought given to financing such a club. Each of the partners appears to have had a slightly different vision of what their enterprise, called the Pajarito Club, would be. Just what Pond had in mind is not clear because he was not clear about it himself. This lack of focus doomed the club.

For the club headquarters Pond chose the remaining buildings of the lumber company in Pajarito Canyon and began planning a clubhouse and small log cabins for the use of his partners and guests. He persuaded Hazel to join him there in late February 1914 and hired architect I. H. Rapp to convert an existing two-story corrugated metal building into the family home and main clubhouse.[11] Rapp was then becoming known around the state for his design of the Territorial capitol building as well as for buildings on the New Mexico Military Institute campus in Roswell. Photos of his remodeling job for the Ponds show flower-filled window boxes, handsome stone fireplaces, polished wood floors, and stuccoed interior walls similar to those Rapp designed for St. Vincent's Sanatorium in Santa Fe.

That spring Joy and Chapin came out to inspect their purchase, which Pond extolled in letters to them, and soon furniture was shipped, an orchard planted, and a handyman and cook hired. The Pond children joined their parents that summer for what seemed an idyllic time with the plateau as their own private playground.[12]

Soon enough, the shaky nature of the enterprise began to emerge, complicated by the fact that Pond's role was never clearly defined. The Detroit men considered him to have some voice but not an equal voice since he had not contributed an equal share of the purchase price. On his part, Pond felt that his opinions were ignored when his friends regularly vetoed his ideas and requests for funds. They, in turn, had no accurate understanding of what was possible on undeveloped land far from urban centers and reached only by primitive roads. Moreover, the timing was poor, with the shadow of war in Europe causing uneasiness among American businessmen. In the three years

Fig. 1.1

Interior of main building, Pajarito Club, 1916. Ashley Pond on
floor at right, Katherine and Harold Brook seated behind him.
Courtesy Los Alamos Historical Museum Archives.

that Pond managed the club, Chapin and Joy came out only two or three times
and the Grays apparently not at all.

As on-site manager, Pond was a source of constant worry to his partners.
In May 1914, still months before the purchase was finalized, Pond requested
authority to purchase two hundred head of cattle, to build barns in which to
store grain, and to build "eighteen miles . . . of good gravel road." For their
part, his wary partners felt they must "hold Ashley down on any expenses."[13]

For the next two and a half years this pattern of frustration and uneasiness
among the five men was repeated time and again. Pond requested additional
money almost weekly and often made purchases without his partners' prior
approval. The Detroit men agreed to install a water system to replace the cum-
bersome hauling of water from the canyon's small stream, but they approved
little else.[14]

In the meantime guests arriving at the club, sent by the Detroit men or
invited by Ashley himself, expected comfortable and attractive accommodations.

Among the visitors were a trustee of Columbia University, an editor of the *Boston Herald,* two Metropolitan Opera singers, writers for the *Saturday Evening Post* and *Collier's Magazine* gathering material for "western stories," artists sketching the Indian ruins, a New York financier and associate of J. P. Morgan, and historian Samuel F. Bemis, a recovering tubercular who spent most of the fall and winter of 1916–1917 at the club. Ashley was an affable host, but he complained that he and Hazel were working themselves to the bone caring for the guests. The idea had been to invite people who would want to invest as members of the club, but no one did. Although Pond had fallen in love with the Pajarito and rhapsodized about it to his partners, others were quite satisfied to spend time there as guests with no financial commitment.

In the summer of 1915 Clara and Templeton Johnson and their young sons Winthrop and Alan, the Ponds' friends from San Diego, spent some weeks at the club.[15] Their visit apparently was the catalyst for Ashley's renewed thoughts about forming a school. Two years earlier, Clara, concerned about the quality of their children's education, had started a Progressive school in San Diego modeled and named after the school her nieces attended in Chicago, the Francis W. Parker School.[16] The California Parker School emphasized health and outdoor physical activity, work with the hands, scientific evaluation, a limited amount of book learning with small-group instruction geared to each individual's needs, and group projects emphasizing cooperation and responsibility to the community—all parts of the Progressive canon.[17] Templeton Johnson had studied architecture at the Paris École des Beaux-Arts, and the innovative building he designed for the school had open-sided classrooms built around an outdoor courtyard. There were lively discussions that summer as the Johnsons and Ponds talked about the San Diego Parker School and its Progressive program. Ashley's dream of a school for sickly boys was rekindled, and two years later many of these progressive themes appeared in the Los Alamos Ranch School program. Eleven years later the Johnsons' son Winthrop graduated from the Los Alamos Ranch School.

In the fall of 1915 Hazel took the children to San Diego, where all three attended the Parker School. Left to his own devices on the plateau, Ashley needed to find someone to help him with the club. He turned to Harold and Katherine Brook, neighbors north of the Ramón Vigil Grant who were struggling to eke a living from their homestead ranch, named Los Alamos by Katherine for the cottonwoods that grew along canyon streams.[18]

Although Harold Brook's timbering venture on the Ramón Vigil Grant had come to grief, on the Los Alamos homestead he put into practice modern farming methods learned while earning a degree from the Illinois College of Agriculture. He was the first resident to bring the twentieth-century cash economy and modern farming machinery to the Pajarito. Burdened by the financial losses of the failed lumber company, he struggled with the difficulties of dry-land farming and ranching in the often rigorous and capricious climate of the plateau. When Pond offered the Brooks positions as general manager and hostess at the club they saw a way to supplement their ranch income.

There had been no mention of a boys' school in Pond's correspondence with his Detroit friends before the summer of 1915, but subsequently references cropped up to running a school on the grant. Pond continued to bear a large portion of the operating costs of the club, while appealing to his partners for more money. Finally, in April of 1916, the Detroit men bought out Pond's fifty shares in the corporation for $5,760, although Pond remained as the on-site manager and the venture continued to unravel.[19] His letters took on a bitter and complaining tone, and he accused his friends of blocking his plans to start a school on the Ramón Vigil. But as was so often the case with Pond, as one venture died he sighted another possibility and charged off, abandoning the one, in this case the Pajarito Club, but with high hopes and enthusiasm for the next.

In June of 1916 Pond entered a partnership with Harold Brook to start a boys' school at the Los Alamos Ranch and in the interim to run a dude ranch there, the Cliff Cities Pack Outfitters. The incorporation papers of September 1916 bear the unmistakable imprint of Pond's impractical nature, stating that the Los Alamos Ranch's purposes would be to "sell milk, deal in fruits, raise stock, operate slaughter houses and stockyards, build sanitariums, maintain dispensaries, hotels and training schools for nurses, to buy and lease lands, maintain a summer resort and park and deal in real estate; to handle mortgages, to prospect for ores, to bore for oil and gas and seek coal; [and last but not least] to establish . . . a school."[20] Pond later explained that in these various activities he hoped there would be found some means of supporting the school. In August of 1916 he sent Roy Chapin a brochure for "Los Alamos Ranch: An Outdoor School for Boys," with an accompanying note on a letterhead that proclaimed "A Sound Mind and a Healthy Body."

That fall his dream of a school appeared to be in danger of dying once again as he and Brook had a falling out. Clearly their very different personalities and backgrounds made working together difficult. Brook was a practical rancher who had spent ten years trying to wrest a living from the plateau. Pond was an impulsive dreamer and now, at forty-five, having come into his full inheritance, he offered to purchase Brook's portion of the ranch. The twenty-thousand-dollar purchase price included the livestock, equipment, and "all of his plans regarding buildings and proposed school."[21] Harold Brook left the plateau in early 1917, with his pregnant wife, Katherine, to become the Doña

Ana County agricultural agent, but his hard struggles with the plateau and an earlier bout with tuberculosis took their toll, and he died eight years later.[22]

Just how Brook and Pond thought they would finance a boys' school is not clear. Brook certainly had no financial resources, although he may have thought that Pond did, given the freedom with which he spent money. Pond told his Detroit partners that he had spent over ten thousand dollars on the club, and he was now assuming the additional burden of the Los Alamos Ranch. In October he purchased a house on Palace Avenue in Santa Fe, and in November he bought a new Cadillac (apparently feeling no loyalty to his friends with the Hudson and Packard Motor companies).[23] But living well is one thing and establishing a school is another: Pond realized that he would need more money as well as someone capable of organizing and bringing the school to life.

Pond found the funds in the person of Philo Carroll Fuller, a family friend from Grand Rapids, Michigan. In October Pond went to Michigan, where he asked Philo Fuller for financial backing. A contemporary of Pond's father, Fuller was a Yale graduate from a distinguished colonial family, a wealthy lumberman, and in 1917 the mayor of Grand Rapids. His wife had died after childbirth many years previously, leaving him with two daughters and a son, Edward, who was partially paralyzed and unable to speak clearly, the result of a bout with polio as a young child. Edward was now twenty-nine years old, and although not mentally impaired, his disabilities were such that participation in business or social life was difficult.[24] When Pond asked Philo for financial assistance, the father saw a possibility for a new life for his son. With his father's money, Edward purchased the ranch mortgage and was given a position with limited responsibility on the school staff.[25]

It was a happy solution for all concerned: Pond had a financial ally who held the mortgage; Philo Fuller was assured his son would have a place of his own and the dignity of valid work; Edward not only had the responsibility of a job, but the companionship of other men and boys in a place where his disabilities were of less consequence than in the usual social settings. On February 16, 1917, it was announced that Edward Fuller had given Ashley Pond a promissory note of $15,500 with the ranch as security.[26] From that time on Edward Fuller made Los Alamos his home.

It is to Pond's credit that he realized his inability to run a school on a day-to-day basis, although it is doubtful he would have wanted to be tied down by that responsibility in any case. The man he chose to direct the school was forest ranger Albert J. Connell, whom he had first met on February 20, 1914, when both were guests at the DeVargas Hotel in Santa Fe. Over the next several years the two became acquainted when Connell was stationed first at the Bland

Ranger cabin on the Pajarito Plateau southwest of the Ramón Vigil Grant and later in the Pecos Forest east of Santa Fe. Connell's reputation in Santa Fe as an exemplary Boy Scout leader undoubtedly recommended him to Pond. Not only was Connell adept and insightful in his work with boys, but he was skilled at organization and, as a consummate detail man, the antithesis of Pond. Connell was to prove decisive in not only the survival of the school, but in its movement away from Pond's loose Progressive approach. His vision, coupled with a dominating and authoritarian personality, colored everything at the Los Alamos Ranch School.

In many ways, however, Albert Connell seemed an unlikely person to head a school. Never having attended college and, by his own confession not "a school man," he had few formal qualifications for the job. A lifelong bachelor, he had spent the previous six years working for the Forest Service, first as a draftsman, then a ranger. Like Ashley Pond, ill health led him to New Mexico. Both men were twenty-eight when they arrived, a decade apart, in what was then the New Mexico Territory, and both fell in love with the outdoor life of the West.

Connell was born on March 17, 1882, into a well-to-do "lace curtain" Irish American family in the Bronx, the next-to-youngest of the five children born to Edward James and Emma McGean Connell. His mother's family had been in the New York City area since the 1840s; his father was born in England and came to the United States with his family about a decade later. Their families were part of the educated Irish American middle class that emerged in New York City after the Civil War. Albert's father was a banker, his mother a school-teacher before her marriage, and both families had deep roots in the Catholic Church. Edward and his brother Hugh were founding members in 1871 of the St. Xavier Union, which later became the Catholic Club of New York City, an organization devoted to encouraging "'virtue and Christian piety among the educated Catholic young men of the city . . . [of a] certain social and financial class.'" Emma Connell's brother, James McGean, was a graduate of St. Xavier College and priest at the oldest Catholic parish in New York City, St. Peter's.[27]

The family home was a large house near Fordham University, in the Bedford Park section of the Bronx, and the children grew up roaming the still rural parts of the city, playing in the woods and sailing boats on Pelham Bay. New York City was rapidly expanding with the extension of the subway system into outlying areas, and the family participated in the cultural life of the metropolis, attending the symphony and opera. All of Albert's siblings attended college, the three older boys St. John's College (later Fordham University), and his younger sister Mary (called May) The Academy of the Sacred Heart (later Manhattanville College for Women), much-favored by affluent Catholics for their daughters. The eldest brother, Edward Jr., went to

Fig. 1.2

Cardinal Gibbon and A. J. Connell's uncle, Msgr. James McGean,
New York City, 1890s. The boy half hidden behind McGean
is Albert Connell. Courtesy of John Curtis.

Cornell Medical College and established a medical practice in New York City. Middle brother William became a highway engineer, and Walter, next in age to Albert, went into banking. May spent several years in the mid-twenties on the fringes of the Paris art colony and always considered herself an artist. Of the five children, only Albert did not attend college, although he may have had some post-secondary school training in draftsmanship. He worked for Louis Comfort Tiffany, probably as a designer. His artistic flair and sense of design were later revealed in the buildings and furnishings of the Ranch School.[28]

In 1899 Walter Connell came to Los Lunas, south of Albuquerque, leaving his New York City banking career when he became ill with what was feared to be tuberculosis but in fact was only severe bronchitis. Having recovered his health, Walter entered the sheep and wool business in New Mexico, Colorado, and Arizona and within a few years married Emma Huning of Los Lunas and formed a partnership with her brother Fred in the Huning-Connell Mercantile Company. In 1909, at age twenty-eight, Albert followed his brother to New Mexico, by which time Walter was a well-established businessman.[29] Albert stayed with Walter and Emma for six months before becoming a surveyor for the Forest Service in the Gila National Forest near Silver City.

One can hardly imagine a world more removed from that of Connell's youth and young adult years in New York City than that of a forest ranger in the Gila National Forest, then wild country. Why did Connell leave New York? He had been quite ill at one time in his youth, and family lore says that he spent the better part of a year living with his father's cousin, a doctor in Connecticut, spending the nights on a screened sleeping porch. It was feared that he had tuberculosis, but it proved to be an intractable case of severe bronchitis. Years later Connell himself said that health brought him to New Mexico, and so it may have been a recurrence of a bronchial infection that sent him West. Fear of the "white plague," as tuberculosis was sometimes called, sent legions of anxious persons, fearing the worst, to the high desert climate of New Mexico.

Connell's choice of such a completely different life invites speculation. Certainly the West offered freedom from eastern ways and family expectations, as well as the opportunity to change life roles, to be his own man. The family's deep involvement in the life and liturgy of the Catholic Church contrasts sharply with his infrequent church attendance in New Mexico. Did he come to New Mexico in part to escape what to him was a stifling family involvement in the church? Or even perhaps, as the only unmarried son in a family devoted to Catholicism, to escape pressure to enter the priesthood? Connell had an Irish genius for hard work and attention to detail that the church often sought in its priests. The Ranch School, which he intimately shaped, was nondenominational, and he told parents that he believed religion should be freely chosen, not forced on anyone.[30]

Never in robust health, why did he choose the demanding life of a forest ranger? The answer may lie in part in Connell's strong streak of Irish romanticism. The West held great appeal in the popular imagination, and the image of the forest ranger had joined that of the cowboy as one of the mythic western characters—riding alone into the mountains, where he confronted danger in its many forms, the self-sufficient western man who brought civilized order into the chaos of the natural world. This role must have appealed to Connell, who fell in love with the mountains of New Mexico and with a ranger's life on the trail.

The Forest Service, established in 1905 with Gifford Pinchot as chief, was charged with enforcing policies and regulations on the public lands. Beyond controlling fires, its responsibilities included stopping grazing and timber trespassing, controlling mining, reforesting logged areas, and protecting wildlife. The remoteness of the public lands made the work a challenge but was also part of what lured men to become rangers. An early recruit described the appeal of life in the infant Forest Service.

> Beyond great valleys stretched range after range of blue mysterious mountains, threaded only by trails, with here and there a ranch or cabin or little mining camp. There were few roads, few telephones, few intrusions of the outside world. To cover their far-flung districts the Old Timers jogged along on their horses 15, 20, or even 30 miles a day, trailing their pack horses or sharing the proverbial hospitality of ranches [or] cow camps.[31]

The romance of such a life drew a wide variety of men, few with any formal training in forestry or related fields, a motley and colorful collection of "ex-cowboys, stockmen, lumberjacks, timber cruisers, or miners—frequently lacking in formal education but rich in the lore of the West—a general sprinkling of engineers, artists, pharmacists, health seekers, ministers, and outright adventurers . . . attracted . . . by the lure of a . . . new and worthwhile adventure."[32]

Not only was the work itself an adventure, but in it a man was judged solely by his ability, not his background, education, or family connections. The work of a forest ranger fit perfectly into Progressive concepts of the social democrat: hands-on, active outdoor work in public service, with success measured only by one's ability to do the job. For Connell, it seems to have been the perfect match. Furthermore, the land and the rough characters that inhabited it appealed to his romantic nature and made a deep impression on him, and for years his stories of "timber cruising in the Mogollon" and other adventures on the trail enthralled the Los Alamos boys.[33]

Southern New Mexico, where Connell entered the Forest Service, was only a few decades removed from skirmishes with Apaches, and the forest lands were rugged and dangerous, fraught with violence. Grazing was the primary use of southwestern forests at that time, and when the railroads made large-scale ranching profitable, cattlemen competed with sheep barons, leading to range wars throughout the region. Prospectors driven by dreams of gold or silver pushed through the mountains, with mines and connecting webs of rail lines following. Homesteaders fenced off claims and water sources, and periodic drought added to concerns over depletion of the West's resources.

In addition to competing legal uses of the public forest lands, there were the inevitable illegal ones, among them cattle rustling and bootlegging in remote canyons. The Datil National Forest, north of the Gila Forest, was described as a place "where frontier conditions obtained and the residents of one of the principal creeks were said . . . to be as hard a lot as existed on any Forest in the Nation."[34] Caught between violently competing interests, no ranger would consider being without a gun; it was a natural and necessary part of life. Danger lay not only in the violence sometimes aimed at rangers trying to enforce Forest Service policies and regulations, but also in the nature of the work itself—made tragically clear the year Connell entered the Service, when firestorms in the northwestern United States killed seventy-eight firefighters in less than forty-eight hours. Whatever the threat—wild animals, fire, violent men, or extreme weather—the ranger was often alone on horseback, miles from any settlement, and had to be resourceful and self-reliant.[35]

Reinforcing a ranger's authority was his uniform, a broad-brimmed Stetson hat, heavy olive worsted made up into cavalry-style riding breeches, and puttee leggings. This practical gear was not yet required in 1910, but a Forest Service memo urged rangers to adopt it because of its "'economy, efficiency, and . . . adapt[ation] to the needs of the work.'"[36] These principles—economy, efficiency, and adaptation to the particular needs of a situation—were wholeheartedly embraced by Connell and became central in all that he did.

The Gila National Forest, north and west of the mining center of Silver City, was being mapped by the Service at that time as part of a larger project to produce accurate topographic maps of the southwestern Forest Reserves. On October 8, 1912, the *Silver City Independent* reported that Connell, a member of the survey team that had been mapping the Gila for the previous three years, would be staying in Silver City over the winter to draft the maps. That December Connell took the civil service exam required to become a ranger and was assigned as assistant ranger on the Mimbres section of the forest, later becoming the ranger in charge there.[37] Having spent at least two years mapping the Gila Forest, Connell was as familiar as anyone with the lay of the land.

Connell—who from his Forest Service days was known to friends as A. J., not Albert—was in Silver City regularly and enjoyed the opportunity to socialize and participate in a popular local theater group as his work allowed. The town was a bustling regional center, a sometimes uneasy combination of fading "wild West" and urban sophistication brought by the faculty of the New Mexico Normal School and health-seekers from around the country, who came to the Cottage Sanatorium on the outskirts of town or to nearby Fort Bayard, a sanatorium for military personnel.

Life in the industrial United States was widely seen as taxing to the strength and health of men and women alike, and there was a general concern and preoccupation with health. By 1912 the nationwide search for health had become a major industry in New Mexico and a primary source of income for Silver City, which advertised the benefits of its year-round mild climate. Tuberculosis was the great scourge of the age, rightly and greatly feared; it was rampant, highly contagious, and most often afflicted the young. Treatment was uncertain and often futile, with victims enduring slow lingering deaths. Only in the 1930s did effective medication become available to control the dreaded disease. Before that time, "climate therapy"—a combination of three popular treatments—was favored by many doctors. Its elements were found in abundance in New Mexico: high altitude, dry air, and sunshine.

New Mexico became one of the leading centers in the United States for tuberculosis treatment; by 1922 there were forty-eight sanatoria in the state, the oldest established in 1865. It has been estimated that 20 percent of the state's population was associated in one way or another with the disease. As in other towns where sanatoria were located, hardly a week went by without publication of at least seven or eight obituaries in Silver City newspapers. The steadiest income in town appears to have been that of the coffin maker.

Vestiges of earlier lawless days remained, giving Silver City life a raw edge. It was the central shipping point of the area for gold and silver bullion—in July of 1912 a single shipment of fifty thousand dollars in gold and silver was sent to the U.S. Mint. The presence of such wealth drew crime, and bank robberies and holdups of trains and horse-drawn mail coaches were not uncommon. The mines and railroads attracted a colorful and polyglot population, including immigrants with exotic-seeming customs and bands of gypsies who camped outside town.[38] His years in Silver City provided Connell with rich material for riveting campfire stories.

Connell's involvement in boys' work began when he became scoutmaster for one of the Silver City Boy Scout troops in February 1913. There had been a troop in Silver City since at least 1911, shortly after the formal founding of the Boy Scouts in the United States, and when its scoutmaster moved away the large troop of sixty-five boys was split into two groups, with Connell leading the older boys.[39] Although no records survive of Silver City troops in Connell's day, newspapers reported regularly on the Scouts' activities, which centered on camping and hiking. In Boy Scouting, embraced with great enthusiasm across the nation in the teens and twenties, Connell found the perfect vehicle for his life, and on it he later based the Los Alamos Ranch School program.

The Boy Scouts, along with other boy-centered groups of the time, among them Ernest Seton's Woodcraft Indians and Daniel Beard's Sons of Daniel Boone, issued from a widespread concern in the early twentieth century known as the "boy problem." Parents saw their sons as weak and passive and feared for their moral and physical health. These fears stemmed from changes in American culture in the decades around 1900, when industry and cities grew rapidly. It was a cynical and tumultuous age, roiled by labor strife, immigration influx, and large-scale social movements urging the enfranchisement of women, the prohibition of alcohol, and health and safety regulations for food, water, and the workplace.

For generations parents had considered cities dangerous and unhealthy for their children, metaphors for evil and decadence leading to premature sexual encounters and the ruin of susceptible youth. Yet the economic realities of an industrial society dictated that increasing numbers of Americans, both native-born and recent immigrants, live in or near cities, where life was stressful and impersonal. Alien customs grew where large numbers of immigrants settled, crime and gangsters flourished, and flappers and speakeasies flaunted convention.

Beyond this, boys lived sedentary lives and appeared to have far too much free time in which to test dangerous waters. At home and under the supervision of women more than in agrarian times, with as yet few after-school athletic or activity programs to occupy their time, parents worried that boys were becoming effeminate. Ernest Seton echoed the fears of many when he stated that "the rise of industry and growth of spectator sports had turned boys into 'flat-chested cigarette smokers with shaky nerves and doubtful vitality.'"[40]

Congruent with the vision of urban life as dangerous was a changing attitude toward the nation's wild places—the mountains, forests, and expanses of land empty of human settlement—located primarily in the West. Increasingly, the remaining wild places of the country were seen as finite treasures rather than as something to be conquered, as refuges from civilization's stresses and inspiration for the soul. Wilderness could revive the fainting spirit, Washington Irving had said, and "produce . . . manliness, simplicity, and self-dependence."[41]

Yet the West provided the resources that fueled the cities and industry as well as opportunity to grow rich for those willing to work hard. Both views saw the West as a testing ground for body and spirit. Perhaps more than anyone of the age, Teddy Roosevelt, the Chief Boy Scout, embodied the sometimes contradictory views of Americans toward their western lands.

The highly organized Scouting organization, as well as the YMCA and other groups, sought to address parental fears by steering boys away from undirected passivity and to what its founder, Lord Baden-Powell, termed "recreation in which the boy would be insensibly led to educate himself." Its organized and detailed program of awards and ranks kept boys busy, thereby assuaging parents' fears that "a boy's first idle moment is the starting point of whatever trouble he makes in the world."[42] Influenced by the work of psychologist G. Stanley Hall, Scouting sought to control what was called the "gang instinct" by placing boy leaders, under the control of adult scoutmasters, over their companions. The emphasis placed on "scientific" efficiency, self-reliance, and outdoor activities, as well as the program's tone of moral earnestness, held great appeal for parents.[43]

The heavy emphasis on outdoor activities promoted nostalgia for a mythical, innocent West. The uniform, as the 1930 *Scout Handbook* explained, was designed to symbolize "the ideals and outdoor activities [that] help the Scout identify himself with the great traditions of our outdoorsmen—the pioneer, explorer, scout, and cowboy." Some of these outdoorsmen were known to Connell at firsthand, and the discipline and survival skills that Scouting taught were vital for life as a forest ranger.

Furthermore, the Scouting movement proclaimed good health to be one of the greatest benefits of its program.

> The outdoor life in particular has brought to the Scout health values lost to increasing thousands, because of our having so much of the indoor and sedentary in modern life. Fresh air with vigorous action which calls for deep breathing; the sunshine with its germicidal action, its cell stimulation, its ultra-violet light storing Vitamin D; the rest to the eyes in the outdoor 'greens' and distances and 'large-seeing'; the vigorous appetites; the restful sleep after such action. President Theodore Roosevelt, as a young man, built his puny body into a strong one by this very formula.[44]

Connell knew what it was to be plagued by illness and appreciated the rejuvenating powers of an outdoor life. All aspects of the Boy Scout program resonated deeply with him, and its themes—striving for the ideal, doing things right, being useful and an unselfish contributor to the group—later echoed throughout life at Los Alamos. Henceforth Connell was deeply committed to Scouting.

Connell's tenure as a scoutmaster in Silver City ended in February 1914, when he was transferred to Santa Fe. He made the three-hundred-mile trip alone on horseback, a dramatic gesture entirely typical of Connell. He arrived on February 24, the very day Ashley Pond was in Santa Fe to meet Hazel's train, preparing to show her the Pajarito Plateau and the site he had chosen for the club headquarters. Both spent that night at the DeVargas Hotel, quite likely their first encounter.

Connell's first assignment in northern New Mexico was in the Jemez Forest Reserve at Bland, a small gold-mining town at the southern end of the Pajarito Plateau. The Bland Ranger Station was among the closest stations to the Ramón Vigil Grant, and undoubtedly Connell and Pond became acquainted as Connell patrolled the forest near the grant. He served at Bland at least through the summer of 1914, but by May of 1916 (and probably earlier) he was transferred to the Panchuelo Ranger Station in the Pecos Mountains east of Santa Fe.[45]

By then, Connell was again a scoutmaster, this time for the Santa Fe troop. The Scouts spent several weeks in June camped at the Panchuelo Station near the headwaters of the Pecos River and throughout the summer worked under Connell's direction building a cabin for the troop's use in Santa Fe Canyon. That fall, as war in Europe aroused national passions, the weekly Scout meetings featured military-style drills along with first aid lectures by Dr. James Rolls. Connell made sure the boys were "useful" in serving the community, committing them to keeping Santa Fe's roads cleared of rocks and as escorts for arriving teachers at the State Teacher's Convention.

Connell's leadership skills and knowledge of how to engage boys in "men's work," rather than mere busywork, were manifested in the cabin the Scouts built in the summer and fall of 1916, and Santa Feans were clearly impressed.

> Under the supervision of the Scoutmaster, A. J. Connell, they cut down the trees making the crosscut saws and axes hum; they learned all the terms the lumberman uses; they snaked the logs down to the site; they put them up; they roofed and floored and furnished the cabin.
>
> Now they need to build on a big sleeping porch so that when the whole troop goes out to the cabin in winter they won't have to stack the boys up like cross ties to find dormitory room. They [also] need more equipment for the summer camp on the Pecos.[46]

To complete their cabin and acquire more equipment, the troop planned a fundraising project early in 1917, "a novel and delightful entertainment entitled

'The Boy Scouts' Camp on the Pecos.' Saturday the boys went out with Mr. Connell and brought in from the forest a whole truckload of properties, logs and trees and scenery."[47] The show, which played to packed houses on the afternoon and evening of February 17, included musical numbers, live burros, and amusing skits poking fun at local notables. Connell was in his element: he loved theater and had a flair for the dramatic.

Four days later, on February 21, it was announced that Connell was leaving the Forest Service to become director of Ashley Pond's new school. Exactly when Pond approached Connell about coming to the Ranch School is not known, but most likely it was after his trip to Michigan the previous fall when he lined up the Fullers' financial support. Finding a suitable director was the next thing needed to get the school off the ground.

In the early spring of 1917 Connell moved up to Los Alamos, joining Pond, Ed Fuller, and Samuel F. Bemis, whom Pond had enlisted as the school's first secretary-treasurer, in preparing to open the school on May 17 with hoped-for students. The Big House was complete, and furniture, linens, and supplies were ordered. A commissary was established, stocking school and recreational supplies, a selection of Indian and Hispanic craft items, and practical necessities of life for local homestead families. The library at Santa Fe's Palace of the Governors furnished the school with a list of recommended books "of such character as to appeal especially to boys gathered around the campfire or out on a hike."[48] Saddlery and a string of horses were acquired; kitchen and housekeeping staff hired; ranch hands were shown how to involve city boys in the less dangerous and demanding chores. All utilized Connell's organizational skills to the fullest.

Realizing that a feminine presence was needed to reassure boys and parents, Pond hired Aileen Baehrens, a vivacious young widow recently returned from life abroad with her son Deric, to be the hostess and matron that first summer.[49] Her artistic talents and Connell's sense of design combined to attractively furnish and decorate the Big House with the work of local artisans. Operating the ranch was a full-time job in itself, and Connell turned to a former Forest Service associate, C. V. Shearer, as the first ranch foreman.

Although Pond's second brochure, printed in the spring of 1917, stated the school would open in mid-May, it is doubtful any boys were there at that time. In early June the Santa Fe Scout troop held a two-week camp in Los Alamos Canyon, and it was from this root that the well-regarded Los Alamos summer camp grew and blossomed.

The first student—John Kauffman, from Des Moines, Iowa—arrived sometime in the summer or fall of 1917. Records of the first boys at Los Alamos are incomplete, but by the time Lance Pelly arrived, in early 1918, George Wetherill, from Virginia, was at the school. Kauffman had left to finish his schooling else-where, although he returned in 1919 for a postgraduate year.[50] Connell's nephew, Louis, spent the summer of 1917 at Los Alamos, and Bill Rose, along with several others of the Santa Fe Scout troop, came up for weekends and holidays, providing companionship for any boys at the ranch. Most likely the school operated in part as a dude ranch during much of 1917. Several boys arrived in the spring after Lance came, and by the fall of 1918 eight or nine boys, including Bill Rose and Ashley Pond III, were enrolled at Los Alamos.

With fewer than six boys present for much of 1917–1918 there was little need for any formal program. The scheduled activities, many of which utilized skills Connell acquired as a forest ranger, were listed as horsemanship, exploration and mapmaking, animals and their habits, forestry and silviculture, mountain climbing, livestock and grazing, modern ranching, archaeological explorations, marksmanship, rope-throwing, nature study, and saddle and pack trips. Every activity's educational value was viewed through a Progressive lens; even rope-throwing was said to be "of value as a recreative exercise for the quickening of hand and eye." Based on his own experience, Pond believed that boys would gain stamina under the watchful eye of a director who saw to it that they ate and slept well, were outside most of the time, and occupied with useful activities that strengthened their bodies, fired their interest, and engaged their minds.

John Dewey and other Progressive educators sought to draw schools away from study of abstract concepts to practical, hands-on learning that occurred out of doors, preferably in a group setting. This reflected perceptions about health and the moral benefits of outdoor living coupled with beliefs about the value of experiential learning. The Progressive underpinnings of Los Alamos were vividly illustrated in the 1916 brochure, which pictured a boy seated at his desk before an open book, daydreaming of being far away, happily seated astride a horse. The brochure stated unequivocally that Los Alamos was to be a health school. Academic concerns were referenced only in one brief statement to the effect that a boy wishing to keep up with his class work might "arrange for tutoring in subjects of the preparatory curriculum." Initially, it was thought that boys would be at the school for only a few months, a year at most. The school's regimen would teach healthful habits to temper their young bodies into strong, resilient vehicles for a useful life. Having become physically fit, boys could complete their schoolwork elsewhere.

Los Alamos was kindred to what were called "fresh air schools," where classes were mostly held out of doors. One such school had operated in Santa Fe for a few years just prior to the founding of LARS, with classes held in the owner's orchard.[51] At the San Diego Parker School, Templeton Johnson had designed the school buildings around open-sided classrooms, with many of the activities conducted in a central open courtyard. A variation of fresh-air schools was the western ranch school, where horses provided the common focus for outdoor life, as was the case at Los Alamos. The earliest of these ranch schools was the Thacher School in Ojai, California, founded in 1889. By the late 1930s there were at least seventeen others across the pedagogical spectrum, all with horses as an integral part of school life.[52]

Pond's new school was slow to attract students, in part because of the war and the great flu epidemic of 1918, but also because the program was very loosely structured. Samuel Flagg Bemis, the school's secretary-treasurer, by his own account helped Pond develop the program and wrote one of the first school brochures. A Harvard Ph.D. and recovering tubercular, Bemis had been at Sunmount Sanitorium before spending the fall and winter of 1916–1917 at the Pajarito Club with Pond. Initially quite enthusiastic about the school, he chose to disregard warnings given him in Santa Fe about the sometimes mercurial nature of Pond's friendships. While assisting Pond with the school, Bemis worked on a diplomatic history that was to earn him the Pulitzer Prize, and his devotion to that work evidently irritated Pond, who felt Bemis was slacking in his commitment to the school. As the relationship between the two men soured, Connell began exerting more control over what he soon considered his school, and Bemis was fired. He moved on to Colorado College and later became a prominent professor of diplomatic history at Yale.[53]

Pond himself was not involved in the daily operations of the school after the summer of 1917; by that October he was in San Diego hoping to be trained as an army aviator. He continued to spend time in San Diego, but Santa Fe was home for the rest of his life. He was a member of the Ranch School Board of Directors until his death in 1933, but having sold the mortgage to Ed Fuller, he had no financial interest in Los Alamos. He had, after all, fulfilled his dream of providing a place where boys could build strong and healthy bodies.[54]

Pond's influence can be seen in the unfailing commitment of LARS to boys with health problems, in its Progressive foundation, and in the population from which the school recruited students. Without Pond's contacts among the wealthy and prominent, Los Alamos would not have had entrée to the world of elite boarding schools, nor could it have succeeded in recruiting students from families able to pay the school's fees. A list of the school's endorsers in the 1917 brochure reflected Pond's broad contacts in business, industrial, and academic circles, and included Gifford Pinchot, the former Forest Service director. Pond's hero, Theodore Roosevelt (whose sons attended an Arizona ranch school), turned down the request for an endorsement because he had no personal knowledge of the school.[55] Prominent Santa Feans on the list included archaeologist Edgar Hewitt, businessman Frank Springer, and physician James Rolls; Levi Hughes, a Santa Fe banker, was on the Board of Directors.

The hub of school life was the Big House, built by Pond during the fall and winter of 1916–1917. Its design of vertical ponderosa pine logs dominated the campus and its layout encapsulated the health goals and Progressive ideas of Los Alamos. The architect is unknown, although Clara and Templeton Johnson surely had an influence on its design. Other influences may have been I. H. Rapp and archaeologist Jesse Nusbaum, both of whom had been with Pond at the Pajarito Club and might have been persuaded to draw plans for the Big House. The portal on the east face (soon enclosed to provide more classroom space) evoked the posts and corbels of the Spanish-style portal designed by Nusbaum for the Palace of the Governors in Santa Fe. Nusbaum had worked with both Rapp and Johnson at the San Diego Panama-California Exposition in 1915 and had the building skills to design and create such a sophisticated log building.[56] Rapp, for his part, had earlier worked with Pond on the Pajarito Club buildings, and the architectural firm of Rapp and Rapp had just finished building Sunmount Sanitorium with its many sleeping porches. Another likely candidate for architect of the Big House is Allen Pond, Ashley's cousin, whose

Fig. 1.3

Architect's drawing of the Big House, 1916,
in 1917 LARS brochure. Fermor Spencer Church Collection.
Courtesy New Mexico State Records Center and Archives.

Chicago firm of Pond and Pond designed buildings at Purdue and the University of Michigan as well as Hull House and other Chicago settlement-house buildings. Allen Pond was listed as an endorser of the school, and he may have contributed the design from his firm as a favor to Ashley. Whoever the architect, the Big House, the largest log building in New Mexico at the time, was a fitting symbol of the program Pond envisioned for his outdoor school.

The main room of the Big House centered on a great hearth built of local volcanic tuff that, campfire-like, was open on all four sides. Four thick ponderosa timbers set on stone pillars defined the corners. The chimney breast was stepped like a ziggurat, recalling the nearby mountains. Around this hearth the community of boys gathered each evening while a master read to them. At one end of the room were the dining area and study tables, and at the other, shelves of books (which served as the school library), games, and a Victrola. At the foot of the stairs was a locked gun rack for rifles and shotguns. Around this central communal space were classrooms, offices for Connell and the faculty that soon were a part of LARS life, and the infirmary. Between the summers of 1918 and 1919 the portal was enclosed to provide more classroom space and an area for ping-pong and pool tables, and on the third floor, originally an attic, dormer windows and rooms were added.

Students' rooms were on the second and third floors. Each boy and his roommate had an inside room where they dressed, studied, and kept their belongings, and although not luxurious, the rooms were hardly the bare cubicles of some eastern boarding schools. The boys and the single masters (who lived in small apartments in the building) slept on the two-story screened porch located on the west side, where heavy canvas shades could be pulled down to keep winter snow from blowing onto the beds. The canvas shades and piles of blankets were concessions to comfort in a regime intended to toughen up boys. In contrast to some of the era's more Spartan boarding schools, Los Alamos from the start had indoor plumbing, hot showers (the Groton School in Massachusetts had only cold showers), and electric lights. Eventually the school provided a separate dormitory, Spruce Cottage, for the older boys, but for more than a decade all boys lived together in the Big House, and it remained the main school building where students lived and attended classes.

Pond's impractical and unfinished ventures led some to dismiss him as ineffectual, a good-hearted remittance man, yet he accomplished no small feat in founding a school on the isolated Pajarito Plateau and erecting there a distinctive building that embodied his ideals.

By early 1918 Ashley Pond was gone from Los Alamos and no longer directly involved in the school's operations. Edward Fuller was neither interested in nor capable of shaping a school. The way was clear for Connell as director to create his own vision. At the request of Mrs. Pelly, he instituted some academic class work in the spring of 1918 and by that fall had hired a Yale graduate as the first schoolmaster. In October he registered the students as Boy Scout Troop 22.[57] Pond's loose Progressive model was replaced within a year or two with a more structured regime, although Progressive elements were retained. Connell shaped a unique program intended to develop health and moral character in boys through a disciplined regimen and a robust outdoor life centered around horses and Boy Scouting.

"Los Alamos Ranch: An Outdoor School for Boys"
from the Spring 1917 brochure written by S. F. Bemis

The principal aim of the school is to take advantage of the unexampled natural features of the best part of the great Southwest in a way to build up the constitution of boys from eastern cities by an active but well-guided outdoor life. The climate of Los Alamos is peculiarly favorable to this; its altitude is especially conducive to strengthening the circulatory and respiratory organs; the clean, pure ozone that drifts down from the peaks of the Rocky Mountains is the greatest natural revivifier to be found anywhere on the continent.

[The] regimen is calculated to produce complete health and a strong and resilient constitution that will carry the boy through the more arduous and demanding years of later education, and enable him to enter upon his professional or business career without the exhaustion that so frequently follows the pressing scholastic and social requirements of modern university life.

The strain and competition inseparable from modern city life and the conditions under which boys, as well as their parents, are often forced to spend the greater part of their lives, tend to wear down the health of a young man before his constitution has been fully developed. It is hoped that the time spent at the Los Alamos Ranch: (1) in natural development of the body by such exercises as horseback riding, mountain climbing and other recreation in this truly wonderful country; (2) attracting the boys' attention to the mind-quickening activities of outdoor life, such as marksmanship, exploration, mapmaking, the study of the habits of wild animals, the floral and mineralogical features of the land, will on the whole produce that perfect health that is the aim of the school, and that elevation of spirit which is essential to future success. A good digestion, a bounding pulse, and high spirits are true elements of happiness that no external advantages can out-balance.

The Los Alamos School aims to take those boys whose parents find them suffering with no constitutional malady; but nevertheless aenemic, under-developed, or under weight, nervous, restless and generally under par . . . to end their ceaseless ailments and pull them back from the brink of chronic bodily disorder.

The strong will and untiring activity which are the products of abundant animal vigor will go far beyond compensating for a trifling postponement of further education.

Everything for a Reason

The Los Alamos Program

"At Los Alamos, everything is done for a reason," Connell proclaimed in word and deed. This philosophy was a hallmark of the Los Alamos Ranch School evidenced in all aspects of life, from horseback riding and choice of equipment to the varied and nutritious meals. With meticulous attention to detail, Connell carefully organized school life into a highly rational and ordered existence reflecting his beliefs and personality. His aims were boys' healthy physical growth and character development, goals fully in the mainstream of Progressive-era concerns. Using skills acquired and refined in the Forest Service and Boy Scouting, he organized the school around outdoor activities within the framework of a Boy Scout troop. In his view the school, the ranch, and the community that grew up around them existed to support the overarching goals of developing robust health and moral character in boys. The academic program was of secondary importance to him.

The only area of Ranch School life where Connell did not exert direct control was the academic program, which seemed almost incidental in 1918 but later assumed equal importance with the rest of the program. Otherwise, Connell was "the boss" of community and school life, the dynamic center around which Los Alamos revolved. As director, he was clearly in the mold of the traditional New England headmasters. A description by a 1928 student at the Kent School in Connecticut of the relationship between his headmaster and students applies equally well to the relationship at LARS between Director Connell and his students.

It was a one-man school from start to finish, run by a peculiar but inspired man, one in which every boy had a personal relationship with that man. The relationship may not have been a good one. It may have been based on fear and avoidance—as mine was—but there was nothing phony or institutionalized or plastic about it. It was real.[1]

Organization

Ranch Setting

From the first incorporation of Los Alamos Ranch by Pond and Brook, the purpose of the ranch was to support the school. When Ashley Pond took over Harold Brook's ranch, it was a substantial operation of approximately 730 acres and soon thereafter was fully capable of supporting a small community. Initially the school's only mechanical transportation was a Dodge truck, but there was a tractor, threshing machine, hay baler, silo filler, and a wide assortment of other machines and tools. By 1921 the livestock included—in addition to the two-hundred-head herd of range cattle—work horses, dairy cows, bulls, hogs, hens, turkeys, ducks, geese, and rabbits. Only three school buildings existed in 1921—the Big House, a masters' cottage, and the infirmary/guest house—but there was housing for the cooks, houseboys, laborers, ranch foreman, and poultry man. A large barn, water tower, silo, smokehouse, sheds, corrals, and a commissary completed the physical plant. Overseeing the operations of this sizeable ranch and the fledgling school was a strenuous challenge, as Connell was to discover.

The ranch was vital to the survival of the isolated school, particularly in the early years when its distance from any other settlement made it necessary to have an on-site support structure. Connell was proud of the fact that Los Alamos produced nearly all its own food, allowing him to assure parents that their sons were provided the very best of tables. There was an extensive vegetable garden, and fresh fruit was supplied by workers' families in the Española Valley. Once the school was firmly established, the ranch typically employed about one hundred people, who with the school faculty, staff, and their families comprised the Los Alamos community, while the student body ranged from only nine in the early years to a maximum of forty-eight students.[2]

Los Alamos was a significant and stable economic resource in job-poor northern New Mexico. In addition to those who looked after the livestock and gardens, the Ranch School employed a night watchman, electrician, plumber, auto mechanic, and general laborers. As buildings were added, carpenters and stonemasons were employed. Some were seasonal, part time, or off-site employees such as Edith Warner, who lived at the Otowi railroad crossing on the Rio Grande and ran a tearoom there. She was paid thirty-five dollars a month by LARS to act as the school's baggage agent for the mail and supplies that came on the daily run of the D&RG.[3]

It was a small and intimate school family in which students came to know the masters and the school staff and their families, as well as some of the ranch hands, particularly those who worked at the interface of ranch and school. The school's houseboys and waiters were about the same age as the oldest students, but there was little interaction between students and local boys. The houseboys' duties included stoking the buildings' big wood-burning furnaces early in the morning, taking breakfast to Connell in his rooms, turning down his bed at night and setting out his books, and assisting with general chores and cleaning. Waiters, dressed in colorful costumes that varied over the years, tended the dining tables where students ate family style with faculty and school staff.

For many boys, the mentoring they received from one or another of the older ranch staffers was an important part of their Los Alamos educational experience. The horse wrangler, Ted Mather, was a colorful character who must have seemed straight out of a western movie, but he was the genuine article. He had a swaggering "tough hombre" look, complete with slouch hat, pistol, and large black mustache fortified with lamp-black. His dramatic appearance and extensive knowledge of horses made a lasting impression. To boys who helped him with the horses, Mather occasionally showed the scar where an arrow pierced his upper leg in a skirmish with Apaches when he was a boy in Arizona. Another who provided a sympathetic ear and counsel for some was Benceslado (Bences) Gonzales, who helped run the Trading Post and was the much-admired cook during the summer camps. He was also a crack shot and knowledgeable fisherman who taught boys how to catch the native trout that abounded in the mountain streams. For other boys, the ranch electrician and mechanic, Floyd Womelsduff, was a fount of information about electrical equipment.

Floyd was one of a trio of brothers, part of an extended family that worked for many years at Los Alamos. His brother Jim was the ranch foreman, brother Frank the public elementary school teacher, and Jim's father-in-law, Fred Crangle, the dairyman. The family of an earlier Los Alamos foreman, Ben White, homesteaded on the plateau, and Ben's brother George was the school dairyman. In the mid-thirties Edna Rousseau, wife of the business manager, became the elementary school teacher, assisted by Amador Gonzales, brother of Bences. Connell often hired multiple members of a family, thereby benefiting from the labor of most who lived at Los Alamos as well as creating family loyalty to the school. Most plateau homesteaders had at least one family member employed by the school at one time or another. The homestead community scattered across the central Pajarito Plateau was in some measure a "company town," with Otowi as its postal address.

Further development of the physical plant was essential to the school's long-term survival. Completion of the new sections of road west of the Rio Grande in the early twenties made travel to and from Los Alamos easier and more convenient. A Nash automobile was purchased in 1922, the first in a series of sedans used for conducting routine school business in Santa Fe and Española as well as for trips of small groups of boys around northern New Mexico. A new power generator and water system installed in the early twenties provided improved and more reliable utilities.

The Big House continued to dominate the landscape until 1928. Throughout the twenties a number of smaller buildings were added, their style prefigured by that of the Big House, which bespoke the school's image as a combination of the best of West and East. These log buildings linked the school to the rural frontier and the ideal of rugged manhood as well as to the inspirational quality of the mountains and forests. They were not crude, haphazard log structures but carefully designed homes, attractive and comfortable, blending into their setting at the base of the Jemez Mountains. Many apparently were designed by Connell himself and reflected his artistic bent and training as a draftsman. Cultivated lawns and flowerbeds were planted in the thirties, relieving the raw frontier look of the first years and creating a sense of rural sophistication, joining the school to the cultural world of the East Coast and to comparable private school settings there.

Initially Connell had an apartment in the Big House, but in 1924 he moved into a small cottage with two apartments, one for himself, the other for a master. Several buildings were added that year: a house for the school mechanic, a bunkhouse, icehouse, and a new one-room log elementary school for children of the employees. A public elementary school, attended by the children of ranch workers and homestead families, and later by masters' children as well, had been held in various small cabins for some years, but this was the first purpose-built school.

The school's single masters usually lived in small apartments in the Big House; as married men arrived, small cottages were built for them. Over the years faculty and staff moved from house to house as personnel changed and families grew. Most of the early cottages were built of logs, but Connell designed a stone and stucco house for his sister May, who lived at Los Alamos for brief periods of time. By 1936 there was a row of neat stone or log buildings, most of them faculty homes, ranged in a line west of the Big House. In the middle of this row was the handsome Arts and Crafts Building, given by a generous parent, housing classrooms, science lab, woodworking (where only hand tools were used), and paint shops. Near the south end of the row stood the earliest cabin, originally called the Pyramid for its unusual peaked roof, by 1935 expanded and remodeled into a residence for the oldest boys and called Spruce Cottage. Last in the line was another early log building, now with a stone addition, variously used as a guest house or infirmary.

South of the row of cottages was the other main school building, erected in 1928 and named Fuller Lodge in memory of Edward Fuller. It was financed largely through the sale of bonds to parents and friends. The dramatic central room of the three-story Lodge served as the school's dining hall and social center; other rooms were for club meetings, the infirmary, and living quarters for the nurse, masters, and Connell. Construction of Fuller Lodge marked the beginning of a lasting partnership between the Ranch School and one of New Mexico's most influential architects, John Gaw Meem, whose office designed most of the Los Alamos buildings added after 1927.

Fire was a continuing problem, affecting not only the physical plant but the program as well. In 1923 an untended wood stove started a fire in the Commissary, destroying that building and all the school records. Only a shift in the wind saved the Big House from a similar fate. The Commissary served the plateau's scattered community and offered, in addition to the required school supplies and uniforms, canned goods, rope and wire, and a variety of basic items. Essential to both school and the larger community, it was rebuilt immediately after the fire and renamed the Trading Post. As part of their obligation to the community, students pitched in to help with rebuilding by peeling the logs. A small hand-drawn fire engine was purchased at that time, but it was not always able to avert disaster. In the bitterly cold winter of 1930–31 the water pipes froze and water had to be hauled from the Rio Grande. When fire broke out in the cabin where Connell and the headmaster had apartments, there was little anyone could do but watch grimly as flames consumed the building.[4] Fires also destroyed the school powerhouse and a cabin where the houseboys lived, seriously injuring two of them.

The most spectacular fire, vividly etched into boys' memories, was in November 1935, when the ranch's large dairy barn burned in the middle of the night. All the livestock was saved, but there was great loss of equipment in addition to the structure itself. At that time Connell dropped the school's dairy operations and began buying milk in Santa Fe. It had been increasingly evident that maintaining a dairy was not cost-effective, particularly during the Depression, and the greatly improved roads made purchase of commodities in Santa Fe an obvious choice. As fire-destroyed buildings were rebuilt, stone was used increasingly, likely with an eye to fire safety.

Recreation facilities grew apace with the school. Most obvious was the addition of a pond, irresistibly dubbed Ashley Pond by William Mills, an early faculty member "known for his large size, good humor, and fondness for bad puns."[5] The pond was created in a shallow depression, heretofore known as the Duck Pond, by overflow from the new water system built in early 1923. It became the site for swimming, canoeing, ice hockey, and skating parties. Tons of ice were cut from it in especially cold winters to be stored in a nearby icehouse; in warm winters ice was shipped in on the D&RG. Another notable early addition was a toboggan slide adjacent to the Big House, built by the boys and masters in 1919–1920, where many learned to ski. Over the years tennis courts, a basketball court, baseball diamond, polo ground, boxing ring, rifle range, and trapshooting pit were added, most often built by the boys and masters working together.

Two facilities that significantly impacted school life were gifts from parents.

Fig. 2.1

Toboggan slide built by students and masters in 1919–1920.
Courtesy of Carolina Waring Stewart.

In 1922–1923 a log cabin, the gift of Chicago's George and Edith May, was built on leased Forest Service land high on the eastern slopes of the Jemez Mountains west of the school. Known as Camp May, this alpine cabin became an important part of the outdoor life enjoyed by the boys, providing a base camp for weekend expeditions into the mountains and for skiing and hunting trips for the oldest boys. Another generous parent, the father of Sam Hamilton, gave funds in 1926 to acquire and fix up a small cabin east of the school in Pueblo Canyon. Located near the Otowi Indian ruins then part of Bandelier National Monument, the cabin had previously been used by an entrepreneur, a Mr. Coomer, as a base for tours of the plateau's Indian ruins. Camp Hamilton, like Camp May, was used by the school under a Forest Service special-use permit and was particularly important in introducing new boys to Los Alamos life. It was accessible by road so boys could be driven there before they became proficient horseback riders. Usually one of the first trips made after arriving at the school was to Camp Hamilton, where the boys clambered around the ruins and cliffs, exploring the canyon and its small intermittent stream. At a lower altitude than the school itself, Camp Hamilton allowed boys a first taste of the wonders of the plateau and of sleeping in the rough.

The special-use permits under which the school operated Camps May and Hamilton effectively enlarged the grounds without entailing any purchase. The school grounds did grow in size, however, with a gift of land from Connell himself. In 1931 he gave the school forty acres west of Los Alamos for the sum of one dollar. Known as the upper fields, this land previously had been leased from the Forest Service, but Connell traded land he owned elsewhere in the state for the tract.[6] Eventually the school owned almost 780 acres and it had use of the surrounding thousands of acres of national forest and park lands. The school also used nearby private lands, particularly the Ramón Vigil Grant and the Baca Location Grant in the central Jemez, both of which were owned for a time by northern New Mexico businessman Frank Bond, a partner of Walter Connell's in the Bond-Connell Wool Company.[7]

By the mid-thirties the Los Alamos campus was complete and reflected the settled status of the school within the northern New Mexico community as well as its growing national reputation. The only recognizable remnant from Brook's homestead and the school's earliest days (other than the Big House) was a small cabin used as storage for the pack outfits; today its vine-covered chimney is all that remains.[8]

Finances

The cost of attending Los Alamos Ranch School was never within the reach of most families. A brochure in the early twenties unabashedly stated, "Our

Fig. 2.2

Camp May. Photo by T. Harmon Parkhurst. Meem Collection, no. 23845. Courtesy New Mexico State Records Center and Archives.

Fig. 2.3

Camp Hamilton. Photo by T. Harmon Parkhurst. Wirth private collection.

school is necessarily limited to boys whose parents are able and willing to pay for the best."[9] Fees at Los Alamos were comparable to those at other western ranch schools of the day, where annual tuitions in the years around 1920 ranged from eleven hundred dollars to eighteen hundred dollars.[10] Moreover, Pond's extensive contacts provided a pool of well-to-do families who could afford these amounts.

The first LARS brochure, printed in the summer of 1916, gave the cost of attending Los Alamos as $150 per month, which included "board and lodging, medical attendance, use of horse and saddle—everything . . . except personal laundry." This reflected Pond's initial vision of Los Alamos as a place where boys were accepted year-round but were at the school only for as long as it took to build up their health and strength. In 1918–1919 the cost dropped to one hundred dollars per month, with students now *expected* to stay year round. Parents who wanted their sons at the school for only the months of the standard academic year had to make special arrangements with Connell. Most of the eight or nine boys present that year did indeed stay over the summer months, with additional boys recruited for the summer and charged $125 for each month. It soon became obvious that most parents whose sons were at LARS during the academic year wanted them home for the summer, and eventually those who attended the summer camp were by and large a different group of boys from those who attended the school.

Like other western ranch schools that lacked the financial advantages of proximity to municipal services, Los Alamos was among the more expensive boarding schools in the country. Isolated on the Pajarito Plateau, the school had to bear basic infrastructure costs along with the expense of maintaining a working ranch and a stable of horses for boys and staff, as well as a pack outfit. By the fall of 1920 the cost of the academic year at LARS had increased to eighteen hundred dollars, and camp fees for that summer were four hundred dollars. The following year school fees were raised to two thousand dollars per year, where they remained until the late 1920s. For most of the years after 1928 the fee was twenty-four hundred dollars annually, although during the worst of the Depression it was temporarily lowered. Operating costs were always high, but financial management was neither Connell's interest nor strength, and he feared that cost-cutting might damage the school's carefully cultivated reputation for a program of high quality. It was not until the last decade of the school's life that serious attention was paid to controlling costs.

A corollary to the high cost of operation was the low salary paid to the faculty. Like many other schools, Los Alamos took advantage of young men starting their careers by paying near the bottom of the wage scale. Because the faculty lived in school-owned housing and ate in the dining hall, in many years the school prorated the value of this room and board and recorded it as part of each person's salary.[11] Connell's justification for the salaries was that the physical setting and lifestyle made up for the low pay. For some, however, there was a nagging suspicion that they were being taken advantage of, and in some cases this feeling became strong enough to drive faculty from Los Alamos to eastern schools where the pay was better. So long as the expenses remained high, however, there simply were not the funds available to pay higher salaries. "We worked for the love of it," recalled Art Chase, one of the core faculty. And so long as the size of the school remained small, the cost-benefit ratio meant that the cost of operating school and ranch remained high. Without an endowment fund, Los Alamos continued to pay for facilities and equipment in part from its operating budget, although most often parents and the bank provided the funds for capital improvements.

Families who sent sons to Los Alamos were mostly from the business and professional classes, with substantial financial resources, but Los Alamos never developed a clientele of the truly wealthy. The Evans School in Arizona attracted a galaxy of largely New England scions of wealth—Saltonstall, Roosevelt, Vanderbilt, DuPont, and Pulitzer being some of the names connected with that school.[12] For families of some LARS students the fees plus additional costs of travel to and from New Mexico and for the required uniform and gear were a difficult burden. Parents frequently complained about the costs, particularly for what seemed to them like nonessential extras, and this was the primary reason cited by parents for not returning their sons to Los Alamos.

To one parent who complained about his son's six-hundred-dollar bill for the year at the Trading Post (several hundred dollars more than the average boy's yearly bill), Connell gave a detailed analysis, explaining that the required leather coat, helmet, boots, and Stetson hat should last for two years, and the bedroll, blankets, quilt, and sweater for three years. In part, he said, the bill was greater than average because the boy bought, with parental permission, English riding boots and a .22 rifle, but much of it could be "attributed to the carelessness of the boy in losing, destroying, or otherwise disposing of equipment which it is absolutely necessary for him to have. . . . Small articles which are constantly lost such as Scout knives, Scout whistles and match safes are articles which we consider necessary for the boy's protection in the mountains should they through any accident become separated from the party or lost." Connell was touchy about parental charges of needless expenditures and defended his policies while keeping an eye on what boys bought at the Trading Post. He felt that parents were often negligent in allowing their sons unlimited freedom to charge on their accounts.

Connell was committed whenever possible to providing financial assistance to families who could not afford Los Alamos. In his role as boss at Los Alamos, Connell felt a responsibility and fatherly interest in sons of his employees and enrolled several of them at reduced cost. Among these were Ashley Pond III, who graduated in 1925, and Andrew White, son of dairyman George White, who attended LARS from 1923 to 1927. After the mid-twenties, two formal scholarships were awarded in some years, the Edward Fuller and Fay Curtis scholarships, and Boy Scouts were regularly given financial assistance for the camp. During the Depression years, Connell lowered the fees for many, with reductions ranging from two hundred dollars to thirteen hundred dollars per year. In the late thirties approximately one-fifth or more of the students received some financial aid, which the school could ill afford at the time. If Connell really wanted a boy at the school whose family could not afford it, and if school finances allowed (or even sometimes when finances did not), Connell offered the family a reduction in fees with no formal scholarship designation.

Parents played a significant role in helping Los Alamos financially and with acquisition of equipment and facilities, over the years providing funds for everything from pianos to tennis courts to scholarships to buildings. The LARS physical plant always tended to be somewhat Spartan, albeit of top quality, with minimum classroom and laboratory equipment. Even though parents stepped in to fill some of the gaps, the school's perennially tight budgets allowed for little beyond the basics. Students were generally unaware of this, however, and felt no lack in the amenities of Ranch School life.

Daily Routine

On first arriving at Los Alamos each boy was weighed and measured, then under the watchful guidance of Bences Gonzales or another staff member, outfitted with a uniform and other required gear from the Trading Post. He was assigned to a Scout patrol and given a room in the Big House, a roommate, and an official school name. Because every person was considered a unique individual, no two boys at the school at the same time were to be called by the same first name. For instance, if two boys named "John" were enrolled, the boy senior in arrival at Los Alamos kept his name and the later arrival was given a nickname such as "Juan" or "Jack." Likewise, a second "Jim" might become "Jaime" or even some seemingly unrelated nickname. Connell's insistence on the use of his chosen names was meant to emphasize everyone's individuality and circumvented use of nicknames that might be derogatory in nature.

Daily life was regimented to a degree, as at most boarding schools, and although minor variations occurred over the years, the basic pattern continued for the life of the school. Boys rose at 6:30, drank a glass of water, pulled

Fig. 2.4

Early morning calisthenics, 1919. From left, Tony Taylor, Whitney Ashbridge, Connie Wetherill, Robert Bates, Lance Pelly, Ashley Pond III, Sam Martin, Herman Haskell; Bill Rose leading. Courtesy Los Alamos Historical Museum Archives.

on their shorts, and lined up outside in all weather for fifteen minutes of exercises led by one of the masters or an older boy. Unless it was snowing or extremely cold, they were expected to be shirtless for exercises; in moderate weather Connell sometimes expected the boys to exercise in the buff. He wanted to toughen them up, and so they were encouraged to go shirtless as much as possible when out of doors.[13]

Following a hearty breakfast and room inspection, classes began at 7:45 and continued until 12:55, with a mid-morning break for milk and cookies. At 1:00 the main meal of the day was served, and after a short rest period the afternoon was spent in recreation. In keeping with Pond's founding vision—and the Progressive belief in hands-on activities—in the first two years the afternoon activities consisted of "the work of the various departments of the ranch, horseback rides and hikes in the mountains . . . when the boys [are] instructed . . . by actual contact, in forestry, botany, mineralogy, geology, orthnology [*sic*], wood craft, topographical mapping, and surveying. It is our aim to fill every minute of the boys' time with some profitable work made as interesting as play."[14] Just how and under whose guidance these early activities were carried out is unclear, but initially the program was likely very informal and sporadic in nature.

These instructed activities and the ranch work, called Industrial Training, were discontinued after two or three years. In their place were Boy Scout activities and what was later termed Community Work [CW]—regular weekly hours when students assisted with any number of jobs necessary to keeping the school functioning well. This included building trails, maintaining the gardens, grounds and facilities, and working with the horses or in the library or office. There was never a lack of jobs, and boys with particular skills were assigned where they would be of most use. One course credit was awarded for this work, which was evaluated for "effort and achievement" as well as attitude.

At least two afternoons each week boys rode with their Scout patrol and a master. Sports and Scouting activities filled the other afternoons. Supper was at 6:00, like all the meals served family style with a master or staff person at each table, and was followed by a half hour when all gathered around the Big House fireplace to listen to a master read aloud—perhaps a Tarzan story or a tale by Ernest Seton or Jack London. Given that the entire student body for most years was no more than forty boys, these evening gatherings emphasized the school's family role. Evening study time was instituted in the twenties, presided over by a master or an older boy, with attendance required for those not doing well academically. The youngest boys were in bed by 8:15, the oldest ones by 9:00.

Once a week everyone was weighed and measured by the nurse, with Connell always present, and these figures provided parents a detailed record of their sons' physical growth. The measurements correlating weight, height, and rate of growth were based on something called the Taylor Standards, one of the era's "scientific" approaches to health. On Saturdays the patrols rode all day—perhaps to Camp May or some of the plateau's canyons and Indian ruins, or to the Rio Grande to swim or ford the river and climb Black Mesa, or perhaps to ride into Española. Only the length of the ride limited their options. On many Saturdays after 1920 each boy cooked his lunch over his own fire, which was evaluated as part of his CW grade.

Sundays were less regimented, the only scheduled activity being the weekly evening meeting of the student body as a Scout troop and in some years an evening nondenominational service. Once a required weekly letter home was written, there was time for reading and games. In the first years boys were intrigued by "the latest thing in toy engineering," the Erector Set; when Monopoly came out in the mid-thirties, the boys went crazy over it. Speakers, musical performances, holiday parties, athletic events, and area trips regularly broke the routine. In the thirties invitations to tea, supper, or perhaps a game of bridge at faculty homes were welcome diversions, especially to the homes of popular faculty like Tommy Waring, whose wife Anita was the beautiful sister of early student Bill Rose. She was an accomplished artist who designed sets and costumes for school theatrical productions and gave dancing lessons and advice to those smitten by girls from Santa Fe's Brownmoor School for Girls. Every year Brownmoor and LARS put on formal dances for one another and collaborated in hosting cultural events. And Los Alamos always celebrated St. Patrick's Day in style, fittingly enough the birthday of Irish-American Mr. Connell. As Rogers Scudder, 1930, and a former master, put it, "There was never any monotony at Los Alamos."

The Mission

Health

At the core of the Ranch School's mission was a concern for health. For both Ashley Pond and A. J. Connell, their experiences as sickly children were a powerful motivating force in creating the school. Connell said that he had "worked with boys for years . . . the outcome of volunteer work prompted by love of youngsters and a great desire to help them physically as no one knew how to help boys when I was one."[15] School literature stated that it accepted "sickly boys" who were "below par."

Poor overall physical fitness was a real concern of the era, not merely anxious hand-wringing of overprotective parents. The 1917 Selective Service Act that drafted men for service in World War I revealed to the country the generally poor condition of most young men, and this finding gave impetus to the movement to bring physical-fitness training to public schools. There were a multitude of conditions that could afflict a boy, among them infantile paralysis (there were over ten thousand cases in the United States in 1916), rheumatic fever, infections such as mononucleosis, poor nutrition, a lack of sunlight in polluted city atmospheres, and the presence of harmful concentrations of minerals such as lead. Lifestyles without any outdoor exercise led to weakened bodily systems. Of course parents themselves—especially mothers, it was thought—may have contributed to boys' problems by overprotecting them, responding to every sniffle by keeping them inside and in bed. And there were certainly boys who used illness as an attention-getting device with parents who neglected them. Above all, however, it is important to remember that the Los Alamos Ranch School existed before the age of antibiotics, before modern pharmaceuticals and diagnostic tools, and before widespread public health measures governing waste disposal, pollution of air and land, and the safety of food and water.

The Ranch School was adamant in refusing to take boys who had tuberculosis. Several students were known to have had the disease before enrolling at Los Alamos, but they were accepted only after their doctors certified they no longer had an active form of tuberculosis. The most prevalent disease among the Ranch School students was asthma, and a small but consistent percentage of each year's students suffered from it. Like tuberculosis, it was greatly feared, in part because its attacks are often unpredictable and can bring sudden death. Victims have a terrifying feeling that they are suffocating. As one of Theodore Roosevelt's biographers described it, living with asthma is like

"living with a time bomb." The attacks are a shattering, numbing experience—always, no matter how many times it has happened before. Parents become intensely wary of anything that might bring on an attack. They grow increasingly protective, often engulfing in their good intentions. And if, as the years go by, the child shows no improvement, they begin feeling desperate and depleted. Some mothers "just about go crazy" with worry.[16]

While the nature of asthma is not completely understood even today, in the 1920s it was known that the emotions, dust or animals, foods, or climatic conditions could trigger an attack. Like tuberculosis, the recommended treatment for asthma at that time included "fresh air day and night; a simple nutritious diet. . . . [and a] dry climate."[17] Life at the Ranch School fit this prescription, and some boys had been so severely affected by the disease that their doctors urged sending them to Los Alamos without even a day's delay.

Spring and fall pollen counts in Los Alamos are often quite high, and students were constantly around horses with their accompanying dander and stirred-up dust, and so it seems an illogical place to send an asthmatic. Yet a number of students, perhaps even most who were asthma sufferers, had no further difficulties after a few months at the school and were never again troubled by asthma. Some reasons for this seem apparent: the atmosphere at Los Alamos was far less polluted than in the cities from which the students came, and the daily regimen enforced very healthy habits. Student recovery also may be explained in part by considering the emotional triggers for attacks. Connell's word was law, and he had complete faith that boys would recover from asthma—or almost any other illness—under his care. He flatly stated to parents that their sons would have no further problems with asthma at Los Alamos, and often there *were* no further attacks after a boy settled into school life. Connell apparently read extensively to stay current with ideas regarding health and disease and thus may have been aware of a theory that held that sustained exercise was beneficial to the lungs, which the outdoor life at Los Alamos promoted.[18]

Most likely it was a combination of factors that helped create Connell's success: the healthy lifestyle at Los Alamos, the relative lack of airborne particles in the unpolluted atmosphere of the Pajarito Plateau, Connell's intolerance of illness and his certain belief in the efficaciousness of his "cure," and the simple fact that as boys responded to a healthier lifestyle and as they matured, their immune-system responses to irritants changed. Whatever the reasons, Los Alamos achieved a deservedly wide reputation for success in creating healthy adolescent boys.[19]

A central element of the healthy regime at Los Alamos was the extreme importance of fresh air, widely considered to be of utmost importance to health. Belief in the salutary qualities of fresh air was a core principle of the era's "fresh air" or "outdoor schools" and western ranch schools. Many homes at that time had sleeping porches for health reasons as well as for summer comfort before the days of air-conditioning. Ranch School boys slept on the screened sleeping porches of the Big House year round and were urged to spend as much time as possible outdoors, in all but the coldest months without shirts outside of the classroom and mealtimes.[20]

Connell was a devotee of ritual "sun baths" in the first few weeks of school and camp, whereby boys turned this way and that at preordained intervals, exposing their pale city skin to the bronzing and supposedly health-giving effects of the southwestern sun. (Those who in later years battled skin cancer may eventually have rued this aspect of Los Alamos life.) Some recall being encouraged to ride horses and participate in outdoor activities in the nude while on the school grounds. While not a problem in the school's secluded location or in remote mountain valleys, this could cause concern when the boys returned home. One father in the 1930s complained to Connell about his son, who was quite healthy, but "our only difficulty with him now is that it is hard to make him keep on any clothes; he has hardly had anything on beyond his shorts excepting for social occasions."

Not only did Los Alamos boys breathe fresh air every day, but it was the thin air at seventy-two hundred feet, important because living at a high altitude was believed to build strong lungs. Thus any outdoor activity was considered more beneficial when it occurred at the Ranch School—an aspect of school life that Connell was quick to point out to parents of prospective students. Just as boys needed time in which to gradually expose their skin to the sun, so too they needed a period of time to adjust to the elevation of Los Alamos. No strenuous activities were scheduled for the first weeks of school, and boys were watched closely to make sure they did not overexert themselves.

Los Alamos boys rarely minded spending time outside wearing few clothes, but there was a steady chorus of complaint about a third element that made up Connell's health regime—carefully balanced and nutritious meals. Like many of that time, Connell placed great confidence in the "curative qualities of a proper diet," part of the growing celebration of science that emerged in the late nineteenth century.[21] School meals, whether in dining hall or mountain camp, were always "scientifically planned," Connell said, with a balance of essential elements—protein, carbohydrate, fat, minerals, and vitamins (where research was just beginning to provide much new information). There was some justification for Connell's obsession with diet. Digestive problems were a major public-health concern, so much so that one medical dictionary devoted five pages to the problem of constipation and provided lengthy lists of recommended foods and even a recipe for bran muffins. These lists are striking in their emphasis on a variety of whole grains, fresh vegetables, and fruit, and in their caution against too much meat or dairy products—exactly the diet Connell insisted upon.[22]

Connell's "eccentric tyranny" in regard to food was famous among all associated with the school.[23] When one parent wrote asking if his son could be excused from eating *atolé,* a traditional New Mexican blue-cornmeal gruel that many boys disliked, Connell replied that he would not change any of "my regulations in regard to diet. This is one of the strictest rules in School and Camp. Our boys are never permitted to refuse any of the food provided. . . . When a scientifically planned balanced meal is arranged, it is only balanced as long as all of it is used." The logic was unassailable, and Connell maintained that if he allowed one exception he would be "obliged to allow other boys to refuse the various things they might not like." He explained to the father that as much as he wanted his son to return the following year, the boy would be accepted only if he agreed to eat everything served to him. Even masters were expected to eat everything, much to the shock and dismay of several faced with such perennially unpopular items as liver. Connell made it clear they would be dismissed immediately—although none ever were—if they did not eat every food offered.[24] In keeping with this policy, no one was allowed to receive food—candy or otherwise—sent by family, nor were boys allowed to bring purchased food back to the school. At Los Alamos there was no choice but to tolerate Connell's eccentricities in regard to diet, whether atolé or bread made with lima bean flour or any other healthy food that Connell felt was good for boys.[25]

The elements Connell promoted as the core Los Alamos health program—an abundance of fresh air, exercise that promoted deep breathing, a healthy diet, sunshine, and high altitude—were medical treatments in vogue for a variety of ailments. Today no one would argue the benefits of such a lifestyle, particularly in the developmental stage of adolescence, but it would be viewed primarily as *preventive* rather than *therapeutic*. What made LARS unique among health schools was Connell's rigid insistence on adhering to a healthy regime *no matter what*. Most schools planned balanced meals, but rarely included such a wide variety of foods, nor enforced their consumption so rigidly. Some emphasized the benefits of fresh air, but it was rare for boys to spend not only half of every day outside but also to sleep virtually outside in a mountain climate year round. Likewise, calisthenics were rarely insisted upon outside in rain, snow, and sun as they were at Los Alamos. Given the character of Los Alamos student life, it is no wonder the school acquired a reputation as an eminently successful health school. Connell was very careful, especially in the school's first decade, to nurture that reputation.

Connell planned his recruiting trips as much as possible to coincide with medical conventions, seeking out doctors who specialized in diseases of childhood and adolescence, explaining to them the school's routines and seeking their endorsement of its program. He was, he said, the doctor's ally in seeking the best for boys. He visited asthma and ear-nose-throat specialists around the country, some of them nationally recognized authorities such as Dr. Oscar Schloss of New York City, an authority on pediatric diseases.[26] Connell's efforts paid off and a number of boys arrived at Los Alamos as the result of his careful cultivation of doctors (including several who came at the urging of Dr. Schloss). As in so many things, it was Connell's untiring and meticulous efforts to promote the school that helped make it a success.

From the beginning, the school was sought by parents anxious about their sons' health. Lance Pelly came because his parents had heard that it helped sickly boys, and concern for health was apparently the reason Antonio and Thomas Taylor came to the first LARS summer camp in 1918. The Taylors' mother was a devotee of Dr. John Kellogg and a regular visitor to his sanitarium in Battle Creek, Michigan. Kellogg and Connell shared much the same approach to health, considered eccentric at the time, and some of their practices, such as sunbaths and drinking copious amounts of water, remained a part of students' adult lives.[27] In 1941 almost half of the parents whose sons enrolled for the first time that year mentioned health as a reason for selecting LARS. By that time, however, the school's reputation was based on far more than health-building. As one applicant stated: "Its splendid reputation of the right spirit of sound and balanced education, physical development and true comradeship and to be amongst . . . boys of good character" were all reasons for choosing Los Alamos.

In fact, most boys at LARS were neither ill nor even particularly prone to illness. Less than one-quarter of the boys who attended the Los Alamos Ranch School suffered from any chronic or out-of-the-ordinary illness. Most came for reasons other than health but of course benefited greatly from the life there.

Character

More important to Connell than a boy's health was his character, a special concern of Progressive educators. Much of the Los Alamos program reflected John Dewey's philosophy—mastery of manual skills and tools that educated the "whole" person, learning related to everyday life, and active participation in interesting activities and in the community. "Moral character" was seen in "shared social relationships, the disposition to determine one's conduct and attitudes with reference to the welfare of the group."[28] Connell's evaluation of each boy's character looked at his behavior within the greater Los Alamos Ranch School community. While each boy was seen as a distinct individual, he had to fit himself to the community's needs.

Boys participated formally in the Los Alamos community in their required weekly hours of Community Work [CW]: in 1918, one hour five afternoons a week, in 1928 changed to three hours on Monday afternoons. This formal commitment of time to the welfare of the community, a common theme at schools such as Millbrook in New York and Putney in Vermont, made up only part of each boy's CW evaluation, however.[29] As the catalogs stated, CW was the boys' "effort and achievement in all non-academic activities, and general deportment." It was in the quality of one's relationships with others that character was most clearly revealed.

Hazing of fellow students was not tolerated in any degree. Selfishness, meanness to others, disrespect for women, lying, deviousness, "crabbing" or complaining, and lack of cooperation were behaviors Connell abhorred. In typically blunt fashion, he wrote one set of parents that their son was "very much spoiled, always wants to be made an exception to every rule, has no idea of obedience or his duty towards others. A boy unwilling to do his part can never hope to make good in the West or any where else." Behavior and interactions with anyone—fellow student, master, staff, or ranch hand—could earn one plus or minus CW points. "In running a school we must consider carefully the effect of each boy on the group of boys, also on the staff," Connell said. In numerous instances boys who did not get along well with others were not asked to return. Infraction of rules and poor academic performance were not in themselves reason for dismissal from the school in Connell's view. So long as boys showed evidence of trying to improve they were given repeated chances to redeem themselves. In explaining to one set of parents why their son was not asked to return, Connell said this was the result "of our despair of ever accomplishing much improvement in his conduct." Masters evaluated the boys, but Connell was the ultimate judge, rarely allowing for any difference of opinion about a student's conduct.

If Connell did not like a boy for any reason, and if the boy transgressed in some way that deeply upset him, he would on occasion dismiss a boy from the school out of hand. After four and a half years at Los Alamos, sixteen-year-old Lance Pelly was not asked to return because he accepted and drank a bottle of moonshine from a ranch hand. Connell felt betrayed and wrote the Pellys that he was so disappointed in Lance that he did not want him back.[30] In the days before legal protection for students and parents, there was little recourse from these sometimes arbitrary actions. The school head as chief character-guide and authority figure was a well-known role in American boarding schools, one echoed in the scoutmaster. Connell's absolute power was not unusual for the time, and parental protest was to no avail.

What Connell hoped to develop in Los Alamos boys was a spirit of cooperation and service to the group, a hallmark of Progressivism. Boys who earned his highest praise were those whose actions showed respect for individuals and for the community. In a college recommendation for a recent Los Alamos graduate, Connell praised the boy for having "real moral force of character . . . qualities of manhood, truth, courage, devotion to duty, sympathy for and protection of the weak, kindliness, unselfishness, and fellowship." Among the behaviors that earned boys positive CW points were displaying leadership, exhibiting energy on expeditions, "zeal in Scout work," "perfect equipment," and having the week's best room or cooking fire. Emergencies or extraordinary events provided opportunity for displaying community spirit. In the spring of 1941 heavy snowmelt caused a dam to overflow in Los Alamos Canyon, washing away part of the road. The entire school except for the youngest boys spent many hours rebuilding the road, thus displaying what Connell called "their fine spirit of cooperation . . . considered [the] true 'School Spirit' at Los Alamos."[31]

The Progressive view—and Connell's—was that one should be useful to one's community; otherwise, you were a parasite who gave nothing back. *Useful* was one of Connell's favorite words, occurring more frequently than any other in his correspondence with students and parents. He repeatedly told parents that if their son was to be of any *use* in life he must uphold his responsibilities and participate so that the community as a whole functioned well. There was no place at Los Alamos, he told them, for anyone who wouldn't play his part. If one boy "falls down" on his responsibilities, the whole community suffers. "This school was founded and is operated for the purpose of bringing boys who are not strong to a robust *useful* manhood" [*my emphasis*]. This standard was applied to himself as well. In 1919 he wrote Mrs. Pelly that "I love boys, and their love, admiration, and respect of me means more to me than anything else in the world. When I fail in that I believe my usefulness is past."[32]

This emphasis on public service, on one's duty within the community and being of use to society, grew out of the Social Gospel movement and

Progressive-era thinking and was subscribed to by many traditional boarding schools. The idea that wealth and position brought not only privilege but responsibility was deeply imbedded in the values of the era. Theodore Roosevelt, Ashley Pond's hero, preached this constantly and carried out his life on this foundational belief. For Los Alamos boys, by and large from well-to-do families, the message of the school—both implicit and explicit—was that they had to shoulder their community responsibilities like men.

Character had to be taught and shown to boys by their parents and especially by the faculty, as surrogate parents and professional educators. In Connell's view, this could happen only when a boy gave "instant and unquestioning obedience." More than anything else, this demand separated Connell from most Progressives, who cultivated a more democratic atmosphere where children had true voice in their affairs. In this, however, Connell was in accord with "scientific" theories of education proclaimed at the time. Professionals, or "experts," knew better than parents how to raise children, and Connell was quite blunt in telling parents that he knew better than they what was good for their sons.

He did not mince words with boys or parents. Typical is this letter to a student's parents:

> I am very much afraid . . . unless he is more firmly handled and absolutely required to do the things he should do regardless of his own choices you are simply going to pile up trouble. . . . He is already far from desirable . . . tricky, inconsiderate . . . extremely fresh and impertinent.

Only by imposing a strict routine could Connell, a self-declared expert on boys, teach them good habits for life. He often called the youngest boys at LARS his "gibbons"—a species of tailless ape, he told them—therein revealing his concurrence with the views of psychologist G. Stanley Hall and others that the "school must lead the child to freedom by leading him away from his primitive self. . . . Its likes and dislikes must be subordinated to civilized wants. . . . The essence of the enterprise is discipline."[33] Wearing the mantle of surrogate father and expert on boys, Connell expected and demanded obedience at all times.

Any questioning of his statements or authority might cause blistering outbursts of anger from which no one—boy, faculty, or staff—was exempt. He was known, behind his back, as THE BOSS, as indeed he was. His anger could be triggered by something as trivial as one boy calling another by an unofficial nickname. The recipient of this anger was expected to acknowledge that he deserved the "bawling out" and to take it in good grace for his own good. Connell expressed his pleasure with one boy "because he has tried to do well and never resented my criticism which has at times been quite harsh." So long as a boy obeyed Connell and sincerely tried to behave as expected, he was given repeated chances.

Connell's tirades left lasting impressions, if not scars, on boys and masters, and some chose not to return because of one too many encounters with these very public and caustic tongue-lashings. Those able to look beyond Connell's irascible and tyrannical behavior could perhaps see his essential fairness and deep concern for boys.

Without the consuming passion and devotion of this autocrat the school might never have survived. It is impossible to imagine the Los Alamos program without him. Yet one of the tragedies of A. J. Connell was that he could brook no challenge to his authority, nor even any disagreement, and age only made him more rigid in this regard. In direct contradiction of his exhortations to others to be kind and considerate, he rode roughshod over the opinions and wishes of all who dared differ in any degree from his edicts, exhibiting an almost violent disrespect. In his view he was merely carrying out the duty inherent in his authority as the director.

In the final analysis, however, most boys at Los Alamos learned how to avoid him and his anger. As Jay Rice, 1930, wrote his parents after receiving a dressing-down from the director, "the good part . . . is he doesn't hold a grudge. He can shift from fury to pleasantness in no time."[34] In their adolescent view, he was an adult eccentric who provided the framework, albeit sometimes disagreeable, within which they enjoyed a life close to what the early School literature called "every boy's dream."

A Boy's Dream

Outdoor Life

Daily life at the Ranch School was a full, rich experience, with much to occupy boys outside of their schoolwork. The Pajarito Plateau and the Jemez Mountains were their backyard to explore. It was a robust world, far removed from the city life that was all most had known, and it contained a good deal more danger than perhaps parents realized. While boys were almost always under the watchful eye of a master or staff member, life on horseback amid nature and wild animals always carried an edge of risk to life and limb.

Many years after his time at Los Alamos, Earl Kieselhorst, 1923, wrote a short reminiscence of his student years, describing his entry in the summer of 1919, along with his two brothers, into "a strange and adventurous new world that would fill [us] with the keenest and most delightful memories of a lifetime." At a time when the cowboy was the great American hero, they plunged with enthusiasm into the work of the ranch itself, assisting with "round-ups, branding, castrating, de-horning, inoculating and riding bucking steers." The ranch hands responsible for the work may have been less than enthusiastic about having city boys as helpers, but they were invariably kind to the boys. And although ranch work was dropped within a year or two from the scheduled activities, still the "daily experiences with animals were rich and abundant."[35]

Horses were ubiquitous in both ranch work and school life, and pets were always around, especially dogs, Airedales prominent among them. Connell and several staff members had dogs, and boys were allowed to bring their dogs to school. Replying to a mother who asked if her son could bring his dog to camp, Connell wrote:

> I am sure I will like the boy who will not come without his dog. Of course he may bring him. There are nine dogs in the School now. . . . I have never objected to the boys having good dogs here, in fact, I am accused of encouraging them. All that I ask is that each boy takes care of his own dog. While on pack trips he can have his dog in his tent.
>
> I get quite a thrill out of the sight of all the dogs that escort us whenever we ride out. The dogs seem to be having as good a time as the boys. When I told Miss Ranger, our matron, that a boy wanted to know if he could bring his dog, she was much amused as there were seven of various kinds basking in the warmth about the fireplace before us.

Connell clearly had a soft spot for dogs. He wrote a poignant letter to a camper after one summer's end, telling him of the death of a favorite dog. Connell did not want the boy to hear of it secondhand and assured him the dog was never in pain.

Other pets arrived at the school through various circumstances, wild animals "tamed" by the boys—coyotes, foxes, badgers, prairie dogs, owls, chipmunks, and squirrels. During the 1919 camp a pair of bear cubs whose mother had been killed intrigued and amused the boys. The cubs were given free run of the grounds but as they grew became a destructive nuisance. After efforts to find them a zoo home failed, they were shot and served to the boys for dinner.

There were vivid lessons in the harsh realities of nature. Unlike pampered city dogs, the ranch dogs had to be able to survive in a wilderness setting. More than once one of the feisty Airedales returned to the ranch bleeding and near death from an encounter with a bear or mountain lion. Sometimes Los Alamos horses or cattle were killed by wolves, bears, or mountain lions inhabiting the Jemez. Earl Kieselhorst wrote of a time when the students cut a Christmas tree from the forest: "We could hear the wolves howling and were

Fig. 2.5

Riding from Fuller Lodge accompanied by one of the
ever-present dogs, c. 1930. Photo by T. Harmon Parkhurst.
Courtesy Museum of New Mexico, neg. no. 1131.

fearful of being attacked. However, as a precaution . . . our two schoolmasters
stood guard with rifles."[36]

Hunting and trapping, in which most boys participated, reinforced the
mystique of living at the edge of wilderness and were integral parts of Los
Alamos life. Only older boys were allowed to hunt; younger ones were encouraged to run trap lines. Experienced men taught hunting and trapping skills
and the ways of wild animals. Kieselhorst learned to set traps from an ancient
trapper who stopped at the ranch, and Homer Pickens, a fabled New Mexico
lion hunter and predator-control agent, and a regular ranch visitor, enthralled
boys with his accounts of capturing wolves and mountain lions. Forest Service
men were given special rates for the school guestrooms, and Connell arranged
for those with expertise in firearms, archaeology, animal science, or forestry to
talk with the boys.

Students were allowed to bring guns to the school, which were kept in locked
racks at the Big House, never in the boys' rooms. Boys were encouraged to
become members of the Junior Rifle Association and to earn their sharpshooter
award. Four- or five-day hunting expeditions were scheduled during deer season

each fall, always with an accompanying adult—either a master or trusted staff person such as Bences Gonzales or, on occasion, a hired expert guide such as John Davenport. The return from a successful hunt was always exciting, with every boy photographed with his kill, and venison served the next day.

Often boys sold the skins, with even skunk skins sometimes bringing two dollars apiece. One year some boys enrolled in a taxidermy correspondence class, hoping to learn to cure their own skins. Unable to take time from their studies for a hunt and desperate for animals on which to practice their skills, the boys took to trapping mice, understandably not very satisfactory.[37] Yet as former student John McDonough described, trapping at Los Alamos and experiences with raw nature sometimes turned young men away from hunting.

> Each student was assigned a specific area in a canyon or on a mesa where he could set out animal traps. We caught anything that walked into the traps—skunks, coyotes. We hoped to catch a bobcat. Trapping was considered . . . a macho thing to do. You had the animal's hide tanned and hung it on the wall of your room instead of a Harvard pennant. In the afternoon after classes, you got your horse and rode your trapline.
>
> It wasn't always fun. [I] caught a coyote once. When I found him, he was suffering with his foot half torn off. It was too late in the afternoon to get a master to come with a pistol. I had to beat him to death with a club. It cured me of killing.[38]

Not all boys were interested in killing animals, but everyone was encouraged to take the initiative to pursue whatever interested them so long as they were out of doors.

An early brochure explained that formal athletics were not featured because "the great wild mountain country, filled with a thousand interests for the boy, is so close." However, intramural sports were always a part of Los Alamos life, and everyone participated in at least one. In sharp contrast to most traditional boarding schools, however, LARS sports were relatively informal and tended to be those in which a boy competed against himself or a few individuals in events such as archery, riflery, tennis, boxing, or fencing. In any given year the activities varied depending on the interests of the boys enrolled at the time—yet another of Connell's Progressive approaches. Fencing was popular in early years, polo for a few years in the late 1930s. The student body was never large enough to field competitive sports requiring large teams, and Connell did not allow vigorous contact sports such as football. In early years the school fielded competitive basketball teams, but they usually lost; tennis was the only sport in which

Fig. 2.6

The fall deer hunt, 1922. From left, Earl Kieselhorst, Philip Clay, George May, Robert Lewis (in back), Bill Regnery, and A. J. Connell. Courtesy Los Alamos Historical Museum Archives.

LARS regularly and successfully competed statewide and in several years won state championships. Connell particularly encouraged tennis because, he said, it was a sport that could be practiced for a lifetime. In cold winters ice hockey was played on Ashley Pond, and after the late thirties, on Douglas Pond—the gift of a parent, built in Los Alamos Canyon where deep shade provided consistently better ice. The boys managed their own teams, and always the "athletics [were] suited to the entertainment and development of the boy, rather than to making a reputation for the school."[39]

Skiing was practiced at Los Alamos from the start, well before the modern sport caught on nationally. One photo taken in the winter of 1918–1919 shows two boys mounted on their horses, ready to ride west to the mountains carrying their long wooden skis and single wooden pole. The following winter the toboggan slide was built and when packed with snow provided a convenient slope on which boys could practice basic skills. A favorite pastime was "skijoring," whereby a boy on skis holding a rope was pulled along snow-

Fig. 2.7

Philip Clay with bobcat, and skunk, raccoon, fox, and coyote pelts, 1922. Courtesy Los Alamos Historical Museum Archives.

covered fields by a galloping horse and rider. Skiing gradually grew in popularity at Los Alamos, but not until the mid-thirties were downhill trails cut above Camp May on Pajarito Mountain and a ski hill developed southwest of the school at Sawyer's Hill.[40] Until then, there was no organized skiing or instruction, and boys "played in the woods on [skis], alone" or in small groups.

"Climbing cliffs was one of our favorite diversions," Kieselhorst wrote. "Connell encouraged it because he thought it was good character-building."[41] Lava tubes were explored along with the multitude of caves in the cliffs. For truly inclement weather and the darker winter hours there were pool and ping-pong tables, cards and games, and the woodworking and photography shops. Several attempts were made at having a school newspaper, and there were occasional special-interest groups like a stamp club and a small orchestra. Outside the confines of regularly scheduled classes and outdoor activities, boys were encouraged to take the initiative to pursue their interests. Connell's aim was to develop the man, as the school's last brochure stated: "Recreation in school should develop the interests that are most likely to be continued after school and college into adult life."

Just as sports became more varied as the school developed, so did other extracurricular activities. Theatrical productions were given once or twice a year after the late twenties and usually included a Gilbert and Sullivan operetta in which most of the school community participated, with an audience invited from Santa Fe and the surrounding area. Connell's love of drama was infused into Los Alamos life in everything from the log buildings on the spectacular stage setting of the Pajarito Plateau, to the costumed waiters and the school uniform, to the graduation ceremonies and the ordered procession of the school pack train, all equipment gleaming, winding its way through the mountains. Central to the drama and rhythm of Los Alamos life were Scouting and horses, which combined on the Pajarito to create what Connell claimed to be the first mounted Scout troop in the country.

Horses

On arrival at Los Alamos every boy was assigned a horse to ride and care for during the school year. Riding was an integral part of everyday life on the ranch and regularly scheduled for the boys at least two afternoons every week and on Saturdays. Former student Peter Dechert, 1941, described it well when he said that "the chief item . . . outside of academics was our relationship with horses."[42]

The dominant role horses played in Los Alamos life is described in the 1942 catalog.

> Each year groups are organized, as interest indicates, for polo, gymkhana, jumping, bareback riding, or 'flat' saddle equitation. At the end of the year a Saturday is reserved for contests and show classes to note and reward achievements in horsemanship during the year.

So important were horses and outdoor life that "proficiency in horsemanship and camping" was a requirement for graduation. After all, life on the trail and in camp was one of the founding dreams of Ashley Pond and A. J. Connell.

Most boys coming to the Ranch School would have ridden a horse at least a time or two, but few well-to-do city boys would have had experience in caring for horses or have ridden in a pack train. During the first weeks of school, boys were shown how to care for horses and equipment and then how to pack a horse for an overnight trip. They learned to ride the high-cantled western saddles made for the school by a Silver City saddler. The 1942 catalog stated that since "a good horseman should be able to ride well any style, boys are . . . [also] encouraged to own and use eastern riding equipment, and to ride bareback." The greatest challenge was learning how to load camping gear and cinch it tightly on a packhorse using the "Los Alamos diamond hitch." This took much practice and coordination between boys, but provided a real sense of accomplishment when finally mastered.

Mack Wallace, a student in the mid-thirties, recalled his introduction to the school horses. There were about thirty horses, he said,

> gathered in the corral when we approached it. We were first ushered into the tack room within the big white barn, and our saddles and bridles were pointed out. Back in the corral, the first day, a young man haltered a horse and watched while I painstakingly put on the bridle, then placed the saddle blanket and saddle on his back and fastened the girth. I was wise enough to note that my mount had ballooned his belly and with a great heave on the girth I countered the measure. As we rode back to the "Big House" horse and rider became acquainted. His name was Nogales, and he was magnificent. This was an animal that I came to love and trust, and I think maybe he reciprocated in his way.[43]

Each boy learned the personality and idiosyncrasies of his horse and in so doing acquired a deeper understanding of himself, learning patience and self-control as well. Another student, Jeremy Taylor, recalls "Smoky, the ultimate plug and [my] first-year charge, an ego-wounder to one who fancied himself quite a horseman after years of experience on Eastern flat saddles" and "Alazon, [my] much friskier second-year charge, an ego-deflater when, spooked by a rustling poncho, he shied and dumped his would-be rider on the ground in the initial attempt at mounting."[44] Wrangler Ted Mather saw to the overall care of the horses, but every boy spent time with his horse daily. He was responsible for grooming the horse and for keeping his equipment polished and in top-notch shape, and woe to any who mistreated or neglected a horse or his equipment.

Boy Scouting

The organizing principle of Ranch School life was Boy Scouting. Connell wholeheartedly embraced the philosophy of the Scouting movement that had swept the country with great fervor before World War I, and it was no accident that the first activity associated with the Los Alamos Ranch School was the two-week Scout camp held in Los Alamos Canyon in June 1917. Connell registered the school as Boy Scout Troop 22 in October 1918, and the basic organizational format of school life was the Scout patrol system. All students were members of the troop by virtue of their enrollment in the school and were required to achieve the rank of First Class Scout in order to graduate, although this requirement was dropped sometime shortly before 1942.[45]

In setting up the school troop, Connell sought to improve on the Boy Scout patrol system. Rather than dividing the student body into academic levels or age-based patrols as was standard Scout procedure, he placed boys in patrols according to their physical size and maturity. At the start of each year all the boys lined up for inspection by the masters and Connell, who then sorted them into patrols. The intention was to avoid having adolescent boys of the same age but widely varying sizes, strengths, and physical maturity grouped together. With Connell's arrangement, activities could be planned around any patrol's general physical abilities without having to worry about large, physically advanced boys intimidating smaller weaker ones. It also avoided having a group of small boys holding back larger, more physically able ones of the same age. In fact, most of the boys in any patrol were usually about the same age and maturity level.

What this organizational structure did not address, however, was the varied emotional and mental maturity of boys, nor changes in boys' interests with increasing age. Daily life was centered around the patrols: the sleeping porches were segregated according to patrol; roommate assignments were made by patrol; Saturday rides and other weekly activities were carried out in patrols. Thus older boys entering puberty late or who had small physical builds sometimes chafed at having to do activities with a group of boys younger than themselves. In such situations when a boy resented his placement and complained, Connell stressed his responsibility to "show the way" to his younger comrades. Over the years, however, Connell did tinker with the patrol structure in an attempt to address such problems.

For the first decade there were three patrols—Junior, Intermediate, and Senior—but eventually these were replaced by four patrols named after native evergreens, with the smallest boys in the Piñon patrol, and the other boys graded by size up through the Juniper, Fir, and Spruce patrols, the latter being the most physically mature boys. In the early twenties Connell instituted one of the most far-reaching elements of school life: every boy was ranked within his patrol, with each patrol led by its number-one-ranked boy, and the school led by the number-one boy in the oldest patrol group. Rank was assigned by Connell with input from the masters and was based on their evaluations of each boy's character, attitude, leadership ability, and how he performed his required community work. Academic performance played no part in patrol ranking, so a boy who was trying hard but doing miserably in his courses might be a patrol leader. Ranking provided a clear hierarchy at the school so that in any given situation there was always one boy who outranked the others and who thus bore the responsibility for the others. This was especially important when boys worked together on camping expeditions, in the pack train, or in any situation where some danger might be involved.

In one sense it was a very democratic system, with reward based solely on each boy's performance, but the evaluation and ranking were done by adults, not a boy's peers. Ranking was intended to encourage leadership ability; boys were given increasing responsibility as they were able to accept it. In theory at least, a boy new to the school at age twelve would likely start near the bottom of the Juniors, or later the Piñon Patrol, work his way up in a year or two to becoming for a few months at least the leader of that patrol, and then as he matured be transferred to the next patrol, where he would once again be near the bottom in the rankings. He would thus have experience with obedience as well as opportunity to be the leader of his patrol. Of course, some were more suited to a disciplined environment where instant and unquestioning obedience was required. Those who bridled under the demand for obedience often did not do well in the rankings. Nor did boys whose early growth spurts placed them in a patrol with mostly older, more emotionally mature boys. Ranks were evaluated and changed weekly as necessary; promotion or demotion might occur on the spot as a result of any observed behavior. Connell did not tolerate boys who were overbearing in their behavior toward lower-ranking boys, and demotion was the result of any perceived arrogance of leadership, whether hazing or mean horseplay or just selfishness and a cynical attitude.

Before 1919 Los Alamos boys did not wear Scout or school uniforms, but were encouraged to wear corduroy or other sturdy clothing, all of the best quality, offered at the Commissary. Connell insisted upon practical gear and would have nothing to do with anything that smacked of tourism or "dudes." He did not allow students to wear cowboy boots or spurs, which were impractical for mountain riding, or to refer to their Stetson hats as "cowboy hats." The "red cowboy boots with four rows of stitching" worn by the director of the Aspen Ranch School, a short-lived endeavor north of Santa Fe, must have appalled Connell.[46] Drawing on knowledge gained during his Forest Service days, Connell told parents that "the equipment we have has been selected after much experience in the field." Preoccupied with detail and with "doing things right," Connell did not leave any more to chance than was absolutely necessary.

By the 1919–1920 academic year a school uniform closely resembling the Scout uniform of the day was required, consisting of khaki flannel shirts and riding breeches, winter breeches, high lace boots, heavy shoes, and puttees. Black, army-regulation ties were required for class attendance and formal occasions. Heavy leather gloves and chaps were practical gear necessary for riding in the brushy country of the plateau and Jemez Mountains. Everything except underwear and pajamas was selected by Connell and stocked at the Trading Post, where parents were obliged to buy the required outfit. Experience soon added such required items as a waterproof Scout cape. Minor modifications to the official Scout uniform were sanctioned by Scout headquarters in New York City for the Los Alamos troop: the shirt collar was slightly different; the shorts were an inch or two shorter; a variety of patterned neckerchiefs was available to chose from; the hat was a Stetson modeled on the Forest Service hat, which Connell favored.[47] Eventually students wore the Scout shorts year round and on all occasions, from ice hockey games and skiing to formal dances with private girls' schools. For their part, the masters were required to wear similar uniforms, but unlike the boys, theirs included a jacket and long trousers for formal occasions.

Connell continued to lead the Santa Fe troop, of which the Ranch School boys apparently were members, for the 1917–1918 academic year, but when the Los Alamos troop was registered, Fay Curtis was the scoutmaster. In later years, Cecil Wirth served in that post, along with several deputy scoutmasters, including Harry Walen. Connell maintained his involvement with the Scouting movement, serving on district boards and the National Council, regularly attending national meetings and visiting Boy Scout headquarters when he was in New York City.[48] He was given Scouting's Silver Beaver award in 1931, and when the national Scouting program experienced difficulty retaining older boys, they turned to Connell, among others, for assistance in planning what eventually became the Explorer Scout program.[49]

Boys who enjoyed Scouting worked their way through the Scout manual to earn badges, progressing from Tenderfoot through First Class Scout to Eagle Scout rank. Badge activity leaned heavily to the outdoors and provided a lengthy program of purposeful, educational play to fill afternoons and weekends. There was an extra edge of determination and enthusiasm to skiing when a boy was working toward a ski badge, or to swimming or packing a horse when one wanted a lifesaving or horsemanship badge. This fit perfectly with Connell's overall goals and beliefs, and his letters to parents often echoed Boy Scout literature of the day.

Not everyone, of course, enjoyed Scouting. In the spring of 1919 Lance Pelly became unhappy and wanted to leave Los Alamos, in part because he disliked Scouting. As was Connell's habit with unhappy or rebellious boys, he had a heart-to-heart talk with Lance, who agreed to stay if he didn't have to become a Scout. Connell reluctantly agreed to this, writing Mrs. Pelly that Scouting "was to me like religion, no boy should be forced into it."[50] Lance's situation was an exception, probably because the school was not yet firmly established and needed every student. Connell was also genuinely fond of

Lance and did not want him to leave. More typical is Connell's reaction to a camper who made no effort to learn basic Scout skills as required. Connell wrote the boy's father that his son would have to fulfill the requirement before the day was over or he could not continue at camp. This was not an arbitrary requirement; successful participation in the weeks-long summer pack trips or the Saturday rides during the school year required knowledge of such Scout fundamentals as building fires and camp cooking. Boys had no choice but to complete basic Scout work, but for those who weren't interested in going beyond these requirements, sports or special projects, music or theatre, occupied their afternoons.

Connell was quite perceptive in his application of Scouting to the school, especially in terms of older boys who might consider the Scout uniform and activities too juvenile. Such boys tolerated the Scout uniform because it was the *school* uniform, a common requirement of preparatory schools at that time. Likewise, many of the Scouting activities at the Ranch School appealed to older boys because they were purposeful *men's* work—pack trips, hunting and trapping, horses, sports such as riflery or boxing—not merely woodcraft projects to fill up time.

Scouting's appeal to Connell was in its discipline, structure, and moral tone, which encouraged hard work followed by the rewards of the evening campfire under the stars. Although he met Santa Fe neighbor and fellow Boy Scout Ernest Thompson Seton, founder of the Woodcraft Indians, there is no evidence that the two ever spent time together, even after the leadership institute at Seton Village opened in Santa Fe in 1932.[51] Both men were eccentric and shared similar views of the West and concerns about boys, but Seton's unkempt "natural man" appearance and romanticized vision of American Indians placed him at odds with Connell, a pragmatic perfectionist.

Scouting and the Ranch School were never part of the social-activist strain of Progressivism (which likely would have made some of the school's corporate executive parents uneasy), but their roots lay in the same troubled ground. Conservative in character, both responded to the concerns of middle-class American parents, who began to look to western schools as places where boys who appeared to be growing soft or who were frequently ill might find health and strength.[52] Typical is one father's statement of why he wanted his son at Los Alamos.

I want to get [my son] away from the softening and enervating influences that surround a boy in a suburb of a big city, where most of the parents give their sons luxury and pamper them—I want to get him away from movie pictures, girls, cars and all that sort of thing—

I want him to be *clean,* truthful, manly and courageous, taught that work is the greatest of all blessings, and fitted to stand on his own in the battle of life, and taught to depend on his own efforts, not on what his parents may or may not leave him.

The West could test a boy's strength and stretch his growth. There, parents believed, he could learn the value of hard work and find heroes to emulate—the hard-working miners, ranchers, forest rangers, and cowboys. As well, the West provided the fascination of the American Indian and his "ruined cities" to add spice and romance to a boy's life.

In the Los Alamos Ranch School Connell provided a unique answer to parental concerns. He brought the pervasive discipline of a Scout troop to a life lived in the semi-wild setting of the Pajarito Plateau and nearby mountains. Parents whose sons were ill were attracted to LARS because of its location in an area of the country renowned for its health-giving properties and because of Connell's strict health regimen. Parents concerned about urban or feminine influences on their sons were reassured by the school's remote location away from towns of any size, by the discipline and masculine flavor of the school's daily life, and by the opportunities provided for extensive time on the trail and in the mountains. Connell modified the structure of the Scouting program to fit his authoritarian and perfectionist personality, which thoroughly colored Los Alamos life and made it unique among western ranch schools.[53]

Both the founder and director of the Los Alamos Ranch School subscribed to certain core Progressive ideas—emphasis on useful hands-on work through which knowledge and skills were gained, on the individual, on physical health, and on responsibility within the community—and Connell was a member of the Progressive Education Association. The core values of Los Alamos were based on a modified Progressivism combined with the Scouting organization, but Los Alamos nevertheless lacked a pervasive or consistent Progressive philosophy or pedagogy. (In actuality, few Progressive schools—witness the Putney School and to some extent the Progressive-leaning Millbrook School—were ideologically consistent in their application of Progressive principles and struggled to balance student-centered programs with the preparatory curriculum.)

Los Alamos was a western school focused on outdoor life and the powerful role of place, with academic standards that placed it in the upper tier of independent boarding schools. This combination gave a distinctly western flavor and Progressive foundation to a boarding school in the mold of traditional headmaster-centered New England schools.[54]

Everyone Must Do His Part

The School Community

After a year of trying to run a Progressive health school with no academic program and a small fluctuating corps of boys, Connell realized a change of direction was necessary if the school was to survive. In June 1918, a year after Los Alamos opened, Connell turned to Yale seeking someone to teach math and the classics. He wrote that Pond's original plan for the school had not worked.

> We would not take boys who were actually ill, and when a boy was well enough to stand this life his parents usually thought he was well enough to keep up his studies. This development made it necessary for me to plan a regular school.[1]

Thus it was in response to parental concerns that Connell instituted a conventional academic program, at the same time retaining many Progressive themes. He kept what to him was quintessential—outdoor life within a framework of Scouting whose purpose was to build character and health—and recruited masters from Yale and other leading universities, allowing them free rein to establish and guide the coursework. Students were carefully mentored from their first arrival at the school through graduation and sometimes in their subsequent academic careers.

A community with varied talents and backgrounds formed around the young male faculty, enriching the boys' lives and bringing fullness and depth to an otherwise exclusively masculine society. The 1921 brochure emphasized the importance of this community. "Owing to our isolation, social responsibility is essential at Los Alamos. We are limited to our own community for happiness. . . . Everyone must do his part toward making the community happy." Life on the isolated Pajarito Plateau was not easy, but those who came to terms with it—and did their part—found the rewards to be great.

Connell established the school's routines with single-minded devotion, although the demands of running both a ranch and a school stretched his abilities. He successfully met a series of crises in the early twenties, and when the first headmaster died suddenly in 1926 the school moved smoothly from one era to another. Connell did not address, however, the school's most serious problem, its shaky financial underpinnings, until the late thirties.

Faculty

Within two weeks of writing to Yale, Connell received a reply from Fayette Samuel Curtis Jr., a June graduate, and soon the two were discussing the terms and conditions of the job. The school could afford only one master to teach all subjects to the handful of boys, and because Los Alamos operated year round, the job was full time with only a short summer break. Curtis was ill with tuberculosis that spring, and Connell assured him there was no better place to recuperate than Los Alamos, where he could participate as he wished in the afternoon outdoor activities.[2] In September Fay Curtis arrived at the school with his widowed mother Leila.

There were between six and nine students at Los Alamos in September 1918, some like Ashley Pond III staying on after the summer camp. (Records for the first several years are meager, with conflicting accounts of who was enrolled.) School began with a staff of four—Connell as director, Ed Fuller as supervisor of junior boys (with no teaching responsibilities), Fay Curtis as master, and his mother Leila as matron.

Curtis clearly had the academic qualifications to meet parental expectations. He was from Boston, his father deceased by 1910 when he entered the Taft School in Connecticut. The Taft yearbook shows a slender, dark-haired boy whose nickname was "Cowboy" and who hoped for a military career. Poor eyesight and health problems prevented the fulfillment of this dream, but surely someone called "Cowboy" would have been happy to teach at a ranch school. The romance of the West was in full bloom on the East Coast, and many young men like Curtis were lured west by a sense of adventure. At Yale he was a classics major and captain of the fencing team; his years at LARS would prove him a true scholar. Perhaps spurred by the shadow cast over his life by tuberculosis, he rapidly became a proficient scholar of Spanish life in northern New Mexico.[3]

From the start Connell let Curtis determine the nature and content of the academic program, but he made it clear that morning classes were never to interfere with the afternoon outdoor activities. The academic program that took shape in 1918 remained largely unchanged throughout the school's life, with course sequences offered in English, history, mathematics, science, foreign languages, Latin, and mechanical drawing. In setting up the curriculum, standard for the day, Curtis drew on his experience at Taft and knowledge of eastern preparatory schools.[4]

Bible study was offered only once, in 1918; like Hotchkiss, Choate, and other nonsectarian schools, Los Alamos Ranch School had no religious affiliation. Protestant services were variously held at the school monthly or weekly, conducted by ministers from Santa Fe or Española, but these clearly were an incidental part of school life. A Catholic priest regularly came to the ranch to conduct mass for ranch families, but Catholic students usually attended mass at the Cathedral in Santa Fe. The school had no chaplain until the later years, when brochures listed the Dean of the Episcopal Cathedral in Albuquerque as the chaplain. He likely spent only one or two afternoons a month at the school, and his appointment appears to have come as Los Alamos moved into the upper ranks of boarding schools, many of them affiliated with the Episcopal Church. When the school closed there was a small but growing fund on the books designated for a chapel. Connell did not consider the formal teaching or practice of religion necessary to forming moral character, although he accommodated individual parents' wishes for their sons to have opportunities for worship.

The academic year was divided into eight grading periods, and at the end of the year Fay Curtis wrote evaluations of each boy's character and academic ability.[5] Although these reveal an oblique and acerbic turn of mind with a rather dark and critical attitude, the students apparently enjoyed Curtis, and Connell and the parents were pleased. Connell sent letters to parents for the first time that November, reporting on their sons' academic progress, health, and character development, and at the same time instituted a requirement that students write weekly letters home. Eventually his practice was to write parents once a month and include grades and comments from the headmaster. He always put academic performance into the context of his evaluation of the boy as a person.

As the only instructor to the small group of boys, Fay Curtis was a busy man, and additional faculty was needed if the school was to develop. The following summer Curtis returned to Yale and recruited Lawrence Sill Hitchcock as the second master. There could not have been a more fortuitous choice. Hitchcock, an army veteran, had graduated Phi Beta Kappa in June 1919 and was

looking for a job when Curtis convinced him to try teaching at Los Alamos. He accepted the offer because he considered it "a call to adventure, a chance to spend a year in the West."[6] Late that summer Hitchcock made his first trip west: two days on the train from Chicago, an overnight in Santa Fe followed by a mid-morning ride on the narrow gauge railroad from Santa Fe to Buckman, where Fay Curtis met him with a horse, and the two men rode the ten miles from the river to the school. They divided teaching the approximately twenty boys between them, with Curtis now in the position of headmaster.

That fall as Hitchcock assessed the Los Alamos job, he wrote his mother that he believed the unpleasant part of it—that is, "pumping knowledge into unwilling craniums"—would be encountered anywhere he taught. The particularities of the Los Alamos situation were quite attractive, though. "The variety of subjects I teach, and the possibility of getting my results in my own way and being answerable only for results and not for methods, and of course, the outdoor life, all appeal to me very strongly, and the pay appears to be as good as I would be likely to get anywhere."[7] This statement sums up the appeal of Los Alamos to many of the young men who in future years came to teach there. It also points to one of the keys of the school's successful academic program, that the masters were free to teach their subjects as they chose. The only thing that mattered was the success of their students, assessed in frequent testing.

The sometimes unconventional teaching methods were well remembered by former students. Many years after leaving LARS Earl Kieselhorst wrote Hitchcock, reminding him of "how you used to shoot craps with George May and myself, using assigned algebra problems and Latin lines as currency, and luck determined whether our daily assignment was to be longer or shorter."[8] Another master, Fermor Church, impressed students with his ability to use the surrounding environment to vividly illustrate principles of physics or geology, pointing out angles of gradient on ski slopes or demonstrating the effects of gravity by having boys plunge their hands into boiling water at ten thousand feet. Yet another, Arthur Chase, was adept at using classroom games to make a point in his English or Latin classes. Overall, the pedagogical methods were conventional, but the sense of freedom instructors felt to improvise and experiment as needed gave the academic program great vitality.

LARS academic life was also enriched by the high intellectual quality of

Fig. 3.1

Lawrence Hitchcock reading to the boys after dinner in the Big House. Photo by T. Harmon Parkhurst. Courtesy Los Alamos Historical Museum Archives.

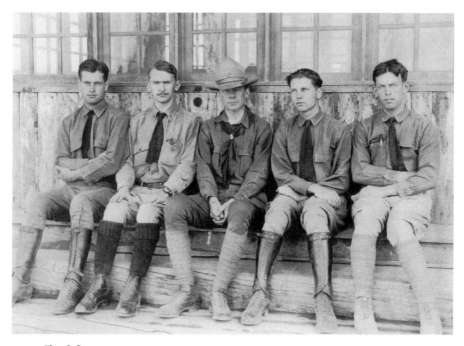

Fig. 3.2

Faculty and staff, 1921–1922. From left:
Lawrence Hitchcock, Fayette Curtis, A. J. Connell,
Fermor Church, Edward Fuller. Courtesy
Los Alamos Historical Museum Archives.

mind that Curtis and Hitchcock, who had been friends at Yale, brought to the program. They set high standards, and at Los Alamos they regularly enjoyed evenings together reading Dante aloud. Both pursued intellectual interests outside of school life: Hitchcock took advanced studies at the University of Chicago and the American School in Rome, as well as a Masters degree in classics at Yale; Curtis catalogued an Hispanic weapons collection for the Museum of New Mexico, served as an editor of the *New Mexico Historical Review,* and was an acknowledged and published Spanish scholar who prepared a major translation of the Spanish poet-historian Villagrá.[9]

Yale, with a reputation as a strong trainer of teachers, sent other men to teach at Los Alamos, and recruits also came from Harvard, Princeton, and leading universities primarily on the East Coast. From 1918 to 1943 forty men taught at Los Alamos, but less than a dozen remained for four or more years. Most moved on to other schools, as young men starting their careers are prone

Fig. 3.3

Faculty and staff, 1936. From left, back row: Oscar Steege,
Charles Shain, Arthur Chase, Cecil Wirth, Robert French. Front row:
Helen Sulier, Lawrence Hitchcock, A. J. Connell, Fermor Church,
Thomas Waring. Photo by Laura Gilpin. Wirth private collection.

to do. Some were unable to adjust to the rigors of an isolated life at Los
Alamos; others sought higher pay elsewhere, and some clashed sharply with
Connell. For many, especially those who stayed, the school was a unique and
exhilarating place. Unfortunately, no faculty or academic records survive to
supplement the student files. Some faculty now are only shadowy figures preserved in memory or a few written student reminiscences.

One such person is the third master hired at Los Alamos, Henry W. Ruhl,
another Yale man. Ruhl was the first married master at the school, but his tenure
was tragically short. In late October 1920, six weeks after the beginning of school,
Ruhl and a student became lost in a snowstorm while deer hunting. They shel-
tered under a rock ledge for the night but were unable to start a fire, and the next
morning the student found Ruhl, who had been badly wounded in World War
I, dead. Fortunately the boy had the wits to follow Connell's training and hiked
down the Alamo Canyon drainage to the Rio Grande, which he then followed

north to Buckman. It was a traumatic experience for a young city boy and for the school itself. Connell arranged for the Rev. Walter Trowbridge, Episcopal rector in Santa Fe, to talk with the boys a few days later.[10]

Hitchcock persuaded his good friend and fellow Yale graduate, Leicester Bradner, to fill in for the remainder of that school year, and in the fall of 1921 the first non-Yale faculty member arrived. Fermor Spencer Church was a Harvard-trained engineer and like Curtis and Hitchcock, a New Englander. Similarly, this was his first exposure to the West. He was to teach math and science, a relief to Hitchcock who willingly gave up teaching physics.

In each of the four years following 1922 a new master was hired to teach languages and history, but each left after a year. In the late twenties a core faculty began to come together, with Henry Bosworth (math) and Thomas Waring (French and Spanish) arriving in 1926 and Arthur Chase (English and Latin) and Cecil Wirth (math and history) in 1929. By 1930 six of the long-term faculty (those who stayed for four or more years) were in place, joined in the next decade by three more.[11] Of the core faculty, three were minister's sons: Hitchcock, son of a Congregational minister, Chase, son of an Episcopal minister, and Oscar Steege, a Lutheran pastor's son. Several students returned for short tenures as teachers at the Ranch School. In 1923–1924 a LARS student (although not a graduate) of three years earlier, Richard Slaughter, was hired to teach history, and in the thirties three LARS graduates briefly joined the faculty ranks—Edward "Caesar" Nicholas, 1925, Henry "Heb" Newman, 1927, and Rogers Scudder, 1930.

Connell believed with absolute certainty that Los Alamos could restore almost anyone suffering from illness to full health, and several of the masters apparently came to the school in part for health reasons. Curtis and Ruhl were the first of these, followed by Slaughter and Nicholas, who were in remission from tuberculosis. It is doubtful that parents were aware of these men's illnesses, given the prevalent fear of the highly contagious disease and Connell's declaration that no tubercular boys would be admitted to the school.

Students

In the spring of 1920 Connell made the first of what were to become semiannual recruiting trips, traveling through the Midwest and East to visit with parents of prospective students and of boys already at the school. Initially it was largely Pond's contacts that provided the pool of families from which to recruit, but Connell handled all recruiting and admissions. To be admitted to Los Alamos one had to pass his judgment. On paper the entrance requirements were simple: "Any boy of good moral character over twelve years of age, whose physical condition does not disqualify him, and who has completed the sixth grade."[12] In fact, Connell chose only boys he felt he could work with, reserving the right to reject anyone with no explanation given. As he explained to a parent: "A great deal depends upon a clear understanding and a certain amount of attraction between the man and the boy. I have met but few boys that I could not reach and I believe I know at once whether I can do anything worthwhile with a boy."

Connell always interviewed new boys in their homes, believing that a boy's behavior at home revealed his character.[13] He showed photographs of the school and northern New Mexico and films of school and camp activities, impressing parents with the school's use of the latest technology and the quality of its program. Drawing on his middle-class background and work at Tiffany's, he was charming and at ease with his well-to-do clientele, inspiring confidence and leading some parents to assume that he was a college graduate. One application in the records states a consistent theme: "We met Mr. Connell at La Jolla last year, liked him very much and felt willing to trust [our son] to his guidance." Friendships developed over the years, and Connell was warmly welcomed on return trips.

When possible, these trips were arranged to coincide with medical or Boy Scout national conventions, in part to remain current with health and Scouting issues, but also to make LARS better known. When in New York City, he consulted with Boy Scout headquarters and visited with medical specialists and doctors who had referred boys to Los Alamos. He knew the value of public relations and was an adept practitioner of the art, however abrupt or authoritarian he might be in the school setting. His efforts paid off well; by the mid-twenties there were waiting lists every year until the last year, when World War II affected enrollments.

Recruitment was concentrated in the large cities of the Midwest, Northeast, and the West Coast, as was reflected in the school's largely urban student body. Connell never recruited in the South and only a couple of students came from that region. Texas and Oklahoma provided a handful of students, but school records reveal that some of the New England faculty were prejudiced against students from Texas in particular. This seems to have been based largely on Texas speech patterns, offensive to their New England ears, and a perceived laziness. New Mexico, lacking a reservoir of prosperous families, sent few students. The greatest number of boys came from two cities—Chicago followed closely by New York City, both sending nearly three times more students than any other city. A majority of the other students came about equally from California and Ohio cities and from Detroit, St. Louis, Dallas, and Houston.[14]

Applications clearly show a pattern of networking in the early years, with most parents learning about the school via word of mouth. As LARS grew, so grew the number of satisfied parents recommending it to friends. Advertisements were taken in leading magazines and newspapers, along with an annual listing in Porter Sargent's *Handbook of American Private Schools,* which Hitchcock said was known in school circles as falling "somewhere between advertising and blackmail." Sargent's trenchant descriptions of schools could be quite acerbic, but he "apparently thought well of Connell" and Los Alamos. Advertising was an unavoidable and substantial portion of the yearly budget—in 1921 advertising and printing costs were $2,655—but this expense decreased as the school became better known.[15]

Boys were accepted between the ages of twelve and sixteen, but in most years a few younger or older boys were enrolled. A few eighteen year olds came for a postgraduate year or a "western experience." Ten year olds rarely did well, not yet having the maturity to endure LARS discipline. A surprising number, perhaps a third, came from public schools, but most were from small private country day schools. In the twenties some came from other outdoor or Progressive schools such as the John Burroughs School in St. Louis. Connell was adamant about maintaining a small student body, and enrollments never exceeded forty-eight boys, and in the first decade, never more than thirty-four.

Corporate families increasingly selected Los Alamos for their sons when it began to achieve academic stature in the ranks of private schools. Some of the family surnames are familiar across the country: Cudahy (Cudahy Meats), Colgate (Colgate Products), Burroughs (Burroughs Adding Machines), Douglas (Douglas Aircraft), Hilton (Hilton Hotels), Pullman (Pullman Car Company). For others, the family business association was less obviously revealed in names: Clarkson (Indian Detours Company), Gardner and Wood (Sears Roebuck), Chapin (Hudson and American Motors), Poole (Boeing Aircraft), Reed (Santa Fe Railroad), Veeck (the Chicago Cubs). Also among the parents were bank presidents and chief executive officers of such companies as Humble Oil, Texas Pacific Coal and Oil, Continental Oil, and Palmolive. Most LARS families were at least locally or regionally prominent. In New Mexico, the Thomas Catron and Howell Earnest families of Santa Fe sent sons to the school, as did some of Connell's friends from Forest Service days, among them Dr. Leroy Peters and A. H. Hilton, who was a colorful promoter of New Mexico tourism. Archaeologist Alfred Kidder's sons attended the camp and only sudden illness kept Aldo Leopold's son, Luna, from the summer camp. Ashley Pond's son and one of his grandsons were graduates.[16]

Some students later became renowned in their own right, among them Wilson Hurley, artist; John Crosby, founder and director of the Santa Fe

Opera; Jim Thorpe, owner of The Bishop's Lodge outside Santa Fe; Gore Vidal and William S. Burroughs, authors. In general, little is known of the careers of most former LARS students, although some suppositions can be made from information compiled at the time of three school reunions in the 1970s and 1990s. Consonant with their families' roots in the business and professional world, most LARSmen seem to have followed this same path, becoming businessmen or entering the legal, military, or teaching professions.

The Anglo-Saxon cast of the Los Alamos student body was typical of that time. No African American attended, but one Hispanic was enrolled in the school's last year. A Native American attended briefly—an orphan with a substantial amount of oil money and a bank-appointed guardian who wanted to educate him without "any parents to hinder my experiments." (This boy from a rural Indian reservation was unhappy and ludicrously out of place at Los Alamos and ran away before the year was out.) A number of boys came from Roman Catholic families, and records show at least a dozen Jewish students attended school or camp, although it is likely there were more than the records reveal. In a time when anti-Semitism was rife and the Ku Klux Klan resurgent, many Jewish families chose to blend into society and did not acknowledge or declare their heritage or faith. Compared with boarding schools in the East, most of whom maintained exclusionary practices, Los Alamos stands out in its acceptance of Catholic and Jewish boys, who apparently felt little if any overt discrimination at LARS. Of course, Irish Catholic Connell would hardly discriminate against Catholics. College references written by the headmaster for Jewish graduates mentioned their Jewish heritage, but usually coupled this with high praise for their character and academic abilities. Given the prevailing sentiments of the day, he must have felt it necessary to mention this but hoped to win acceptance for any boys Los Alamos felt worthy of its diploma. With few exceptions, however, the Los Alamos student body reflected the extant white Protestant male power structure of American society at the time.

A persistent perception among parents complicated the school's efforts to establish its own identity and program. While parents saw Los Alamos as a place where an invaluable western experience could be gained, they felt their sons needed the added prestige and college connections that finishing at one of the established eastern schools such as St. Paul's or Choate could give. While Los Alamos faculty made some progress in fighting this perception, it continued to plague the school for its entire history. Fay Curtis wrote a father who had asked that his son's courses be tailored so he could enter St. Paul's the next year: "You have misunderstood the nature of Los Alamos Ranch School. We do not make a business of preparing boys for other preparatory schools but for preparing for entrance into college." However much Los Alamos wanted that to be the case, the reality was that most boys left the school before graduating and finished elsewhere. Of the approximately five hundred boys who attended the Los Alamos Ranch School or Camp, only eighty-eight graduated from the school. For the most part, Los Alamos was a feeder school for other preparatory schools, primarily nonsectarian Hotchkiss, which graduated thirty-seven LARSmen. The caliber of the Los Alamos program is indicated by the fact that former LARS students did well at such schools, surprising Hitchcock whose informal estimates sometimes underestimated their future success.

By the end of its second decade, as it became more widely appreciated for its own unique program, Los Alamos was graduating increasing percentages of its own students, and some whose parents intended them to return East did not want to leave. In 1935, near the end of his third year at LARS, Douglass Campbell wrote several letters seeking to convince his parents to allow him to stay at Los Alamos. St. Paul's was too formal and religious, he said, and Hotchkiss "turned out many hundred pancakes (boys who are all alike, all having a typical Hotchkiss characteristic) per year." The thing he liked most about Los Alamos, in addition to the intimacy of the small student body, was that "everyone is different, and we are not pancakes, nor does Mr. Connell try to give us a typical Los Alamos characteristic." Campbell also felt that "in an Eastern school, with competitive athletics, I would not be on any team or anything, whereas out here everyone can play all the sports." And as he pointed out, Los Alamos was "very high scholastically, ranking at the very top with Hotchkiss."[17] Campbell's parents relented, and Douglass graduated from LARS the next year, joining the growing ranks of boys who found a Los Alamos education excellent preparation for the Ivy League.

Of the school's eighty-eight graduates, the greatest number, at least fifteen, were loyal to the school's origins and attended Yale. An almost equal number, thirteen, attended Princeton; fourteen were equally divided between Cornell and Colorado College; five attended Williams College. The rest enrolled at prominent state universities or other Ivy League colleges. Harvard, with its reputation as a more liberal school than Yale, drew only five LARS graduates. Hitchcock's sketchy notes reveal at least a few elected to Phi Beta Kappa. Clearly, Los Alamos graduates could hold their own among those from the more well-known, established boarding schools.

As with any school, some students loved their time at Los Alamos, whether one summer or six years, and others hated every minute they were there. Even parents who felt Connell to be overbearing and self-righteous wrote to thank him for what he did for their sons, commenting, as one parent did, on how "buoyant, radiating happiness and contentment" their sons' letters were. Boys who found the school congenial often considered their months or years there as one of the most important and memorable times of their lives. Student files contain many letters testifying to how deeply they were influenced by Los Alamos. After Lance Pelly died in 1928, his mother wrote Connell that Lance's "happiest years" were those he spent at Los Alamos; indeed, his nickname at LARS had been "Happy."[18]

Two aspects above all else seem to have most deeply imprinted LARS boys: the sweep and grandeur of the western landscape and the character-building lessons so dear to Connell's heart. More than thirty years after the close of the school, one student wrote of his memories of "the cottonwoods . . . in Frijoles Canyon . . . , [the] pattern of the cliffs and caves and erosion . . . , the thrilling all day ride from the school to Santa Fe with water up to the saddle when we forded the Rio Grande. The sight of Redondo [Peak], Tchicoma [Mountain] and Guaje Canyon, their form and coloring are [all] still so vivid."[19] Another, writing twenty years after his year at LARS, said that he "had gotten more benefit out of my seven months out there with you than at any other time and place in my life. It was much more than an experience; it really molded my character and spirit." Even some who clashed with Connell wrote, as one did in 1934, that "despite our several little differences . . . I remember my year at Los Alamos as one of my happiest and certainly the most advantageous from a physical and mental standpoint."

Whether one enjoyed it or not, life at Los Alamos *was* demanding. Those who were unhappy found plenty to push against before withdrawing or being asked to leave. This was particularly true if one was inclined to a dreamy, sensitive, or nonconformist nature, as Ashley Pond's daughter Peggy noted, or if one did not enjoy outdoor activities or horses. Gore Vidal commented that "'for a sensitive lad like me, roughing it at the Ranch School was, well, too much,'" and he considered his time there an "awful year."[20] (With typical perceptivity, Hitchcock noted in the year Vidal was at LARS that he was a nonconformist genius.) Billy [William S.] Burroughs, who attended the camp for three summers and the school for two years, chafed under the school discipline and several times was in trouble for use of drugs and alcohol.[21] Many enjoyed some aspects of Los Alamos life while other aspects caused them misery. Parents sometimes rode roughshod over their son's desires or were so removed that they had no idea of, nor interest in, the boy's happiness. And finally, Connell's demands for conformity and obedience were suffocating to some boys and faculty.

If a boy's unhappiness boiled over into outright defiance and rebellion or if he ran away from school, his parents were asked to withdraw him immediately. Trouble cropped up particularly as boys entered puberty and began asserting themselves, testing their individuality and independence. One boy, leaving at the end of the year with no desire to return, defiantly set fire to the Big House sleeping porch just before driving away with his parents, doubtless knowing that Connell was a stickler for fire safety. (Luckily the fire was discovered before much damage occurred.) Older boys often ran up against the ban on smoking, allowed only in designated areas to eighteen year olds with parental permission. In the thirties a smoking room was set aside for these boys, where they smoked their allotted single cigarette after dinner; they were forbidden to smoke in the presence of any who did not have permission. With smoking widely promoted as a manly and sophisticated habit, it was inevitable that teenage boys would flaunt the smoking rules, and probation and sometimes dismissal were the result of repeated violations. Connell's rigid food rules also invited rebellion, and a few boys were asked to leave after repeatedly being caught trying to dispose of unwanted food. More than one boy commented in later years that the requirement to eat everything only caused some to acquire sneaky habits.

Alcohol was permitted (and more socially acceptable than smoking) for older boys at Los Alamos, and they were allowed to share a beer with Connell or the masters from time to time. On occasion visiting sports teams were shocked when beer was provided for the LARS boys after sporting events. In later years Connell regularly invited a few older students to enjoy a drink while listening to classical music with him in his rooms before dinner.[22] Success at Los Alamos ultimately meant following Connell's rules, however arbitrary they might seem.

Connell realized that only certain boys could succeed at Los Alamos, and that those who didn't "fit in with his plan" should not be there. School brochures emphasized the importance of fitting into the community: "Occasionally we find a boy, who, although he commits no offense for which dismissal would be justified, fails absolutely to fit in . . . , is himself discontented and makes others miserable. In such a case the parents will be requested to withdraw him quietly." Nevertheless, it was often difficult for Connell to let a boy go because he truly believed he could transform boys from small savages to civilized young men. Several boys stayed on for years with little by way of academic achievement—or much else—to recommend their presence, which caused great frustration to Hitchcock in particular, who did not suffer fools gladly. In part this was because the income from every boy was needed, but also at stake was Connell's pride in maintaining his reputation for transforming boys. His mission was to create health and moral character in boys, and academic success was only a secondary goal for him. He encouraged several boys not interested in college to pursue other options, sometimes exasperating ambitious parents. For him, success in life depended on one's character, not primarily one's education.

Although a grade below sixty was considered failing, there was no written policy regarding how many times a boy could take a given course and no standard for how many courses a boy could fail before being asked to leave. Everyone's situation was considered on its own merits. Each spring the faculty decided which boys would be asked to return, basing their decisions on how each boy measured up to his perceived potential, his efforts to improve in all areas of Los Alamos life, and on whether they felt their efforts would produce results in the boy. While Connell did not participate in these faculty discussions, he did discuss each boy with the headmaster, and his opinion held ultimate sway. Boys asked to return were given a slip of paper on which to indicate if they wanted to return; only after indicating their desire were parents informed. Connell's explanation for this procedure was that the school would thereby have only those boys who wanted to be there. Given the mercurial nature of puberty, however, boys who were happy one year might be miserable the following fall, or a particularly harsh encounter with Mr. Connell might cause a boy who enjoyed Los Alamos in his first months to want to leave as soon as possible. It was one thing to have boys sign a statement that they wished to return, but quite another to assure that every boy was happy to be there and willing to do his part in accordance with Connell's regime.

School Staff and Families

Those with the most reason to be unhappy at Los Alamos were women. Connell made no secret of the fact that he thought women spoiled their sons, a widely held view of the time. It was thought that women worried and fussed over their sons far too much, thus creating weak and timid boys. He and Ashley Pond intended the Ranch School to be a rugged, masculine place where soft city boys were tested, stretched, and shaped up. They wanted no feminine distractions or interference with their ideas and plans. In 1918, when Fay Curtis asked if his mother could come with him to Los Alamos, Connell replied that it would be best if she stayed in Santa Fe.

However, Leila Curtis was soon living at Los Alamos with responsibilities as matron and hostess. Aileen Baehrens, the first matron, had left Los Alamos after a few months, and for most of the 1917–1918 school year Connell employed various ranch wives to help with the distaff side of school operations. As he began his second year as director, Connell realized that a full-time motherly presence, under his control, was needed for the boys, someone who could also serve as hostess to parents and visitors.[23] Leila Curtis was more to Connell's liking than the beautiful and cultured Aileen, around whom men swarmed like bees to honey. Mrs. Curtis was "a very nice New England lady, not interested in being fascinating, and anxious to help everyone without 'butting in,'" Connell wrote Hazel Pond. He grudgingly acknowledged that women had definite and important roles to play at the School, but he ran the show.

The women Connell liked best were those who didn't "butt in" but who stayed in the background, invisible but available when called upon to help or to teach boys the finer social skills. So long as women did not challenge or interfere with his power or his vision of how the school should operate, Connell was often gracious and charming to them. He tolerated faculty wives only because he could not expect to retain faculty otherwise, but he saw their presence as distracting to the total commitment to Los Alamos that he expected of the faculty.

Leila Curtis moved to Santa Fe after a year, and in 1919 Genevieve Ranger arrived to fill the combined position of matron and school nurse. Miss Ranger had been nurse to asthmatic student Philip Clay in San Francisco before he came to Los Alamos, and his family recommended her to Connell. She "never loses her temper and is very level-headed," the family said, surely good qualities for a school nurse. The position proved more than one person could reasonably handle, and when allergy problems forced Miss Ranger to leave in 1924 Connell split the position. During her five-year tenure, Genevieve Ranger was the only female at Los Alamos, except for the wives and daughters of ranch workers who lived at the school.

As much as Connell wanted the faculty to be as single-mindedly devoted to the school as he was, he could not forestall the inevitable, and in 1924 Fermor Church married Ashley Pond's daughter Peggy, who thus became the second faculty wife. (Henry Ruhl's wife Virginia was the first.) Peggy was joined two years later by Fay Curtis's wife "Daisy," but she too left the plateau after her husband's death. Nevertheless, a tiny but close-knit community of masters, staff, and their families began to form.

In 1927 Helen Sulier arrived as nurse, remaining for the duration of the school's existence. Mrs. Sulier was a German immigrant, a divorcee with two young daughters, and a recent graduate of St. Vincent's School of Nursing in Santa Fe. Unflappable and capable of dealing with a variety of emergencies, she was held in much affection by the boys. No doctor was in residence at the school and so the nurse was on the front lines of any medical situation. Not only did she need to know about adolescent diseases and asthma, but also had to be able to treat anything from bee stings to campfire burns to horse kicks. Broken bones from skiing accidents or falls from cliffs were treated by the school doctor in Santa Fe.[24]

Genevieve Ranger returned as matron in 1928–1929; Santa Fe resident Doris Barker filled that position in 1930–1931 and again in the last two years of the school. In between Barker's tenures the matron was Lucille Sheffield, a widow whose son Wallace was a LARS graduate, and a southerner of grace and enough "steel" to hold her own with A. J. Connell.[25] The kindly smiles of these women and the faculty wives, or the gentle competent touch of the nurse when a boy was ill, must have been balm to many boys who at one time or another felt rubbed raw in the masculine regimen of Los Alamos. The female staff—Ranger, Sulier, Barker, and Sheffield—were capable women of grit and substance, able to work in the Connell-defined world of Los Alamos. All maintained a remarkably cordial relationship with him.

True to his nature, Connell left little to chance and wrote out detailed lists of the duties of both the matron and his secretary. He gave minute descriptions of every duty throughout each day and the exact times they were to be performed. The matron's duties were extensive and required considerable organizational ability. Her responsibilities included planning the meals, ordering food as needed from Santa Fe, overseeing all aspects of the food preparation and service (including training the waiters and planning food for lengthy pack trips), and the housekeeping for half a dozen school buildings. Some of the ranch wives, among them the foreman's wife, Abbie Womelsduff, assisted the matron with these duties. The indomitable Mrs. Sheffield exercised "firm control over her sometimes fractious staff and tolerated no interference from any source, including A. J. Connell himself."[26] Above all, these women gave warmth and a feminine perspective to the male world of the school, and with the long-term faculty wives—Peggy Church, Anita Waring, Virginia Wirth, Betty Walen—they formed a close-knit and supportive sisterhood.

Two other women were briefly on the staff and faculty of the school. In the fall of 1930 Connell hired his sister May to teach voice, music appreciation, and painting. A self-described artist recently returned from several years in Paris, May moved to the ranch, perhaps as early as the mid-twenties, with the intention of making it her home. Connell designed and built a house for her there with good north light for her painting. However, May was a strong woman with opinions of her own, which she did not hesitate to express, and a prickly personality as well. Brother and sister clashed, and after teaching at LARS for only a few months May moved to Santa Fe, where she spent the rest of her life, returning only intermittently to Los Alamos. For a few years she taught at the Brownmoor School for Girls, but for most of her life A. J. and other family members provided financial support.[27]

Esilda Pepper holds the distinction of being the only female master at Los Alamos Ranch School. Connell steadfastly refused to hire women as masters, even when World War II made keeping male faculty extremely difficult. However, when the school's French instructor was drafted at the end of

December 1942 and the school was committed to accelerating the academic year's instruction into the final weeks before army takeover, Connell had no alternative. He hired Mrs. Pepper, the wife of Jerry Pepper, the master who replaced Cecil Wirth in the fall of 1942, to teach French for the final two weeks of school.

At first Connell employed female secretaries from Santa Fe who came to the ranch for a day or two a week to type reports. He preferred, however, to have full-time male secretaries who could live at the ranch. The first of these that we know of, Hamilton Beasley, stayed for a couple of years and was hired in part for his musical abilities, the idea being that he could help organize entertainment for the boys. He encouraged them to listen to jazz, much to the disgust of classicist Hitchcock.[28] Louis Connell, A. J.'s nephew, worked as his secretary for a time in 1927. His successor, former LARS student Francis Reynolds, became one of only two accidental deaths ever recorded at the school (Ruhl being the other one) when he drowned in Ashley Pond in the summer of 1929. (The pond was not deep, but apparently Reynolds hit his head as he dived off the wooden diving platform.) Perry Merrill held the longest tenure as A. J.'s secretary, from 1933 to 1943. The boys were particularly intrigued when Merrill married the beautiful Zoe Bunting, a teacher at the Brownmoor School.

In 1928 the Ranch School hired L. A. "Fred" Rousseau, yet another New England transplant, as business manager. Fred managed the Trading Post as well, and his wife Edna taught at the public elementary school. Having arrived in New Mexico from Vermont some years earlier, Rousseau came to Los Alamos after drought forced him out of his work as a "banker, store-keeper and deputy sheriff in Estancia, New Mexico."[29] His business acumen, along with Hitchcock's fiscal abilities and steadying influence, were indispensable to Connell. The Rousseaus became part of the long-term core community at Los Alamos, and their son Francis was one of seven sons of staff members who attended the school.[30]

Photography played an important role in advertising and promoting Los Alamos, and school brochures were always well illustrated. Photos of daily activities, particularly of boys exploring canyons and mountains on horseback, were given to boys or made available for purchase. In the first years these photos were taken by Ed Fuller and by one of Ashley Pond's acquaintances, T. Harmon Parkhurst, a Santa Fe photographer who had sometimes accompanied Pond's guests at the Pajarito Club.[31] He taught Hitchcock to develop film in 1921, at which time Connell built a darkroom for the use of both faculty and students. Parkhurst became the official school photographer after Fuller's death, and many of his broad panoramic shots were later favorites of the boys. Students recall "T. Harmony Packrat's" large presence huffing and puffing on expeditions into the mountains, lugging his heavy camera equipment and the required glass plates. In the early thirties he began sharing his school duties with photographer Laura Gilpin, whose imaginative use of light marks many of the later school photographs. The sophistication of her photography matched the growing sophistication of the school.[32]

Two musicians—Wilbur Wiswall and Charles Kinney—came to the school in different years on several days a week, coordinating the school's musical productions, providing instrumental lessons for boys desiring them and teaching a sometimes-required course in music appreciation. Wiswall, a published author and photographer, was married to Santa Fe artist Etna West. Kinney taught at both LARS and the Brownmoor School, whose students were yearly guests at LARS functions. The LARS drama group, the Koshares, put on an annual play (sometimes written by LARS faculty) or, the highlight of later school years, an annual Gilbert and Sullivan production, which was truly a community effort. The boy soprano casts were supplemented by masters and their wives, with Peggy Church usually providing piano accompaniment and masters sometimes playing lead roles—Oscar Steege several times was cast as the lead female. Invited guests included Santa Fe friends as well as the Brownmoor girls, who reciprocated with their own all-girl productions of Gilbert and Sullivan operettas.

Opportunities for adults to socialize outside Los Alamos were limited by the isolated location and by Connell's demand for total commitment to the students. Some like Fay Curtis felt they had to escape the twenty-four-hour presence of boys and the confines of the ranch for Santa Fe as frequently as they could manage. Others like Hitchcock were content to putter around the ranch, which was, after all, home. Free time was a rare commodity. Connell's entire life was the Ranch School, and he expected 100-percent dedication to the school's needs from all who worked there. Doris Barker discovered this when interviewed by Connell for the position of matron. Asked about time off, Connell replied: "'Take all the time off you want to as long as your job is done.'" Barker continued: "Time off as I discovered, meant ice skating; in the early spring time to look for wild flowers to put in the lobby and on the tables in the dining hall; in the summer we had time for horse back rides, although we always had to have a male escort."[33]

In the early years Hitchcock organized "bailes," dances held at the nearby McCurdy Sawmill or sometimes at Los Alamos, with a local fiddler and any residents of the plateau who could be gathered for the occasion. In keeping with the small family atmosphere of the school, students were sometimes included in these parties, although they had to be in bed long before the event wrapped up in the wee hours of the morning. The faculty were young and energetic, mostly in their twenties, and as Hitchcock wrote his mother, he wanted "a chance to prove I can stay out all night, and yet live through the next day." When Oscar Steege broke his arm roughhousing with fellow master Tommy Waring, one student guessed that there was "some bottled cheer" involved. During Prohibition there appeared to be no shortage of alcohol on the plateau, and at least Hitchcock and fellow masters Art Chase and Fermor Church maintained a supply of "Pojoaque lightning." Parties held at the school in the first years included ranch and school staff as well as friends and family from around the plateau and Española Valley.

Santa Fe provided the greatest opportunity for socializing, and Los Alamos employees were there regularly tending to school and personal business. Both Connell and Pond attended dinner parties given by Progressive Party member Bronson Cutting, later senator from New Mexico. (True to his

Fig. 3.4

Young masters Hitchcock and Church with their dates at San Ildefonso Pueblo, 1922. Hitchcock Collection. Courtesy Los Alamos Historical Museum Archives.

New York Irish heritage, Connell was a dyed-in-the-wool Democrat.) Staff attended Santa Fe Fiesta activities at the end of each summer, along with any boys at the school at the time, and in the 1920s both Curtis and Hitchcock were actively involved with the organization and running of Fiesta. Single masters dated Santa Fe women, and all at the school enjoyed parties and dances there.[34] In turn, Santa Fe residents were frequent guests at Ranch School musicales, lectures, and other events.

The most popular social events in the early years were "house parties" held at the school. The first of these was at Thanksgiving in 1919, when a bevy of Santa Fe girls and young women came to the ranch for the weekend. Among them were some of the Santa Fe Girl Scouts from the troop started by Hazel Pond, including Peggy Pond and Anita Rose, sister of student Bill Rose and later wife of master Tommy Waring. A dance was held with records played on the school's Victrola, and during the day boys served as escorts for horseback rides and other activities. In the late twenties dances were regularly held with the short-lived Santa Fe School for Girls, which was modeled on Los Alamos and advertised itself as "the only ranch school for girls in New Mexico."[35] After Brownmoor was founded in 1931 the Los Alamos parties were held exclusively with girls from that school.

Often there were a couple of students who because of asthma could not go home during Christmas break or between the end of camp and the start of school. One of the masters or Connell himself was then responsible for these boys and thus not able to travel or come and go freely. Occasionally an asthmatic student's family spent a winter or summer holiday in Santa Fe, and a few mothers rented houses there for the year so as to be near their sons. This did not mean they saw their sons often; Connell strongly discouraged frequent visits and allowed no boy extra time in town to see family—or for any other reason. Winter holidays were in general lonely times for staff or students at the ranch, with most of the school community gone and themselves far from convivial company and seasonal parties. Connell gave a Christmas dinner party every year for the ranch staff and their families, complete with a staff member dressed as Santa. Presents were given to all—one year all the ranch children received ice skates—and ranch children's memories of Connell are of a kind and generous man. Any students present at the time helped with these events and were included in invitations to holiday parties in Santa Fe.

Parents were encouraged to leave their sons at Los Alamos for the one-week spring break so they could participate in school trips. Those who lived within five hundred miles of LARS were allowed to go home, but Connell told visiting parents they could not take their sons more than five hundred miles from Los Alamos. An additional fee was charged for the spring trips to such

Fig. 3.5

Spruce Patrol boys Miron Neal and Tom Rutledge playing bridge with Cecil
Wirth and Art Chase, Camp May, 1936. Wirth private collection.

places as the Grand Canyon and southern Arizona. Typical was one in 1926,
when Hitchcock took a group south to Carlsbad Caverns, El Paso and Juarez,
the new Elephant Butte Dam, and Albuquerque, a thirteen-hundred-mile trip.
The most popular spring trip of the late thirties and early forties was to one
of the Colorado ski resorts. These trips were enjoyed by boys and masters
alike, providing opportunity for relaxed discipline and escape from the
confines of Los Alamos and the ever-watchful presence of Connell. For wives,
of course, it meant more long days of family separation.

Wives coming to Los Alamos coped as best they could with the over-
whelmingly male-dominated place, each carving out time for family life as
much as possible given the demands on their husbands, who were at Connell's
beck and call. The masters ate most of their meals with the students and often
had evening duties, which complicated family life. Few conveniences eased isolated Los Alamos life for the women. Connell believed in heating with wood
rather than coal or oil, which would pollute the atmosphere and harm the
boys' health. In the early years the only telephone was at the school office;

eventually there were phones in faculty houses, all connected to the single Forest Service party line that served the school.

Peggy Church's experiences were typical of the rigorous life faced by faculty wives, although this eased somewhat in later years. When Fermor and Peggy were first married, they lived in one half of the small peaked-roof Pyramid just north of the infirmary, the other half being occupied by Connell's male secretary. There was no hot water in the cottage so Peggy bathed at the Big House when the boys were in classes, an awkward situation that resulted in at least one embarrassing incident when Connell was showing visitors around the school. The only kitchen facility in the Pyramid was a small two-burner hot plate, so the Churches took their meals with the boys. Connell expected Peggy to clean their rooms as well as those of his male secretary. Like the Big House, the Pyramid had a sleeping porch, and Peggy described awakening in the depths of winter under piles of blankets to find her face nearly frozen to her pillow.[36]

Soon there were children to raise, gardens to be kept, and sewing and handwork to be done. Some like Peggy Church had their own horses and rode with or without companions. Fermor built her a small one-room cabin on the edge of Pueblo Canyon, to which she retreated to write poetry.[37] Families could use any of the school's sport facilities not being used by the boys. There were gatherings in one another's homes to play bridge or listen to classical music, and the Churches' upright piano provided many pleasant hours. The development of nationwide radio in the mid-twenties lessened the sense of isolation, and on Saturdays they could listen to the Metropolitan Opera or Toscanini concerts. On occasion masters taught informal classes for one another. In 1922 Curtis taught Spanish to Hitchcock, Church, and Genevieve Ranger on three evenings a week; Hitchcock reciprocated by teaching the others Greek on two evenings. In some later years a few masters and their wives met weekly for Bible study classes.[38]

Peggy Church poignantly captured the texture of life for many of those who, for their part, contributed to the life of Los Alamos—the women and children.

Electricity for the school was provided by a power plant which was only just adequate for the necessities; an electric space heater or electric iron could easily cause an overload, at least in the early days. The . . . faculty wife learned to do her ironing with a set of old fashioned "sad irons" that came in three sizes with a detachable handle. Two of these irons would be getting hot on the woodburning Great Majestic cook stove while the housewife was ironing with the other—and usually getting pretty hot herself. Mornings and evenings a big copper teakettle simmered quietly. Bread could be put to rise or milk to clabber for cottage cheese in the warming ovens at the back of the range. Cake and cookies baked erratically. It took a lot of practice to learn just when to expect a roast to be done; the pitch sticks flamed up fast and other greener sticks sometimes took an exasperating lot of coaxing.

After the arrival on the scene of bottled gas, the wood cookstove was replaced by a more modern green enameled range. The drippy icebox on the little screened back porch gave way to a gas-fueled refrigerator. The wind-up Victrola was discarded for an "orthophonic" radio phonograph and winter evenings were livened by broadcasts of Toscanini conducting Sibelius or Beethoven.

During the winters, wives, both of staff and employees, pored over catalogs—generally referred to as "wish books"—from Sears Roebuck and Montgomery Ward, selecting everything from circulating stoves to fabrics to pots and pans to bassinets and snowsuits for children. This was the age before Kleenex and before zippers. Keeping children's noses wiped and getting them in and out of arctics and winter clothing took a lot of the housewife's time. It was also, of course, the age before washing machines and laundromats. At first the housewife did the diapers herself in a deep, built-in tub adjoining the kitchen sink. Later the laundry was sent out to the wife of one of the ranch employees, or one of his pretty daughters came in to clean or to wash in the new wringer type machine.[39]

I remember the fragrance of the weeks before Christmas when the women busied ourselves in our kitchens, burning stacks of sweet smelling pitchy pine wood in our cast iron kitchen ranges. Edith Warner and Tilano always sent up from Otowi Bridge little neat bundles of pitch pine tied with red ribbon to kindle the fire in our fireplaces.

I seem especially to remember the winter moonlight. The moon that seemed to be the mistress of shadow. . . . How much I loved that world covered with untrodden snow, or the silence of snow falling at night among the pine trees, the almost soundless rustle.

New Mexico has been called the Land of sunshine. But has anyone noticed it is also the land of moonlight.[40]

Above all else, there was special compensation in the beauty of the place—the sweeping views bound on the horizons by high mountains, cottages nestled under a clear blue dome of sky, brilliant sun, moonlight and stars undimmed by city lights, a peaceful quiet unknown in cities, and the broad plateau where children could roam unafraid. For most of the community, life at Los Alamos had, at least in retrospect, a magical quality that continued through minor changes in the routines and details of daily life.

Close attention was given to detail in all aspects of the boys' lives. The major themes of school life, established in the first years, were refined with creative and distinctive traditions, so necessary to forming school loyalty—exemplified in the logo designed by Santa Fe artist Gustave Baumann, the trademark use of brown ink in all correspondence, or the school's unique and dramatic graduation ceremony. These gave a special texture to Los Alamos life.

The careful mentoring given by the young, energetic faculty was of great importance to a number of boys, and frequently lifelong friendships were the result. While some families made up for their sons' long absences from home by regular correspondence and close attention to their sons' activities and academic progress, others—whether from neglect, illness, or business pressures—seemed indifferent and distant, an all-too-familiar situation in private boarding schools across the country. Perhaps typical of such boys, Antonio and Thomas Taylor arrived at LARS in June of 1918 and returned home only a year later even though their mother died in September 1918. They were not told of her death, in accordance with their father's wishes. After a month at home in June 1919, Antonio returned to Los Alamos for another twelve months.[41] For some like Antonio, Los Alamos became almost the only home they knew, and the masters and A. J. Connell their male role models. Connell in particular took this responsibility very seriously, writing a parent that "my affections are deeply involved [because I think of myself as a] temporary father to the boys I have here." Many letters in student files indicate the genuine affection some had for Connell. Jay Gilchrist wrote that Connell "became my warm and much beloved friend before I left the ranch in 1931 and my return visits were always a sort of 'homing.'"[42]

Of the approximately twenty boys at the school in 1919–1920, most hailed from St. Louis, New York City, Chicago, or San Francisco, and they arrived in Santa Fe via train, as did most future students. After new roads were added, boys rode the D&RG from Santa Fe to Otowi, where the school truck met them. (In later years, when the narrow gauge railroad was reorganized as the Denver and Rio Grande Western, students dubbed the accident-prone D&RGW the "*d*angerous and *r*apidly *g*rowing *w*orse.") As enrollments grew in the thirties, a Pullman car was chartered on the Santa Fe Railroad, with a staff member and sometimes an older trusted boy chaperoning the group of students.

Los Alamos seemed on surer footing in 1920–1921, having survived the first crucial years and the transition from Progressive health school to more conventional boarding school. There were three faculty and twenty-two boys that year, two of whom—Bill Rose of Santa Fe and Wallace Kieselhorst of St. Louis—became the school's first graduates in June.[43] The graduation ceremony, with New Mexico Governor M. C. Mechem as the speaker, was held northeast of the Big House at a place still known as Graduation Canyon. Guests were seated on boulders and Indian blankets spread on the ground. Philo Fuller and Ashley Pond, who awarded the diplomas, were among the one hundred guests. The carefully staged ceremony described in the *Santa Fe New Mexican* revealed Connell's theatrical flair and set the pattern for all future graduations.

> At a signal from a Scout posted on the mesa rim above the amphitheater the Los Alamos school boys appeared at the top of the trail on their ponies, the leaders bearing Old Glory and the Los Alamos flag, and wound down the path to the "hall," parking their ponies in a row and taking their seats around the edge of the cliff.
>
> The most picturesque feature of the day was the serving of refreshments by seven San Ildefonso Indian boys and men in native dress, some of them with bronze torsos bare from the waist up, and bravely adorned with beads and feathers and silver ornaments. These waiters served the eatables in basket shaped pottery bowls made especially at San Ildefonso for the occasion as were the immense pitchers.[44]

After Fuller Lodge was built in 1928 graduations were held on its east-facing portal, but the drama remained, with a formal entrance of the mounted student body singing the school song as they paraded past the assembled guests. San Ildefonso Indians sang and danced, their performances supplemented in later years by the Villeros Allegros, a mariachi group from the La Fonda hotel in Santa Fe. It was an impressive and memorable scene. Prizes were awarded, as at every subsequent graduation, to those with the highest and second-highest yearly averages and to the boy who showed the greatest overall improvement for the year. The actual prizes were selected by each boy at the Trading Post, for Connell did not "believe in giving useless medals."

Over its quarter-century life span, Los Alamos awarded diplomas to some of the thirteen boys who came for a postgraduate year. If their deportment and academic work, not duplicated elsewhere, met Los Alamos standards, exceptions were made to the two-year residence requirement for a diploma. Some few boys whose behavior met Connell's standards but whose academic performance did not meet the school's standards were awarded Certificates of

Work Accomplished as a reward and validation of their time at the school. One such certificate read in part:

> He has exhibited high qualities of responsibility and leadership . . . as Senior Patrol Leader and Troop Leader in the School . . . [and] demonstrated high ability in horsemanship and camping. His academic program has been specially adapted to his needs and ability without regard to college preparation.
>
> This certificate carries the full recommendation of Los Alamos Ranch School, except the recommendation to continue with academic work of college grade.

These certificates were yet another way Los Alamos emphasized the importance of character building in its mission.

Connell turned forty in the spring of 1923 and found himself tested by the demands of running both school and ranch. Believing that ranch operations took too much of his time and energy, he sold the range cattle in 1922, keeping only the dairy herd. The Camp May cabin was added that same year, reflecting the shift in focus away from ranch work and toward direct experiences with nature on the trail. In June, Connell confidently wrote Edith May: "'The tumult and the shouting dies, the Captains and the Kings depart,' and I find myself again practically alone on my mesa, calmly considering in this quiet atmosphere the accomplishments and failures of this past year and strange to say, I am fairly well satisfied." However, a month later the expenses of new water and power systems made it uncertain that the school could open in the fall. Enrollments, after an initial spurt in 1919–1920, had been flat or had decreased, this at a time when every student's fees were of critical importance to daily operations. Connell turned to the Irish solace and curse, drink, and offended a boy's mother, a staunch supporter of the school. After apologizing, he said he "realized that my condition has become steadily worse and that I must get away if I am to run the School in the fall." It was common knowledge among faculty and staff that Connell drank heavily at times, but he was obviously shaken by this situation and had too much at stake to allow it to happen again. Later that summer, he wrote that he was "planning some changes in my way of living. I must cut out the 24-hour duty. I am remodeling some rooms in the cottage and will have two rooms there." He established a policy that no students were allowed to stay at Los Alamos between the end of the school year and the beginning of camp, the only time during the year when there were no students present.

With financial assistance from Philo Fuller, parents, and the bank, the school did open in the fall of 1923, but barely a month after the opening of school, the Commissary and the school's records were destroyed by fire, and on December 9, Edward Fuller died after an illness of several months. The following spring the school was quarantined with scarlet fever, and in May, Fay Curtis took a year's leave of absence when his tuberculosis flared again.

The previous fall George May II had written Connell:

> Do you know I'd hate to have to wrestle you for a living. You can be thrown down but you can't be *pinned*; always coming back for more. One would think that disastrous fires were mere exercise-stunts, from the calm and casual way you write. It's the way you and your bunch rise to emergencies that counts most. Courageous self-command. That to me, is the essence of Los Alamos spirit.

At the peak of his powers, Connell was full of energy at midlife and met these challenges with determined vigor. What he did not do, however, was address a critical weakness in the school's foundation, one that ultimately affected its ability to respond to crisis—its financial operations.

Ashley Pond held the original mortgage on the ranch with Edward Fuller's promissory note; in 1919, Fuller foreclosed on the mortgage and assumed ownership of Los Alamos. Following his father's advice, in 1920 Fuller incorporated the school, with himself as president and principal stockholder. In the spring of 1922 Connell assumed control of the common stock and at Fuller's death became the principal stockholder, thus solidifying his control of the school. After 1923 neither Ashley Pond nor the Fullers had any substantial financial involvement with the school, and none of the wealthy parents invested heavily in the corporation, although at critical junctures some provided emergency funds for operations or equipment. Connell held the controlling interest, and various parents and employees held smaller amounts of stock. When Connell referred to LARS as "my school," it in fact was.

The school depended on enrollment fees for both operating expenses and capital improvements; a small endowment fund on the books in the early years soon disappeared. For most years the school operated with a slight profit margin, but in several years ranch accounts had a net loss. Capital improvements were vital to the school's growth, the new road and power and water systems being only the first of many such improvements. The period from 1927, when the Pyramid was remodeled to serve as a dormitory for Spruce Patrol (providing for more beds and a larger enrollment), to 1936, when John Meem completed several new buildings and additions to older ones at Los Alamos, was a time of rapid growth in the physical plant. Funds for these or any other projects came from the operating budget or from bonds issued by the school, large bank loans, and donations from parents, of critical importance to the school's survival. Among these generous parents were the Marston, May, (Lafayette) Hughes, and Regnery families, who invested in Los Alamos bonds or stock and occasionally provided funds to keep the school operating.

Although the school survived the challenges of the twenties and early thirties, its vulnerability was recognized by Hitchcock, Rousseau, and others. In the late thirties Connell reluctantly agreed to changes in the school's organizational structure laid out by Hitchcock and other staff members. In 1939 LARS was instrumental in passage of a state law allowing not-for-profit incorporation, under which law it reorganized and established the Los Alamos Foundation, whose goals were to retire the school's indebtedness, establish an endowment fund, and place control of the school in the hands of a board of trustees. Connell became director of the Foundation, but he was no longer able to wield sole power. Unfortunately, the timing of these changes was not fortuitous—the Depression continued, and war once again darkened the horizon—and ultimately the changes came too late.

The school's shaky financial basis had not yet come into focus in the fall of 1926, however. Connell had successfully overcome the troubles of the previous three years, Fay Curtis had returned to teaching in the fall of 1925, his year of rest having apparently cured his tuberculosis, and enrollment was steadily growing. In June of 1926 Curtis married Rosa Margaret Parker, known as Daisy, of Santa Fe.[45] Fermor and Peggy Church had moved into their own house in 1925, so Fay and Daisy moved into the Pyramid. In 1926, the previous year's secretary, Henry Bosworth, a former forest ranger at Bland, stayed on to teach math. Hitchcock left to pursue a Master's degree in classics at Yale, and Charles Jenney was hired to teach Latin in his absence. Enrollment in the fall of 1926 was higher than ever before: thirty-four students, nine of them new. Los Alamos was increasingly known for its high academic standards—as Fay Curtis wrote a college dean that October, "our passing grade is 60 and an average of 80 is unusual for us." Some colleges, among them Vanderbilt and Amherst, had begun to grant Los Alamos "certificate privileges," meaning that they would accept the school's graduates on the strength of their Los Alamos diploma, without College Board examinations. The school seemed on solid ground.

Daily routine continued much as it had throughout the decade, with morning classes and afternoon rides and other outside activities. As early as 1921 movies were shown on Sunday evenings, and in later years boys enthusiastically embraced the newest invention, radio. (Connell specified Kadette radios for the boys since they drew less electrical current.) Speakers and musical events were regularly scheduled; in 1926 one performance featured

"Princess Tsianana and Oskenonton, the famous Indian singers with Homer Grun, the composer."[46] Boys old enough to have a driver's license and whose behavior met expectations were allowed to drive school cars around the ranch or on official trips with a staff member to and from Santa Fe. Senior Patrol boys, or those with good grades or high rank, were allowed special trips to such places as Eagle Nest, Acoma Pueblo, the hot springs spa at Ojo Caliente, or to Santa Fe for sightseeing, the movies, and "junk" food, allowed in moderation only on trips away from school.

The ranch itself was functioning well, with a new foreman, Jim Womelsduff, who took over after Ben White left. Another scarlet fever epidemic infected three boys in October, but otherwise all was well. Connell was in and out of Santa Fe attending Kiwanis meetings and a scoutmaster course, part of a Boy Scout Awareness Program sponsored by the Rotary Club. Curtis was preparing a paper entitled "Spanish Armor and Weapons in New Mexico" to present at the State Educational Association meeting in November.[47] Before that happened, disaster struck. Early on the morning of November 4, Fay Curtis was taken ill and died within a few hours.

Years later Hitchcock wrote that Curtis died of tuberculosis; accounts at the time of death gave conflicting causes, but it seems certain that recurrent tuberculosis weakened Curtis's always less-than-robust health. He had resumed teaching more than a year earlier, but the fact that he left explicit instructions about his funeral and burial seems odd for a thirty-year-old newlywed. Although an undertaker was summoned from Santa Fe, he was sent back because Curtis wanted to be buried on the rim of Pueblo Canyon within twenty-four hours of his death. His body was placed on a pine plank, covered with an Indian blanket, and lowered into a grave that had been dynamited out of the rock. The boys stood at attention as he was buried.[48]

Curtis left not only his distraught new wife, but a school bereft of its academic head.[49] Connell remarked to the newspaper that "No man has had more to do with the success of Los Alamos [than Curtis]." He immediately notified Hitchcock, on leave at Yale, who told the university that he would have to leave his work unfinished. When Connell made him a formal offer of the headmaster's position, Hitchcock accepted. The pull of life at Los Alamos was strong by this time, and he returned to LARS for the start of school in February 1927. Lawrence Hitchcock was now in a position to influence the caliber and direction of the school, and he was to develop a close working partnership with A. J. Connell over the next fifteen years. In fact, 1927 marked the start of the mature phase of the Los Alamos Ranch School.

An Inspired Partnership

The Leadership

Lawrence S. "Hitchcock's judicious nature and general unflappability . . . provided an invaluable counterpole to A. J. Connell's more temperamental Irish genius," Peggy Church reflected from her perspective as the founder's daughter and a faculty wife.[1] Pooling their skills and acting in concert, these two very different men were a team almost from Hitch's arrival in 1919 as a young army officer reservist and teacher fresh out of Yale; explicitly when he became headmaster in 1927; and then demonstrably a full partner, even after he was mobilized for army service after Pearl Harbor and until A. J.'s death in February 1944. Connell was the romantic—a master builder at the ranch; a visionary who dreamed up the Scout-based organization of the student body; a charmer who recruited the students while visiting parents in their homes; and a classic *patrón* who relished his role as "The Chief," or boss over all. Hitchcock was austere, the practical idea man with an eye for budgetary details who discovered a talent for administration. Introspective, scholarly, serious, he was the foil for Connell's enthusiasms.

In this division of labor, the overall program, the equipment, and the setting stemmed from Connell's vision, but the academic program was Hitchcock's domain. They developed clear spheres of authority, but with areas of overlap; this was the strength of their partnership and each man respected the other. They conferred about finances, too, especially when Hitch revealed a talent for analyzing budgets in contrast to A. J.'s rather cavalier approach to the bottom line, which was always precarious at Los Alamos.

Connell was not, as he put it, "a school man." His credibility came from hard-riding service in the New Mexico backcountry as a forest ranger and his local fame as a Boy Scout leader. Thanks to Pond's contacts, he already had access to Yale and to well-to-do families. But in order to round out LARS's reputation as a health school he needed to achieve academic credibility. This the first headmaster Fayette S. Curtis provided from 1918 until his untimely death in 1926. With their rigorous academic standards and Yale degrees, Curtis and Hitchcock positioned LARS to associate with the world of eastern boarding schools, and in the school's later years to compete with them for students. What made the difference in the tenure of each man is that Hitch had the vision and aspiration to put LARS in the top ranks of boarding schools as well as the leadership ability and drive to accomplish that vision. Possessed with broad learning and a questing mind, Hitch was a strong role model for faculty and students alike.

Connell was unquestionably an autocrat, Hitchcock the more balanced and judicious. A. J. enjoyed being boss of both school and ranch, and as the spokesman and recruiter for LARS he was excellent in this outside role as well. However, his public persona masked private vulnerabilities that became more noticeable as he aged. A private person, Hitch was both disciplined and self-assured, traits that enabled him to grow in stature as both he and the school matured. Both men loved Los Alamos and had deep insights into boys.

At Los Alamos, "the school was totally centered on the kids and we were all dedicated to the care of these kids," Oscar Steege recalled.[2] Their welfare always came first. This is a hallmark of a successful boarding school and adult mentoring is the key to it. Both Connell and Hitchcock, in their different ways, were strong role models.

Connell prided himself on understanding boys and developing their character in the school's group-centered, outdoor program. Hitchcock agreed wholeheartedly that the boys should prove their mettle in the LARS program, but he also wanted these students to meet high academic standards and the school itself to achieve excellence rather than to be ranked with some of the other western ranch schools, where the goal was often enough for young men to regain their health and then hope to get into college by virtue of wealth and family connections. In their dealings with students, Connell tended strongly toward the hortatory and liked to deliver moral homilies, whereas Hitchcock with his quiet authority was excellent one-on-one. Hitch was eighteen years A. J.'s junior, but he never seemed "young" to the boys. By virtue of his reserved personality and high standards, Hitch seemed mature beyond his years, even though at first he was only five years older than some of the boys. Their comments in the student files make fascinating reading, a point counterpoint of concern and insights into what made a given student tick.

Connell always sought to reach a boy if he at least tried to meet the academic program and was unselfish and caring toward the group. Hitchcock had less patience with a boy who could not achieve decent academic work, but he would go the extra mile for the capable student who tried. A good example is Bernon Woodle, 1932, who, failing geology during his freshman year at Harvard, received a classic Hitchcock letter from his former headmaster. Hitch wrote: "I am inspired to write you by the hope that we shall in two or three weeks have from Harvard a more favorable report than the one that came to us at mid-term." Characteristically, Hitch checked into the course and found that it was not very difficult. Bernon could and should do better.

> You will remember Mr. Connell and I frequently talked with you when you were here about the defects of excessive individuality, from which you were inclined to suffer. It is, fortunately or unfortunately according to one's point of view, necessary in college as in any other position in life to achieve a certain measure of conformity to normal social expectations; it is never possible for us to do precisely as we like. I feel less hesitation in urging you to swallow your probable dislike for the course since I know that you should have no natural difficulty with any of your college courses.[3]

Woodle was intellectually gifted, an individualist, an original, an interesting challenge for Hitchcock, especially since Hotchkiss School had given up on Bernon and passed him on to LARS.

In similar vein, a graduate with very poor grades at NYU was reminded that he had been in this situation several times before at LARS, but pulled out and brought his grades up. Following up with the NYU dean, Hitch said he was "glad indeed to help you in any way possible with this boy as we by no means consider our responsibility entirely finished when the boy graduates from our school." Hitch kept careful records of many boys' college grades in their freshman and sophomore years. Indeed, careful mentoring of graduates in their fledgling college years enhanced the school's reputation.

Careful mentoring of the boys at LARS was a matter of course. To a father whose son was transferring to Hotchkiss, he wrote in 1930: "I am afraid that his anticipation of the greater freedom he expects to enjoy at Hotchkiss has made him rather careless of the obligations we expect to be done here." A student in 1933 was profiled as "capable of doing excellent work, so his failures are inexcusable." Commenting on another student who was doing poorly, Hitch wrote in 1937: "I know of no way to make the horse drink; the impulse must come from within, there is no question that we are generally able to help inspire that impulse, but this isn't a very good answer to a father whose boy hasn't yet shown any desire for good work." Another student was asked not to return in 1937 because of a poor attitude, being "careless and inattentive, thoroughly undisciplined and disorganized." To Collier Baird, however, who had just scraped by with a sixty-point average, enough to graduate in 1943 with the last group ever to receive LARS diplomas, he said with a wink: "Well Collie, you are the first person at Los Alamos I've given a diploma to for exactly passing." Baird was no student, but he had tried hard and this is what really mattered to his headmaster and to Connell.[4]

The two men came at the quest for excellence from different directions, but instead of clashing seemed to intersect, which strengthened the school community as a whole. For example, in the early 1930s Hitchcock lamented that "we have done little to educate [a particular student] who in his 5 years at Los Alamos . . . has done less than two year's work, passing in only seven courses. While he has done his best to cooperate, I think that his influence in the school has been bad as it has been an example of the lack of any necessary standard of performance to remain in school." He concluded: "I do not exactly regret our keeping him but feel that in the future in so far as is possible, we should not take or retain such. There must be a sufficient number of health cases in the country that we can choose those who are promising scholastically." Connell saw it somewhat differently, feeling that LARS "did him good." Emphasizing the boy's character, he reported to the boy's father that "as leader of the Spruce Patrol he did very well. He was also a great help to his roommate." Although the boy's "academics were difficult," Connell put great stock in this boy's unselfish behavior and willingness to assume responsibility. Seeing potential, he did not hesitate to appoint him to the top senior leadership position despite poor grades.

Early on, Connell was impelled to tighten up Pond's very loose, expressive model in order to convince parents to send their sons to a remote ranch school that soon enough had ceased to be a working ranch. But he continued to believe that the most authentic test of character was mastering outdoor skills in a structured group program, and his approach to safety issues was rooted in this conviction.

It was because Connell was a stickler for safety that the school's accident record was superb, no mean feat given a vigorous schedule that brought boys in daily contact with horses, and that stressed outdoor activities such as hunting, setting out trap lines, exploring Indian caves, climbing cliffs, and building trails during their community-work program. Connell's insistence on "instant and unquestioning obedience" was not simply the exhortation of a commanding personality. Rather, the school's remarkable safety record owed much to the insistence by Connell and his faculty on responsibility and doing things right. The director harped on safety to the faculty, as well. "There is no such thing as an accident," A. J. would say. "You need to think ahead to anticipate danger."[5]

The potential for accidents was high in the Ranch School setting. Connell himself learned this lesson the hard way when Henry Ruhl died of exposure on October 30, 1920, while deer hunting with a student. In public, Connell said the boy survived because of his Scout training, but in private he was shocked to learn that neither of them had known how to start a fire with wet wood. Spurred by this incident, "Mr. Connell took all the boys of the school down into the canyon and gave tests and instructions on how to start a fire when all the available wood is apparently wet. I picked up much information which was as new to me as to some of the boys," Hitch said. There was nowhere "in the immediate vicinity where dry wood cannot be found in abundance by those trained to look."[6]

As part of their training in basic survival skills, boys were required to carry a whistle, match safe, knife, cook kit, and other equipment when they were away from the ranch. Survival skills included cooking, as well. Each patrol during the all-day Saturday ride learned how to cook lunch in their Scout mess kits over coals from an individual campfire. The motto exhorting Scouts to "Be Prepared" was no abstract principle at the Ranch School.

Fire danger was severe during certain months, particularly in the summer of 1922 when the Pajarito Plateau suffered a prolonged drought. That year, the Commissary burned down because of a faulty stove, and the fire could not be put out for lack of sufficient water pressure. All the heating was by wood stoves except for the kitchen in Fuller Lodge (built in 1928), which used coal. In winter 1931 the cottage where Hitch and A. J. were living burned to the ground; it could not be saved because the water pipes were frozen solid. Hitch lost everything, including his books and papers. For several hours the flames flickered with an intense blue glow, fueled from a thirty-gallon keg of "Pojoaque Lightning." (This being Prohibition, Hitch, Ferm Church, and Art Chase had stashed corn whisky there for safekeeping.)[7] The dairy barn burned to the ground in the mid-1930s, the cause being spontaneous combustion.

The worst accident took place in the fall of 1929, when Francis Rousseau plunged sixty-five feet from the cliffs above Camp Hamilton in Pueblo Canyon and bounced on the talus below. Rousseau survived with a broken pelvis, but Arthur Chase, the young master only one week on the job, was badly shaken. Quite likely, Connell admonished Chase for letting this happen on his watch. Several years later Ransom Lynch, another new master, was dressed down for failing to stop students from rolling rocks into the canyon below. It was Connell's practice to chew out new masters in front of the boys; it reinforced his role as boss, while delivering a necessary message.[8]

The year 1941 saw its share of incidents: a summer camper with a deep-cut knee extracted by car from the Valle Grande, a skier with a broken leg brought down by sled from Camp May. Gilbert Davis, 1941, might have been the hero of this skiing accident. Riding back alone from Camp May through deep snow to get help at the ranch, Gil was terrified that Connell would chew him out for breaking a cardinal rule: never ride alone. Avoiding Connell, he reported the incident to Cecil Wirth (his brother-in-law), and recalled years later that if A. J. knew he never mentioned it. Of course the boss did know: the rescue was a success, but Harry Walen, the master in charge, got the chewing out.[9]

Even more important were the accidents that did not happen, thanks to careful planning and procedures. Firearms safety was taught at the rifle range. Older boys in the Spruce Patrol could go on the fall deer hunt. This three- or four-day event entailed riding out on horseback from Camp May and coming back each night full of stories. John Reed recalls the fall hunt in 1932 when his team of three under Tommy Waring became disoriented in the canyons southeast of the Valle Grande. "It was a cold November day with snow on the ground. After scaling one mesa after another we were utterly lost. It was getting dark and Mr. Waring said he couldn't continue and thought he was getting a heart attack. We were obviously scared and with my 30.06 I fired the prescribed 3 shots of lost persons. To our great relief we heard answering shots and after one more ridge found we were right back [at Camp May]."[10]

Being around horses almost daily was a manageable risk, but something could go wrong, as happened to Harry Walen one rain-soaked afternoon while he was helping the boys harness their horses to go on the daily ride. "We always assigned a new, unknown horse to a master," he recalled, "until we felt we knew where it could be safely assigned." As he prepared to mount Buddy, a large, strong, fractious horse of unknown quality, the horse half-turned, kicked, and knocked Walen into the muck. Buddy then "whirled around as he reared up on his hind legs, and came down with his sharp front hooves aimed at my head. Hitch saw what was happening, and already was plunging through the muck to rescue me. He flung the reins in his hand at Buddy's head, just enough to deflect him, so that the hoof came down beside my ear instead of on my head."[11] Alertness to danger saved the day, and Harry went to the hospital with a banged-up knee instead of a concussion, or worse.

Lawrence Hitchcock subscribed completely to the outdoor program developed by his boss. Early on as a young master, Hitch was asked to give the talks on fire safety, reminding everyone of the precarious water system, made all the more serious because they lived surrounded by forest. He developed a roster system so that the school could know where any student was at a given time. Although he had little prior experience in riding and camping, Hitch soon mastered these skills under Connell's direction, and with Fermor Church he developed the elaborate logistics and procedures of the Los Alamos Summer Camp. He loved riding out with the boys on afternoons during the school year. Unquestionably, however, the academic program was his domain.

Los Alamos's reputation for good teaching rested not so much on the curriculum itself, which offered the conventional spread of college preparatory courses, but on small classes, some with one-on-one instruction, where individual students could advance as rapidly as they mastered a subject area. Upon entering LARS, a course plan was established for each student based on prior preparation, entry test scores, and goals, regardless of age. For example, a fifteen-year-old proficient in Latin might take advanced work with Hitchcock, and at the same time take an intermediate history class and perhaps a beginning math class. Under the patrol system based on physical maturity, students

Fig. 4.1

Oscar Steege's Ancient History class, late 1930s.
Courtesy of Barbara Steege.

were ranked on the basis of their individual achievement in all aspects of the program (including academic effort, but not grades), but there was no class standing. Academic marks were given on the basis of frequent tests. Honor lists were posted weekly, and academic high achievers were given prizes and special trips, but it bears repeating that, true to its Progressive origins, the LARS program was designed to develop the whole boy, with success in academics an important but not the most important goal.

The courses each master taught varied from year to year, depending on the specialties of other faculty and on student needs, with Hitchcock teaching upper-level Latin and Fermor Church most of the science courses. To be sure, the small lab for teaching physics and chemistry in the Arts and Crafts building was rudimentary at best. But because masters were creative generalists who took teaching seriously, the lack of lab equipment was not serious. In 1935, Los Alamos became the first western boarding school to provide an examiner at

Fig. 4.2

Harry Walen's English class, Arts and Crafts Building, June 1941. From left: W. C. "Christie" Luhnow, Collier Baird, Baird Tenny, Ted Church, Gary Sutcliffe, and Henry Walen, master. Photo by T. Harmon Parkhurst. Courtesy Museum of New Mexico, neg. no. 1299.

the College Board: Art Chase, on the English board, was followed by Harry Walen. The college placement record was strong, and the faculty took pride when in 1926 and again in 1936 a LARS graduate was ranked first in the freshman class at Princeton.

The group of long-term teachers was in place by 1929, but LARS still depended on recent college graduates, some of them its own graduates, to fill out the teaching staff. That salaries were cut across the board during the Depression was taken in stride by men who were grateful to the director for giving them a job. Hitchcock himself took periodic leaves to do graduate work at Yale and the University of Chicago, and the fact that LARS had a liberal leave policy, enabling men to do advanced work in their fields, owed much to Hitch and his example. Men left for one reason or another—the low pay, isolation, another job, the difficulties of working under Connell—but they shared with the longtime masters a sense of joy for having lived in the Los Alamos community. Another attraction, surely, was the freedom to teach what they wanted within the broad subject areas of the preparatory curriculum.

Taking Ferm's geology course or reading classics one-on-one with Hitch—"Virgil in the wilderness," Rogers Scudder, 1930, called it—were highpoints for the strongest students. To this day, former LARS-men recall with glee the mannerisms of certain masters such as Warren "Lefty" Page, former pitching star on the Harvard baseball team, an impatient teacher who enjoined his students to shape up, or to laugh at the right time, with well-aimed volleys of chalk. Art Chase knew how to liven up his Latin class for even the slowest students, as, for example, the day he challenged a boy to decline correctly or receive a zero for the day's grade. For each wrong answer the student was asked to take one step back toward the door. Backward he plodded, but at the very last step lightning struck and he found the correct answer. Hitch was rarely without his curved pipe in hand and Harry Walen also smoked. One day in English class students saw smoke curling up from Walen's jacket pocket, which began to smolder. Suddenly Harry noticed himself and raced out of the room and into LARS lore.[12]

A highpoint of the Hitchcock regime was his close working partnership with George Van Santvoord, the head of Hotchkiss, who bestrode that Connecticut boarding school like a colossus. Known as "the Duke" (as the headmaster was universally referred to, but never to his face), Van Santvoord was (like Hitchcock) a product of Yale's strong emphasis on undergraduate teaching, and he may even have taught Hitch when he was briefly an assistant professor of English at Yale. The two men were much alike: confirmed bachelors until well into middle age, committed gardeners, fierce in their advocacy of high standards, and not shy about displaying their intellectual breadth and brilliance. Hitch and the Duke became headmasters just one year apart, and their partnership waxed with Los Alamos's growing reputation as a top western school whose students were welcome to finish up at Hotchkiss, and to which students not ready or suitable for Hotchkiss could be referred (as happened with the gifted, but difficult Bernon Woodle, profiled above). In the arrangement worked out between them, after a year or two of the vigorous outdoors life at Los Alamos, some thirty-three boys transferred to Hotchkiss before going on to Yale or Princeton, for the most part.[13] It was primarily through Hitchcock's personal connection with Van Santvoord that LARS became well known in the boarding-school world. This West to East link is fondly remembered by many of the LARSmen who went on to Hotchkiss, where they found themselves academically, physically, and morally prepared by Los Alamos to flourish under the rigorous, high-minded, and at times eccentric ministrations of the Duke.[14]

Stories about Connell's mannerisms abound. Having been a sickly child himself, A. J. was a strong believer in positive thinking. Walking back from the Big House toward the Lodge one day, Rogers Scudder, 1930, mentioned to A. J. that he thought he was coming down with a cold. "No you are not!" Connell reproved the young master in no uncertain terms. "Don't even think of it." And Rogers didn't catch cold, after all. Connell had a horror of anything that recalled funerals, including certain flowers. When a visiting family brought calla lilies to the Lodge, he thundered: "Who brought these damn lilies?" "I did!" replied the student's grandmother. A. J. much preferred Adolfo's gladioli, which grew in the fields in theatrical profusion and festooned the Lodge during summer months. And yet, when someone did get sick, the capable nurse Helen Sulier would work wonders, aided by the fact that in her infirmary boys could listen to the radio at will.

Adolescents appreciate adults with style, especially if they are offbeat characters like Connell, with his many mannerisms. Connell let boys drive the 1930 school Packard on the road to Santa Fe, thrilling for boys learning to drive, terrifying, perhaps, for the passengers. When taking boys into Santa Fe on weekends, he would permit them to buy only one ice-cream soda or sundae apiece—what A. J. called "garbage" (pronounced "gahbage")—and then, returning to the ranch, he would stop his car in the middle of Otowi Bridge to check for comic books, melodramatically casting same into the river. In his upstairs quarters in the Lodge on Friday nights, the director would occasionally host a musicale, organized by one of the Spruces. Boys noted that Connell preferred Ravel's *Bolero* and Wagner's *Ride of the Valkeries,* which they found a bit much. As a strong FDR Democrat, he also liked Paul Robson's "Ballad for Americans." Irreverent boys knew how to stir him up, as when they dubbed the ancient Indian trails worn into the stone at Tsankawi ruin—a cultural site Connell wanted them to appreciate—"Broadway and Forty Second Street."

No profile of A. J. Connell is complete without mentioning his opinions. Boys learned to tolerate his one-sided conversations, related with some amusement in a letter home by Jay Rice, 1930. "I had a talk with Mr. Connel [sic] yesterday on a ride. We spoke of everything from co-education and Mr. [John L.] Lewis, to wildcat trapping. His ideas were evidently deep set, cause whenever I commented to his distaste, he became harsh and generally nasty; toward the end of the conversation I agreed with him even before he spoke."[15] Former student John Reed recalls visiting the school in the summer of 1936 following his freshman year at Yale, and arranging to spend a month there with his roommate as paying guests.

> It was a wonderful vacation; we were assigned a horse and had the run of the country all to ourselves. . . . We usually dined with A. J., but unfortunately 1936 was an election year. Tom and I were Republicans, though too young to vote, and of course in A. J.'s eyes FDR could do no wrong. We made the mistake of arguing with A. J., who soon told us that if we continued to express our stupid views he would send us home. Needless to say, the "discussions" ended forthwith.[16]

Sometimes irascible, often melodramatic, the director with his homilies and stories and particular style was revered by many. Upon receiving the customary birthday card a graduate wrote Connell in the early 1940s: "it rekindles a warmth of memory, which is never long dormant, of very happy days. I doubt if a day goes by that I do not recognize as having been most useful some large or small item of knowledge or training which I got either in camp or school. . . . To this day I find myself trying to make the items of existence of a haphazard world conform to [the school's] neat and efficient regularity." Many similar testimonials stud the student files, and it is important to note that these very qualities of "neat and efficient regularity" were among the things that Hitchcock himself liked the most about Los Alamos. "What I had learned in Los Alamos," Edward Hall wrote, was "a lifelong obsession with doing things right, with the maintenance of all equipment, and with the importance of quality. These ideals were shared by most of my classmates when I met them later in life."[17]

Longtime faculty members accommodated the Boss's whims, and he in turn (thanks to Fay Curtis and Hitch) gave them ample freedom to teach how they wanted, coupled with a liberal leave policy to pursue graduate studies, as long as they paid for it themselves. However, A. J. had another difficult trait: he enjoyed putting junior faculty down in front of students.

At meals, new faculty members who made the cardinal mistake of not finishing everything on their plates were skewered by Connell in a booming voice in front of the boys: "At Los Alamos, we eat everything." A camper recalls Connell berating a new master for sitting on his legs before dinner in the Lodge: "pull your legs out like a man," A. J. scolded. This show of power was hard to take and some men soon left.

Most everyone put up with Connell's imperious style while resenting the fact that "you couldn't tell him anything." One who didn't play along was Ransom Lynch, a young math teacher who left after two years in 1939 for what became a lifelong career at Philips Exeter Academy. Having won the faculty bridge pool, Lynch made drinks for everyone at the year-end faculty party and spiked Connell's cocktail with an extra strong dose of whiskey, causing him soon to leave the party. Sweet revenge, but Cecil, Virginia, and Oscar felt this was going too far.[18]

Still others made fun of Connell at his expense, as when the veteran Tommy Waring and Rogers Scudder, a youthful master from the class of 1930, spoofed him at Santa Fe parties, which inevitably got back to the Boss and was hurtful to him because they were all friends. When "Mr. Connell turned the N. East room [in Fuller Lodge] into his home with magenta damask curtains, bedspread and chair covers and an aroma of incense, I joined him often for a drink before dinner," Chase recalled. Connell liked scotch, and sometimes arose late in the morning with a hangover. "One evening when A. J. was in Santa Fe, Rogers Scudder, who has since become one of the leading Latin scholars in the country, took a flying leap with his shoes on into the middle of the magenta bed just to demonstrate his independence."[19]

It was a life shared by men and boys together, whether in the Big House with its open-air sleeping porches; or on afternoon rides—sometimes one-on-one with a master, which was one of the highpoints of the LARS experience; or on trips during spring break; and of course in the classroom with never more than ten students (and usually less) every morning. "Kids felt free to come to our rooms," Oscar Steege recalls. "We had lots of contact with the kids. Some of them were a lot of fun."[20] To be sure, the horses, the big sky, and even the huge trees around the school intimidated some of the boys until they learned to love living on the mesa with that grand view of the Sangres. For most, but not all the boys, this theatrical setting would work its magic and for Connell this was very much a part of his grand design.

A draft for a school song entitled "Sing ho, for saddle weather" includes various typed verses describing the landscapes discovered "when we ride out together." Then, in Connell's hand, the themes of fellowship and joy are penciled in:

A verse about returning over the range from a pack trip
  —sudden view of the ranch on the mesa far below
  —pine smoke curling up from the many chimneys
  —the promise of comforts after hardships enjoyed
  —warm showers
  —the dining room
  —the completeness
  —gaiety and larger companionship of the School.[21]

This same romantic vision was lovingly depicted as a star-strewn winter evening, with skiers and bonfires outside Fuller Lodge, on the 1928 Christmas card sent to parents and friends of the school.[22]

Fuller Lodge, beautifully rendered by the Santa Fe architect John Gaw Meem, brought this vision to completion. Tramping the woods together, Connell, Meem, Ashley Pond, and a forest ranger selected massive Ponderosa pines growing nearby for the portal. However, when the forester marked some of the trees in a grove just west of the school, A. J. later painted over these marks, because he didn't want any of those trees cut down.[23] Meem recalled that he and Connell were careful to site the Lodge "in such a way as to give it ample room in front, for the ceremonies incident to Commencement time."[24]

The Lodge, with its distinctive vertical lines, mirrored the Big House built by Pond in 1917, and also owed its inspiration to the Evans family ranch house in Colorado, which Meem had visited when he was studying architecture in Denver at the Beaux Arts program. Planning began in 1926 for a formal dining room large enough to seat sixty or seventy people where musical events, plays, and lectures could be held; rooms for guests, activities, and single faculty were also included in the overall design. Navajo blankets hung on the wall on both sides of the fireplace and over the east doors. Chimayó rugs hung on all the balcony railings. Another prominent feature of the great hall was the large elk's head over a massive fireplace on the south wall. A deer's head graced the facing wall. A portrait of Ashley Pond hung above the fireplace in the foyer. Dining-room tables and chairs were fashioned in rustic style. Large wrought-iron lighting fixtures, with the LARS logo designed by Gustave Baumann, hung from the portal. Stairs led to the mezzanine level and the infirmary, where the matron and the dietician had small apartments. The third floor housed Mr. Connell's apartment, as well as Mr. Hitchcock's, while in earlier years a third apartment was occupied by a single master, later by Connell's secretary and his wife.

"In designing the building," Meem recalled, "I was impressed with the possibility of making the dining area somewhat monumental in character with trussed ceiling and with balconies on one side and rear. The beautiful tufa stone also gave me a chance to feature the fireplaces. The vertical columns of the east porch also gave dignity and an exciting impression of strength to the design of the structure."[25] Construction began in the fall of 1927 and was completed one year later when the academic year began.

In Fuller Lodge, LARS now had a distinctive focal point, and the school's national reputation grew apace. Meem became the school architect, and what remains today of the LARS physical plant is largely representative of work coming from his office. Remodeling included work on the Church house, and expanding the faculty quarters at Spruce Cottage in 1935 to accommodate Cecil Wirth and his bride Virginia. To the west of Ashley Pond, the WPA grade school for children at the ranch was another Meem design. By 1937 the school occupied a dozen smaller buildings and three large ones, including the once all-inclusive Big House, Fuller Lodge, and the Arts and Crafts building.

Fig. 4.3

Valentine's Day dance with Brownmoor School girls in Fuller Lodge, 1941. Bottom center, Cecil Wirth; bottom right, Lawrence Hitchcock. Photo by Laura Gilpin. Courtesy Los Alamos Historical Museum Archives.

John Meem charmed Connell, as he had Hazel Pond, for whom he built two residences in Santa Fe, one of which included an apartment for A. J.'s use while tending to business in town. Built in 1932, at the nadir of the Depression, the Arts and Crafts building was a multipurpose unit containing classrooms, a small laboratory, and workshops where the students used only hand tools. Although Meem was a master at handling difficult clients, the micromanaging parent donor drove even him to distraction until, after Hitchcock tried and failed to handle the situation, Connell took charge and told her what *he* wanted for her building, and that she should stay in Pasadena during the actual construction. She died before the building was finished, and in due course Meem invited her husband to visit the tufa and half-timber structure made possible by her fifteen-thousand-dollar gift. "Mr. Connell," he wrote, "had a large number of Santa Fe people out to the school recently for an afternoon of music, and supper afterward, and I was glad to hear the comments in connection with the building." Turning on the charm, he concluded, "I believe that Mr. Connell and Mr. Hitchcock are both happy with the results and I hope you too will be."[26]

Connell's friendship with his architect was typical of the close relationships he had with several prominent Santa Feans. He was a longstanding member of the Rotary Club, where Daniel T. Kelly of the Gross Kelly Co., and Ferdinand Koch, owner of the Santa Fe Electric Laundry, opened doors to the local business community for him. Much of the stock of the Trading Post was supplied by Gross Kelly (wholesalers). "Dan Kelly was a great friend of all— and a patient creditor during the depression years," Art Chase recalled. With Dr. Frank Mera of Sunmount Sanitorium and Miss Isabel Eckles, the city school superintendent, Connell served on the board of the short-lived Santa Fe School for Girls, which was modeled on Los Alamos, sleeping porches, horses, the outdoor program, and all.[27] LARS students staying over for Fiesta could lodge at Sunmount, which served a good table and was safely removed from the heavy drinking that went on in town.

From all that has been said so far, it is clear than Connell and Hitchcock were interesting men. Connell's character and background have been described. What do we know about Lawrence Sill Hitchcock?

Among Connell's talents was the ability to attract and hold the loyalty of key subordinates. The youthful Lawrence Hitchcock was hired by Fay Curtis right out of Yale in 1919 and, with his military training and gift for organization, soon achieved the status of a trusted advisor even before he took over the academic program after Curtis's death. Unlike A. J. with his upper-middle-class Irish Catholic origins in New York, Hitch was a Congregational minister's son whose family was shabby-genteel. He was the fourth generation of

Hitchcock men to be inducted into Phi Beta Kappa at Yale. Disciplined, serious, and scholarly, Larry, as he was then known, worked his way through Williston Academy and Yale with the help of scholarships and served briefly in the U.S. Army at the end of World War I. Upon arrival at Los Alamos, Connell called him Hitch, and Hitch it would be from now on.[28]

Burdened with a distant, difficult mother, with whom he carried on a voluminous correspondence during his twenty-three years at LARS, Hitch may have found in Connell a substitute father figure for his own, much older father who was ineffectual. When it came to camping, pack-trips, and the outdoor life, he took immediately to everything that Connell had to offer. LARS became his true home, providing the structure and order that he craved. He was one of the few masters who did not own an automobile, but Hitch was not a recluse. While preferring to stay at the ranch, he enjoyed Fiesta parties as much as any of the young masters, even though he was in no hurry to get married. Hitch dithered and talked so long about the house he was designing for Charlotte Bosworth, the beautiful sister of LARS master Henry "Boz" Bosworth, that she gave up on him. However, he did have a long-term relationship with a Santa Fe woman.

One of the enduring memories of Hitch is of him assiduously planting iris bulbs along the paths at Fuller Lodge. "Some time in 1930," Doris Barker recalled, "Hitch in his own meticulous way, had planned and executed a border of Iris for an odd shaped area in front of my cottage. He made a chart of the blooms beginning with purple and deep blue tones down through the light blue to white and then up the scales of tones from cream color and pale yellow to bronze and brown."[29] Since boyhood, he was a dedicated gardener. Helen Sulier, the school nurse, pitched in with her own flower garden, tended lovingly year after year near the Lodge.

Many years later Mac Wood, 1932, provided an alumnus's perspective on the formidable headmaster. "Hitch was and is the greatest," he wrote. "He taught himself Sanskrit late at night, worked on a strawberry garden between the Big House, the baseball diamond, and Fuller Lodge before dawn in the mornings, coached track, and was cool in the saddle on long all day rides. In addition, he headed the academic program at the School, without interference from Mr. Connell."[30] Severo Gonzales recalls catching sight of Mr. Hitchcock as he emerged from Bences's cellar with a jar of homemade wine. He relished Wednesday night poker with the ranch hands. That he did everything meticulously and well, but was available to ride one-on-one with students on a given afternoon, and was indeed "cool in the saddle" was the Los Alamos community's measure of the man.

In the early 1930s Hitch began making a yearly analysis of school balance sheets, looking for ways to cut expenses and shore up the school's precarious finances during the Depression. In doing so, Hitchcock hoped to convince Connell that a casual approach to operating this high-cost operation was outmoded. A self-taught skill at budgeting enhanced his indispensability to Director Connell.

Hitch was dedicated to lifelong learning, and took several summers off at the University of Chicago to perfect his knowledge of Greek and Sanskrit. He kept up with his field and enjoyed a summer spent at the American Academy in Rome, which was intellectually stimulating and confirmed his vocation as a classicist. He spent the 1935–1936 academic year earning an MA in classics at Yale, where he was offered a professorship if he would stay another year and turn his MA thesis into a dissertation.[31] A cousin, Richard Seymour, was president of Yale, and the Classics Department wanted Hitchcock on the faculty. Once before, Hitch had left for a year of teaching and study at Yale, in 1926, the year Fay Curtis died. His plans cut short, Hitchcock had returned to be headmaster. Ten years later, he faced another career crossroads.

The opportunity to become a university professor was both flattering and tempting. Years later, after a second career in government service, he wondered if he shouldn't have taken the academic path his college roommate Leicester Bradner had followed in a long career of teaching English at Brown. Yet the pull of loyalty to Connell and the entire way of life at Los Alamos was stronger, and he agreed to return after first visiting several eastern prep schools and colleges to get their views on the future of boarding schools in American education. Among the established boarding schools he visited was the Progressive school Putney, recently founded in 1935 in a farm setting in Vermont.

On the basis of knowledge garnered during this trip he sent a searching, highly critical letter to Connell that changed the course of LARS, and without destroying their relationship. Unfortunately, the original Hitchcock letter no longer exists, but there is firsthand testimony of Cecil Wirth, who wrote his wife Virginia in June 1936, after their first son John was born:

> Mr. C. left this morning with Fred [Rousseau]. He was a very tired man and quite broken in spirits because of Hitch's letter . . . and I am afraid the summer might turn out to be a long round of conferences because it looks as though the spirits of Mr. C. will break completely before he gives in too much. I hope I am wrong and that he gets a new perspective on things because I am sure we must change a few things to keep pace with our maturity. He felt so badly about Hitch writing what he did and expressed himself so conclusively against the written word that I have decided against writing what I originally thought as

I think what Hitch had to say needs to be digested first and after that I will be able to see which way the wind blows.[32]

Evidently, Hitch agreed to return only if several conditions were met. First, as Virginia recalled years later, the academic program would have to be strengthened at the expense of Scouting, so dear to A. J.'s heart. Furthermore, LARS should outgrow its earlier role as primarily a feeder school, and (as soon happened) graduate more of its students. Second, as seems evident from the changes subsequently set in motion, the autocratic director could no longer run such a one-man show; a more collective leadership under a board of trustees would have to be established. Third, the school's finances, always precarious, should be bolstered by a fundraising effort to pay back debt, support a scholarship program and build endowment under a new foundation. Among the younger men, Oscar Steege felt that the school was financially precarious and recalls talking about this with Cecil. Faculty salaries were too low, a primary cause of teacher turnover, which A. J. always shrugged off but Hitch saw as a sign of institutional weakness. It bears repeating that direct evidence of Hitchcock's conditions is lacking. What is clear is that these changes were implemented after Hitch's return.

By 1940 the LARS model was mature and the school had reached full enrollment: forty-eight boys. Although Connell was majority shareholder in the Los Alamos Corporation, which ran the school, it was reorganized as a nonprofit corporation, with Connell agreeing to become chairman of the board and president of the new Los Alamos Foundation. The officers were Connell, Hitchcock, Church, Rousseau and J. O. Seth, the school's Santa Fe lawyer. Connell was still boss, but more in the sense of *primus inter partes,* because the Board and the Foundation had voting members. Under the leadership of General Robert E. Wood, the powerful head of Sears, Roebuck and a very satisfied former parent, the endowment campaign was begun. He was assisted by Lafayette Hughes, 1934, whose Colorado family was a major bondholder of the school.

It is much to Connell's credit that he gave way, even if he had no choice: without Hitch he could not run the school. In truth, neither man alone could have done it. "You are too austere to be Director," Connell told his partner in the direct style they both preferred. And Connell, as Hitch told the trustees after A. J.'s death, was too cavalier with figures.[33] Connell's was the classic dilemma of the strong-willed school founder who has outlived his original mandate. It happened to Carmelita Hinton, founder of the Putney School, when her power was challenged, then curbed, in the bitter faculty strike of 1947.[34] What emerged at Los Alamos that summer of 1936 was a new leadership core comprised of Connell, Hitchcock, and Cecil Wirth, who became assistant to the director and head of the summer camp, which Connell had abandoned after the 1932 season. Hitch himself assumed the additional title of treasurer, which he held until 1943.

With these new structures in place, Los Alamos could weather the loss of Art Chase, who, tired of Connell's authoritarian style, resigned in 1936 while completing an M.A. in history at Yale before going to the Berkshire School in western Massachusetts, where he taught for many years and served as assistant head. A buoyant person full of song and one of the best-loved teachers, Chase initiated the weekend camping and skiing activities for the older boys at Camp May. Evidently, Art tired of A. J.'s constant interference and paternalism. Starting in

Fig. 4.4

Cecil Wirth, Lawrence Hitchcock, and A. J. Connell,
with his dog Peggy, 1936. Wirth private collection.

Fig. 4.5

Berthod Pass, Colorado. Spring ski trip, 1936, led by
Art Chase and Cecil Wirth. Wirth private collection.

1937, however, Art returned every summer to run the summer camp with Cecil. Fed up with Connell, Tommy Waring left in 1939 to start his own school in Santa Fe. Of the faculty hired in LARS's first decade, only Fermor Church (and Hitchcock) remained. Twice he served as acting headmaster in Hitch's absence, including the school's last year, and reported to him and the director.

As for Scouting, fewer boys were interested in pursuing Scout activities and the students themselves were now petitioning Connell to devote more time to skiing in the afternoon program in place of riding. "Skiing has gained tremendous popularity at Los Alamos during the present year," the alumni *Bulletin* for Spring 1936 reported. "More trips were taken to Camp May than in any previous year, and every available afternoon when there was snow the slopes back of the ranch were dotted with skiers." Art and Cecil took the older boys to Berthod Pass and Winter Park in Colorado during the spring break.

The next year the boys were invited to Aspen where pictures of their skiing through deep powder were used for publicity purposes by the fledgling ski resort. Cecil Wirth and Harry Walen now ran the skiing program. The alumni *Bulletin* reinforced the point: "skiing is . . . coming into its own at Los Alamos. The ranch men during the summer, and the boys of the school in early fall, built ski trails at Camp May which open unlimited possibilities for skiing on weekend trips. A trail [dubbed the Pitz Palu] was cut from Camp May to the top of Pajarito mountain, and a small jump and practice hill near the cabin was built." The riding, pack-trips, and the rest of the well-established outdoors program continued, but Scouting itself for many boys had become old hat.[35] Because of skiing, there was less time spent on Scout activities, but this also reflected the declining national interest in Scouting. This change impacted directly on Connell's dream; even his constant harping on Troop 22 being "the first mounted troop in America" had become something of a cliché. Furthermore, it seems likely that the college admissions officers to whom Hitchcock talked looked askance at the program of a major school—as LARS now regarded itself—being so closely identified with Scouting.

It is clear that admissions standards at Ivy League schools were tightening, and even though in retrospect they were still bastions of elite preference in the 1930s, the winds of an emerging meritocracy were blowing even then, as Hitchcock sensed.[36] To remain competitive, Hitch maintained, LARS would have to hone its academic edge. The school was placing well, but for how long? College boards, testing, assessments by outsiders—all were encroaching on the LARS model.

School leaders as different as Groton's Endicott Peabody, Putney's Carmelita Hinton, and Los Alamos's A. J. Connell were motivated by higher ideals than test-taking and college preparation. Peabody's deeply felt preference for character-building was impinged upon as early as the 1890s by Harvard professors attempting to impose academic standards geared to college preparation. A Harvard evaluation panel "found Groton at best mediocre, academically, and weak in its teaching staff; but, grudgingly, strong on character. In short, Groton was found to afford 'mediocre instruction, but excellent education.'"[37] The relentless march of test taking and evaluations by outside experts is nothing new. In fact, the struggle between elite secondary schools with a mission and universities seeking trainable students has gone on for a century!

To evoke a parallel example: Carmelita Hinton, founder of the Progressive Putney School, sought to develop in her students the ideals of individual creativity, with ample space for music and the arts, community service, and trips abroad to encourage internationalism. However, in the face of parental demands for access to top colleges, she made space for an assistant director in charge of academics. While not destructive, the tension between these cross-cutting goals runs like a geological fault through the entire history of the Putney School.[38] In still another example, L. L. Nunn, the quirky genius who founded Deep Springs, another ranch school in the California desert in 1917—the same year LARS was founded—abhorred test-taking for the sake of meeting outside standards, and isolated his students on the ranch, the better to couple a vigorous cowboy life in the morning with high-minded discussions of books and ideas in the afternoon.[39]

Connell stressed the importance of community work in the overall LARS experience. Robert D. Stuart Jr., 1933, relates: "We had to do one afternoon of C.W. after class each week to work in gardens or on pathways, etc. Since some of us were quite charmed by Anita Waring, Tom Waring's wife, we competed to work in her garden. But over and above our favorite places to work, the idea of doing something for the school community was excellent. I think we all learned to do our part in later years in our own communities perhaps as a result."[40]

All of the school heads mentioned above emphasized community service. Putney had its Work Jobs two afternoons a week, and a separate summer work camp that built and maintained the physical plant while (hopefully) generating community-spirited applicants for the school. Los Alamos had its Community Work day on Mondays. Groton sent its students to tutor in the public schools and ran a summer camp for disadvantaged urban youth. And it bears repeating that for the directors of these three very different private boarding schools the development of character and service to society was a higher goal than simply getting their students into college. Yet their preferred emphasis on character, family, and communitarianism over academics was coming under increasing pressure before the Second World War, and Hitchcock's response to the encroaching meritocracy was to strengthen the academic program within the context of a more modern and a more open school.

Again like Peabody, Connell was interested primarily in the development of character, the academics being a secondary if necessary concern. Give him almost any boy, Connell told the parents, and Los Alamos would work its transformation. For his part, Peabody stressed that Groton was first and foremost a church school, "primarily designed to build character, only secondarily meant to be a 'mere' preparatory school." Furthermore, Peabody believed "that the best environment in which to build character was the family; therefore Groton would be a family. The persistence and intensity of the use of the familial image to describe institutions is astonishing," a historian of boarding schools relates.[41] Connell felt the same way about "his boys." In this respect, LARS was akin to the mainstream of eastern boarding schools established in the late nineteenth century. And along with Scouting, the CW at Los Alamos was a ritual of the character building that Connell sought to foster. "In retrospect, we were lucky to have so much emphasis on character building," Stuart wrote."[42]

Hitchcock fully subscribed to Connell's ideas about the importance of character, developed in a carefully supervised program of extracurricular activities. As he told students and guests at the 1927 graduation, "we must teach young people how to weigh the consequences of their acts, to understand and accept responsibility . . . and implant the desire to do things creditable to one's self. Do as you see fit," he counseled the graduates, "but be sure and see that the consequences are such that you will take full responsibility for your acts." To a parent who wondered why the report letters were so full of his son's doings outside the classroom, Hitch responded: "Los Alamos exists to give health and strength to boys who would not find them elsewhere; in that sense it might be said that the curriculum is of secondary importance. We have found, however, that the education of the whole individual helps in the education of all the aspects of the personality."[43]

However, Hitchcock also worried about the small applicant pool of students whose parents could afford LARS or other elite boarding schools, especially now that war clouds were gathering and families might keep their children closer to home. It happened that 1940 was not a good year to launch the endowment campaign; even a corporate leader of General Wood's stature could not get it off the ground. Yet even in the last half-year of operation enrollments, though diminished, had come in. "The School has started rather well," A. J. wrote Hitch in September 1942. "Every boy whom we wanted is back with us this year. [Furthermore] we have a promising staff, but it will be hard on Ferm as well as on me to break in so many new men."[44] Soon two full-paying students had to be dismissed for disciplinary reasons, and the percentage of scholarship students went up while the bottom line of revenues took a beating. But he always did look for the silver lining.

Hitchcock's relationship with Van Santvoord of the Hotchkiss School was that of intellectual equals filling similar roles, although the Duke was in charge of everything and of course Hotchkiss was a much larger, well-established school. Hitch's relationship with A. J. was more intimate and complex. For one thing, Hitch found himself and his calling in the well-ordered world of Los Alamos, which was Connell's creation. Los Alamos was his home. For another, Hitch discovered a talent for budgeting as well as academics, and A. J., while still the Boss, could not have run the school without him. For still another, Hitchcock was the rock on which Connell could anchor his mercurial temperament.

Art Chase is one of the few contemporaries who committed some (but by no means all) of his candid thoughts on Connell to paper. "Since I lived for some years next to A. J. at the top of the Lodge and took a number of trips with him (and more than a lot of drinks) I probably could do a life-sized portrait of him after a few more years," Chase wrote in 1974.

> "At the reunion last fall," Art said, "I sensed a great uncertainty in the minds of alumni as to what they should say about A. J. I think there was a latent feeling that he would descend like a fiery *deus-ex-machina* to punish any who did not show 'instant and *unquestioning* obedience.' My initiation under him made all subsequent headmasters like rolling down hill. . . . He was a remarkable, opinionated, terrifying 'boss-man.'"[45]

Students themselves were terrified by the prospect of a tongue-lashing by Connell in his room upstairs. Some of his more arbitrary decisions were buffered by senior faculty: for example, the interventions of Cecil Wirth are mentioned in alumni letters. Admirous of the school, fathers counseled their sons to work things out with Mr. Connell, because they knew he had high standards and cared about the boys. Faculty wives bridled at his chauvinistic attitudes toward women, and there was little private time for the hard-working masters to spend with their families. And yet, contributing mightily to the success of LARS, Peggy Church recalled on hearing of A. J.'s death in February 1944, was "the loyalty to the school, the sense of community that in spite of all the ups and downs did seem to keep us pretty well knit together at Los Alamos."[46]

Rogers Scudder, who was fond of Connell, recalls that he was always concerned with discipline. Upon hearing of an incident when students defiled the chapel at Groton, A. J. told Rogers that "'Mr. Peabody seems to have lost some of his control.'" In fact, "A. J. was an autocrat in the style of school directors then, who built schools as projections of their own personalities," Scudder observed.[47] Connell's method was to control outright by being ever-present and delivering swift rebukes to miscreants. "There was no effort to play down a boy's faults."

Self-confident and imperious as always on the outside, A. J. expressed private doubts to Hitchcock on whom he relied heavily to share the burden of running the school and enforcing discipline. In February 1942, with Hitch away on active duty, Connell wrote:

> I have missed you here a great deal. I miss you in the usual little discussions of the various problems which you and I have had together for so many years, not merely actual school work, but on the business

end of things. I also feel that your being here always strengthened my disciplinary measures. I have had the same feeling that I had during the year of your absence [1935–1936], that I was in the position of being the only policeman on the place. I am trying to get that situation in hand by expecting others to do their part. Too many feel that everything will be all right, and experience has taught me that nothing will be all right unless you make it so.[48]

A more classic statement of Connell's controlling philosophy would be hard to find.

The A. J.-Hitch partnership continued through the harrowing last year, when faculty called to active duty were replaced with men who were themselves almost immediately called up. Hitchcock left LARS in early 1942, shortly after Pearl Harbor. He had kept up his reserve-officer status, attending army summer camps, and held the rank of lieutenant colonel of field artillery when he was mobilized. Harry Walen, a five-year stalwart teaching English, was lured away by Groton offering half-again the salary that LARS was paying. Connell took this in bad grace.[49] A life-threatening illness forced Cecil Wirth to leave in May. Through it all, Hitch exchanged letters with A. J. and Ferm (the acting headmaster) several times a week and stayed in close touch with LARS business even when the school closed in February 1943 and the office was moved to Santa Fe.

In truth, in the later years the director had been unable to face the idea of letting go of his domain, telling faculty members that he didn't care what happened to Los Alamos after his death, making arbitrary decisions just to show his power, worried about losing control, drinking more. Of course he did care deeply about Los Alamos, taking out life-insurance policies that, in the event of his death, would cover outstanding liabilities at LARS. That Los Alamos had hit its stride in the last five years or so before 1942 is abundantly clear. That, increasingly, it was evolving beyond him also seems apparent. For all its strong sense of community and loyalty to the school, the faculty had wanted a more collective, less authoritarian style of leadership, one more welcoming to women, one that granted more private space. But these faculty concerns were now mooted by the exigencies of war.

For all the positive sides of Los Alamos Ranch School—particularly the lives of boys and families forever changed and influenced for the better—there was another side. To touch upon it is to confront what might be called "the Thomas Jefferson dilemma": how to deal with an aberrant facet in the life of a great contributor?[50]

Adolescents often take to adults who are characters out of the ordinary, quirky, as long as they are authentic, and are who they say they are. Mercurial, melodramatic, at times irascible, A. J. Connell and his ideas were admired by many of the boys. "Stand tall, think tall, act tall, and be tall," he would exhort the boys, but without always doing so himself. Most took Connell's behavior in stride; of this, after a close reading of the archives and many interviews, there can be no doubt. Even so, some of the liberties that this powerful man presumed to take with the boys, whom he affectionately called his "gibbons," raise questions about his behavior and personality.

The 1922 summer camp was idyllic, a former camper told his son years later, except for Mr. Connell appearing suddenly out of nowhere in the Big House, in effect sneaking around and playing "gotcha." Typical is a graduate's response to a questionnaire circulated for the 1970 reunion honoring Hitch. (Held at the Yale Club in New York City, this was the first LARS reunion.) When asked what values, skills, or other experiences gained at Los Alamos had seemed most important to him in later life, he wrote: "1. I came to have an undying respect for L. S. Hitchcock [and] 2. I learned to avoid people like A. J. Connell."[51] That Connell was overly familiar is an undisputed fact; for boys who were subject to Connell's attentions, the scars inflicted on some lent at the least a bittersweet taste to their school days in Los Alamos. Connell's attraction for young men is alluded to in works by Gore Vidal and William S. Burroughs and their biographers. While it is through the writings of these two prominent American authors that Connell has in recent years become known to a wider public, to a degree these accounts reflect the personalities through which the facts were filtered.[52]

To the best of our knowledge, Connell never went beyond inappropriate touching of certain boys. First-person accounts of Connell's actions are credible: his predilection for examining a boy alone in his office, or private room, or, at the infrequent times when no one else was around, for suddenly coming upon a boy changing clothes in his Big House room.

Students quickly learned to avoid him in situations where they might be vulnerable. And while boys knew about it and talked about it, Connell's behavior was experienced by only a few boys in any given year and, as far as is known, was experienced only occasionally by any one boy during his years in Los Alamos. If they mention it at all, some graduates today say it was not a big deal. At the time, students made fun of Connell because he enjoyed watching them swim in the nude—just as they spoofed his other mannerisms. Yet as a graduate who had endured Connell's attentions relates: although he knew at the time that it was clearly strange and "far out" behavior, because Connell was The Boss it never occurred to him to tell a master or especially his parents. Here, then, is the familiar pattern of behavior that, to use an expression from that era, "goes over the line": the perpetrator's position relative to the victim is one of some authority by age or position.

The faculty, particularly the longtime masters, being aware that Connell was vulnerable to temptation, arranged for the physical exams—an important feature of the health program—to be held in the infirmary, with the school nurse or other adults present. The core faculty did what they could in a quiet way to protect the boys from being caught in a vulnerable situation with Connell. If he was steered away or even admonished from time to time, it would likely have been done by Hitch, given their close partnership. Because Connell owned the school for most of its history and held ultimate control, however, the faculty could do little as individuals except to cope as best they could or, of course, to leave for another school.

For all his faults, A. J. Connell had considerable insights into individual boys and demonstrated time and time again a deep concern for their welfare. "A. J. was a kindly man, and was interested in you and the boys liked him for this," Scudder recalled.[53] Yet the emotional strain on a leader who built his school around traditional Scout values must have been considerable. The tensions set up by this deep caring, juxtaposed with his urge to touch boys inappropriately, must have been unbearable to contemplate or acknowledge on any conscious level. It was at least in part these tensions that led to his drinking, particularly as he aged and felt himself becoming less connected to the pulse of the community.

When all is said and done, particular dissonances were there, undoubtedly, but did not sink the school or, in any fundamental sense, sour the melodic whole. The professional achievements of the graduates, the high quality of the faculty, the loyalty of the ranch staff, the strong sense of community in which everyone shared, all relate in the most intimate ways to the school's core values. Moreover, it must be stressed that most LARSmen never experienced untoward behavior from Connell. Extant letters show that several continued to write to him over his lifetime, and these letters contain no hint of anything other than genuine affection and respect.

In the end, it is the assessment of the large number of LARS boys who praised the school that most clearly indicates what the Los Alamos Ranch School was and what it accomplished. Looking back to his school days from the perspective of sixty years, Bill Baird, 1936, writes: "Despite my reservations, my Los Alamos experience was tremendously positive. My whole life was given a great boost, not just healthwise." Writing for the 1991 reunion, Peter Dechert, 1941, captured the essence of Connell's legacy:

> Authoritative, perceptive, vain, imperious, charming, capricious, sometimes outright coquettish, he did indeed scar a few of his friends, and of ours. But to most of us, the important fact today is that the goal of training each student, each camper, to be both able and ready

to realize individual personal responsibility was the absolute keystone of A. J. Connell's educational philosophy. And on the Los Alamos Ranch we were constantly inspired to attain the Boss's goal. The automatic exercise of reasoned personal responsibility was the hallmark of a successful Los Alamos boy.[54]

In short, doing things right, responsibly, unselfishly, for the good of the community, became part of one's internal moral compass. It is for this symphonic whole of values that A. J. Connell and his school on Los Alamos Mesa are best remembered.

Conceptually, the school was largely A. J.'s creation; educationally and operationally, it owed much to Hitch. Hitch's role in helping A. J. to cope with emotional distress and his drinking problem is undocumented, except by inference.

Connell, a complex, interesting man, should be seen as a great contributor. He was a respected member of the Santa Fe community and provided an important source of jobs for Anglos and Hispanics. He was loyal to his employees, and affectionate with their children. Doubtless, some of the things people did not like in him are fairly common to individuals who have the drive to create their own vision. The irony is that certain behaviors of Connell's could have damaged the whole thing, but didn't. Instead, out of the blue Los Alamos Ranch School became "a war casualty."[55]

As for Lawrence Hitchcock, he is universally admired in the recollections of alumni, former colleagues, and the staff. In truth, he was wholly centered upon Los Alamos and the Chief, and when these were taken away he was never again so happy or fulfilled.

We Ride! We Ride!

The Los Alamos Summer Camp

Of all the things that have to be learned, such as balancing both sides of the load for even weight, padding noisy items like rattling tin cans that might spook the horse . . . the most important thing to know is the knot that keeps it all together. It's a knot that keeps the cinch tight and holds the load so it can't be scraped off a tree, bucked off in a frenzy, or rolled off in a mud wallow.

The knot that prevents these catastrophes, used from Alaska to Texas in infinite variation, is the diamond hitch.

Sid Marty, *Men for the Mountains*, p. 48.

Camp Song

Los Alamos high on the Mesa,
Looking out on the swift Rio Grande.
Here we live near the ancient pueblos
Of the Indians who cherished this land.
Let's remember the far Chihuahueños
And the trout in del Indio's stream
And the view from the top of Chicoma
As home from the mountains we ride.
WE RIDE! WE RIDE!

The pack outfit left the ranch at ten, Ted Mather the wrangler in the lead riding Joe, the black horse with the white star and a single-foot gait, and Cecil

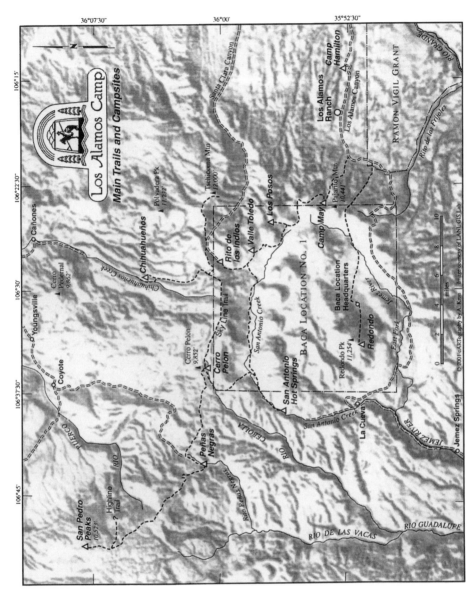

Map 2

Los Alamos Camp, Main Trails and Campsites.
Cartography by Andrea Kron.

Wirth, the camp director, bringing up the rear on Chili, the spirited red horse whose mane was streaked in white. With more than thirty people riding, in addition to fifteen packhorses and Mike the mule and the Churches' dog Jamie, the outfit on line of march was a majestic sight. Boys new to riding learned how to keep up with Joe's fast pace without trotting; otherwise, their horses would develop saddle sores and the pack loads would begin to shift. The train was moving right along in order to reach the first camp at Rito del Indio by four so that Bences Gonzales and his helper could set up for dinner, while the boys pitched and ditched their tents. And then, with dinner over and the fire built up, Art Chase would lead the singing and tell stories. Soon the boys would be in their bedrolls and the horses, hobbled, let loose for the night, but the exhausted staff might perhaps have time for a few hands of poker before turning in themselves. Wind whispered in the ponderosas. Stars in all their brilliance shone over the camp and the nearby vast expanse of the Valle San Antonio.[1]

So went the first day of the famous long camp in August, shortened to sixteen days under Wirth from the full three weeks when A. J. Connell ran the camp. San Pedro Peaks was their destination, fifty miles by trail through mountains and open grasslands, and several campsites away from Los Alamos Ranch. It was the last of three pack trips into the mountains behind the ranch that summer, the culmination of a superbly run, unique group experience of living together in the wilderness—learning to care for horses and to use and maintain good equipment, putting boys in daily companionship with enthusiastic adult mentors, building character and self-confidence, while hiking, riding, fishing, and having fun. It was the essence of Pond's vision of Los Alamos that had been played out every summer since 1917, except for four years during the Depression. But this was early August 1941—as it happened the last time the outfit would ever ride out on the traditional long camp again.

Records for the first camp under Connell from 1919–1932 are abundant; less well documented is Wirth's operation from 1937, when he revived the camp as an independent operation, until his last camp in 1941. (Connell ran a much-reduced operation in 1942.) However, the historical record of the second camp is recorded in several color movies. This leads to a curious perceptual imbalance. We know more about the details of how the first camp under Connell was organized, but the still photographs in black and white give it an old-fashioned cast. In contrast, the second camp under Wirth has a vividness and immediacy that was captured on amateur movie film and slides, as well as black and white photos by Parkhurst and others.[2] Yet the differences between the two camps were ones of nuance and style rather than substance.

Ideologically, the Ranch School was an extension of the summer pack-camp. Connell went along with the college preparatory program in order to attract students, but his heart was in the outdoors program and Scouting. Moreover, he always felt that a student should, preferably, have attended the camp first before going on to LARS. In this, he was the ideal man to carry out Pond's vision. "The summer camp was the clearest expression of the dream of the founder of Los Alamos Ranch School," Fermor Church wrote years later, when he deposited camp records in the New Mexico State Archives. "Careful planning and great detail went into each year's program as these reports [to Connell] testify."[3] In this, A. J. revealed another of the reasons for his effectiveness: administrative ability, attention to detail, and the capacity to motivate others to carry out the vision. He sought nothing less than to make this summer camp unique in America, using tested methods and equipment devised by him and the camp staff.

Connell already had a feel for the Pajarito backcountry and its peoples from his service as a forest ranger based in Bland. A. J.'s experience going into nature on pack-trips was part of his carefully nurtured persona. "A word in regard to the moral training of Los Alamos," he wrote in 1919. "Going on the principle that there is nothing bad in nature, such close contact with her, under the guidance of clean men, backed by the splendid principles of the Boy Scouts of America, must produce a clean boy and develop the best that is in him."[4]

Furthermore, he had the contacts to gain and maintain access to a vast area in the Santa Fe National Forest and the Baca Location around and west of the ranch's eight hundred acres. His brother Walter's partner, Española merchant Frank Bond, had extensive grazing leases on the Pajarito Plateau. In 1918 Bond purchased the Ramón Vigil Grant from Pond's Detroit backers, and one year later he bought the ninety-five-thousand-acre Baca Location No. 1, in the Valles Caldera. The Bond-Connell Sheep and Wool Company was dissolved in 1926, but by then A. J. was closely allied with Bond, who in turn provided access to the Valles for the summer pack-camp.

Hal Rothman has described in detail how Bond, the homesteaders who were beholden to him, Connell, and other landowners sided with the U.S. Forest Service in its struggle with the National Park Service beginning in 1919. The Forest Service, promoting development through logging and grazing, and the Park Service, seeking to protect ruins and promote tourism, were at loggerheads throughout the entire twenty-five-year history of LARS. A proposed Ancient Cities National Park would have incorporated Frijoles Canyon (which did gain monument, but not park status), pueblo ruins at Puyé (later administered by Santa Clara Pueblo), Otowi, Tsankawi and Navawi'i, the whole of these Pajarito Plateau sites backstopped by the huge Baca Ranch (which only passed into federal control decades later, in July 2000). Wanting access to grazing for his sheep and flocks under contract, Bond had no interest in seeing the national forest lands on the Pajarito Plateau and the Baca itself become a new national park. In turn, Connell fought to preserve isolation for his program, including very limited automobile access to the Pajarito. The establishment of a national park would threaten these advantages. With close links to the Forest Service and the nearby pueblos of Santa Clara and San Ildefonso, Connell was a powerful local voice against the park concept.[5] Thus, the nature he wanted to preserve for LARS had an ongoing political dimension.

Connell had reason to be concerned about encroaching roads. As early as 1922, Lawrence Hitchcock reported seeing several carloads of fisherman coming up from Albuquerque to fish the Rio Cebolla and the Rio de Las Vacas just west of the Baca Location. The boys had poor fishing at the campsite there in comparison with 1921. Considering that the limit then was fifty trout per day, the arrival of the automobile heralded not only the onset of pressure on the fishing, but also the loss of wilderness in certain parts of the Jemez. The San Pedro camp, by contrast, was inaccessible by car or wagon teams and "should be good for some time to come."[6] Time proved Hitchcock right: much of the territory used by the camp north of the Baca was opened to logging roads in the 1960s, but San Pedro remains off limits to timbering and roads as a designated wilderness.

Given these alternative futures, the lovely mountains, valleys, and meadows behind Los Alamos that provided the setting for Los Alamos camp were already deeply marked by the hand of man. Crossed for millennia by Indian trails, the Pajarito had been heavily impacted by sheep, then by cattle grazing at the time Los Alamos was founded in 1917. An extensive trail network used by woodcutters and homesteaders also provided access. In reality, the sense of isolation and living in a remote wilderness was already something of an illusion, very much in the eye of the beholder, useful to the marketing of the camp and the school. Indisputably, this was still predominately horse country, and to this day a well-articulated, if rarely used, network of horse trails still exists along most of the Los Alamos camp routes.[7]

During his twenty-five-year reign, Connell was deeply attached to the mission of Los Alamos, of which the summer pack-camp was the heart. The burdens of organizing and running the highly regarded camp, with no break from the regular school year, were exhausting. The camp was a source of revenue and recruitment for LARS, but almost every fall Connell threatened not to run it again. But "the trouble is," he wrote one parent, "I like it so much that I cannot bring myself to give it up." The joy of it, as well as of trips using the same horses and equipment during the regular academic year, was a main reason why men of the caliber of Lawrence Hitchcock, Art Chase, Ferm Church, and Cecil Wirth stayed on, working on low salaries for the love of it.

Fig. 5.1

A. J. Connell in summer camp, 1920s. Gilchrist Collection.
Courtesy Los Alamos Historical Museum Archives.

Goals and Organization of the Summer Camp

Campers signed up for the whole eight-week program, although exceptions could be made. The basic plan for this pack-trip camp included short periods at the ranch preparatory to increasingly longer pack trips until the August three-week trip, which initially was held in the Pecos country in the Sangre de Cristo Mountains, then, starting in 1922, out to the San Pedro Peaks in the Jemez. "We sure had a good time on our big trip [in the Pecos]," Antonio Taylor wrote in 1919. "We were gone 3 weeks and covered 200 miles. We sure camp comfortable, plenty of grub and a good cook, a tent to every 2 boys and each boy has a bed roll consisting of a quilt and 3 blankets. All of this is carried on pack horses and each boy has a horse to ride." On the way home they were given a dance by the Girl Scouts in Santa Fe, and arrived back at the ranch the next night.[8] In 1920 there was a five-day pack-trip at the end of June into the northern Jemez range, a seven-day trip into the southern Jemez in July, and in August a three-week trip riding across the Española Valley to the Pecos country. Although the locations changed, this three-trip format remained the focus of most summer camps through 1941.

The camp was dear to Connell's heart and central to the skills and habits he wanted to teach boys. The educational philosophy behind it was grounded in group experience. "It was A. J. Connell's firm conviction, shared in large measure I am sure by those who worked for and with him," Hitchcock related, "that the individual in any cooperative enterprise is happiest playing his assigned part in a smoothly functioning whole, in the success of which, and in the pride and satisfaction from that success, all share. The presence of an occasional bolshevik, resentful of direction and hostile to any control, reinforces rather than vitiates this rule."[9]

Under Connell, the camp was tightly controlled, even authoritarian, but for good reason, Connell felt. "In my opening talk to the boys of the camp I always emphasize the absolute necessity of instant and unquestioning obedience," he wrote to the parent of a rebellious camper who was asked to leave in 1927. It was "of paramount importance in a camp of this sort, and I would not for a moment consider taking these big pack trips with boys who did not conform to this rule. The danger of accidents would be too great." This approach carried over into the school as well. "'Instant and unquestioning obedience' was a phrase indelibly imprinted on my mind by A. J. and used forcefully in each of his opening talks to the school body in September," Jim Anderson, 1938, recalled.[10]

Of a boy who was sent home before the long trip in 1930, Connell wrote: "[Your son] has been . . . extremely disobedient, which has resulted in one accident, fortunately not as serious as it might have been. Against absolute orders plainly announced to all, and after being reminded by one of the boys, he insisted on trying to ride and jump a horse that was assigned to another boy, resulting in the horse kicking one of the boys and inflicting a painful injury. In a camp of this kind disobedience is dangerous." In fact, he added, "it is very seldom that I have dismissed boys from the camp . . . only . . . in cases where necessary for the protection and safety of the boys entrusted to me."

Boys who improved their skills and helped the group go—"learned group responsibilities," he would say—were rewarded in the weekly ranking system. Those who exhibited selfishness were the object of his withering, public scorn. A 1924 camper who was awarded the prize for greatest improvement was praised for never complaining to Connell or his parents despite "being constantly bawled out. He never seemed to get discouraged. Each calling down seemed to increase his determination to overcome his faults. With such a boy anything is possible." On the other hand, a 1928 camper had "not taken hold well . . . is the poorest camper . . . constantly crabbing, always objecting to everything, trying to tell his superiors how to do things." Unless he "shows a more manly attitude," A. J. was prepared to send him home before the big trip.

To reinforce desired behaviors, prizes were given, Best Camper being the top award. Others were awarded for having the neatest tent, for the greatest improvement during summer camp, for being the most unselfish boy, and for catching the most and/or the biggest fish. Campers whose behavior needed improvement were singled out in a series of bulletins, as were their good traits. "Remember," Connell enjoined the 1924 camp in Bulletin no. 7, "that the greatest fault in the world is selfishness, avoid that, it pays. Think over the people you know and I am sure you will agree that the unselfish people are pretty well taken care of, and naturally so as everybody likes them."[11] This mix of praise and criticism was the classic hallmark of the strong-willed school director type in the early twentieth century. As such, tough love often brought results. In achieving these results, the school was in seamless connection with the values of Connell's camp. Writing in 1924, a college freshman thanked A. J. for his influence on him. "Being away from home is as enjoyable now as eating one of those old campfire meals made by Bences. . . . I wonder what would have happened to me if I hadn't come out to your camp last summer. It was the turning point in my life. That's straight goods, sir."

Connell acted out of deep conviction. Among his most salient characteristics was the frequently demonstrated fact that one couldn't tell him anything; boys took the strong-willed director on his own terms or not at all. "He is always right and you are always wrong according to him," Bill Carson wrote home in 1942. "I sit at his table and he tells us we must eat everything like men while he eats just what he pleases." Later, Bill reported that, during an announcement period, every boy in the camp was told his faults and what he should do to improve.[12] Connell's core beliefs were solid, straightforward, and unchanging. "There is no place like camp to bring out the man in a fellow," he wrote a parent in 1920. "I like [your son] and was pleased with his progress. Our trips are a man's job. A boy must come through or lose out."

The staff both internalized and reinforced these values. Applying for a military commission in the early days of World War II, a former camper requested his 1925 camp record and a letter from the school. Fermor Church wrote: "He made a very good camper and received valuable instruction in caring for himself and equipment under mountain conditions, in the New Mexico Rockies. The camp work stressed discipline, leadership, and general responsibility of both the individual and the group."[13]

The 1929 camp had gone exceptionally well, Connell wrote to the parents of a boy whom he had criticized quite severely. "This summer's group of boys not only showed exceptional ability in learning to handle their part of the camp duties but also displayed a splendid spirit of cooperation and cheerfulness which never relaxed under most trying circumstances." These were the values of Scouting in action, and boys in Connell's camp had to register with Troop 22 upon arrival at Los Alamos. "All of our boys are expected to become Scouts the first month of camp," Connell wrote in 1919. "I have just discovered . . . that [your son] is the only one who has made absolutely no effort to do so. I have told him that he will have to be prepared before tomorrow or he cannot go on the long trip." Mirroring the school's own Scout-based organization, boys were assigned one of three patrols, each with its senior and assistant patrol leader. Spruce was for the older, more experienced boys; Pine was for intermediates; and Fir was for young boys, the minimum age being twelve.[14]

As at the school, each boy knew where he stood in an explicit chain of command, which facilitated carrying out the duties and details of camp life. As Hitchcock recalled:

> A rank list, revised before the start of each trip (and occasionally during the trip) determined who was in charge of small groups, even between two individuals; tent mates were determined and lists posted before we started. By the time of the big trip of the summer packing and unpacking was by crews, which were the units of the order of march. On arrival at the camp one boy or a crew of two put up a tie line and brought in saddle horses, which had been merely turned loose on arrival at the camp ground until the packs were unloaded and the camp set up. Individuals unsaddled and hobbled their own horses and stowed their saddles only when their camp-making-crew chores had been completed. Then there was a pole crew (if we had camped at that spot before, poles had been carefully hidden when we left, but some new ones generally were needed.) The tent crew, or crews, pitched the tents, including front and back and corner guys, and did the ditching. And finally, last of the assigned crews, garbage hole and latrine trench.[15]

Such attention to detail bears all the hallmarks of the Hitchcock touch, and indeed the camp was one of the first fruits of the long A. J.-Hitch collaboration. With almost no camping experience, Hitch caught on fast and found himself filling in for Bill Rose [the senior counselor] on the 1921 long trip with A. J., and in 1922 he became assistant director of the summer camp and led the long trip by himself. The indispensable Hitchcock was soon vetting the suggestions of junior staff for improving the camp equipment and routines, and in a series of elaborate reports he and Ferm fine-tuned what was now being called "the Los Alamos Organization and Procedure."

A. J. Connell's Camp, 1919–1932

In general, the camp followed U.S. Army practice for packing mules. From the army transportation manual Hitchcock and Church adapted and developed

Fig. 5.2

Connell Camp Staff, 1930. From left, Fermor Church (master),
Heb Newman (counselor), Tom Waring (master), A. J. Connell,
Art Chase (master), Fred Hall (counselor). Photo by T. Harmon
Parkhurst. Courtesy Los Alamos Historical Museum Archives.

the "Los Alamos Diamond Hitch." Proficiency in tying this diamond hitch was
highly prized; beginning campers spent hours practicing on a wooden mule
between camp trips. Essentially, the four-sided shape of this knot puts an
equal strain on all points of the load so it can be pulled off in a hurry if a mule
or a horse gets hung up in timber. Learning the Los Alamos diamond differ-
entiated the top campers from those who could master only the less complicated basket hitch. In addition to being singled out for praise, the best packers
(often the best riders) got to assist crusty Ted Mather with the horses. On the
trail, riders leading well-packed animals, each with balanced loads tied down
properly, were doing things right. Little wonder that the Los Alamos Diamond
loomed large in the camp's mystique.

In 1926, the adult staff was divided into two divisions, logistics and activities. The rather grandly named Department of Transportation, Communication
and Supply, or TCS for short, was created by Ferm Church and run for the first

time under Hitch. The two men then alternated so that both could stagger their summer leave; Ferm was TCS again in 1929 and 1930 before Art Chase took it over through the last Connell camp in 1932. Among the responsibilities of TCS was "looking to the health and suitability of saddle and pack animals, and the state of the equipment, training boys in saddling, hobbling and packing, operating the field telephone we carried, and, in consultation with the cook, making menus and chuck lists."[16] In sum, TCS was responsible for all logistics, including the rendezvous with resupply trucks at various points on the line of march bringing fresh laundry, mail, and food. TCS coordinated closely with Bences and the cooking staff, and made sure that Ted Mather and his helper were backstopped by campers bringing in firewood, a job they liked to do as a way of showing off horsemanship; doing the packing, a job whose performance figured in the ranking; and helping with the morning roundup, a prestige job for the best riders.

The activities director handled in-camp activities including sports, singing, and the daily rides, and back at the ranch was in charge of the Big House and daily activities, including leatherwork and carving. Boys were divided into Buffs and Browns for intramural sports and, as in the school, Community Work was in the schedule. They swam in Ashley Pond or in the Rio Grande, after which they finished up with lemonade and chocolate cake at Miss Warner's nearby teahouse. There were side trips to ruins, Spanish mountain villages, and the Cowboys' Reunion in Las Vegas, and a high point was the Santo Domingo Corn Dance on August 4. Henry "Boz" Bosworth and Tommy Waring both filled the job of activities director. One of Waring's innovations was adding several New Mexican songs in Spanish to the campfire sing. An important part of his job, as stipulated by Connell, was to supervise the daily "sunbaths" during which boys gradually achieved the deep tans and robust outdoors look that were the hallmarks of the Los Alamos camp.

Connell's own enthusiasms were expressed in various ways and at times his interests bordered on the bizarre. He was on top of every detail of camp life, to the extent of requiring a series of different whistle toots that indicated the pack outfit was to move forward; or that all were to pay attention, stop talking, and listen for orders; or all were to assemble and gather round the whistle; and so forth.[17] (How much of this caught on is a matter of conjecture.) It was an honor to serve as Connell's "orderly" and arrange the director's camp cot. A portable two-holer of his design was dubbed the CCCCC, for "Connell's Comfortable, Collapsible Camp Can"—soon shortened by the boys to CCC, for "Connell's Collapsible Crapper." Perfected year by year, this indispensable device served the camp for twenty seasons.

Los Alamos camp was renowned for its elaborate equipment. At the Trading Post, Bences fitted every boy with the standard school uniform, including several sets of shorts, and a Dakota Stetson or a Worth, the less-expensive alternative. Each boy carried his own canteen, scout knife, match-safe and whistle, camp ax or hatchet, and, under Connell, a mess kit that apparently was rarely used in camp. (Mess kits were always used on Saturday rides in the school.) Horses, chaps, and saddlery were supplied by the camp. Hitch ordered pack frames of his design from Abercrombie and Fitch in New York. It was all first-class stuff. However, a glance at the camping gear shows it belongs to the days before lightweight equipment and synthetic fibers were invented. The bedroll was heavy and bulky: a canvas shell holding sheet and blanket. Tents were made of canvas duck, and while a group camping out today might still want to line up the tents and ditch them to prevent being flooded in a rainstorm, as in Los Alamos days, the lightweight gear now used bears no comparison.

Fig. 5.3

Packing mules with the Los Alamos diamond hitch, 1920s. Photo by T. Harmon Parkhurst. Courtesy Museum of New Mexico, neg. no. 1103.

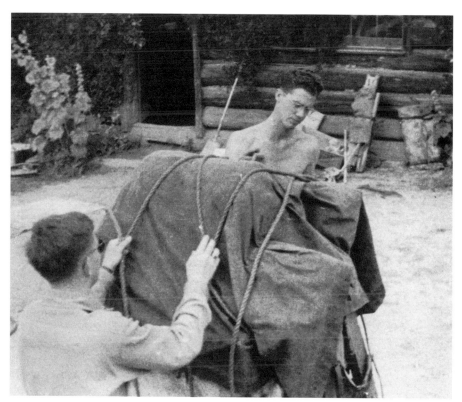

Fig. 5.4

Practicing the diamond hitch on a wooden
mule, 1942. Courtesy of Maurice Lonsway.

Neophytes learned to pack on a wooden mule at the ranch, and by the end
of the summer most were proficient and proud of their ability to tie the diamond hitch. On the live mules (used in Connell's camp) and the pack horses
(used in Cecil's camp) loads were carefully balanced, evenly distributed, and
weighed on a portable scale before starting off. (Connell preferred mules, but
Wirth felt that packhorses were easier for boys to handle.) The most proficient
riders were assigned the honor of rounding up the horses each morning with
Ted Mather. Learning to care for horses was part of camp life. Neglecting animals was high in the pantheon of sins, along with selfishness and inability to
accept authority.

Camp cooking was the domain of Bences, who was a master of the Dutch
oven. Typically, 120 pounds of the heavy iron pots would be packed, for there

was no aluminum substitute for the slow, even cooking that was achievable with cast iron. Over the years, Bences and the boys built raised cooking altars at each of the camps, where the Dutch ovens rested on a deep bed of cooking coals and were easier on the back. His *sopaipillas* were legendary and occasionally, fresh lamb could be obtained in the field from herdsmen. After the boys had bedded down, a special treat for the men was to pass around a pit-roasted sheep's head. Savoring the brains and tender parts of *barbacoa* was a time-honored New Mexico tradition. (See Glossay page 197).

Addressed as Mr. by the boys, the two or three counselors who served in every camp were invariably among the most successful LARS graduates—chosen for their proficiency, character, and ability to serve as role models. In the chain of command from small boys to adults, these high-spirited and enthusiastic young men provided an essential emotional and practical link. The first was Bill Rose, a Santa Fean who ran the first camps with Connell in 1919, 1920, and most of 1921, when there were fewer campers. The Kieselhorst brothers (Wally and Earl) came next. Cecil Wirth was equally fortunate in the counselors he had, including Jim Anderson, Charley Ripley, and David Hughes. Counselors served without pay, for room and board and the joy and privilege of coming back to the ranch. Others, such as Rogers Scudder—a former camper, student, and master—came back several summers in a row to help out at the Trading Post and the corral. Henry "Heb" Newman, 1927 (who lasted only one year teaching math at LARS—he felt the school was too isolated and austere), relished coming back five years in a row as a senior camp counselor while teaching at the Fountain Valley School. All this created highly positive links of fellowship between the camp, the ranch community, and the school, just what A. J. wanted.

As Hitch relates in his autobiography, "the pack outfit, designed and maintained at first for the summer camp, got more and more use during the school year. There were frequent weekend trips to our cabin [Camp May] at the ten-thousand-foot level in the mountains behind the school, and for skiing during the winter and as a base for all-day rides further into the mountains in the spring and fall. The outfit was also available to, and occasionally used by, school graduates who wanted to demonstrate their skill acquired to family or friends."[18] It became a tradition for the older boys to go on a long pack-trip over Memorial Day weekend before graduation. "Just got back this morning from the wettest trip I have ever been on," Dave Hughes related in 1937. Four days of steady, cold rain caused miserable, even dangerous, conditions. "It was not as bad a trip as it might have been though, for Mr. Hitchcock was in charge, and he had the organization down to a finite system."[19]

In the general scheme of things and certainly in Connell's mind, the concepts of the camp energized the school. To him the Ranch School was an extension of the camp, and in this sense it remained an "outdoors school for boys." Thus "in some ways," Ferm and Peggy recalled, "these summer pack trips came closer to Ashley Pond's original [Progressive] dream than most of the activities associated with the School itself."[20]

One questions whether anything so elaborately planned and equipped could be called in today's parlance "a wilderness experience." Indeed, it was not, and by design. Year after year, Connell relished telling the boys his story about the woman guest (inevitably, it had to be a woman) at a dude ranch talking to the ranch hand. "My," she said, wiggling up to the cowboy, "Don't you just love roughing it?" "No ma'am," he replied, "I enjoy smoothin' it." So with the camp. In their clean outfits every day—thanks to laundry service by the truck relays—and with their balanced meals, mail deliveries, and the carefully planned mixture of fun and assigned tasks, the boys were having a group experience in Nature, rather than experiencing Nature on its own terms. Not that being caught in a sudden mountain hailstorm wasn't terrifying, or learning to control horses with lightning crackling all around wasn't scary. It required staying power to endure days on end of intermittent rain, as sometimes happened in the mountains, and stamina to complete the occasional twenty-mile ride between camps. The swarms of deer flies in the Valle Toledo could test boy and beast's capacity to endure. What mattered was that Connell and his men had developed the organization and the equipment to cope with and to master almost any situation in camp or on the march. "The Camping technique developed by Los Alamos can be more accurately described as a science, as every detail concerning camp equipment, packing, camp cooking and the care of the boys has been carefully studied."[21] What they called "the Los Alamos Organization and Procedure" was elaborate, effective, and unique.

Safety always came first, and it is noteworthy that in the many years this camp operated serious injuries were virtually nonexistent. From the start, a telephone connection with the ranch was intermittently available by hooking onto the Forest Service line, and early on Ferm Church speculated that the job of staying in touch would be vastly facilitated once radios became more portable. If someone were seriously hurt, it was possible to extract him within hours by alerting a school car to rendezvous with one of the trailheads. Liability concerns do not appear in the surviving camp reports. Clearly, however, all the adults were enjoined to put the boys' welfare at the center of their concerns.

For campers who bought into the experience, and for the adults, many of whom returned year after year, these summer-camp trips into the lovely Jemez country behind the ranch were tremendous fun, almost addictive. Among the core faculty, Tommy Waring was an early enthusiast; Art Chase served the summer camp for a total of eight years, and starting in 1937 ran the camp with Cecil; Oscar Steege only missed two summers during his tenure on the faculty. What enthralled them all, in Peggy Church's words, were

> the long days of trail-riding; the exhilarating mountain air; almost daily thunder storms that dripped chill rain from Stetson and slicker, flashed lightning, roared with thunder, then cleared suddenly away; bathing in mountain pools, fishing in clear mountain streams; tents carefully pitched at night and trenched against sudden downpours; the daily care of saddle and pack animals, each with its special blend of wisdom and orneriness; the tinkling sound of bells on the hobbled horses at they began moving to graze just before dawn—a warning that the wranglers must quickly crawl out of their cozy bedrolls to catch them, for as soon as the sun rose the horses would stop moving, the bells would stop tinkling, and finding a motionless horse in a thick spruce or aspen forest could seriously delay the setting out of the pack-train.[22]

Moreover, the shortcomings of those who did not measure up to this challenging and highly structured group experience were posted for everyone to see, and a boy who refused to shape up could be asked to leave. For recruitment purposes, a nonconformist could be accepted but he was then expected to change his behavior; the adults from Connell on down determined what was acceptable. William Burroughs, later a renowned Beat Generation author and counterculturalist, attended the camp for three summers running with mediocre ratings, whereas his brother Mortimer tried harder and was deemed Best Camper.

The basic plan was to begin with short rides and training sessions at the ranch preparatory to increasingly longer, more demanding, pack-trips traversing the Baca Location until the August three-week trip to the San Pedro Peaks. Long rides of up to twenty-five miles, which taxed horses and boys alike, were more common in the early years than later, as the routes and campsites were perfected. Basically, what developed was a preference for holding the first, four- to five-day pack-trip in the Valle Grande, then running the intermediate trip lasting some six to ten days out to San Antonio Hot Springs and La Jara west of the Baca, and ending with a long, three-week trip to the San Pedro on trails that followed a roughly inverted L route.

The first camps were small—eleven campers in 1919, six in 1920 and only five in 1921, and ten in 1922—and included some roundup activities when the school was still a working ranch. The 1922 camp under Hitch followed the routes and campsites pioneered by A. J. and Bill Rose, but he systematized the planning on the basis of a week's reconnaissance trip, during which he and two Santa Fe companions (Hap Horgan, younger brother of writer Paul Horgan, and Neal Rennehan) covered about one hundred miles in six days. The three young men pioneered the San Pedro Peaks area and decided that going farther north below the pine line into the hotter piñon-juniper country around Coyote was not feasible.

Before taking the long trip that year the boys had a house-party with six or seven girls, including Peggy Pond (who married Ferm Church in 1924) and Anita Rose (Bill's sister, who became Tommy Waring's wife). The big trip left on August 8, stopping the first night in the Valle Grande; then on to four nights at Redondo Creek, where the boys played strip poker—last garment off immediately followed by a plunge in the creek. The next camp was at Rio Cebolla, where two of the boys reported in sick and were taken by wagon to Jemez Springs to see a doctor. The first truck relay appeared, bringing fresh food, clean laundry, and the mail. On the seventeenth, the outfit moved through heavy rain to the Rio Las Vacas, at the junction of the Rito Presa. Another relay reached them before the pack train left for San Pedro mountain, which they reached via the Palomas Trail. There, Ed Fuller caught his full limit of fifty fish, while Hitchcock and several of the boys searched for traces of the famous Highline Trail, "said to run from the summit of Tsicoma [Chicoma] to San Pedro summit along the divide separating the streams flowing generally south [and north] into the Rio Grande." This trail "was little used in 1922; various ones of us from Los Alamos had ridden and . . . cleared out much of the eastern portion, but we could not find . . . the trace where it would leave San Pedro summit."[23]

The boys asked to stay longer than their allotted three days at San Pedro, but the outfit moved on via Coyote and descended into lower-elevation hot country. "We covered at least twenty, maybe twenty-five miles that day, were in the saddle eight and a half hours, and got to eat supper at quarter after eight."[24] Moving the next day to the Upper Cebolla, near Cerro Pelon, was an easy ride. From there they took the Highline (Skyline portion) for Chicoma, clearing the trail as far as Chihuahueños Canyon, where they stopped for lunch before following the trail across grassy slopes to a cabin under the summit. Hitch continues: "the sole point of this camp was ease in reaching the summit of Tsicoma, highest point in the Jemez, with magnificent views eastward over Los Alamos and to the Pecos range on the other side of the Rio, to the south to the Sandias, east of Albuquerque, and to the west over the country in which we had been camping on this year's trips." From there it was a short ride down to the divide between Santa Clara

Canyon and the Rito del Indio, and on to the last camp at Rincon Bonito. Of the 1922 camp, Hitchcock reported that all of the boys had gained weight over the summer, while he had lost ten pounds, and "all the boys whose opinions had won the respect of the staff over the summer said they had a wonderful time and seemed to mean it."[25] In addition to further developing the best routes, in this summer the ranking system with posted bulletins was fully developed. Before setting out on the big trip he exhorted the boys in Bulletin no. 14:

> This trip is rightly known as our BIG TRIP. It is a greater opportunity than any offered to boys in this country; as great as any ever offered to visitors to our Southwest. A successful trip will be something to remember as long as you live; that success depends on all working together to the limit of their ability. LET'S GO![26]

By all measures the camp was incredibly ambitious. Initially, none of the boys were experienced in Los Alamos camp methods, but they showed willingness to learn. Not yet twenty-four, Assistant Director Hitchcock berated himself for some shortcomings in detail—especially the still shaky relay supply system—but the camp was a success. "By my figures," he reported to Connell, "we traveled with the pack horses about one hundred fifty miles during the big trip, [and] we went possibly seventy-five miles in addition on our side trips. At least half of the total distance traveled with the outfit was during the last week."[27]

Starting in 1925 the camp was attracting well over twenty campers each summer, and the route system was further refined. Most areas west of the Baca were dropped, and by 1927 the long trip included the Chihuahueños meadow with its slow, meandering stream, a favorite of the boys. That year's camp of twenty-three boys sported eighteen tents, including a cook tent, a saddle tent, and the toilet tent. On the long trip, three relays brought supplies to camps at Redondo, American Creek, and Cerro Pelon.[28]

Reports show that the system was being steadily perfected year by year. Ferm was a mainstay of the camp during these years. Hitch himself "took a good many reconnaissance trips, even in years in which I was not working

Fig. 5.5

Rito de los Indios campsite, 1930. Photo by T. Harmon Parkhurst. Courtesy Museum of New Mexico, neg. no. 124/.

with the camp, usually in the interval between school and camp, to locate new sites or new approaches to old ones, and quite a few purely pleasure trips with other members of the staff or with guests." By 1930 the camp system was fully mature.[29]

Judging from camp enrollments, the Depression seems not to have affected operations much until 1931, when only twenty-one boys signed up and discounts were offered to fill up enrollments. However, in 1932 the camp with thirty boys was fully subscribed, including eleven campers from Michigan, of whom at least five were scions of the families who owned and ran America's automobile and glass industries. "I consider [this] the most successful camp we have ever had . . . , thirty boys which is the largest group I have ever taken out. This is a particularly happy situation for me as it is the last camp session for Los Alamos," Connell wrote to a parent.

Just why Connell decided to make this his last camp is unclear. After a discouraging camp season in 1921 he had decided to discontinue the camp but was talked out of it by Porter Sargent, the Boston educational consultant, who told him it would be a great mistake to give up the camp.[30] His heart was in the camp but his health was never robust, and he found the strain of overseeing the ranch, the school, and the camp sapped his strength. Connell told at least one parent unhappy with the discontinuing of the camp that he simply couldn't give the school the attention it needed and also run "his" camp. In 1932 Connell was fifty, which seems young today but it was not so then. Perhaps the deepening national Depression made recruiting for the camp that much more difficult. Still, since the income from the camp was so important to the finances of the school, how did Connell manage without it? By cutting back on salaries is one obvious answer.

Although ably served by loyal, long-term staff, and the core faculty, it seems likely that the camp in all its splendor did not measure up in one critical area: producing a stream of seasoned, tested applicants for Los Alamos Ranch School. Overall, there *was* a strong demand for the camp; there *was not* a strong preference on the part of most camp parents for the school. Thus the linkage that Connell wanted was problematical, because the camp was not a reliable feeder into LARS.

In truth, Connell was also a victim of his own expectations and devices. As Hitch recalled:

Camp enrollment was quite separate from school enrollment. AJ did not favor a boy who had been with us during the school year, and was to return in September, being in the camp between the two school years, and rarely allowed it. There was no recruitment for camp during the school year (A. J. was critical of a common arrangement in which a master in a school operated an independent camp and filled his list from contacts in the school), but the reverse was not true. We frequently urged the parents of a camper who had done well physically and socially (and showed student promise) to consider leaving him with us for the school year. In fact, the full enrollment for my first year at Los Alamos [1919–1920] was produced by the staying of a sizable group from what had been a very successful camp in the summer of 1919.[31]

Of that camp with eleven boys, six went to LARS, a ratio never equaled afterward. And of the few campers in 1920 and 1921, only George May of Santa Fe attended LARS. Little wonder that Connell thought of quitting. How well did he do in later years?

In the decade from 1922–1932 the ratio of all campers to those who became student applicants fluctuates between 20 and 30 percent. Although records are not complete or fully consistent, it is clear that aside from 1919 the camp never was a robust producer of applicants to LARS. On average, it appears that only three or four campers each year went on to attend the school. While that represents almost 10 percent of the student body, it probably was not a cost-effective recruitment method.

The number of brothers attending camp together is striking, beginning with the Kieselhorsts—Wallace, Earl, and Sidney, who all came to the 1919 camp. Additionally, Wally and Earl served as counselors for two summers each between 1923 and 1926. The Gilchrists, James and Robert, had nine years between them in A. J.'s camp. The Burroughs, Mortimer and Billy, came for three years each in 1925–1927. Bruce and Bill Carson had seven summers riding out with Cecil. Although Connell occasionally offered a reduced rate to families who sent more than one son to the camp, he resisted parental pleas for an automatic discount in such cases.

What happened in the Depression years, when the discounted though still steep tuition was more than many of Los Alamos's rarified clientele could pay? Twenty-eight boys attended the 1930 camp, but only four enrolled. In 1931, six enrolled out of a reduced camp of twenty-one, an excellent return. But in 1932, with a full camp enrollment of thirty, only five went on to LARS. For the time and energy spent recruiting, and for the money tied up in facilities, horses, and staff salaries, the conclusion must be that the camp under Connell was a success in terms of vision and experience, but a disappointment with respect to providing a large enough stream of seasoned campers to both flesh out and enrich the LARS student body.

Mountain Scouting

After discontinuing the camp, Connell devised the Mountain Scout program—an experiment in advanced Scouting and another way to link the special advantages of Los Alamos with Scouting. He had been offering a special scholarship to an outstanding Scout from the Rio Grande Council (to which Troop 22 reported) to attend the summer camp. As well, Connell was helping Scout headquarters to develop the Explorer program (which still exists) as a response to the national decline of interest of older boys in Scouting. In 1934 several Scout executives from New Mexico and New York visited the ranch to talk with Cecil Wirth about the Mountain Scout idea, which was Connell's inspiration, for A. J. himself was absent on his spring recruiting trip. This idea bore fruit, and at the 1935 commencement Eagle Scout Francis Rousseau received Scouting's highest award, the gold palm, from Cecil, who also announced that Los Alamos had established a new division in national Scout work, Mountain Scouting, which would parallel other programs then being developed for older Scouts including Explorers, Timber Scouts (in the Northwest), Rovers, and Sea Scouts.

As reported in the *Santa Fe New Mexican*: "The 'Mountain Men,' who emulate the achievements of southwest pioneers like Kit Carson, are divided, said Wirth, 'into Mountaineers, four badges; Packers, five badges, who must be able to carry through one phase of a pack trip; and Rangers, five more badges, who must be able to handle a whole pack train in the woods for three days.'" Rousseau was made senior patrol leader of the new Mountain Scout program developed at Los Alamos, and was slated to put on a mountain program during the ten-day national Jamboree in Washington, D.C., that summer. The Jamboree was canceled because of a polio epidemic, but Rousseau did serve as a leader in the council's Scout camp held two miles from the ranch, where some 135 New Mexico teenagers spent three weeks. After organizing and leading a one-week pack trip for twenty-five boys, Rousseau received his Mountain Scout badge, designed by Anita Waring, which bore the motto "Prepared." Very few of these badges were ever given, because (Rousseau recalled) the facilities for leading a pack-trip were more or less limited to Los Alamos at the time.[32]

In retrospect, the Mountain Scout idea must have been A. J.'s last attempt to make Scouting the centerpiece of the LARS experience. Mountain Scouting, with its evocation of Kit Carson, has all the earmarks of Connell's romanticism, but in the more academically oriented Los Alamos program that Hitchcock wanted, the role of Scouting was diminishing. Furthermore, by the mid-1930s fewer LARS students were taking Scouting seriously. They still had to achieve the rank of First Class to graduate, but only a handful went on to become Eagles, a prerequisite for achieving the rank of Mountain Scout.[33]

Cecil Wirth's Camp, 1937–1941

In the reorganization following Hitchcock's return from Yale in 1936, the camp was revived as an independent operation under Cecil Wirth. Connell was listed as the camp advisor, but the actual operation of the camp was entrusted to Cecil and Art Chase, who returned as associate director every summer from 1937 to 1941 from the Berkshire School where he was then teaching. These two younger men were close friends and brought complementary skills to the operation. Having served two years as TCS under Connell, Chase was intimately

Fig. 5.6

Wirth Camp Staff, 1941. From left, Ransom Lynch (counselor; former master), Art Chase (assistant director; former master), Bud Turner (counselor), Cecil Wirth, James Anderson (counselor), Bud Wieboldt (counselor). Photo by T. Harmon Parkhurst. Wirth private collection.

familiar with the Los Alamos pack-camp system. The fun-loving Chase was renowned for his physical strength and repertoire of campfire songs. For his part, Cecil came to the job of camp director with ten years of experience at the highly regarded Cheley Camp in Estes Park, Colorado, rising to associate director under Frank Cheley, who saw Cecil as his protégé and right-hand man. More guarded in his personality, Cecil was the natural leader. In Peggy's words: "Assisted by recent graduates of the School who had become expert with horses and camping activities, these two men with younger, freer ideas, built up a new camp spirit on the old framework."[34]

Under the new regime, Cecil and his bride Virginia did the recruiting together. Connell stood aside while the dashing young couple turned the spring trips to Texas and the Midwest into social events as well as work. Running the camp as an independent operation, Cecil's financial arrangements with Los Alamos are lost to time, but he must have returned a portion of his earnings to LARS while paying for certain items such as stationery, salaries, and day trips out of his own earnings. Before taking over, Cecil conferred with Bences, who assured him that the help was on board and that he would continue to produce the camp meals that were a centerpiece of the Los Alamos camp experience.

If the Boss no longer wanted to go out on trips, his proclivity to meddle could not be entirely walled off. For example, Cecil's brother-in-law Gilbert Davis, 1941, was an expert rider who attended the camp for three summers and in 1939 was honored as Best Camper. (Watching Gil jump the spirited horse Chili was poetry to a small boy.) As Gil remembers, he was showing the younger boys how to pack one day when Connell appeared and told him, "No, you're doing it all wrong," and then proceeded to do it his way. After Connell left, Gil complained to Cecil, who, irritated, said, "He's wrong. Now do it *your* way."

The camp under Wirth was less authoritarian, but for reasons of safety and the director's personality it was still run as a tight ship. Bruce Carson was struck by the difference between Art Chase and Cecil Wirth. By then an experienced third-year camper, Bruce enjoyed trips "more when Mr. Chase, not Mr. Wirth, is in charge. The latter is far too regular and quiet. He allows very little freedom, while Mr. Chase believes in letting everyone have a good time in his own way as he pleases (with restrictions, of course.)."[35]

Gone were such things as the whistle signals and elaborate bulletins setting out the in-camp tasks during Connell's day. But the ranking system was still in force. Under it, the Carson brothers flourished, each rising to patrol leader. But others, for example Bill Baird, were unhappy that ranking was so ingrained in the camp experience:

Each person was ranked by the staff on some criteria which were never shared with us. The top ranked person was patrol leader. It wasn't just that they picked a leader. They said A is over B who is over C who is over D. I never was A, but usually I was high enough that I didn't get a complex about it like somebody on the bottom might have. In retrospect, I believe that this was a cruel system with little to recommend it. The boys at the bottom usually stayed there, and it cannot have done much for their self esteem. While in a tight situation the system was to provide a leader at all times, I am not at all sure that a person of lower rank would have always done what the person of higher rank told him to.[36]

If the self-regulating system developed by Connell and controlled by adults was active until the end, Scouting itself now played no role in the summer-camp program, and in retrospect the ranking system itself seemed ripe for revision. However, mastering the Los Alamos diamond was still high on the list of camp achievements, and in defense of the ranking system, it did reflect how hard a boy tried, as well as his spirit of cooperation.

The pack train was shaped up as ever. A former Albuquerque boy remembers his astonishment at seeing it on the move. After days of camping in the mountains his own group was grubby—rained out, unshaven, their equipment a wreck. However, in the LARS group "every boy was in a fresh uniform; all gear was bright and shining; the leather looked as if it had just been polished. [The Albuquerque] friends were speechless while this equestrian apparition passed."[37]

As in the Connell era, so under Wirth: the routes changed somewhat year by year, but the basic scheme of one short trip, one intermediate trip, and one long trip was maintained for the Montaneros, or older boys, 1937 through 1940. The Villeros, or younger boys, had separate pack-trips until 1941, exploring different parts of the Valle Grande. The younger boys rode to the tent rocks and St. Peter's Dome and stayed closer to the ranch; the older boys took longer rides and did more fishing. According to the 1939 camp catalogue, "three, four, five, ten, and twelve-day pack trips are taken into the big range country."[38] Running so many different trips in a separate two-patrol system must have required some complex logistics.

In 1941 the two groups took all their pack-trips together, lasting four, ten, and sixteen days, respectively. By then, the long trip was just over two weeks, the route progressing from Rito del Indio to Cerro Pelon and on to Peñas Negras, the camp farthest from the ranch, from whence San Pedro Peak was climbed on a day trip. The outfit returned on the Skyline Trail via

Chihuahueños, a twenty-mile ride from Peñas Negras. Meeting the second relay coming up from Santa Clara Canyon, they then spent the last three days in the Valle Grande taking side trips before returning to the ranch.

With the changeover from mules to packhorses, the younger boys no longer did their share of the packing.[39] Cecil felt that mules were temperamentally unsuited to handling by adolescent boys, and horses were both more pliable and reliable. They were also big. Ted Mather, the wrangler, was so short himself that he had to balance a pannier on his head before hooking it over the pack frame. Doing this without first removing his hat was one of the things that delighted young boys.

The equipment changed but little—somewhat better tents, but the same heavy bedrolls and Dutch ovens. Campers did not bring mess kits with them, but each boy had his match-safe, knife, and whistle. All wore short pants, having abandoned by 1930 the riding breeches and puttees that were standard in the first few years under Connell. Chaps were now the order of the day. Nobody used cowboy boots, only high shoes or boots. And one of the first things a boy learned was never to call his Dakota Stetson a "cowboy hat."

Fishing with flies was the ideal, made easier to master because the small streams they fished were astonishingly productive of little brook trout. And, as always, each camp provided a base for day trips—climbing Chicoma, exploring new territory or once, riding up Redondo Peak under Jimmy Anderson, having to beat a hasty retreat when they encountered an Indian ceremonial taking place.

It seems that activities at the ranch between pack trips were somewhat more structured than they had been before, when the pack-trips took pride of place. As announced in the 1937 Alumni *Bulletin*: Mr. Wirth and Mr. Chase "are planning a program based on horseback riding, equestrian sports, camp and pack trips into the mountains for four or five days at one time, and rather an extensive 'in-camp' program, as well as various automobile trips to points of interest in this part of the country."[40] Set aside for this season at least was the famous three-week pack-trip, in favor of shorter pack-trips in a more balanced program, including more emphasis on leather craft and woodcraft, side trips, and a three-day stay at Camp Hamilton, where the whole camp climbed the cliffs, searched for arrowheads, and played games such as Capture the Flag. The summer now culminated in a one-day Gymkhana for campers to show off their horsemanship, and a round of parties for parents, visitors, and staff. At the close of the 1939 camp, Professor Carson wrote in his diary: "Elegant lunch—sopaipillas—made by Bences—in the woods. After the gymkhana mint julep party at the Wirth's. Closing banquet."[41]

Cecil's years at Cheley learning how to run a camp combined with his leadership skills, Art's four years with the Connell camp (including two as TCS), and his exuberant good cheer and sense of fun, and finally the counselors' high spirits combined with their role as exemplars of the finest LARS had to offer—all these things came together to produce a most memorable experience. In line with Cecil's more fluid directorship, the TCS position, formerly a faculty responsibility, was now entrusted to the most experienced junior counselor. Having been a camper himself in 1932, Dave Hughes, 1937, a skilled horseman who had run the tack room for his Community Work assignment, was the first TCS under Cecil. Rising enrollments were the sure sign of the camp's success. Cecil's best year ever was 1941, with twenty-five campers. The season had now returned to featuring three pack-trips: the first a four-day trip to Los Posos; the second for ten days camped at Toledo, the San Antonio Hot Springs, and La Jara; and the third, for sixteen days, camped at the Rito del Indio, Cerro Pelon, Peñas Negras, and the beautiful Chihuahueños Canyon, before returning to the ranch on August 27.[42]

The Summer of 1942

Although a brochure announcing the 1942 season was sent out, with America now at war, Cecil gravely ill, Art and the others in—or soon to be in—military service, the camp that actually took place was a different experience. "The spirit of Mr. Wirth, Mr. Chase and Mr. Anderson is missing," Bill Carson wrote after the first week at camp in July. Connell's methods were quite different, more like the school's, Carson felt.[43] Know-it-all Connell had to be dealt with, but Bill carried out his duties as patrol leader with aplomb and had a good summer (his fourth in a row). Connell and Church coped as best they could, making do with shorter pack-trips and a revolving door of counselors as draft calls came in. They considered canceling the camp, but business manager Rousseau insisted that his hard-pressed budget needed cash from the camp. Connell managed the camp, but did not take pack-trips himself, announcing to parents that this would be the last season for the duration of the war. Ferm Church stayed for the first month—he hadn't been out in the summer for at least a decade—and Hitchcock, the other early camp stalwart, had been called to active army duty months earlier. Oscar Steege, who was to have been associate director under Cecil that summer, stayed on after camp's end to see that the fall crop of LARS students was properly uniformed and installed in the Big House before he, too, entered the navy. Dave Hughes, one of Cecil's most experienced and well-liked counselors, was inducted into the Army Air Corps before the camp was over, and so it went.[44]

Afterglow

How to assess the summer camp, an experience unique to that time and place? "In addition to my work during the school year," Oscar recalled, "I was offered the opportunity to spend several summers in the school's pack-trip Camp as an aide to one of my close friends and colleagues who was its Director—an experience whose richness is difficult for me to describe."[45] Friendships made during camp endured over the years. The Carson parents and the Wirths were close. Professor Carson wrote to his wife, Elizabeth: "Cecil says that if his boys grow up to be as fine as ours, he will be very proud."[46] Charles Jenney, a former master returning to assist with the 1929 camp, befriended camper Rogers Scudder. Later, while Scudder taught at Brooks School and Jenney was at Belmont Hill School, the two classicists collaborated on a series of well-regarded Latin-language texts.[47]

"I loved the crisp mountain air, early morning looking out of my tent, the smell of the campfire, the wonderful food, the good fishing, and the fine men who were in charge," recalls Bill Baird, who was in the 1940 and 1941 camps. "It was two of the best summers of my life."[48] When all is said and done, the experience of men and boys sharing together in beautiful country, with horses and good equipment, and in the full flush of youth, was sufficient.

A War Casualty

The Closing of Los Alamos

The taking of Los Alamos for military purposes was hardly unique: as America entered the vortex of total war, hundreds of properties, including schools, church lands, parks, and private lands passed rapidly into federal control.[1] Disrupted lives and loss of place was, for everyone involved, part of the price paid for becoming, in FDR's ringing phrase, "the arsenal of democracy." Those making their homes at Los Alamos Ranch and the homesteads nearby were no exception. What remains unique, of course, was the extraordinary achievement of the Manhattan Project, of which Los Alamos was the place selected to design and manufacture the first atomic weapons.

The site-selection criteria are well known: isolation for purposes of security; ample surrounding lands already in federal ownership and the ease of acquiring title to the remaining 10 percent owned by the school and the Hispanic homesteaders; and a compact physical plant that could support what was initially thought would be a small research laboratory.

Lab director J. Robert Oppenheimer's familiarity with northern New Mexico, coupled with his prewar practice of holding physics *tertulias* (conclaves) for graduate students and colleagues at his ranch near Cowles, in the Pecos, were contributing factors to the site selection.[2] Also, Dr. Ernest Lawrence, director of the Radiation Lab and Oppenheimer's mentor at Berkeley, knew about Los Alamos through Ferm Church, whom he befriended when Church took a sabbatical leave from LARS to do graduate work at Stanford in the Bay Area.[3]

Less well known is the important role of Los Alamos parent Percival C. Keith, a brilliant chemical engineer at the Kellogg Corporation, and a member of the planning board set up in December 1941 under the Office of Scientific Research and Development to supervise engineering procurement and plant construction for what was soon to become the Manhattan Project. Known as a forceful and strong-willed manager, Keith was an early advocate for locating the laboratory and the uranium enrichment facility together in New Mexico—in the Four Corners area or at Los Alamos—which had abundant reserves of natural gas and was more isolated than Oak Ridge, Tennessee, near the eastern seaboard. It is probable that Keith was connected with the April 1942 flyover by a military plane, which methodically surveyed the Pajarito Plateau and the ranch. Keith's proposal to locate the uranium gaseous diffusion separation plant and the laboratory together did not prevail, but by his own account he was well placed enough to have kept the idea of a New Mexico location for the laboratory alive during the months of frenetic meetings and consultations that led to the final, definitive selection of Los Alamos for the laboratory site in November 1942.[4]

It is therefore likely that Keith was the one primarily responsible for choosing LARS, since he was the one who brought it to attention in the first place and who kept it there throughout the selection process. Oppenheimer came into the picture only later, with the final site selection.

In summer 1941 Keith had visited Los Alamos, where his sons Percival and Christopher were campers. There he met Connell and "fell in love with the school."[5] Percival, thirteen, stayed on at LARS, and both boys were slated to return for the 1942 season. Although Christopher did attend the camp that summer, Keith informed Connell on August 24 that the boys would not be returning and invited him to spend the night at his house in New Jersey, despite A. J.'s longstanding policy of not staying at any student's house. It was unusual for Connell to travel east in late summer—his recruiting trips took place in the late fall and early spring—but Keith's letter must have contained enough hints that Connell accepted his invitation and visited him immediately. Accompanying the campers home and recruiting was a good cover.

According to Keith's recollection years later, he intimated that something would soon be happening to the school and, in turn, Connell told him that the school was in financial difficulties and asked "what I could do, if anything to have the school taken over temporarily so that it could be used by the Army or other branch of the service, and after the War he could take it over again."[6]

Enrollments *were* down, "as apparently most schools are," A. J. wrote Hitch. "The rumors of many schools failing to open in the New England and the East Coast areas would indicate great difficulties. [Closer to Los Alamos,] the Fresnal Ranch School is closed, also the Evans School." In leaving to teach at Groton, Harry Walen wrote to Hitch and A. J. expressing doubts about the viability of Los Alamos. "Poor Los Alamos is having a very hard time, I am afraid," Cecil wrote from New York, where he kept in close touch with school matters while he was receiving cancer treatments.[7] A. J. and Ferm had to recruit an almost entirely new faculty that fall, and the call-ups continued. Yet they were determined to stay open, and the most that can gleaned by inference from the tone of Connell's letters that summer and fall of 1942 is that he saw himself managing a setback, and not (until the very end) a crisis.

Keith's account is plausible, at least to the extent that Connell, who by now knew something was up, seems to have been willing to entertain some sort of long-term lease. Evidently, when this did not fly, Connell, through Keith, was willing to negotiate a sale "for the duration." That he was prepared, even eager, to sell outright, as was maintained after the war by some, is not substantiated by any of the surviving school documents. What really happened, was related by Fermor Church (in Hitch's absence, the acting headmaster) in his twenty-fifth anniversary Harvard class report just after the war, in 1946: "We rebuffed all advances made by army real-estate men, engineers, scientists, and inspectors of all sorts until a letter from the Secretary of War left us no choice." Connell's reluctance to alienate the property ceased only when Secretary of War Stimson informed him in early December that the entire ranch property was necessary to the government and the United States would exercise the right of eminent domain to secure it by forced sale. Writing several years after these events Church recalled: "We were not 'eager to sell the school.' To those who wished to acquire it we said it would take a letter from the Secretary of War stating it was necessary for the safety of the U.S. (This we thought a most unlikely thing, but it came in short order.) We pointed out that the ownership of the School was in the hands of Trustees who had no power to sell the school; thus the government could acquire it only by condemnation proceedings."[8]

Indeed, Los Alamos had been the prime candidate for acquisition since August and army officers visited the ranch several times; the site was definitively selected during the visit of General Groves, Lieutenant Colonel Dudley, Oppenheimer, and Edwin M. McMillan on November 16, 1942. Then, on the twenty-second, the Corps of Engineers told the school to have its board of directors and attorney on hand the next morning "as a man was flying out from Washington with papers and wished to fly back this evening," Peggy Church wrote to her mother. "Ferm and AJ are both, I think, almost ready for complete collapse. And if the movement takes place it will be a heart-rending and back-breaking job to close up and get all the boys resettled. It simply staggers the imagination."[9] On November 26 Secretary of War Stimson ordered the takeover and his letter, addressed mistakenly to Española, arrived at the ranch in early December. When asked by Oppenheimer "why we could not send the boys home at Christmas and tell them not to come back, [Church explained] that we were under contract with the parents . . . that tuitions had been paid to mid-year, February 8, 1943. Hence, that date was set for acquisition."[10]

Moreover, Connell insisted on completing the school year with an accelerated program. Though stricken with loss, he presided over a hectic but dignified closure even as bulldozers began clearing the grounds and gardens. In due course, Lt. Col. Lawrence Hitchcock, returning on special leave from Washington, handed out diplomas to the last four graduates of the Los Alamos Ranch School on January 28, 1943. Colonel John M. Harman, the first post commander, gave the graduation address.

This ending was profoundly upsetting to those who had to close up the school and leave their homes, their community and their way of life on the Pajarito Plateau. Yet the meaning of these events has almost invariably been written from the perspective of the newcomers and what came next. Their history is different. (And why not? History is almost always written by the winners, rarely by the victims or the losers.) Vincent Jones, who wrote the army history, said, accurately enough, that "the school was having some difficulty getting instructors during the war and was in serious financial trouble," but then concluded that because of this "the owners were willing to sell." In an early history of the bomb project, Stephane Groueff maintained: "Another advantage of the site was that no population would have to be relocated other than the teachers and the students at the school. But what if the owners refused to sell it?" he asked. "Luckily, the school was in financial difficulty and the owners were quite happy to close it down for a good price." In similar vein, even Richard Rhodes, in his Pulitzer Prize–winning *The Making of the Atomic Bomb,* could write:

> The land and improvements, including the boys' school with its sixty horses, two tractors, two trucks, fifty saddles, eight hundred cords of firewood, twenty-five tons of coal and sixteen hundred books, were worth $440,000. The school was willing to sell. The Manhattan Project acquired its scenic laboratory site.

Altogether, 54,000 acres were targeted for acquisition, 3,600 of it in private hands, of which 772 acres belonged to Los Alamos Ranch School. The school's asking price was $500,000, including compensation for good will; the government offered $275,000 for real property and improvements, but would not recognize value for LARS as a going business. The initial offering price was challenged in court. Prolonged haggling into July over the government's next offer of $320,000 (eventually raised to $335,000 plus interest) distressed Connell and other officers of the Los Alamos Foundation. The owners of nearby Anchor Ranch also challenged the government's offer. As for the homesteaders, most of whom were Hispanics, their settlements for patented land and grazing rights were low. (The figure cited by Rhodes includes their payments as well, and the amounts they received were even lower after Sandoval County had deducted delinquent back taxes owed.) Time passes, but the facts are still being bent, as in this quote from a recent history of World War II: "At the site of an Indian school at Los Alamos, New Mexico, the War Department built a special city."[11]

Given these distortions, it is important to ascertain what Connell and his colleagues actually thought and did during these last, anxious days. As Keith well knew, initial plans were to construct the laboratory at Oak Ridge, Tennessee in conjunction with the huge gaseous diffusion plant that Keith, as engineer in charge of Kellex (the Kellogg subsidiary), was responsible for designing. By late summer a separate lab site in New Mexico was being seriously considered, and this is what prompted Keith to invite Connell to be his houseguest. A team of army engineers in civilian clothing had visited the ranch, Bences Gonzales recalled, and by the time Bences returned in late August from what turned out to be the summer camp's last pack trip he knew that the school would be taken over.[12] Soon thereafter, on August 29, while Connell was visiting Keith, his staff received a phone call from the Albuquerque office of the Corps of Engineers, requesting an inventory of school property and a copy of the 1937 school map prepared in John Meem's office.

For his part, Connell knew that Hitchcock had been speculating about the advantages of a lease option. Just before leaving for active duty in January 1942, Hitch had discussed "'the possibility of the government taking us over,'" as Ferm recalled, and he rode over the property and surrounding area with Dr. Carl Anderson from the California Institute of Technology. Anderson was an early candidate for lab director; Oppenheimer was selected after Anderson turned it down. Evidently, "Hitchcock had read about a school in the East which the Army took over for a camp—and thought that LARS might have the same experience, but assumed it would be a temporary thing for the duration of the war—a kind of leasing of the school, not a complete buyout." This option evaporated in November, when Connell was informed that the school would be taken outright. Hitch himself received this news with mixed feelings, in his words, "'due to the failure of our endowment campaign and long-continued doubts as to the existence after the war of the class on which we have depended.'"[13]

Ever the realist, Hitch was nonetheless open to buying back the property after the war, an option that Connell, always the optimist, latched onto. The record clearly bears this out. For example, a Forest Service officer recalled "hearing Mr. Connell say that he hoped eventually to acquire the lands that the War Department had taken over from him." (The Forest Service also harbored hopes of getting its land back after the war, and did retrieve some of it eventually.) General Groves's account confirms this. The school's owners, he wrote, "were very happy indeed to sell out to us *and close down for the duration* [italics added]—and, as it turned out, forever."[14]

A final aspect of the Connell-Hitchcock partnership concerns the role of place itself. The ranch was A. J.'s beloved stage, a theatrical setting of unparalleled beauty that he had controlled for a quarter-century as impresario and boss over all. When the government took over on February 8, 1943, Connell and Fred Rousseau quit the mesa forever in one of the brown Chevrolet sedans with the LARS logo on the doors. (The new post's commander asked if the army could continue using the LARS logo on plates and cups; Connell agreed, but said that the Los Alamos Foundation would continue using it on stationery. Troop 22 still uses it today.) In Santa Fe, A. J. and Fred worked to close the school accounts, which included haggling with government appraisers over the initial settlement, paying off the bondholders, and deciding what to do with the remaining assets of the Foundation.[15]

Throughout, Connell made no attempt to relocate LARS to another site even though "offers of assistance came from many sources." As he explained in an open letter to alumni and friends of the school: "Educational associations agreed to place unusual facilities at our disposal; other school men wrote, and even telephoned over long distance, urging us to merge or otherwise cooperate with them in carrying on Los Alamos; parents and friends offered to provide locations on ranches and summer hotel sites." However, it seems unlikely that, in A. J.'s words, "we [really did] gave thoughtful consideration to many proposals." Unlikely because, at heart, "so much about Los Alamos was indigenous and appropriate only to its surroundings—the whole program, the life, the very spirit of the school developed out of its location and local traditions—that the conviction grew that the school could not be transplanted. There remained the hope that it might be possible to re-establish Los Alamos, and that the Los Alamos foundation might be the means to do this after the war." This is what he really had in mind.[16] To Connell, the army's takeover seemed more like a temporary use of the buildings and grounds at LARS, rather then an irrevocable ending.

In fact, the initial laboratory project had been expected to support a staff of only 265, a number that "apparently was based upon Oppenheimer's idea that 6 scientists, assisted by some engineers, technicians, and draftsmen, could do the job quite rapidly and effectively."[17] While this number rose somewhat to include support staff, the first construction contract let in November 1942 was valued at a mere $300,000. John Meem, who was then completing work for the army at Cannon Field in New Mexico, was contacted by the Corps of Engineers with offers of doing a "little job" at Los Alamos, or of designing an

Army Air Corps flight academy at Roswell, New Mexico. Having greatly expanded his office to accommodate war work for the Corps of Engineers— in the hectic months after Pearl Harbor, Meem had overseen the design of base layouts and two military hospitals—he decided that the Roswell project was more exciting and turned down the Los Alamos job. And so this top-secret work at the ranch went instead to Willard Kruger, a politically astute young architect who in subsequent years designed much of the new Los Alamos.[18]

Connell (and Meem) had no way of knowing that the secret project would soon mushroom beyond a small scientific lab hosting hundreds on Los Alamos mesa to a sprawling industrial facility employing thousands. In fact, "Site Y," as it was called, grew continuously throughout the war. Yet it was not until May 1944, some weeks after A. J.'s death in February, that the Foundation's trustees abandoned all hope for reestablishing Los Alamos on the Pajarito Plateau. As Hitch explained to General Wood:

> We canvassed thoroughly the possibility of reopening on the old prop-erty after the war. Two considerations forced a conclusion that this was not feasible: the possible lapse of some time, which might cause Los Alamos contacts to become less strong; the fact that, from evidence available to us, hearsay and fragmentary it is true but apparently accu-rate, the government has poured so much money into alterations of the property (the three hundred and twenty-five thousand the government paid us seems to have been only a small beginning) that we could not anticipate being able to raise enough even to sweep the mesa clean of the government alterations if the title should come back to us for noth-ing. Therefore we regretfully abandoned the idea.[19]

Looking for a new approach to carry out its educational mission, the Foundation loaned Tommy Waring the funds to move his middle school from Santa Fe to an adobe building in Pojoaque remodeled by John Gaw Meem's architectural firm. Trustees also granted operating funds to Fermor Church, who in 1944 attempted to reopen Los Alamos itself in leased temporary quarters at the Sagebrush Inn in Taos. (Meem developed sketches for a new building to house the Los Alamos School and served on Church's board.) Unhappily, neither school survived. Church, for all his administrative experi-ence as assistant headmaster under Hitchcock, lacked Connell's sure touch with prospective parents and could not attract enough tuition-paying students to keep the Los Alamos School afloat for more than one year. (It shut in December 1945.) The Waring School (1939–1949) was also modeled closely on Los Alamos. However, even with LARS veteran teacher Oscar Steege on his faculty, Waring had difficulty attracting students and could not make a go of it after the war.[20] But what of the other school options?

Months after officiating at the last LARS graduation in 1943, Hitch was feeling adrift and also frustrated with his new job "on the cocktail circuit" at the Inter-American Defense Board in Washington. Instead of receiving a command in the field artillery, for which he had trained dutifully in summer camps with the Reserves, Colonel Hitchcock served as a desk officer for the duration of the war. As Hitch wrote to A. J. in August, "the government, or, if you wish, forces beyond my control, have taken away my home, my job, practically destroyed my first profession, and as much as forbidden me to practice my second [army field artillery]."[21] Although living alone and in poor health at La Fonda, Hitch's old boss and partner tried to be upbeat. "Mr. Connell asked me to write you," Fred Rousseau said, "that he is sorry that you are still not too happy over your work and progress made. He feels that considering everything he does not think you are faring so badly."[22]

On his trip West for the Foundation meeting in May 1944, three months after Connell's sudden death, Hitch stopped in Chicago for a long conversation with General Wood, who discussed investment policy with him and evidently offered to set Hitch up as a school director after the war—in the Midwest. Indeed, even before LARS shut down Hitch had been sounded out by Hamilton Beasley, Connell's former secretary and now the school's Chicago representative, about the possibility of starting a school in the Chicago area. Although he was only forty-four, Hitch declined, saying that he was now too old to start a school and, furthermore, that the budgetary struggles trying to keep LARS afloat had ended his enthusiasm for running a secondary school.[23] Inflation due to pent-up demand would surge after the war, he advised fellow trustees, and this would make the financing of private schools very difficult. Henceforth, Hitch thought he would make business or government service his career. So it was that Hitchcock, the compleat headmaster, a gifted pedagogue and an astute administrator, put the school world behind him. In doing so he was doubtless denying his true self, a self that had been fully realized as a young man at Los Alamos and that unhappily in middle age he did not reclaim—because he thought he could not and should not.

Another road not taken was in Santa Fe itself, where the former Sunmount Sanitorium, now run as the Santa Fe Inn by John Meem and his partners, had been closed for the duration of the war and was now available for purchase. When word of the government's foreclosure of Los Alamos reached Santa Fe, the First National Bank's George Bloom informed Connell that he and the other partners would like to sell the Santa Fe Inn. "Sorry George," A. J. said, dismissing the offer out of hand. John Meem then called up and offered to make the inn available for the remainder of the school year if Connell wanted it.[24] Nothing came of this, and Meem, who felt sorry for his friend Connell having had to leave his life's work at Los Alamos, arranged for him to become president of the Santa Fe Boy's Club.

With Ferm and Fred at his side, but without the heavyweight support of Hitch, and without Cecil as his probable successor, A. J. was too old to start again, which he in fact never considered. Early on, Ferm wrote Hitch on December 1, 1942, that (as Hitchcock reported to the trustees later on), "he and Mr. Connell were not inclined to try to continue at another location, saying 'This is obviously no time to start a new school. To try to carry on elsewhere would be doing just that. . . . The foundation of course continues with all intangibles ready to start a new school at some future time or put its resources to work elsewhere.'"[25] Yet for Connell, clearly, it was "his" school at Los Alamos, or nothing.

Consider, however, what historians call a counter factual. Located at the southeastern end of town, the Santa Fe Inn property backed onto vacant land abutting the national forest with its trails leading into the Pecos Wilderness. The pack-trips that were such a hallmark of the old Los Alamos could have been continued from the new location—if not in the Jemez with the open meadows of the Baca and San Pedro Peaks area, then into the Sangre de Cristo range with its more rugged wilderness east of Santa Fe. Why not? In the school's first years, specifically the summers of 1918 and 1919, the famous three-week-long camp had indeed been held in the Pecos.[26] As a small but cosmopolitan regional city, Santa Fe presented quite a different ambiance than the deliberately isolated, theatrical setting of Los Alamos.[27] Nonetheless, Santa Fe was an exotic, tricultural destination that might well have attracted sufficient and sustained enrollments in the postwar years. It hosted more than a few families with means. Skiing at the postwar Santa Fe Basin could have supported a vigorous winter sports program, without tempting LARS boys to become semiprofessionals while still in high school (which is the lure today that Aspen, with its world-class winter sports facility, exerts on the Colorado Rocky Mountain School, a Putney offshoot in Carbondale). And if LARS had merged with Brownmoor (which, in 1948, moved to Scottsdale, Arizona, before merging shortly thereafter with Judson, a boys' school in Scottsdale), the market for students able to pay the rich tuition needed to support the LARS program would have doubled.

The might have beens (but never weres) are also ironic, in that the vacant land behind the inn became the home of St. John's College in the 1960s, and in 1973 the remaining assets of the Los Alamos Foundation were given to the college.[28] Meanwhile, John Meem's architectural office and adjacent lands became the new campus of the Santa Fe Preparatory School. The inn itself was purchased by the Catholic Archdiocese for a seminary (now a conference center) and a Carmelite monastery, where bells call the nuns to worship in a ritual old as those practiced in the ancient settlements on the Pajarito Plateau.

To be sure, the very thought of Connell officiating over one of the nation's first coeducational mergers would have set him sputtering. In the independent-school world of American education, alliances of established boys' and girls' boarding schools began after the war and became a trend only in the 1970s. In the Ranch School's last year, when obtaining deferments for young male teachers became next to impossible, Connell bridled when the local draft board suggested he hire female teachers instead, although he did hire Esilda Pepper to teach French for the last weeks of school in 1943. (Hitch even teased him a bit over an offer to Connell in 1943 of work at a VD clinic for women.) LARS was indeed "a war casualty," to use Hitchcock's term.

Whether tuition-driven Los Alamos with its expensive infrastructure and rather narrowly based clientele could have survived financially in postwar America, we shall never know. (Hitchcock was dubious.) But if so, it would have had to develop a broader social base, probably becoming coeducational, perhaps with more scope for student-run activities in accordance with its Progressive roots, certainly with more emphasis on the arts. Whatever, it is clear that LARS had just found its stride in the late 1930s when time ran out.

Disrupted Lives

The abrupt demise of LARS was devastating to core faculty and administrators. It is likely that well over half of the five hundred some odd individuals who attended the school or camp were in uniform, including most of the faculty. Students and faculty were gone and the staff had already dispersed when Acting Headmaster Church wrote to Colonel Hitchcock in May: "The most difficult thing for me to get into my head about the whole business (the 'last act') is that there are only four of us left."[29] What became of Connell, Rousseau, Church, and Hitchcock? Ferm and Hitch, the two younger men, were only forty-three and forty-five when the school closed, whereas A. J. and Fred were sixty-one and sixty-six, respectively. Of the four, only Fred Rousseau had been ready to retire.

Fermor Spencer Church (1900–1975) taught for a year at the Cate School in California and then, having started and soon failed to sustain the short-lived Los Alamos School in Taos, he began a new career as a field engineer for rural power companies in New Mexico. Roaming the back roads and tracks of rural New Mexico was Ferm's substitute for the beloved rides into the Jemez country that he had so enjoyed as a young man. Church was a trustee of the Los Alamos Foundation until its dissolution in 1973. An early supporter of environmentalism, he was a founder of the New Mexico Citizens for Clean Air and Water in 1970. Ferm's three sons—Ted, Allen, and Hugh—were children at the ranch and later made their careers at the government's Sandia Laboratories in Albuquerque.

Fred Rousseau (1877–1955), the business manager, initially shared a rented house in Santa Fe with A. J. while they wound up the affairs of the school. He and Edna then moved into a house of their own in Santa Fe, where their son Francis's merit-badge sash, with its Mountain Scout patch and other awards, was on prominent display. Fred also served on the Foundation until his death. The Rousseau's daughter Joan grew up at the ranch and returned after the war to teach briefly at Los Alamos High School before teaching in Albuquerque. Francis sold commercial real estate in California.

A. J. Connell (1882–1944) served as president of the Santa Fe Boys Club and threw himself into raising war savings bonds. But these activities were no substitute for the loss of his beloved LARS, and he died suddenly, on February 11, 1944, in Santa Fe, as much as anything from a broken heart. "It was a sad day for all of us when the school closed," a Boy Scout executive wrote of his old friend A. J. "I remember talking with him several times after he moved down to Santa Fe and I had to hold back tears as he talked of his boys. The last visit was mainly a review of photos of them and their fine military service." John Meem found Connell alone in his room at La Fonda, staring into space. Increasingly, he hung around the Montoya household, now relocated in Santa Fe. Adolfo was like a lifeline, then Connell was gone. "The School had been his life," Peggy Church wrote days after his death to Ted Church, 1943, now a Harvard freshman. "He had given himself to it body and soul, and when it was taken away from him he was like a man without a soul."[30]

Connell had been the majority stockholder in the LARS corporation, and from 1940 to 1944 he was president of the Los Alamos Foundation, to which all his remaining personal assets, including life-insurance policies, were willed. Foundation funds supported pensions for Fred, Ferm, and Hitch and scholarships, including stipends for local boys to attend the College of Santa Fe. In 1973, the remaining assets were transferred to St. John's College.

Cecil W. Wirth (1907–1943) kept in close touch with school affairs from New York, where he recruited Jerry Pepper of Milford School to replace him and run the athletic program, interviewed prospective campers, and received many visits from students and faculty. Shortly before his death, Lawrence Hitchcock sent Daisy Curtis and Cecil a narrative of LARS's closing, including the last graduation. Ironically, Cecil's cancer may have been triggered by a riding accident when, on a weekend trip with the boys to Camp May in April 1942, his horse reared unexpectedly and he received a blow in the saddle. This accident, the school's expropriation, and his own struggle to survive must be happening according to some divine plan, he felt; how else to make sense of it?

Lawrence Sill Hitchcock (1898–1983) stayed in federal service for the rest of his career, serving first from 1942 to 1947 as secretary general of the Inter-American Defense Board, for which he received the Legion of Merit, and then as a senior administrator at the CIA, from which he retired in 1964 with a Certificate of Merit, with Distinction. His last assignment was to oversee construction of the CIA's new headquarters at Langley, Virginia. He too was a Foundation trustee until 1973. Although colleagues regarded him as a confirmed bachelor, in 1947 he married Barbara Singley, with whom he had two children, Charles and Josephine, and then separated. Hitch loved New Mexican cuisine, and during all the years in Washington he would send to Kaune's market in Santa Fe for Ortega's green chili, blue corn meal, and pinto beans, serving the chili on crackers during the cocktail hour. Reflecting on his career late in life, Hitch wrote to Cecil Wirth's widow Virginia: "I am glad if I was useful in my six years fighting the war on the cocktail front for the Inter-American Defense Board and in my following seventeen years as a minor bureaucrat but the twenty-three years at Los Alamos was my real life."[31]

Solicitous for his employees to the end, Connell sent the post commander a list of the staffers whom he recommended the army hire. They were Bences Gonzales, who assisted Fred Rousseau at the Trading Post—with the school for twenty-three years; E. A. "Ted" Mather, the wrangler—at LARS for nineteen years; Adolfo Montoya, master gardener—employed at Los Alamos for seventeen years; Floyd Womelsduff, the head mechanic—with the school for fifteen years; and ranch foreman Jim Womelsduff—with seventeen years of service.[32]

Among the senior staff, Bences Gonzales and family stayed on during the Manhattan Project, where he ran the PX. Doris M. Barker, the matron, also stayed on. Jerry Pepper, whom Cecil had recruited as his replacement, stayed to manage the Post recreation program and helped to revive Troop 22. Jerry and Esilda Pepper were the only faculty to work for the Manhattan Project, although Oscar Steege returned briefly after navy service to teach high school in 1946. After leaving the navy, Ransom Lynch and his wife LaRue, a Santa Fean, gave some thought to working at the Los Alamos Scientific Laboratory, but Ranny returned to Exeter instead, where he gained national recognition as the author of textbooks on the new math.

In 1943 the pack outfit went out again under Bences and his sons, Ray and Severo, who took a group of senior army officers into the Valle Grande. The Gonzales brothers accompanied Kitty Oppenheimer on day rides. Bences protected his Dutch ovens from the widespread pilfering that was the fate of many smaller items (furniture especially) in the Ranch School inventory. And for several years he led Scouts from Troop 22 on pack-trips into the lovely back-country of the Jemez.

Education for a Higher Purpose

Los Alamos was an unusual and creative school. To be sure, the college prep curriculum it offered was conventional for a boarding school of that time. However, boys advanced not by grade but by mastery of a subject, and the brightest students could experience taking advanced work one on one with a master, as for example the future classics teacher Rogers Scudder, 1932, reading Virgil with Mr. Hitchcock, or the future Skidmore, Owings and Merrill partner David Hughes, 1937, designing a dormitory under Mr. Connell and Fermor Church. Again, like most schools in its league, the arts at LARS were weak. But there was room in the program for photography, crafts, piano lessons and music appreciation, and theatrical events.

Los Alamos participated in the content-oriented College Boards, and two of its faculty members served in succession on the English board. Frequent testing to measure mastery of a subject was built into the curriculum. Hitchcock himself had no patience with the Progressive nostrum "that a good student can't pass a test because he is not a good test-taker." However, academic rigor and preparation to do college work was the goal; the ability to take tests was a means, not the end. On the one hand, this approach can be faulted for fostering a certain lack of critical thinking; on the other hand, it was compensated by the individual skills of the best teachers at Los Alamos.

The combination of strong academics with a robust outdoor lifestyle geared to health appealed to families who could afford the high fees and made Los Alamos unusual among well-regarded boarding schools. Through contact with his horse, the Los Alamos boy learned self-mastery while communing with nature in a beautiful place. The de-emphasis of competitive athletics, except for tennis and skiing, was an unusual feature for boys' schools of that era, as was Connell's zero tolerance for hazing.

Looking over quotes from students, it is clear that the things that Connell loved so much—the western life of the trail and the mountains, and molding character—are just what the boys remember and think was most important about their time at LARS. The sense of being in a special place on the edge of wilderness was palpable.[33] Recalling what most impressed them about the Los Alamos experience, alumni are quick to mention learning to live in nature and in the process gaining self-confidence and knowledge of themselves. Pride in the academic program is also mentioned by some, as, for example, Sterling

Colgate, 1943, who recalled that LARS was "extraordinary as a prep school."[34] Taken together, all these things—the dramatic setting; the Scout-based program and organization; the emphasis on character, education of the whole individual, and on accepting responsibility; the ranking system and the caring for horses and equipment and doing things right; and the way the outdoors school overarched the indoors school—made LARS unique.

Was Los Alamos, then, a landmark school? It shared Progressive origins with several schools founded in the early twentieth century, notably Parker in San Diego, John Burroughs in St. Louis, and Deep Springs in the California desert. Under Connell it took a different direction, toward a highly structured, controlled environment. Such an adult-run hierarchy headed by an autocrat like Connell was not uncommon in boarding schools of that era. Still, he remained committed to work jobs and experiential learning—key tenets of Progressivism—and was not unresponsive to student initiatives as long as the individual himself would benefit and do no harm to Connell's carefully constructed program.

LARS was still growing and evolving until the war; it was nationally known and enjoyed a good reputation. If Los Alamos was not yet in the circle of top boarding schools, it seemed to be in striking range. It had a strong and lasting impact on the boys who went there, and many of the faculty recalled their teaching days at LARS with great affection, despite the isolation, low pay, and the necessity of having to deal with the mercurial director. The ranch community is still venerated as a good and special place by the descendants of those who worked there long ago. However, the school did not exist long enough to have a lasting impact on the world of American independent secondary schools.

Scouting was highly developed at Los Alamos. Scenes from the meticulously planned pack-trips were featured in the 1938 through 1942 editions of *Adventuring for Senior Scouts.* Connell himself might have written the section on starting a fire with wet wood: "The Scout who does not get real satisfaction in meeting the challenge of a rainy day on a week's woods trip, lacks something in character and manhood that will prove a handicap through life."[35] However, as discussed above, Mountain Scouting did not catch on nationally as one of the options for older boys in the Explorer Scouts. Connell carried Scouting to new heights at Los Alamos, but his influence on Scouting as a movement was slight.

Today, three generations later, interest in building character as a way of socializing young males has come back into vogue. One concern is that boys, with their identity problems, are falling behind the academic achievement of girls. In catering to the needs of girls through emphasis on bolstering self-esteem and creating more academic space for them, some of the older methods of motivating boys deserve another look. Indeed, as a leading commentator on gender issues writes:

> The traditional approach is through character education: Develop the young man's sense of honor. Help him to become a considerate, conscientious human being. Turn him into a gentleman. This approach respects boys' masculine nature; it is time-tested, and it works.[36]

Character-building is making a comeback today because academic achievement of and by itself has never been sufficient to guide and motivate students of high school age.

In the national meritocracy today, students and teachers shy away from discussing fundamental values. Instead, according to David Brooks, an astute observer of American culture, hardworking kids at elite schools and colleges are geared to achieving self-control rather than self-mastery.[37] Nobody seems to know what character is, a sharp contrast to boarding schools of yore where the most celebrated school heads valued values above academics, in rural settings removed from the frenetic pace of cities, in regulated communities that postponed sex as much as possible in the growing-up experience.

Connell's strong emphasis on hierarchy and masculinity seems excessive and dated by the standards and mores of today. The likening of boys to uncivilized apes—"gibbons," Connell called his students—while not uncommon among schoolmen of that era, was overplayed as part of his rationale for "instant and unquestioning obedience."[38] Even with some of their repressive features as well as their virtues, these schools merit a second look because the good news is that today character-building works well for both sexes, given credible leadership, methods, and goals. Since character building was taken very seriously at Los Alamos, we might learn from it by analogy, at least, with reference also to the other boarding schools that have been mentioned in this book.

The strong-willed directors who ran such different schools as Groton, Hotchkiss, Putney, and LARS before the Second World War are long gone, and two of these schools even followed pioneering Putney in becoming co-ed. However, in his or her quite different ways, each school head mentioned in this book—Endicott Peabody, George Van Santvoord, Carmelita Hinton, and, of course, A. J. Connell—valued character, along with developing a moral compass and service to society, above mere academic achievement. By necessity, they accommodated to the emerging meritocracy, but these idealistic educators stubbornly resisted giving away too much of the special, character-building goals of their schools to outside evaluators and test-givers.

Putney excepted, the schools were training grounds for the nation's corporate and professional elites, yet woe to anyone so bold as to tell these headmasters and directors that when all was said and done this was their school's primary role. Peabody's was a more traditional faith-based view of character building. In *The Rector of Justin*, Louis Auchincloss's novel based somewhat on Peabody and Groton, there is a most poignant scene when the old rector realizes that his businessmen trustees have been playing along with his ideal without seeing it as particularly relevant.[39] The formidable Van Santvoord, after leaving Hotchkiss, played out his secular vision of service by becoming a Vermont state senator. Carmelita Hinton in retirement was active in a number of international causes and organizations. As for Connell, he did not live to see the trajectory of his graduates, but he would be reassured to know that they recall their LARS experience most vividly, in broad brush strokes.

Will a return to valuing the broader educational mission of schools come back in vogue, especially in the wake of doubts now being raised about the utility and fairness of the SAT?[40] If so, revisiting the mission of unique independent schools like LARS can focus attention on the larger purposes of education. Or does the shift to nationwide standardized testing in the public schools mean that the deeper learning that goes on in the best schools will be harder than ever to reproduce?

Of the four schools—LARS, Putney, Hotchkiss, and Groton—Los Alamos was the smallest and one of the few top-ranked western institutions in a boarding-school world then dominated by eastern establishments. Perhaps the school that best exemplifies the legacy of young men living in close and intense engagement with the landscape is Deep Springs College—once a secondary school, now a junior college—founded in 1917, the same year as Los Alamos.[41] In other respects, Deep Springs is ideologically more in tune with the Putney School in the elaboration of Progressive principles. That LARS should be thought of with reference to the leading schools mentioned above is a testament to its achievement.

In today's New Mexico, a modern variant of Pond's vision lives on at Rancho Valmora, once one of his Watrous area ranches, then for many years a leading tuberculosis sanitarium and, since 1992, a special school dedicated to the educational and emotional growth of troubled boys and girls, ages twelve to eighteen. The Valmora program emphasizes "a social learning environment teaching care and concern for self and others." At Rancho Valmora, which is eighty miles northeast of Santa Fe on the Mora River, near where Pond founded his first school, horseback riding and ranch work are important parts of the program that is dedicated to developing self-worth and responsibility: character, in short.[42]

Fig. 1

The big sky—looking east from LARS to the Sangre
de Cristo Mountains. Photo by T. Harmon Parkhurst.
Courtesy Los Alamos Historical Museum Archives.

Fig. 2

Aerial photo, mid-1930s, looking west across the Pajarito Plateau to
Jemez Mountains. LARS fields and buildings at mid-center; the school's
upper fields at base of the mountains beyond the band of trees. Otowi
Hill Road is visible at center bottom, Los Alamos Canyon on left,
Pueblo Canyon on right. Light areas to left and right are homesteads on
adjoining mesas. Courtesy Los Alamos Historical Museum Archives.

Fig. 3

Otowi Hill Road, 1920s. Peggy Pond Church Collection.
Courtesy Los Alamos Historical Museum Archives.

Fig. 4

Ashley Pond Jr., early 1900s. Courtesy of Ashley Pond IV.

Fig. 5

A. J. Connell with Santiago Naranjo, governor of
Santa Clara Pueblo, 1936 graduation. Wirth private collection.

Fig. 6

A. J. Connell with Santa Feans Margaret and Mark Kelly, 1940 Santa Fe Fiesta. Courtesy of Daniel T. Kelly Jr.

Fig. 7

Edward Fuller, early 1920s. Hitchcock Collection.
Courtesy Los Alamos Historical Museum Archives.

Fig. 8

Lawrence Hitchcock and Oscar Steege,
1940 graduation. Courtesy of Barbara Steege.

Fig. 9

Tall in the saddle—Lawrence Hitchcock, 1923.
Courtesy Los Alamos Historical Museum Archives.

Fig. 10

Ferm Church, c. 1922. Photo by T. Harmon Parkhurst.
Courtesy Los Alamos Historical Museum Archives.

Fig. 11

Tommy Waring, 1929. Peggy Pond Church Collection.
Courtesy Los Alamos Historical Museum Archives.

Fig. 12

Art Chase, ca. 1930s. Courtesy of Janet Chase Soldati.

Fig. 13

Cecil Wirth, Rincon Toledo campsite, 1941. Courtesy of James Anderson.

Fig. 14

Virginia Wirth with sons John and Tim, 1940.
Wirth private collection.

Fig. 15

Peggy Pond Church,
late 1930s. Wirth
private collection.

Fig. 16

Bences Gonzales,
1943. Courtesy Los
Alamos Historical
Museum Archives.

Fig. 17

Anita Rose at 1929 Santa Fe Fiesta.
Courtesy of Carolina Waring Stewart.

Fig. 18

Helen Sulier, RN, 1936. Photo by LARS student
John McDonough. Courtesy of Helen Sulier Robertson.

Fig. 19

Edna and Fred Rousseau, 1938. Photo by LARS student Ben Raskob. Courtesy of Joan Rousseau Wright.

Fig. 20

1938 graduates. From left, William H. "Edo" Osborne, James R. Anderson, Charles Pearce, William Cleary, Charles Ripley, J. R. "Budge" Whiting. Courtesy of James Anderson.

Fig. 21

Adolfo Montoya in his garden. Caperton Collection.
Courtesy of Los Alamos Historical Museum Archives.

Fig. 22

Ben White, early Ranch foreman, 1920s.
Courtesy Los Alamos Historical Museum Archives.

Fig. 23

Jim Womelsduff, Ranch foreman, with his Buick roadster.
Courtesy Richard Womelsduff.

Fig. 24

Ted Mather, LARS wrangler. Photo by LARS
student P. Krebs. From Wirth private collection.

Fig. 25

LARS grounds, 1930s. Fuller Lodge on right, Trading Post on left. Photo by T. Harmon Parkhurst. Courtesy Los Alamos Historical Museum Archives.

Fig. 26

LARS graduate Francis Rousseau, Mountain Scout, wearing his badge sash. Courtesy of Juliana Rousseau.

Fig. 27

The graduation procession, 1940. Photo by T. Harmon Parkhurst. Courtesy Museum of New Mexico, neg. no. 1221.

Fig. 28

Architect's drawing of Fuller Lodge, 1927, by John Gaw Meem.
Courtesy Meem Archive, UNM Southwest Research Center.

Fig. 29

LARS Christmas card, 1928. Courtesy of Joan Rousseau Wright.

Fig. 30

The pack train in Valle Toledo, 1941. Photo by LARS
camper Bill Carson. Courtesy of William Carson.

Fig. 31

Overlooking Valle San Antonio, 1939. Photo by LARS student
and camp counselor Charles Ripley. Ripley Collection.
Courtesy Los Alamos Historical Museum Archives.

Fig. 32

On the Highline Trail, 1939. Photo by LARS student
and camp counselor Charles Ripley. Ripley Collection.
Courtesy Los Alamos Historical Museum Archives.

Fig. 33

Camper Bill Carson looking northeast from St. Peter's Dome,
Santa Fe National Forest. Photo by LARS student and camp counselor
Charles Ripley. Courtesy Los Alamos Historical Museum Archives.

Fig. 34

Sopaipillas in Dutch ovens on the camp cooking altar. Photo by LARS camper Bill Carson. Courtesy of William Carson.

Fig. 35

Cook tent at Chihuahueños campsite, 1939. Bences Gonzales on left, fixing trout, Amador Gonzales on right, at the cooking altar. Courtesy of Janet Chase Soldati.

Fig. 36

The Big House, 1941. Photo by LARS student Peter Dechert.
Courtesy Los Alamos Historical Museum Archives.

PART II

FAMILIES AT LOS ALAMOS RANCH

Los Ricachones

Hispanic Families at Los Alamos

THERESA A. STROTTMAN

Viewing the Los Alamos Ranch School through the childhood memories of Ray Gonzales, Severo Gonzales, and Margaret Montoya Caperton, whose fathers were key Los Alamos Ranch School employees, reveals an often-unappreciated aspect of the school's history. The school was established and functioned within an already established Hispanic community with deep historic roots. The faculty and students came and then went away, but the Hispanic staff and their families, as their ancestors before them, were at home on the Pajarito Plateau. The school and the Hispanic community became crucial assets to each other.[1]

Los Alamos Ranch School on the Pajarito Plateau shared a landscape of captivating beauty with Pueblo Indians and Hispanics who had used and prized it for hundreds of years. Overlapping Pueblo Indian and Hispanic cultural landscapes of great historical depth lay embedded in the area. The ruins of ancestral Pueblo communities that cultivated beans, corn, and squash—and the trails linking these ruins—are silent remnants of life on the plateau between a thousand and four hundred years ago. San Ildefonso Indians, whose ancestors hunted and danced on the Pajarito Plateau, still go there to visit shrines and gather natural materials from traditional sites for their ceremonies and arts such as pottery.

During the late nineteenth and early twentieth centuries approximately twenty-five Hispanic families formalized their families' traditional use of the Pajarito Plateau by securing patents for homesteads there, which they inhabited mainly in the growing and grazing seasons—spring, summer, and fall. Hispanic farmers who had homes in the communities along the Rio Grande below Los Alamos grazed their sheep and cows and planted crops, mainly beans, on the high plateau that did not require irrigation because it got more rain than their fields in the valley. They made wagon roads from their homes in the valley to their homesteads and blazed horse trails and wagon tracks linking the homesteaded areas on the plateau.

A few Anglos also patented homesteads on the plateau and stayed there year round, in contrast to the Hispanic homesteaders who generally used their Los Alamos homesteads as supplemental cropland and pasture. The Los Alamos Ranch School was established in 1917 on just such homesteaded land that H. H. Brook sold to Ashley Pond.

The forests and meadows on the Pajarito Plateau were extensive at the turn of the last century. The Indian ruins, homesteads, and the Ranch School were small presences in a magnificent wilderness framed by mountain peaks. Moreover, the school was established in a Hispanic and Indian place. A. J. Connell, despite his imperious manner, at some conscious or unconscious level recognized that the school was in many ways a guest in a Hispanic community.

Under A. J.'s guidance Los Alamos Ranch School became a multiethnic community. During the early twentieth century the school recruited wealthy Anglo students along with masters and administrators who, with few exceptions, had Ivy League degrees. Some of the homesteaders and ranch employees were Anglo, although most were Hispanic, and the help also included workers from the nearby pueblos. The Pajarito Plateau was a place where people worked on their own land and for the Ranch School. The multiethnic staff turned the school's buildings and grounds into a place of surpassing beauty and facilitated the efficient, effective Ranch School program of college preparation combined with outdoor activities.

This community on the plateau had no churches or cemeteries. These deep institutional roots were in the Española Valley, where families had centuries-old connections. But the Pajarito Plateau was home to a community of people who worked together and helped each other on a regular basis. This strong sense of community and pride in work done well are central themes in the recollections of Hispanics whose parents were homesteaders on the plateau and key employees at Los Alamos. They remember the Ranch School of their childhoods as a nurturing community that generously provided physical and emotional security, gave them a good education, and encouraged the development of personal discipline and pride.

The Anglo staff at the Ranch School referred to the Hispanic staff and homesteaders as Spanish or *la gente*. Within the plateau's Hispanic community itself, however, people called each other *primo* and *compadre*. Most of the ranch's Hispanic employees were cousins, in-laws, or related through the special ties that bind godfathers, *padrinos,* to the children whose spiritual development they pledge to guard. Among themselves the Hispanics used la gente, coupled with a geographic location, to refer to the people of a specific area, such as *la gente de Santa Fe.*

In northern New Mexico between the two world wars, the Hispanic families who worked for Los Alamos were at the forefront of the transition from the traditional occupations associated with farming, ranching, and sheep herding to wage labor and integration into the national economy. The Denver & Rio Grande Western narrow gauge railroad established in the late nineteenth century and the state highway built in the 1920s were the infrastructure linking the plateau's ages-old network of trails to the outside world. The railroad had enabled the early homesteaders to sell their surplus bean harvests for cash. Later, the railroad and two-lane road heading north from Santa Fe, which connected with the gravel road to the Pajarito Plateau, enabled the LARS to provide the faculty and students with reasonable access to the wider world from whence they came. As the school grew it added its own trails to the ages-old network of Indian and Hispanic trails. Prior to the Ranch School, wage-labor positions in northern New Mexico involved men leaving their homes and families in the Española Valley for extended periods to earn money by herding sheep or by working for the railroads and mines. Working for Los Alamos gave Hispanic families cash income and the ability to stay together year round. Whether by conscious calculated manipulation or by unconscious instinctive exercise of his natural personality, A. J. Connell gracefully inserted himself and the LARS within the geographic and cultural landscapes on the Pajarito Plateau. For the school's Hispanic staff, A. J. was the good *patrón.* Many northern New Mexico Hispanic families worked over twenty years for A. J. and the Ranch School. The senior employees had steady work and owned their own cars. The contrast with relatives working in the Española Valley, where jobs were scarce, was stark. Hence, their loyalty to A. J. was strong. He was their *jefe* and respected for his fairness. A. J.'s management style was similar to that of a classic patrón in that he maintained personal one-to-one relationships with his Hispanic employees. They could approach him directly without having to work through a hierarchical chain of command. He provided houses for Hispanic families and included them in staff parties and entertainments.

Bences Gonzales and Adolfo Montoya were intelligent, quiet, reliable, and industrious employees, each of whom worked at the Ranch School for many years. Most of the information we have about them and their careers at the school is communicated via the memories of their children, who grew up at the school. Both men were loving fathers who devoted time and attention to their children. At the Ranch School, Bences exercised a talent for interacting with people from diverse backgrounds. Adolfo's ability to coax beautiful and bountiful plants from the high desert plateau made the school's gardens visual feasts that delighted visiting parents and the community, while also furnishing vegetables and berries for the ample, well-balanced meals served at LARS.

Most of Severo Gonzales's answers to questions about the Los Alamos Ranch School begin with "My Dad always said . . ." The phrase is simultaneously the authoritative verification for whatever follows and a loving gesture of respect and homage to his father, Bences Gonzales. Bences was a remarkable man who began working for A. J. Connell in 1919, two years after the school opened. Connell had hired Bences's father, Severo Sr., to build the pack house and the small stone fire station that housed a cart with a water tank, pump, and hose for extinguishing fires. Having grown up near San Ildefonso Pueblo, Bences himself served in the army during the First World War and then worked as a cowboy for the ranch. A. J. later asked him to staff the Trading Post, a job he held until the school closed in 1943.

Ray, Severo's older brother, emphasizes the importance of Bences's position in operating the Trading Post. Everyone who studied, worked, or lived at the Ranch School, as well as neighboring homesteaders and sheepherders, stopped at the store, the only one on the plateau. Visitors to the school or tourists passing through the Pajarito Plateau would stop there. Like general stores in many small communities, it was the information hub of the Pajarito. Bences spoke English as well as the Spanish spoken in his northern New Mexican home and became the mediator for a variety of contacts ranging from simply giving directions to solving personnel problems and counseling anxious students. Being bilingual was extremely important because in those days many families in northern New Mexico were monolingual Spanish-speaking. Severo recalls that his father cashed checks for many employees.

One of Bences's properties was a homestead near Anchor Ranch, just south of the school. He married Ernestina Romero, whose family also had a homestead on the Pajarito Plateau. Work, family, and land formed his roots in Los Alamos. He also had deep roots in the rich network of his extended family in the Española Valley. By the time Severo, his second son, was born, in 1929, Bences had made himself indispensable to the smooth operation of the Ranch School. His family grew as the school grew.

Connell's practice was to discuss his needs for workers with Bences, who would then consult his family network and find reliable employees. Ray recalls how his Dad fulfilled this vital function. "So when anything came up, say Jim [Womelsduff, the ranch foreman] needed a carpenter, or a plumber, or an electrician, or something like that, they would ask my father if he knew

Fig. 7.1

The Trading Post, where Bences Gonzales worked. Photo by T. Harmon Parkhurst. Courtesy Los Alamos Historical Museum Archives.

of anybody to come in and give them a hand. My Dad would say, 'I'll have somebody up here by next day or two.'"[2] Then Bences would talk to his relatives, his primos. "Different people that he had known in the Valley would ask him, 'Is there any work?' At that time there wasn't much work in Española. If you didn't know anybody, you just didn't work. So Dad helped his primos by saying, 'Yes, I know somebody,' and bringing them in when the School needed a person. Within the next day or two the boy would be up here, and they dressed him in a uniform and he'd be serving tables, taking dishes, washing dishes, whatever."[3] Bences saw the school's Hispanic employees as the spokes of a wheel with the patrón at the center.

Bences's wheel is a good image for describing how the school's Hispanic employees viewed their social and work relationships. At the hub of the wheel was a patrón or jefe who had one-to-one relationships, the supporting spokes, with each dependent on the wheel's rim. Whether by design or by instinct, A. J. knew how to assume his position as patrón at the hub of the Ranch School wheel. He personally nourished the relationships that kept the spokes strong. There was a coincidence of expectations between A. J.'s administrative style and the patrón system, which was the paradigm through which the Hispanic employees interpreted their professional and social experiences. A. J. made a point of visiting his friends/employees regularly. For example, he would discuss business and socialize with Adolfo Montoya in Adolfo's extensive gardens.

While much has been written about the negative potential for abuse and exploitation within the patrón system, there is also positive potential for people like Bences to assume responsibility and be a mediator who helps improve the community. Bences functioned as a *patroncito*[4] who exercised influence within the Ranch School community while also having a public role beyond the Pajarito Plateau. Severo has carried on Bences's interest in public service and, like his father, participates in the political process. He remembers Bences riding all night from Los Alamos to Bernalillo to deliver the Los Alamos ballot boxes to the Sandoval County Clerk. For several years he took daily readings for the U.S. Weather Service at the station on the school grounds. During World War II Bences served on the Manhattan Project's first town council in Los Alamos.

Just as each spoke needs to be strong to support a wheel, each relationship between the patrón at the hub and the dependents on the rim had to be nurtured by reciprocal exchanges of intangibles, like loyalty, and material considerations, like wages or a share of meat from a successful hunt. Bences expected the primos, *tios,* and *compadres* whom he recommended to A. J. Connell to work diligently and reliably. Severo refers to the people his Dad recommended as "all steady employees, good employees. Dad would get some relation, either a third cousin or even closer relation that knew something about something. That's the way it went. They built homes for them, and they all lived here in Los Alamos."[5]

A dramatic part of A. J. Connell's management of the Ranch School was his emphasis on uniforms. He, the masters, and the students wore a slightly modified version of the Boy Scout uniform. Severo remembers that the Indian and Hispanic waiters in Fuller Lodge wore khakis or, for formal occasions, white pants with a brightly colored silk shirt and a black cloth sash tied at the waist. Ray recalls that Bences and A. J. had to negotiate the uniform issue. "My Dad was considered one of the staff at the School, and A. J. had the idea, because all the masters wore shorts, he wanted my Dad to wear shorts. But Dad said, 'No. My legs are too bony to wear shorts, and I'm not going to wear shorts. If you don't want me here that's fine, but I don't wear shorts.' A. J. said, 'Well, okay. Will you wear khakis?' Dad said, 'I'll wear khakis.'"[6] Ray describes the result of this mutual resolution of the uniform issue: "So my Dad wore khaki pants and a gabardine type shirt that was more like a military uniform. It kind of matched the School uniform. I don't think he wore wool shirts either, but he did wear gabardine shirts."

Hats, good quality hats, also claimed serious consideration. Ray recalls the LARS hat that was called the Dakota Stetson. "It was a John B. Stetson which is the gourmet hat, top of the line. Actually they patterned them after the Forest

Service hat that A. J. Connell used to use. He showed them the one he had and said, 'I want a hat similar to this if you can make it.' The Forest Service had a green band, and then they had it squashed to the side. Well, A. J. wanted it a little different."[7] Ray remembers how the Stetson company accommodated A. J. Connell. "Stetson sent several different styles of hats to the Ranch for the staff and masters to try. They finally chose one everyone liked. The company said, 'We'll make them.' So then they had the pattern and from then on the school would say, 'We need fifty hats for next year.' They kept them at the Trading Post."

Having won the army's sharpshooting medal for marksmanship, Bences was an excellent shot and an accomplished hunter. A. J. Connell gave him a week each year to go hunting with his 303 Savage rifle. He was proud of his hunting skills, part of his identity as a northern New Mexican. From colonial times men hunted to provide meat for their extended families and protect their homes from predatory wild animals. They also defended their villages from Indian raids. Bences's macho pride in his hunting skills and his experience as a veteran, as a warrior protecting his nation, were closely related elements of his personality. Severo recalls, "My Dad would kill a deer and all the primos would get a piece of meat."[8] Bences nourished the community that he helped gather. His continual activity as an indispensable employee and community leader reflected his concern for the strength of the wheel. A bright, social man, Bences was well suited for this role.

Sometimes he used his skill with bravado. Severo recalls a conversation he had about his Dad's hunting skills with Harry Walen, one of the masters. "They were talking and Dad bet him that he could get a turkey. Dad got his rifle, and Harry said, 'How are you going to shoot a turkey with a rifle?' And Dad said, 'Well, I'll take one bullet.' He took this one bullet and off he went, probably towards where the airstrip is now," about a mile east of the Trading Post. Severo recalls the end of this story with great pride. "Sure enough, hour or so later, here comes Dad with a turkey and its head where the bullet had passed through. He won the bet. Dad was a very good shooter."[9]

A. J. and Bences shared an expert knowledge and appreciation of camping, pack trains, and tack for horses and mules. For his part, A. J had developed these skills when he worked for the Forest Service. Bences added what he learned in the army during World War I to the outdoors lore he had absorbed working from a very young age in northern New Mexico. Their expertise became an important focus for the Ranch School's camping activities, especially during the summer camp. These extremely well-organized pack expeditions across the Valle Grande and out to the San Pedro Peaks were memorable adventures for all who participated. A master of Dutch-oven cooking, Bences was the camp cook for these pack-trips. He had the boys build a raised cooking altar every place they camped so that, as Ray says, "my Dad's back wouldn't give out on him lifting up the Dutch ovens."[10] Bences performed culinary magic on those altars. He built fires on the altar and placed his Dutch ovens among the coals. His fresh cinnamon rolls were delicious. He even managed to cook his famous sopaipillas in boiling lard at altitudes over eight thousand feet.

Ray remembers working as his Dad's helper on summer pack-train expeditions. Bences counted as his friends many of the sheepherders who grazed flocks in the areas traversed by the pack outfit. "When the boys were out camping, Dad would buy a sheep and then butcher it. Art Chase and some of the masters would cut the throat and save the blood. When they had cleaned the sheep, they would save all the intestines and then make blood stew."[11] Severo also recalls this traditional preparation. "In Spanish they call it *burriñates*. To make them, Dad would roll the intestines, clean them out real good and stuff them and roll them up and sort of fry them, and they are a delicacy."[12]

Bences also cooked *barbacoa*, a sheep's head buried in a pit with burning coals. This was an evening treat for himself and the adults and counselors to enjoy when all the boys had been put to bed in the tents. Ray remembers the work that went into preparing this specialty. "Dad would dig a hole in the ground and put hot coals in there, put in the sheep's head, then put in more coals and cover it up. At about eleven o'clock or so the campers would be all through with their prayers or singing and then my Dad and me would get together and pull out the sheep's head. All the delicacy was in the head, the tongue, around the brains and whatever is in the head." Bences made this special treat for his friends running the camp with him. "Dad would make a little sauce with chili peppers. Then he and the masters would sit there and tell jokes and stories and get their meat. There was not much of that meat. But it was a delicacy. Art Chase and the others would then eat some of the burriñates."[13]

As Bences was a responsible patroncito, he recognized that A. J. Connell was his patrón. A. J. was called chief, boss, or jefe by the school's masters and the Anglo employees. Connell was clearly in charge, the man in control, but the perceived nature of his role in those relationships with the Anglos was qualitatively different than his role in his relationships with the Hispanic employees. Both Severo and his older brother Ray recall the close relationship between their father and Mr. Connell as one of mutual respect. A. J. consulted Bences regularly on a variety of issues and often supported him when he had rare conflicts with the masters. Severo will hold up crossed index and middle fingers while he says, "My Dad and A. J. were like this."

One day some waiters didn't show up for breakfast. Mrs. Sheffield, the matron, told Mr. Connell, who immediately went to wake up Bences. After dressing quickly, Bences hurried over to the Lodge, helped cook and serve breakfast to the students and masters, and then talked to the striking waiters. Bences listened to their demands and then told them, "You should have been men enough to come over and say we want this or we want that and talk about it. Don't just among yourselves say, 'Let's not go.'"[14] Two of the striking waiters left the Ranch School, and one of them was Bences's half-brother. However, A. J. continued to employ the father of one of the waiters who left. A. J. did not extend his displeasure to entire families, and Bences did not try to insist on retaining his half-brother. Instead, Bences went back to the extended family network and found new employees to replace the strikers who left.

Bences demonstrated a great deal of quiet empathy as he did his job. His daily contacts at the Trading Post with students, masters, staff, homesteaders, sheepherders, and visitors demonstrated his ability to help people solve their problems, as well as provide them with goods and information. Severo recalls how his Dad was a familiar figure in the students' daily routine. "Being in the position that he was, he had contact with each and every kid on a daily basis, except Saturday and Sunday. They came to get their mail at the Trading Post. He knew their names and home towns."[15] Students also got their weekly ration of candy from Bences at the Trading Post. Severo describes how Bences established rapport with the students at the beginning of the school year when they came to be outfitted. "The most important part, he outfitted each individual from socks to shoes to chaps and hat. He had that touch for clothing and shirts. Boys outfitted by Mr. Rousseau [the business manager] would come back and say, 'He said I needed a big hat, and I'd have to stick paper inside.' Dad would help kids exchange sizes. He'd talk to another kid and say, 'Does your hat fit?' The kid would say, 'You know, Bences, it's too tight.' Then Dad would say, 'Well, why don't you change it with him? See how this one fits.' There were rules against exchanging, but the kids got to trust him to make changes for them."

Ray reflects on the fundamental nature of Bences's personality. "He had this way about him. He said, 'you can catch more bees with honey, and you can't catch 'em with a stick anyway.' He wasn't as well educated as the masters, but he had more common sense, more in heart to reprimand a boy, not in front of everybody, but he would just bring him aside and that's the respect that our boys, myself included, had for him because he wouldn't just scream and holler at you. He'd bring you to the side and explain to you what was wrong or what was right. You had that kind of respect after you did something wrong."[16]

The masters, students, and other employees sensed and responded to Bences's accepting manner and personal dignity. Ray remembers how Bences instructed the students in how to pack the animals for an upcoming expedition.

"The same thing with School boys and packing horses. If you beat a horse, he will remember it and hurt you. If you treat him with kindness, that horse will work for you. That's what he used to preach to them. 'You load a horse; you weight the back with boxes of things, and you don't over weight the horse. We're taking one horse to carry extra pounds. If you do as I tell you, you won't find any trouble. That horse, just pet him all the time; talk to him, and he will understand.' That was his way his whole life, with my sisters, with his three boys and all."[17]

Severo remembers how Bences and the masters took the older students hunting in November. Students often vied to hunt with Bences. After the school closed, former masters and students would write and visit Bences. Severo and his wife, Aurora, still maintain some of these friendships with letters and visits.

Adolfo Montoya was another leading figure at the ranch. Around 1918 he established a homestead on the plateau where he grazed cattle and planned to develop a commercial meat-supply business. In 1920 A. J. hired him to manage the vegetable gardens for LARS. Soon after he began working for the school, his father became ill, and Adolfo moved his family back to San Pedro, near Española, so he could care for him. After his father recovered, Adolfo moved his family north to Leadville, Colorado, where he found a job in the mines. However, around 1926 the family returned to San Pedro. As Margaret Montoya Caperton remembers, "Mother wanted to come back because my Dad was beginning to not feel well from working in the mines, all that dust flying."[18] When A. J. heard Adolfo was back in the vicinity, he rehired him to manage the gardens.

A meticulous man who strove for excellence in his magnificent gardens, Adolfo enjoyed his work and showed it. As Margaret recalls, "We had a big garden. We had, oh I'd say, a couple rows of flowers, rows the length of city blocks, and then all his veggies. And he loved his work so much. I remember when the plants were only just coming up and you could barely see them he took all of us out there. There were no weeds. When Mr. Connell had guests he took them over to see Adolfo's plants."[19]

The first priority for the gardens was to provide food and cut flowers for the Ranch School. Margaret remembers, "We had enough vegetables for the School, but if there was anything extra my Dad would give it away to the people who lived there. Nothing went to waste. It was not surprising to see kids run up and pick up a cucumber or tomato from the garden, wash them with a hose, and eat them. We had a big cellar outside the house, and all the shelves were filled. And my Dad had big, and I mean big, barrels where he made sour kraut for the school boys and for us too."[20]

Adolfo planted an eight-acre orchard on his wife's property in San Pedro, where Margaret's home is today. "Whenever the Ranch School needed fruit my Dad would come down here. Whatever we had at our place we sold to the School. And if we didn't have enough, Dad bought from other people around here and then took it up." Because Adolfo was in charge of supplying the school with vegetables and fruits, she said: "If he didn't have it there in the garden or if we didn't have the fruits here, then he got it from the neighbors around here, whoever, relatives really, because just about everybody was related in those days."[21] Looking out her window, Margaret points to an apple tree. "I convinced my Dad not to cut that tree after that terrific frost we had here years later. So he left that one because, being near the house, it wasn't as badly frost-burned as the others. That's all I have left of what was here."[22]

While Adolfo's major focus was cultivating vegetables, flowers, and fruit, he continued to maintain a small herd of cattle. Like Bences, he hunted deer and purchased lambs. Margaret remembers, "My Dad went hunting up in our

Fig. 7.2

Adolfo and Elaisa Montoya planting the school garden. Caperton Collection. Courtesy Los Alamos Historical Museum Archives.

own property. And my Dad used to go to Colorado. We bought lambs from there, and we have relatives there."

Besides bringing students' parents and guests to visit Adolfo's gardens, Margaret remembers that A. J. took an "extra special" interest in the Montoya family. "Mr. Connell took a liking to my brother, Rubel, when he was, oh, maybe twelve. He had Rubel driving him around the ranch, being his chauffeur, this little thing sitting on a cushion sticking his head up over the steering wheel."[23] Rubel remembers working at various odd jobs as a child before he became A. J.'s chauffeur. He set traps in Fuller Lodge for rats and was paid a nickel for each rat he caught. He was a houseboy for A. J. and remembers being invited to listen to classical music in A. J.'s quarters.[24]

Rubel was the first Hispanic scholarship student to attend the Los Alamos Ranch School. He believes that he was chosen for this honor "because my Dad was one of Mr. Connell's favorite employees." When Rubel graduated from the elementary school he remembers his father, Adolfo, telling him that Mr. Connell wanted him to study at the Ranch School and that he would "need to really study." As a student he shared a room in the Big House with Eric Outwater, a boy from Holland. He used the room for rest periods and doing his homework; and then he had dinner with his family and slept in his bed at home. At 6 A.M. he did exercises with the students and joined them for breakfast in Fuller Lodge. He stayed with the students through classes, lunch in Fuller Lodge, and afternoon activities, including studying, until he went home at approximately 5 P.M. He recalls being scared and intimidated at first. Lawrence Hitchcock and Ferm Church encouraged him to "speak up," and within six weeks he relaxed and "became one of the boys." Rubel's favorite subjects were math and history. He naturally excelled in Spanish and tutored other students. Being a LARS student meant that he didn't have time to do chores like chopping and stacking wood after lunch, and student activities like camping on weekends diminished the time he could play with his childhood friends. Unfortunately, he was at the school for only one semester before the War Department condemned the school property and the homesteads on the Pajarito Plateau. However, the Montoya family is proud of Rubel's brief status as a Los Alamos Ranch School student.

Margaret remembers the piano Mr. Connell gave her family when she was in elementary school. "Mrs. White played the piano up there, and she gave me lessons. And in payment my sister Rose fixed her hair every week."[25] When relatives visited the Montoya family, "the children were sent out to play." But Margaret remembers, "They always brought me in to play the piano. My Dad was so proud of it, and I'd learned a little piece. He wanted me to play for them, for his company. And I would hide and they'd look for me. I hated to put on a little show."

Fig. 7.3

Ray Gonzales, Victor Gonzales, and Rubel Montoya
(in his LARS uniform), fall 1942. Caperton Collection.
Courtesy Los Alamos Historical Museum Archives.

Adolfo and his wife, Elaisa, made great efforts to ensure that all their children, boys and girls, had good educations. After they finished elementary school at the stone schoolhouse in Los Alamos, they went to private schools in Santa Fe. "Dad rented a place for us there in Santa Fe. The boys went to St. Michael's School and the girls to Loretto Academy. And then in the summer we would come home."[26] The older girls, Lucy, Rose, and Adelina, remember working at Loretto doing chores such as cleaning classrooms and waiting on tables in the dining room to reduce their tuition fees. The Montoyas' commitment to their children's education is particularly remarkable considering that they were also coping with medical expenses for their son, Art, who has mild schizophrenia. A. J. recommended doctors and a home in Makin, Missouri, for Art. Margaret remembers her parents' difficulties during those years. "All that my Dad had saved was going to pay for his hospital bills. And you know that he hadn't been able to save too much because when you have eight kids."[27]

Margaret fondly remembers the elementary school in Los Alamos. "We started our lessons in one room, but I remember then Mr. Connell built these two new classrooms. And we had the hall and cloakroom, and then the bathrooms, one for the girls and one for the boys." In the 1930s the WPA sponsored school construction in rural northern New Mexican communities. A. J. contributed financial and other resources to build the new school, which was designed by John Gaw Meem, the school architect. Margaret remembers, "In our elementary school one teacher, Amador Gonzales, was paid by Sandoval County, and then Mr. Connell paid for another teacher, Mrs. Rousseau, so we'd have a good education."[28] "We had everything we needed in the way of books and in so many little ways. We had our own library in the school, so we could read books all the time. In fact we used to bring some of our books down to the valley so that our cousins could enjoy them. Then we would take them back up to Los Alamos." Margaret recalls that A. J. would bring Ranch School students' parents to the elementary school. "Mr. Connell would bring all the boys' parents that came to visit over to the elementary school to see our school and how well we were doing. And Mrs. Rousseau would call me up, my first year, to read to them. And she'd say, 'This little girl didn't know a word of English when she came to school.' But I did."[29] A. J. often attended programs and recitals at the elementary school. Margaret remembers that he heard her play piano on one of these occasions. "I played when we had our recitals, and he heard me then. We had the recitals together with the school program, and those who were taking private lessons performed."[30]

Ray, Severo, Rubel, and Margaret all remember "our school" as a place they enjoyed. They all state that they did not experience discrimination as schoolchildren in Los Alamos. However, Margaret's account of nutrition lessons at the public school indicates how polite Hispanic children negotiated questions of cultural distinctions. "The dietitian from the Ranch School used to come to our school to give us lessons. I remember so clearly our books said you always had bacon and eggs for breakfast. Because I was big and strong she would ask me to tell the class what I had for breakfast. Well, my mother used to fix *atole* and I loved it. I used to have a whole cup. I never mentioned that because it wasn't in our books. I figured it must not be something we're supposed to be drinking."[31]

Margaret recollects: "Up there you never felt racial discrimination. We didn't feel discriminated against because we got to do so many things that our cousins in the Valley didn't get to do. We would come down to the Valley to visit my uncles and aunts, and their life was so different from ours up in Los Alamos. We just seemed to be so privileged. We got to go swimming every day with a lifeguard. They didn't get to go ice-skating. Our school was so special."[32]

Ray and Severo, who could compete with the Ranch School boys, remember participating in games and sports with both students and summer campers. Margaret remembers that the younger children of workers' families had times set aside for them to swim and ice-skate when they wouldn't get in the way of the older children or Ranch School students. Ray, Severo, Rubel, and Margaret all remember that pots of hot chocolate were always available at the edge of Ashley Pond when both the LARS students and the workers' children were skating. Margaret recalls that the lifeguard was always on duty during the swimming time set aside for the workers' younger children.

Severo and Rubel were Boy Scouts, members of the Ranch School's Troop 22. (Severo wore Rubel's Troop 22 merit-badge sash at the 1997 Los Alamos Ranch reunion.) In the late 1930s Ray went on the summer-camp pack-trips into the Jemez as his father's "helper," a position held in earlier years by his older cousins. Ray spent much of his days playing and competing with the student campers. Before meals he would change to long pants and a long-sleeved shirt to protect him from the cooking fires. Then he would assume his duties as Bences's assistant.

Ray remembers that in August of 1938, during one of the summers he worked as his father's assistant and played with summer campers, A. J. Connell gave him a formal twelfth-birthday party dinner in the Fuller Lodge dining room. From the first course through the dessert the meal was an embarrassing challenge for the confident young guest of honor who was proud of his ability to successfully compete with the LARS boys at horsemanship, tennis, swimming, and diving. Ray had never eaten an artichoke. A. J. noticed that he was ignoring his artichoke and asked the boy sitting next to him to show Ray

Fig. 7.4

Josie Gonzales and Margaret Montoya skating on Ashley Pond.
Caperton Collection. Courtesy Los Alamos Historical Museum Archives.

how to eat it. How could Ray know that all new boys had to learn to eat an artichoke, a ritual the older boys turned into a trick to embarrass new boys? Further embarrassment occurred when Ray cut forcefully into the top layer of his birthday cake, causing its cardboard base to slide off the lower layer and onto the table. For weeks after the dinner, students asked Ray if he'd "eaten any more artichokes or had any more cake."[33]

The Gonzales and Montoya children were assigned various chores at home and for the Ranch School. Severo raised fowl and sold eggs and birds to the school. Margaret and her sisters cleaned and prepared the amenities in the guesthouse. They remember taking the empty perfume vials that guests discarded and placing them in their drawers to perfume their clothes. They also babysat for the Wirth boys, John and Tim. Adelina Montoya Montaño remembers staying with John in September 1939, when Virginia went to the hospital for Tim's birth. Their father Cecil moved into the student dormitory while Adelina stayed with John, and Adolfo stopped in late every evening to check on Adelina and John.[34] Adelina helped Virginia Wirth with the housework and the Montoya sisters also helped their mother, who "pushed to send us to good schools because she wanted to be sure that we were prepared. She didn't want us to have to work as hard as she did."[35]

Margaret remembers: "We helped Mother make sopaipillas when the school had a Mexican or Spanish meal, holding them down with a big fork, so she wouldn't have to turn them over." Her mother also "washed the students' scarves by hand because they did not want to send them to the laundry. She'd iron those silk scarves very carefully for the boys."[36] Adelina remembers their mother laundering masters' shirts and handkerchiefs. She also did a lot of baking, canning, and sewing.

Elaisa Montoya and Ernestina Gonzales "were midwives" for each other and for the other women on the Pajarito Plateau. "When anyone was born they would help with the deliveries." Every year the women would "all get together in one house and string red chilis to make the traditional *ristras,* and visit, laugh, and talk."[37] Elaisa Montoya spoke Spanish even though she understood English. Ernestina Gonzales, like her husband and children, was bilingual.

Friendships were formed between some of the Hispanic and Anglo staff families. Rubel has fond memories of Helen Sulier, the school nurse. His birth was so difficult that Elaisa was moved into a room in Fuller Lodge, and Helen Sulier aided the delivery. "Mrs. Sulier taught us how to knit," Margaret recalls. "We made scarves, which were displayed in the county office in Bernalillo to show them off. But somebody broke the window and stole everything." Margaret also fondly recalls her piano teacher, Mrs. White. Rose Montoya recalls doing Mrs. White's hair every week.[38]

Rose and Adelina were firm friends of Mrs. Sulier's daughter, Helen, and the Rousseau's daughter, Joan. The girls spent their free time together playing, having picnics, ice skating, and visiting an old Indian cave that was their secret place. The kids had lots to do at the Ranch School, Helen recalls, and when they returned from the Loretto Academy on vacation they skated, used the toboggan, played fox and geese on horseback, and read mysteries in the school library while the boys were away on vacation.[39] On an outing with Ted Church one day, Joan and Adelina were riding double when their horse suddenly took off, stopping finally at the cattle guard where they both fell off. Adelina was a frequent visitor to the Rousseaus, and Joan went to the Montoyas' house, though not for dinner.[40]

Ray and Severo, Margaret and Rubel remember their fathers as loving and strict parents. In Ray's memoir, there are recollections of instances when Bences quietly assessed potentially dangerous things that his sons and other boys were doing, like smoking in a barn full of hay. He would point out the problem with the boys' behavior and suggest safer options in a private, yet firm, manner. Rubel remembers being instructed to call the adult men *Tío* or *Don*. Margaret recollects, "We had to obey everybody up there. I mean there was no such thing as being disrespectful."[41]

The older Hispanic boys interacted with the students in sports and scouting activities. Rubel, in his brief experience as a Ranch School student, was making the transition from the Hispanic workers' community to the students' world of an elite prep school. The type of interactions one would expect between teenage boys and girls did not occur at Los Alamos. Margaret's memories of minimal contact with the students are corroborated by Joan Rousseau's similar recollections. Margaret and her sisters recall observing the students but having few, if any, interactions with them. They talk about watching the (student) boys exercise and play sports. They attended the dress rehearsals and performances of Gilbert and Sullivan operettas with their all-male casts. At school dances, Margaret sat quietly on the balcony in Fuller Lodge and watched entranced as the boys, decked out in short pants, danced with the Brownmoor girls in their elegant formal dresses. Joan, too, does not recall any dating between the boys and the staff/help girls. The boys were tightly controlled.[42]

Rufus Kelvin, a worker, and his wife Roxy are the newly married romantic couple Margaret remembers with a smile as she describes them. "It was so exciting for us to have a newly married couple up there because he had a motorcycle they would ride around the place. She was holding on to him. It was so obvious that they were so much in love, and we enjoyed that." In accordance with familial expectations, the girls focused their time and energy on their families, their schoolwork, and the women's sphere that quietly functioned within the male-oriented ambiance of the Ranch School. The expectations and mores of traditional Hispanic culture regarding women's roles were complementary and symbiotic with Connell's design for the school as a community dedicated to and focused on young men. The Hispanic women and their daughters focused their attention on their homes and families. At an early age, sons and daughters in traditional Hispanic families were encouraged to work and play with members of their own sex. This coincided with A. J.'s expectation that the women at the Ranch School should exhibit minimal presence and visibility. As mentioned, the girls would hike, explore Indian cave ruins, ride the school's horses, ice-skate, and swim. Like their brothers, the girls had the entire Pajarito Plateau as their playground.

Those who were children of Ranch School employees remember the joy and excitement they experienced at the annual Christmas party that Mr. Connell gave for the staff and their families. The party always took place in Fuller Lodge a few days before Christmas. Not only did they have a holiday dinner, but Santa Claus arrived with a present for every child. Margaret remembers the year that, instead of individual presents for each child, each family received a beautiful sled. Additionally, every year each child received a stocking stuffed with nuts, candy, and perhaps an orange. Josefita Gonzales Sandoval, daughter of carpenter Pedro Gonzales, remembers that her father asked his children to save their stockings to share with primos in El Rancho. A. J.'s Christmas party for the staff and their families was a generous personal effort that the Hispanic community saw as proof he was a good patrón. He recognized his workers as individuals, not merely paid staff, and he spent effort, time, and other resources affirming his recognition of their place in the community. It was a classic exchange of mutual social and material obligations, a characteristic of the traditional patrón system.

At that time, northern New Mexico was being integrated into the national holiday cycle: Christmas festivities that concentrated on December 25, the focus of Anglo Christmas celebrations, were established in New Mexican schools by the 1920s. However, in the Spanish-speaking communities during the 1920s and 1930s the focal dates for Christmas festivities were the nine days before Christmas, *la posada novena*. Both Indian and Hispanic communities lit *luminarias* (bonfires) in the evening. When Joseph and Mary were admitted to a home on the last night of *Las Posadas* the spectators followed them in to celebrate with *biscochitos,* sweets, hot drinks, and the singing of Christmas carols, *Vamos todos a Belen* (Let's All Go to Bethlehem) and *Noche de Paz* (Silent Night). Later that evening, everyone would attend *La misa de Gallo,* or midnight mass. This was followed by a breakfast of *posole, menudo,* and traditional sweets. Then children would go from door to door through the village asking for *"mis Crismas,"* returning home with a sack of candy and peanuts in time to join in the day-long family gathering and feast. This was the event to which Pedro Gonzales's children contributed the Christmas stockings that they were given a few days earlier at Mr. Connell's Christmas party for the Ranch School staff. Severo remembers that often the snow was deep and roads were bad at Christmastime, so Bences's family generally stayed at home in Los Alamos. When the weather permitted, they would go to San Ildefonso over the Christmas holidays to watch Indian dances. One of his uncles taught school at San Ildefonso, and another uncle taught at the public school in Los Alamos. Severo remembers accompanying Bences on his regular trips to San Ildefonso to trade with Maria Martinez for pottery to add to the Trading Post's inventory. From time to time Bences also traded surplus stock at the pueblo. Students bought pottery and jewelry at the Trading Post and paid Bences for wrapping and shipping the presents to their families, especially at Christmas.

The condemnation of the Los Alamos Ranch School for military purposes in 1943 mandated the end of Connell's carefully nurtured community. Margaret recalls that in 1942, "My Dad told Mr. Connell he was going to have to leave the ranch to take care of Art [the son with mild schizophrenia] full time. And Mr. Connell said, 'Oh no. I can't let you go now. They're going to close us up.' That's when he told my Dad, and so we were the first ones to know. He told him not to say anything, but that he needed him and wouldn't be able to get anybody for short term. So Mr. Connell arranged for us to take Art to a doctor in Albuquerque, who gave him electric shock treatments."[43]

Ray describes Colonel Whitney Ashbridge's conversation with Bences at the Trading Post when he came to Los Alamos in 1942, accompanied by a group of army officers: "'Do you remember me?' Ashbridge asked Dad. He replied, 'You look like one of the students who was here.' Then he said: 'Bences, it looks like the army is going to come in and build here. Where can we find Mr. Connell?'"[44]

During the first week of February in 1943, A. J.'s carefully assembled community dissolved. Connell and most of the Ranch School employees moved to Santa Fe. In fact, many former employees, students, and masters were already in the service. Fermin Gonzales, Pedro's son, was captured at Bataan while serving in the New Mexico National Guard. He survived the infamous death march, but Adolfo's son Lucas, a Marine, was killed in the Pacific. In 1945, as soon as he was old enough, Ray enlisted in the navy.

Abruptly cut loose from their homes and secure work environment at the Ranch School, the Hispanic families had to rely on their skills and extended family networks to reorganize their lives and, in most cases, relocate. Although he had built a house in Santa Fe in the late 1930s, Bences chose to stay in Los Alamos, live in the home his family had occupied for many years, and take a job with the Manhattan Project. He worked at the PX that was established in the former Trading Post. With Jerry Pepper, the one Los Alamos master who also stayed on, and some Manhattan Project personnel, Bences reconstituted Troop 22. Thus his sons shared with the sons of scientists, engineers, and mechanics something of the pack-trip experience once so central to the Ranch School and summer camp program. Ray and Severo worked various jobs in Los Alamos, including caring for Kitty Oppenheimer's horses and showing her the trails on the Pajarito Plateau. Both attended the new high school.[45]

No longer boss of the mesa, Connell moved to Santa Fe and shared a house with Edna and Fred Rousseau before taking rooms at the La Fonda hotel. Josefita Gonzales Sandoval remembers A. J. coming to their Santa Fe home and asking her mother for sugar so he could have biscochitos made for a Boy's Club party. Mrs. Gonzales gave him all of the family's sugar ration. Although Pedro was somewhat annoyed by the lack of sugar, the family felt that A. J. had been very good to them for many years. Faced with the difficulties of making a new living, paying for his children's education and medical care for his ill son, Adolfo also provided comfort and companionship to A. J., now increasingly lonely and unhappy. Connell was a frequent visitor to the Montoya house before he died in February 1944. Adolfo Montoya's children say with pride, "My Dad was one of the pallbearers at A. J. Connell's funeral." The children of Adolfo Montoya and Pedro Gonzales say, "My Dad and A. J. were very close." Fixed in the childhood memories of those who grew up on the Los Alamos ranch is the knowledge that their fathers and "Mister Connell were very great friends."

When A. J. died the Hispanic families lost the opportunity to request his advice and aid, especially during this period of wartime upheaval, relocation, and personal crises. As patrón, A. J. had nurtured long-term personal relationships with his employees and their families. These relationships were executed through mutual respect, loyalty, and continual exchanges of labor, money, and favors. The relationships involved conversations—within a traditional patrón system, the word of the patrón was accepted without much concern for signed contracts. A. J.'s flamboyant, at times arbitrary, behavior was acceptable for a patrón. Yet, as it happened, his special relationship with the employees did not carry over to the Los Alamos Foundation, which assumed control of LARS assets.

In some interviews it was asserted that A. J. had promised key employees that he would pay for their boys' education at a trade school or college. As mentioned, Adolfo's son Rubel was the first Hispanic scholarship student to attend the Los Alamos Ranch School. Richard Womelsduff, the foreman's son, was also admitted in the fall of 1942, the same year as Rubel. (Andrew White, son of George White who ran the dairy, and nephew of Ben White, an early ranch foreman, was the first child of an employee to attend LARS. Ashley Pond III, Ted Church, and Francis Rousseau, the business manager's son, were LARS graduates.) However, Rubel attended for only one semester before the school shut, losing, as he put it years later, "the chance to get a good education."[46]

In 1940, Hitch and A. J. established the Los Alamos Foundation to build an endowment and establish a scholarship fund for boys who could not afford the Los Alamos tuition. After the closing, the Foundation assumed a different role: control of the money the government had paid as compensation for the Ranch School's assets. After retiring the school's bonded debt, an immediate priority was securing pensions for the core administrators. It happened that in 1937 the entire school community had voted against participation in Social Security when it was first introduced by the federal government. A. J. felt that the Ranch School employees had been well compensated in comparison to local wage rates, and therefore, did not consider pensions for key Hispanic employees like Bences and Adolfo, or for Jim Womelsduff. Connell believed that the administrators who had worked for low salaries to keep his high-cost, shoestring operation solvent deserved pensions to compensate them for the higher wages they could have earned elsewhere. Thus the Foundation purchased pensions for A. J., Hitch, Ferm, Fred Rousseau, and, after A. J. died, for his sister May.

Prior to A. J.'s death in February 1944, the trustees clung to the hope of recovering Ranch School land and buildings after the war. But that spring, piecing together what little they knew of the massive construction project underway at Los Alamos, they abandoned that goal. Its assets now increased from the maturing of Connell's life-insurance policies, and given its overall mission to support education, the Foundation then invested in Tom Waring's middle school in Pojoaque and in Ferm Church's short-lived attempt to reopen as the Los Alamos School in Taos. Later, scholarships were provided to the children of Cecil Wirth and Oscar Steege, who had been two of the longest-serving masters; their sons attended Harvard and Yale, respectively. Richard Womelsduff, the first grantee, received one year of support to attend the University of New Mexico before withdrawing to work at Los Alamos Lab, and then Sandia National Laboratories. However much Hispanic employees expected that A. J. would have helped fund college or trade-school educations for their children, this was not a formal written commitment that the board recognized.

Perhaps the cultural lens of the patrón system explains why the Hispanic families did not feel comfortable in approaching the Foundation on their own behalf. Their arrangements were with A. J. The absence of the patrón who nourished the long-term relationships left them in a void. Lawrence Hitchcock, after A. J. died the leading board member, was away in Washington. He, Ferm Church, and the Santa Fe businessmen on the board did much of the Foundation business via correspondence and telephone. Quite likely, they focused on paperwork and were unaware of the importance of A. J.'s discussions with the employees. In any case, board members were not approachable for the Hispanic families, who considered personal visits and discussions as the proper way to handle important personal business. This would explain in part why Foundation funds did not reach the Hispanic employees, people to whom A. J. was as devoted as they were to him.

In the 1960s and early 1970s Daniel T. Kelly, chair of the Los Alamos Foundation's Western Scholarship Committee, initiated scholarships to St. Michael's College (which became the College of Santa Fe). Four of the six students who were awarded Foundation scholarships between 1960 and 1972 were Hispanics, although they had no connection with the families who had worked for the Ranch School. Thus, twenty years after Rubel Montoya left LARS, the Foundation picked up on the commitment to Hispanic students that A. J. had begun in 1942.[47]

Fifty-seven years after the homesteads on the Pajarito Plateau and the Ranch School properties were condemned by the War Department, there is a surprising tenacity of attachment to the community that flourished there between the two world wars. On a Saturday in October 1997, several hundred Hispanics, Native Americans, and Anglos—all of them related to former Ranch School employees, their children, and grandchildren—attended a reunion at Fuller Lodge. This reunion evoked memories of the colorful Los Alamos Ranch School graduation fiestas. Scouts from Troop 22 led off with "Hio, we sing of the mountains" (the old Ranch School song), mariachis played, and eagle dancers from San Juan Pueblo danced. Severo Gonzales helped the Scouts build a *jacal* like those that Bences had built during graduation, and there were candies and prizes for the little kids.

The reunion featured movies of the school and camp, and the Los Alamos Historical Museum, which sponsored the event, mounted a nostalgic exhibit of photos featuring the Hispanic families and others who worked at the ranch. Above all, it was a time for storytelling, with reunion attendees telling of their families' connection to the Ranch School. Gonzaleses, Montoyas, Churches, Wirths, and Hitchcocks were there along with the children and grandchildren of many other staff members. Speaking in Spanish, ninety-two-year-old Marcos Gomez recalled his connections to the Ranch School. Gathering to celebrate and commemorate their years of service and life in Los Alamos, the reunion rekindled old friendships and reconnected people to the vibrant community that had flourished between the world wars on the beautiful Pajarito Plateau.

In the late 1990s, as Los Alamos County, the Department of Energy (DOE), and other government agencies negotiated disposition of land in Los Alamos, many descendants of the homesteaders filed a class-action lawsuit to get land or compensation for the land that their ancestors cultivated for generations in Los Alamos. News accounts of the DOE offering surplus land in Los Alamos County to the Forest Service and San Ildefonso irritated the descendants of those who received minimal compensation from the War Department for their lands and grazing rights. During World War II almost all homesteaders' descendants signed quitclaim deeds and accepted compensation. In many cases, the compensation was reduced because Sandoval County collected unpaid property taxes before dispensing the compensation checks. Delinquent tax payments were a widespread problem in northern New Mexico during the 1930s. Statistics show that during the Depression more than 80 percent of the landowners in the Middle Rio Grande Conservancy District were delinquent in tax or mortgage payments.[48]

Moreover, it is not true that these families willingly gave up their *ranchos* for the defense effort, although they were and are intensely patriotic. Ted Mather's wife sat on the front porch of their homestead with a shotgun, indicating how *they* felt about the taking. Some Hispanic landowners in Los Alamos considered refusing to sign quitclaim deeds because they believed that the government was going to take the land whether or not they signed. They hoped that not signing would give them better legal grounds for reclaiming their land after the war. At the time of the forced sales, many people had expectations that the land would be returned to the homesteaders after the war was over. A. J. himself believed this, at least initially. His expectation is mentioned in correspondence of the Forest Service, which also expected to reclaim its jurisdiction over properties appropriated by the War Department.[49] The land owned by homesteaders and the Los Alamos Ranch School was less than 10 percent of the acreage held by the Forest Service. However, this statistic does not diminish or negate the individual tragedies precipitated by the War Department's acquisition of the Pajarito Plateau for the Manhattan Project.

The War Department taking a family's land for the war effort is understandable. Less acceptable is knowing that the family homestead became part of a golf course or that lavish homes were built on the family land. As a result of the lawsuit, legislation is being prepared to compensate the descendants of the homesteaders who received minimal compensation for their properties.

Attachment to land is a powerful force in traditional cultures that place high values on cultivating fields and caring for livestock. Even Hispanic educators, lawyers, and computer engineers joined the class-action lawsuit in an effort to reclaim this aspect of their identity. Whatever the outcome, recognition of the Hispanic and Indian landscapes that underlie the Los Alamos National Laboratory and city of Los Alamos deserves serious consideration. Recuperating the social history of Hispanic families who established roots at Los Alamos prior to the Second World War is part of that legacy.

Glossary of Spanish Terms

barbacoa. Sheep's head roasted for many hours in a pit lined with hot coals and covered with earth. (Local usage)

biscochitos. Traditional anise-flavored Christmas cookies.

burriñates. Sausage made of sheep intestines stuffed with lamb fat, blood, and meat that is then fried.

compadre. Affinity relationship or fictive kinship bond.

jacal. Outdoor hut with walls of vertical logs and a roof of cut branches.

la gente. The people.

luminarias. Christmas bonfires lit in Hispanic villages and Pueblo Indian villages.

menudo. Tripe stew with pigs' feet and red chile.

padrino. Godfather.

patrón. Boss (**jefe**) who is protective and paternalistic.

patroncito. Boss who owes allegiance to a stronger patrón, who has charge of a smaller set of resources than his patrón, and who benevolently lends his help to those in his community.

Las Posadas. Traditional Christmas folk drama depicting Mary and Joseph's search for shelter on Christmas Eve, which is enacted as a procession from door to door until they find shelter. A party is held for all participants and spectators at the house where Joseph and Mary are welcomed and offered shelter.

posole. Stew made with dried white corn, pork, and chile.

primo. Cousin (or more broadly, relative).

rancho. Homestead.

ricachones. Rich folks.

ristra. Red chile peppers tied together on a long string.

sopaipillas. Dough puffs fried in deep fat and eaten with honey.

tío. Uncle.

It Was a Good Time and Place to Be a Boy

RICHARD E. WOMELSDUFF

For many Americans, the span of years from 1929 (when I was born) through 1942 would not have been described as idyllic, but it was for me. The Los Alamos Ranch School remained relatively untouched by events in the outside world. The ranch was a self-contained community, as all persons who lived there were in some way connected with the school. The ranch staff in later years included two grade-school teachers in our local public school, which was part of the Sandoval County school system. There was a foreman, combination electrician/auto mechanic/plumber, carpenter, gardener, one or two tractor operators for plowing and harvesting wheat and oats to feed the herd of horses, horse wrangler, night watchman, and several general-purpose laborers. From the 1920s until about 1935, when the dairy barn burned down, there was a dairyman to care for and milk the dozen or so milk cows to provide fresh dairy products for the school dining room. Taking into account spouses and children, the population of Los Alamos was around one hundred persons, not including the approximately forty boys attending the Ranch School during the school year.

A. J. Connell has often been described as paternalistic, but never as patronizing. Considering all that a director would have to deal with—from young boys away from home, their over-solicitous mothers, exuberant young instructors, the worries of financing, and finding employees to build and maintain the school plant that he envisioned—a person with another personality would probably have failed where Connell succeeded. He and my Dad, Jim I. Womelsduff, the ranch foreman, seemed to get along well, as I never heard my Dad voice any criticism or complaint of him. Dad had a lot of practical knowledge, ability, and common sense, and was a man who kept his word. Connell appreciated and honored him for that.

As nearly as I can estimate, Dad came to the ranch sometime between 1920 and 1924. He had spent the winter of 1918–1919, the coldest on record, driving an open-cab truck, finding and hauling feed for the flock of sheep the Bond Company had moved to Buckman Crossing, on the Rio Grande below Otowi, from summer pastures in the Valle Grande. As the ranch foreman, Jim was in charge of all the non-school support workers mentioned earlier, including the dairyman Fred Crangle. Jim was soon followed to Los Alamos by his brother, Floyd Womelsduff, who was the combination electrician/auto mechanic/ plumber. Floyd had spent several years maintaining irrigation pumps and other equipment for farmers in southern California and northern Mexico, around Calexico and Mexicali. In 1925 the two brothers brought their mother, Sallie Frances Ingram Womelsduff, to live with them at Los Alamos.

Sallie Womelsduff had just sold the land in the Española Valley that had been deeded to her in 1914 by her absent husband, John. John Aaron Womelsduff had abandoned his family several years earlier and left Sallie to raise her four children, Jim, Floyd, Lucy, and Frank. The two older boys, Jim and Floyd, in their mid-teens, had to drop out of school and find work to support their mother and two younger siblings. In spite of this, or possibly because of it, they both became quite proficient at several trades and were honest men and hard workers wherever they went. At Los Alamos, Sallie lived with her tall slender son, Floyd, in a log home just a short distance from Floyd's shop.

The duties of the foreman were many and varied, and it was definitely a hands-on job. With the assistance of the appropriate helper, he was responsible for the maintenance of the entire physical plant—the buildings, roads, water system, power plant, and power lines. Jim, with their help, had to keep all the ranch equipment in good repair. This included the vehicles; the diesel power plant, which involved a complete disassembly to scrape out the caked-on carbon; the tractors and plowing and harvesting equipment; the fences and corrals. He also built special items that were unique to the ranch, such as the snowplows that were used with the Caterpillar tractors to plow roads open after each snowfall. I remember that sometimes this snowplowing had to be done for several miles out from the ranch proper.

The foreman and his helpers cut trees in the nearby national forest, following an area rotation pattern approved by the Forest Service, for use as firewood at the ranch. They would cart or truck the logs to the ranch, then cut them into several different lengths with a large circular saw, split the pieces into stove or fireplace sizes, then stock the woodsheds around the ranch. In the winter, they cut blocks of ice from the frozen pond, and hauled them to the icehouse where they were packed in sawdust for insulation, to be delivered to users as needed throughout the year. Come spring, the foreman and his helpers plowed the fields and planted seeds for the hay crops. Then, in the late summer or early fall, they harvested the hay and loaded it into one of the open-sided barns for storage and use over the next year. My father checked the paper chart in the night watchman's time punch clock each day, and I used to watch him wind the clock and install a new chart paper for the next night. And on and on. It was not a cushy desk job.

Pedro Gonzales was the carpenter and a good cabinetmaker. I often watched him as he worked in his carpenter shop, which was located just south of the house where the dairyman Frederick Crangle, my grandfather, had lived. There is a magic about the smell of fresh-cut wood, and the curls of the wood shavings as the craftsman planes the piece to fit his project. Pedro's youngest son, José, was my age, and after we left Los Alamos our paths occasionally crossed in Albuquerque in later years. The next oldest son was Alejandro, who for many years worked in or owned a dental lab in Santa Fe. Pedro had a daughter Josie and an eldest son named Fermin, who later was in the infamous Bataan death march. When we left Los Alamos in 1943, Pedro moved to a home on Artist Road in Santa Fe, where we would visit him and his wife.

Patricio Gonzales was one of the tractor operators, and I remember that he and Dad and I went on a fishing trip to the Lagunitas lakes in northern New Mexico one time. He had two daughters, the youngest of whom, Isabel, was in my class. In 1943, they also moved to Santa Fe and lived just a few blocks from our house on Pueblo Drive.

The Gonzales family best known to Los Alamos old-timers is that of Bences Gonzales, who was the shopkeeper of the Trading Post. Bences clerked, stocked, cleaned, pumped gas by hand, and just did everything that needed to be done there. He also served as the unofficial postmaster under Fred Rousseau. Two of his children were Severo and Ray. All the school's boys knew Bences through their dealings with him at the Trading Post, but he is probably best remembered as the outdoor chef who accompanied them on their long summer pack-trips through the northern parts of the Jemez Mountains, through the valles to the San Pedro Peaks and the Chihuahueños. Bences stayed on at Los Alamos after the army took over, and lived there for many years.

My Dad assisted the summer camp by driving the school truck to meet the pack-train at prearranged relay points with fresh supplies and mail. I never got to go along on one of these trips with him, but I do have a picture of him standing beside the ranch truck with the fresh supplies laid out in order on the ground, waiting to be placed on the packhorses.

The best known of the several Montoya families who lived at Los Alamos was Adolfo Montoya. He was an extraordinary gardener, whose vegetables and flowers are remembered by all who ate at the school dining room or enjoyed the flower arrangements that came out of his gardens. I especially liked the plot of dahlias that he planted by the north end of our new stone grade-school building; they were huge and absolutely gorgeous. The only one of his children I remember was Rubel, who was about my age, although there were several others. Rubel was an expert marble shooter who cleaned me out of all my marbles when I was rash enough to play him for keeps. Rubel Montoya and I were students together at the Ranch School in the fall 1942 term. Two other Montoya families were Henry and Candelaria Montoya, and I believe that they moved back to the Española Valley after leaving Los Alamos. I met one or more of their sons in Española in later years, when my Uncle Floyd was living there.

The combination electrician/auto mechanic/plumber was Floyd Womelsduff. Floyd also ran the diesel electric plant to charge the bank of batteries that supplied the entire ranch with 110 volts of D.C. electric power for lights, radios, washing machines, and so forth. Floyd was single at that time, and he and his mother, my grandmother Sallie, lived in one of the larger log homes allotted to employees of the school. It was located about fifty yards northwest of Fuller Lodge. Jim Womelsduff, my father, lived in another log home a few hundred yards away.

Until the 1930s, when stone began to be used, the buildings on the ranch were made of logs cut in the nearby national forest. Our house was one of the few employees' homes made with the logs placed vertically, although several of the school buildings, such as Fuller Lodge and the Big House, were constructed in that fashion. The other homes were constructed with the logs placed horizontally. Joints between the logs were sealed with concrete mortar, and the inside of the walls could be paneled with various materials. Coal was used in the cook range in the school kitchen, but yellow pine was normally used for cooking by everyone. Both pine and piñon were burned in fireplaces and in furnaces or ranges for producing hot water for space heating by radiators. The aroma of burning piñon in the still winter air still lingers in my memory.

The dairyman for the Los Alamos Ranch School was Mr. Frederick Nelson Crangle, whose wife was Nettie Alice Cavett Crangle. They came to Los Alamos from Sedalia, Colorado, about 1923 or 1924, having moved to Denver, Colorado, very early in 1920 from Nebraska. To them were born four children: Paul, Beulah, Bessie, and Abbie Elizabeth Crangle. The last named was born on March 10, 1904, in Blue Springs, Nebraska, and was to become my mother.

Fig. 8.1

Jim Womelsduff family cottage, 1942.
Courtesy Los Alamos Historical Museum Archives.

Sometime in late 1928 or early 1929, Fred Crangle broke his leg, which, understandably, made it very difficult to feed and milk over a dozen cows. His recently married son, Paul, was living on a farm between Sedalia and Castle Rock, Colorado. Paul moved his wife Bonnye, and her two young daughters from a previous marriage, Otoka and Laverne, to Los Alamos to help his father with the dairy chores until his leg healed enough to take full charge again. Paul Crangle and his family remained at Los Alamos until late 1933. As nearly as I can figure, about the time that Fred and Nettie came to Los Alamos, their pretty young daughter, Abbie, started college at Colorado Agricultural College in Fort Collins, having graduated from high school in 1922. She probably spent school vacations with her parents at Los Alamos. It must have been during these school vacations at Los Alamos that Abbie Crangle met Jim Womelsduff. After graduation from college on June 2, 1927, Abbie served a four-month internship as a dietitian in a Denver hospital, and soon afterward she took a job in a Flagstaff hospital. After her marriage to Jim, Abbie became the dietitian for the Ranch School.

Jim and Abbie, of Otowi, New Mexico, were married on October 2, 1928, at Flagstaff, Arizona. Abbie was twenty-four years old and Jim was thirty-four. They spent their honeymoon at the Grand Canyon before returning to Los Alamos to begin their short life together. I was born on June 14, 1929, and my sister, Janet Loraine, was born on April 2, 1934. After six years of married life, my mother died on November 6, 1934, at age thirty, of an infection following a thyroid operation. She was buried at Fairview Cemetery, in Santa Fe.

The two modern pueblos closest to Los Alamos are Santa Clara, south of Española, and San Ildefonso, south of Black Mesa and near the Otowi Crossing on the Rio Grande, where Miss Edith Warner had her home and tearoom. It was from these two pueblos that Indian boys were recruited and trained to serve tables in the dining room of the Lodge. Some also worked as houseboys for the school staff families. A few Indian girls may also have worked at the school. On special occasions Indians would put on one or more of their ceremonial dances in the dining room of the Lodge, usually a dance connected with the harvest or for success on the hunt. During school graduation exercises, several of the Indian women from these two pueblos who were potters would spread their blankets under the trees on the lawn between the Lodge and the Trading Post to display their finest pottery. I have several pieces from this time, including an early one by Maria Martinez of San Ildefonso Pueblo, when she signed her pottery as Marie.

There were Indian ruins on Los Alamos mesa as well as most places on the Pajarito Plateau. A small ruin mound of about five hundred square feet was located just a few yards to the west of the Big House. It showed a dozen or so small rooms and was worked on from time to time by a science class of schoolboys. The quite extensive Otowi ruins in lower Pueblo Canyon were sometimes worked on by the boys with more enthusiasm than archeological expertise. I found the remains of a single rectangular room just south of our front yard, as the land sloped toward the west end of Ashley Pond, but found no shards of pottery or discarded arrowheads, nor any indication of there being additional rooms attached. I seem to remember another small site toward the southeastern part of Los Alamos mesa, which one of my friends and I found as we were looking for likely places to set traps for the coyote and fox that inhabited the mesa. These ruins were so prevalent all over the area that they were accepted as a normal part of our environment, with little thought given to the people who had once lived and died there.

One of the main physical features of Los Alamos was a pond slightly south of the center of town. At first nothing more than a mud puddle after a rain, the pond was gradually improved so that it became deep enough for a raft with a slide and a diving board. This was placed in the pond during warmer weather and pulled up on shore during the winter. There were four canvas and wood canoes in a shelter rack near the water, used mostly by school personnel. Small-mouth bass and perch, which we called sun fish, were planted in what was called originally the Duck Pond, but which, inevitably, came to be known as Ashley Pond, a punning tribute to the founder of the school.

Before long cattails became established on the south and west sides of the pond, and soon blue dragonflies flitted among them and hovered over the surface of the water. I had a simple fishing pole and line with a bare hook, to which I affixed bright yellow dandelion blooms, and caught perch like crazy! On one occasion Perry Merrill, the school secretary, took me out in a canoe with him to fish for bass. He fixed me a length of clear leader, with several lures attached, ending with a small spinner. As we paddled along I tossed it overboard, only to discover to my horror that it had not been attached to the line on my pole! Needless to say, it sank out of sight and we never did find it. I guess Perry didn't hold it against me, because I did odd jobs for him and his wife Zoe after we all moved to Santa Fe. Perry was in the navy then, stationed at the recruiting office in Santa Fe. They lived four or five blocks from us, almost on my route to Santa Fe High School, so it was convenient to stop by before or after school to feed and water his rabbits.

Several times I made small wooden boats and equipped them with a sail and a rudder cut from a tin can, then set them into the water on the west or up-wind side of the pond and watched them sail away. My boats usually ended up in a patch of cattails, and I had to wade out to retrieve them, in water sometimes above my waist. For many years a small flock of mallard ducks would spend the spring and summer on the pond at Los Alamos. The hens made their nests in the deep grasses around and under the willows between the pond and our house. It was interesting to watch the ducklings hatch and grow big enough to waddle along behind their mothers as they made their way to the pond and safety in the water.

Our home was a short distance northwest of Ashley Pond and the overflow pipe carrying the surplus water diverted from the ranch water lines ran under a dirt road just a few yards to the north and east of our house. The pipe ended almost as a spring coming from underneath the road. The stream flowed past some pussy willows and poplar trees along the eastern side of our front lawn, then turned and meandered southeast through a thicket of willows, until it reached the pond. One of my favorite Los Alamos photographs is a view from near the pond in the winter, showing the little stream and the willows almost buried in snow, with our house in the background.

This stream got me in trouble one day when I was five years old. The small one-room public grade school, for children of the employees of the ranch, was located about twenty-five yards behind and to the side of our house. Most of the dozen or so kids who attended the school at that time had to walk down the dirt road mentioned above to get to the schoolhouse. The teacher, up until

I started school at age six, was my uncle, Frank Womelsduff, who had been crippled by polio when a young boy and had to use crutches the rest of his life. One nice warm sunny school day, the year before I started school, as I was playing in the front yard, that little stream of water talked me into splashing water on several of the kids as they were passing by on their way to school. Uncle Frank, not one to stand for nonsense, gave me a good paddling, and if my dad had found out, he would have repeated the punishment.

Then there was the pile of logs that got me in trouble. Across the pond from our house was a two-story log icehouse. During the winters, if the ice on the pond got to be over a foot thick, the men would cut it into large blocks, and store it in the icehouse, well packed with sawdust for insulation, ready to be used in our iceboxes during the next year or two. Just to the west of the icehouse there was a pile of logs, each around 6" x 8" diameter and about 8' x 10' long. They must have been left over from some building project. Mother warned me not to climb on this log pile. As luck would have it, I soon found myself in the vicinity of the forbidden fruit, and, just as the serpent tempted Eve by saying that surely God would not punish her, that old Devil in the log pile whispered in my ear and convinced me that surely my Mom would not punish me. After all, I couldn't see her, so she obviously couldn't see me, right? Wrong! When I got home after clambering all over that inviting pile of logs, guess what? Mom had seen me, and I got another paddling. Moms seem to see and know more than their kids realize.

One other memorable event that occurred about this time was when the dairy barn burned down. I awoke during the night to the wildest noise I had ever heard. It was the sound of a siren wailing. I had never heard a siren before and it took a while to finally realize what it was. The night watchman had spotted the blaze and set off the alarm. Dad threw some clothes on and rushed out of the house, and then we could see the flames from the burning barn. The light from the fire was reflected on the pond between the barnyard and our house. It seemed like only a few minutes had passed, and all that was left standing was the stone and cement silo. It happened that none of the cattle were killed, but Mr. Connell decided to sell off the herd and obtain dairy products in Santa Fe, thirty-five miles away. These dairies were by now a more sure, safe, and economical source of dairy products than they had been in earlier years. This situation, of course, also meant that there was no longer any need for a dairyman at Los Alamos, and so my grandfather Fred was out of a job at age sixty-one. He and Grandma Crangle soon left Los Alamos and moved to Fort Collins, Colorado, where we visited them each summer. I still recall grandmother's cool basement, where she worked on her oil paintings.

The most significant event in my young life was the death of my mother in 1934, seven months after the birth of my sister, Janet, and five months after my fifth birthday. Strangely, I have no memories of mother's death, or even of her as a person before she died. All the mental images that I have of her are actually from the pictures of her that I have. Perhaps it is, or was, a defensive mechanism, or maybe four- and five-year-old children just do not retain many memories, unless they are particularly outstanding or traumatic. The first five years of my life at Los Alamos were uneventful, and there are only vague memories of a few things that happened.

After Mother died, Uncle Frank and Aunt Ida, who were both handicapped, helped Dad care for Janet and me for several months. Then Dad's sister, my Aunt Lucy, returned from San Diego, California, after her marriage ended. Since she had no home now, she and Dad worked out an arrangement whereby she would help raise us two kids, in exchange for a home and support for the rest of her life. After Mom died, Dad withdrew into a shell of silence and privacy, and the only time he did much talking was when he and other adult friends or family members swapped stories about days gone by. Janet and I grew up without knowing what it was like to have a normal loving family life. I have always been grateful that Grandma Sallie and Uncle Floyd lived nearby; they were an important part of my youth and an example of the important part that caring relatives can play in raising children. Aunt Lucy earned spending money of her own by sewing the silk scarves worn by the school's boys, as well as doing other sewing and mending as needed by the school.

During the summer of 1935, before I started first grade, the Ranch School hired a business manager named Fred Rousseau. This effected a drastic change in the grade school, since Mrs. Rousseau was an elementary schoolteacher, and part of the agreement between the Ranch School and the Rousseaus was that Mrs. Rousseau would be the public grade-school teacher. This, obviously, meant that my Uncle Frank was now out of a job, and so he and Aunt Ida soon moved from Los Alamos. He found a teaching position for a few years in a small Spanish-American community near the Cochití Indian Pueblo and later taught school for several years at Ponderosa, a timber-company sawmill camp in the southwestern part of the Jemez Mountains. I was there visiting Uncle Frank and Aunt Ida the day that the sawmill burned down, and shortly afterward the company shut down and moved out. Uncle Frank then moved to Corrales, just north of Albuquerque, where he soon had an orchard of apple and peach trees, along with a small vegetable garden. Frank taught at the grade school in Corrales until he retired, then moved to Gallup and built a house so that Ida would be close to family who lived there.

During this same summer of 1935, the old grade-school building was converted into a small residence for the horse wrangler, Ted Mather, and his wife.

Ted was a typical old-style western horse wrangler, on the short side, bow legs, a big hat, a big black moustache, and a big six-gun that he let me borrow for a school play, without the bullets. He took care of the horses, kept them fed and shod, and mended bridles and other leather items. Ted was also a mainstay on the summer pack-trips, where he led the pack train with the heavy camping gear, and generally took care of the horses in areas beyond the schoolboys' responsibilities or capabilities. Closer to home, he set up two metal stakes behind our garage and woodshed and taught me how to pitch horseshoes. He was gruff appearing, but was really a nice guy and always had time to talk to a kid.

While a new stone schoolhouse was being built west of the pond, about one hundred yards from our house, my first grade was temporarily held in a log building that had been used as a clubhouse for the employees. The new schoolhouse, when completed, was one large rectangular room, with a pleated divider that could be pulled across the room to divide it into two rooms. It even had a basement with a wood-fired furnace for heat in the winter. Mrs. Rousseau was soon joined by Amador Gonzales. Now we had a new schoolhouse with two rooms, two teachers, and central heating. Amador also took care of the furnace, helped by the upper-grade boys. We had all eight grades, and around twenty students, give or take a few from year to year. As my second-grade year came to a close, it became apparent that I would be the only student in the third grade when school resumed that fall. It was arranged that Aunt Lucy would oversee my daily studies of the third-grade materials during the summer months, and thus I skipped from second into fourth grade. In retrospect, I am not so sure that it was a good idea, from the standpoint of my social and educational development, but I understand the compelling reason for it at that time.

Most of the boys and girls who attended the grade school were children of the Hispanic employees living on the ranch. Occasionally another Anglo family with children would live and work at Los Alamos for a short time. The only other long-term resident Anglo family with school-age children were the Churches, who had three sons: Ted, four years older than me; Allen, one year older; and Hugh, who was two years younger. It happened that Allen Church and I were the only Anglo kids who were together throughout our grade-school years. I got along well with the Hispanic kids and actually spent more time with them than with the Churches. I still consider the ones that I knew best as good friends. One regret that I have about those years is that I did not take advantage of an excellent opportunity to learn to speak Spanish from my playmates. In a strange twist of fate, all three Church brothers and I ended up working in technical or scientific fields at the Sandia National Laboratories in Albuquerque, and I even worked for Ted for a while.

In addition to our regular lessons, I remember Mrs. Rousseau working with us in all sorts of crafts, including making our own glue. We glued cut-up pieces of Christmas wrapping paper onto glass jars and gave them a coat of shellac to make pretty flower vases to give to our mothers. We had music classes and learned to play the sticks and rattles and tambourines. We also put on several plays. One that I remember doing was Charles Dickens's *A Christmas Carol;* I was Tiny Tim. If the winter weather was too bad to go outside, we would have exercises and indoor games, such as pin the tail on the donkey. Someone provided a hobby-type scroll or jigsaw, and Amador taught us how to cut out pieces of wood to make birdhouses and other things. We also learned to use a woodburning pencil or iron, and burned designs into the woodcraft items we made.

During recess time we played outside, making snow forts in the winter, and having ferocious snowball battles. We also had to do our share in keeping the school grounds neat and trash free, and probably some inside housekeeping as

Fig. 8.2

Ranch children and their craft projects, ca. 1936–1937, at the WPA Sandoval County elementary school at the Ranch. From left, Donicio Montoya, Frank Mullins, Lucas Montoya, Rubel Montoya, Allen Church, Richard Womelsduff, Benny Montoya, Severo Gonzales, Margaret Montoya, Nila White, Ted Church, Alejandro Garza. Courtesy Los Alamos Historical Museum Archives.

well. I loved to read, and after I devoured all the books in the small school library Mrs. Rousseau would let me borrow books from her personal collection. Among others, she had sets of *Tom Swift, The Hardy Boys,* the Nancy Drew mystery series, and several of Cooper's *Leatherstocking Tales.* School seemed easy, but unfortunately, I did not learn good study habits, to my future detriment.

My grade-school years at Los Alamos were the idyllic period of my life. The economic situation for all the families at Los Alamos during those years was relatively stable, in spite of the stock-market crash of 1929 and the Great Depression that followed. Everyone at Los Alamos depended on the Ranch School financially, and the school income was derived from the tuition charges paid by the families of the students. For the 1929–1930 school year, the tuition per boy was $2,400, or double my father's annual salary! Even so, LARS did operate at or near its maximum capacity until 1942. If our "outside" relatives were having financial problems, I was never aware of it. We never lacked for food or clothing or our summer trip to visit Grandma Crangle and our Curtis cousins in Colorado.

Along with starting school, I was gradually allowed more freedom to be away from our house by myself. Actually, within the confines of the community, a youngster was almost always in sight of an adult or two, though they themselves might not be in sight. We would shoot marbles, or fly kites or our balsa gliders, or play games like hide-and-seek or kick-the-can, or even help each other with chores or homework. As the years went by, my pals and I would roam farther and farther from sight of our homes, gradually exploring the world in which we lived. As we grew older, Allen Church and I were sometimes allowed to join the Ranch School boys at the rifle range located past the Churches' home and near the edge of Pueblo Canyon. There I had my first lessons in gun safety and learned some basic .22 caliber target shooting, and I loved it. Los Alamos was really a wonderful place for a boy to grow up in the 1930s. We faced none of the problems that beset children on all sides today. Living in an isolated community, there were none of the outside influences that today's children face. When we got into trouble, it was of our own making and was never too serious, unless you would call being sprayed by a skunk serious. . . .

There were many trails crisscrossing the mesas and canyons of the Pajarito Plateau that were suitable for hiking or horseback riding. One trail, starting just west of the Churches' house, went down into Pueblo Canyon to the north of Los Alamos mesa and on to the lower end of Guaje Canyon. Further west, near the upper field, another trail wove its way north along the foothills to the upper end of Guaje Canyon and on northward toward Santa Clara Canyon. Again from the area of the upper field, a trail dipped down into Los Alamos Canyon before climbing upward to Camp May and on over the rim of the mountain overlooking the Valle Grande. A longer trail from upper Los Alamos mesa led south past Anchor Ranch and Water Canyon and down into Frijoles Canyon. It crossed the Rito de los Frijoles several miles upstream from the main ruins at the Bandelier National Monument headquarters, at a place called the Upper Crossing of the Frijoles. From there the trail connected with a whole network of trails leading over mesas and canyons to the south, between Frijoles and Cochiti.

Two trails took off from the eastern end of our Los Alamos mesa, one going north down into Pueblo Canyon to Camp Hamilton and the Otowi ruins. The second went down the south side of the mesa, switching back and forth almost in parallel with the auto road switchbacks climbing up the north side of the ridge to the top of the mesa. This trail led to several ruins between Los Alamos Canyon and the Tsankawi ruins, and included many good stopping places for cooking a noon meal. There was always a sandy arroyo bottom, with enough dry tinder and small dead wood to make a fire. Then a good bed of glowing coals was used to heat a pot of coffee and warm a pan of stew or soup.

Our mesa was about a half-mile wide and several miles long, from where it was rooted in the flank of the mountain to where it abruptly ended at its eastern reach. For the most part it was fairly flat, but sloped gently downward toward the west clearing, with a soil covering of decomposed volcanic ash, pumice, and vegetation. The soil was of good enough quality to raise crops of oats, wheat, and rye for horse feed, as well as the healthful vegetables and beautiful flowers grown by Adolfo Montoya, the school gardener, and other residents. Ponderosa pine trees, many of them over one hundred years of age, covered the mesa, intermixed with almost equal numbers of piñon and juniper, while patches of scrub oak and prickly pear cactus grew in the more open areas. Wild grasses and flowers grew profusely, especially Indian Paintbrush and little daisy-like flowers. Other species of trees introduced for landscaping also did very well; Lombardy poplar, birch, elm, cherry, apricot, and weeping willow are ones I remember. Many flowers also did well—roses, dahlias, hollyhocks, pansies, carnations, and sweet pea, to name just a few. Mountain-grown strawberries and raspberries had an unbeatable flavor. Mule deer, black bear, turkeys, foxes, coyotes, and yes, skunks inhabited the woodlands. The cheerful songs of robins heralded the return of spring. Red-tail hawks, and an eagle now and then, glided gracefully against azure skies. An occasional mountain lion scream could be heard coming from the upper slopes of the mountains to the west.

I can still picture the tall poplars bending with the gentle summer breezes, as several of us played on the lawn between the Trading Post and the Big House. We had balsa-wood gliders, with wings that folded back against the fuselage, and a notch under the nose by which a stout rubber band attached to a stick was used to launch the plane straight up into the clear blue New Mexico sky. When the glider reached its apex, the wings would snap back into normal flight position, and it would lazily glide round and round, carried by the breeze until it returned to earth, hopefully somewhere nearby. Occasionally one would land way up in one of the tall Lombardy poplars, and the owner would have to wait for the winds to shake it loose.

Three fields at the ranch provided hay to feed the school's herd of fifty or so horses. The upper field, which was a large clearing of good soil, was located at the west end of the mesa, at the foot of the mountain slope, one mile from the community. One of the hay barns was constructed near there. The other two fields lay past the eastern boundary of the school, with the smaller one being on the south side of the state road that came directly into the center of town. A second barn was built just south of this field and was used to store hay. The other field also began at the eastern boundary, but on the north side of the road, and extended for almost a mile until that portion of the mesa abruptly ended in a four-hundred-foot cliff. The eastern half (approximately) of this field became the airfield for Los Alamos after the army took over the mesa in 1943. Six years later, as an employee of the Sandia Laboratories, I experienced the first of many flights in and out of this tiny, high-altitude airfield.

We often flew our homemade kites in these latter two fields. Because the prevailing winds were usually out of the west, we could launch the kites from the border of the field just past the residential area. While the hay was growing we had to stay on the edge of the field, but after it was harvested we could venture as far out in the field as we wished, not that it helped the kites fly any better! While the hay was growing, and before it was harvested in early fall, deer would be attracted to the fields in the evenings to browse on the succulent young shoots and ripe heads. It was probably more tasty and nourishing than whatever they found back in their natural habitat.

Three times each week either my Dad or Uncle Floyd, or occasionally one of the other employees, would drive the school truck down the hill to the train stop at Otowi Crossing to pick up the mail and any freight that was dropped off for the school. It was quite a sight to see the little narrow gauge train come up the east side of the river, belching steam and great clouds of black coal smoke, then turn to cross over the river next to Miss Edith Warner's home and tearoom. A. J. Connell had hired Miss Warner to be the school's freight agent, a position that she took quite seriously, and which thus gave us an opportunity to get acquainted with her as we waited for a late train arrival. That old train, called simply the Chili Line by all residents of northern New Mexico, was the beginning of my lifelong love of the old coal-burning locomotives and trains, regardless of what gauge they were.

Interestingly enough, there were two tearooms in our small remote part of the world. Miss Edith Warner made a meager living beside the Rio Grande and the railroad, offering tourists and other passersby lunch and a slice of her famous chocolate cake. Mrs. Evelyn Frey became the manager of a private guest lodge in Frijoles Canyon. Later, after the CCC built the new stone buildings of the Bandelier National Monument, she became the manager for the new Frijoles Canyon Lodge. She lived there for many years, managing her gift shop and the tearoom. My Aunt Lucy would occasionally drive us over to visit with Mrs. Frey at Bandelier or with Mrs. Smithwick at Anchor Ranch, on a mesa south of Los Alamos.

Since either my Dad or Uncle Floyd had to be at the ranch every evening to start and watch over the diesel electric generating plant, only one of them at a time could go down the hill to Española or Santa Fe to buy groceries or get a haircut. One Friday evening, as Floyd was starting out for Santa Fe, a deer headed for the oat field bounded out of the woods right in front of his car. Although he was only going about twenty-five to thirty miles an hour on the dirt road, when the car hit the deer it smashed the grill and radiator back into the front of the engine. It really made a mess of his almost new Plymouth coupe, and he had to borrow Dad's car to make his trip into town. He said that the deer got up and ran back into the woods![1]

During legal hunting season in the fall, Dad would saddle a horse and head for the high country west of town. He always came back with a good-sized buck and we feasted on fresh venison for several weeks. Occasionally, Dad would have a hide tanned, and would make things like watch fobs, boot laces, pouches, and so on—no dandy fringed buckskin jackets, just practical, useful items.

An adequate and dependable supply of potable water had been a problem from the very beginning of the Ranch School. The simple diversion of stream water about two miles up Los Alamos Canyon from the ranch, into a pipe, which carried it to the ranch, was very undependable, especially in dry years. Around the time that I was nine or ten years old, construction was started on a dam farther up the canyon. A spillway carried water over the top of the dam when it became too full. This happened the very first year, almost before it was even finished, after a very wet winter and early spring. The resulting flooding washed small trees, rocks, and debris onto the road below the dam, and even washed out some sections of the road. I have seen pictures of some of the Ranch School staff and students helping clear the road and repair the damage.

During the summer that the dam was under construction, a mother black bear and her two cubs volunteered their services as "dam site supervisors," and they hung around most of the summer. They didn't much bother the workmen, but the men did keep a sharper than normal lookout just the same. The completion of this dam provided for a reliable supply of all the water needed by the Ranch School, with enough of a surplus left over to keep Ashley Pond filled to a respectable depth.

Normal winters at Los Alamos were usually mild, with snow depths from a few inches to a foot or so, and low temperatures in the twenties. Most days would be clear and sunny. If the winter was mild, the ice did not get thick enough to cut and store. On occasion a winter could be severe, with snow several feet deep, and temperatures down around zero. When it snowed, Dad and Patricio fixed the homemade snowplows to the tractors, and plowed the roads open. One of the other men hitched a workhorse to a smaller drag plow and cleared snow from the walkways and paths throughout the community. When the first significant amount of snow fell, we kids would vie for honors in making the best snow angels. I don't remember ever having to miss school because of the snow, no matter how deep it got. Once, when I was small, I got stuck in deep snow that had been thrown back from the road by the plow and had to holler for help. The snow was so deep that Aunt Lucy could hear me, but couldn't find me for a while.

Cutting blocks of ice from frozen Ashley Pond for use in our iceboxes was not the only use for the pond. When the ice was thick enough, ice-skating was in order. The Ranch School boys formed teams for ice hockey, and sometimes, if they were shorthanded, one of us was invited to join them. When concentrating or working hard, I often unconsciously stuck my tongue out a bit. This habit resulted in me biting my tongue rather severely one day when I accidentally got hit under my chin by a hockey stick. The bleeding eventually stopped, but I had to retire from my brief stint as a hockey player. Anyway, I had weak ankles, and even with high-top skates laced up tight I could not keep my ankles straight enough to skate properly, and hence was never a very good skater, but I still had fun. For the most part we just skated around, playing tag or crack-the-whip, and enjoying the outing.

During the schoolboys' absence over the Christmas holidays, we had Ashley Pond all to ourselves. On one or more evenings, the workmen would arrange six to eight large hollow stacks of firewood around the perimeter of the pond. As soon as it became dark, the firewood would be lighted, and cooks from the school kitchen would bring pans of cookies and large kettles of hot chocolate down to tables near the ice. We would skate to the light from the bonfires until we were cold enough to stop for a mug of delicious hot chocolate and a cookie, and we just had a most enjoyable time. During these years Douglas Pond was built down in Los Alamos Canyon, about a mile and a half west of town. Located in the well-shaded canyon bottom, it was cold enough, and for a long enough time, that block-ice production was assured each winter. Ice-skating was also enjoyed for a longer period of time down there where the ice was thicker and the surface stayed frozen instead of partially melting in the bright sun.

Thanksgiving and Christmas at Los Alamos were really special times for me. Grandma Sallie was a very good cook able to make a feast out of meager supplies. Looking back on those years, I know that we did not have a lot of expensive gifts at Christmas or exotic foods at these two holidays, but one thing that we did have was family. Since Grandma Sallie's home had the most space, we would all gather there. There would be a turkey, obtained from a grower down in the Española Valley, stuffed with Grandma's special homemade dressing and roasted all morning in the oven of her wood-burning stove. Boy, did it smell good while it was cooking! It tasted even better when we sat down to dinner. There were all the usual trimmings, ending up with homemade pumpkin pie. In addition to Grandma Sallie and Uncle Floyd, there would be our family— Dad, Aunt Lucy, Janet, and myself. Uncle Frank and Aunt Ida would come from wherever they were living that year. Grandma Sallie's Christmas cactus would be in full bloom, the living-room floor was covered with Navajo rugs, and Uncle Floyd would have a fire going in the big fireplace in the living room. Although it might be snowing outside, inside it was warm, not only from the fire, but also from having all the family gathered together. I enjoyed listening to them telling stories of the "do you remember when" days.

I also remember the Christmas party for the Ranch School employees and their children. It was held in the dining room of Fuller Lodge and Santa Claus distributed Christmas gifts to the children. One year I decided that Santa was actually Fermor Church. We all had a good time, and in later years I came to appreciate the kindness and thoughtfulness of Mr. Connell and the school staff.

Once the snow had melted and warming breezes dried the soggy soil, we were able to resume our explorations where we had left off the previous fall. Actually, Saturdays were the only full days we had until school was out for the summer. We had homework or chores to take care of at home, but once they were done, our time was pretty much our own. It was interesting to see that as time went by we youngsters gravitated into two groups, the ones who stayed closer to home versus the ones who were more adventurous and roamed farther afield. Allen Church and I, and occasionally one or two others, were in the latter group.

As we got braver and gained enough self-confidence, we gradually found and explored most of the trails, previously described, that led down off the mesa into the canyons on either side. In later years, we biked down the road from the upper end of the mesa down into Los Alamos Canyon. We would make a complete loop, descending into the canyon, then all the way down the canyon on a seldom-used dirt road, until it joined the main state road from Los Alamos to Española or Santa Fe off the east end of the mesa, and then back up the hill to home. The loop distance was probably about five to six miles, which isn't very far, except that it was a pretty steep climb up the switchbacks to where the road leveled out on the mesa top. Even with the three-speed gearshifts we had then, the bikes got pushed up most of this section of the road.

Another part of our explorations that I really enjoyed, but which if I caught my own kids doing would upset me, was climbing down and up the canyon walls where there were no trails. As I look back on it, I realize that it was probably a lot more dangerous than we thought at the time, but no one was ever hurt, even though we sometimes got into a tough spot. There is a saying that "the Lord watches over children and fools," so maybe we had a double dose of watch-care.

Starting as a student at the Los Alamos Ranch School in September 1942, I had my first exposure to Scouting. There must have been a specific day and time set aside for Scout meetings. I remember meeting with a group of boys in the main room of the Big House and memorizing the Scout oath and promises and beginning to work on rank requirements.

The one requirement for advancing in rank to Second Class Scout that I remember was the cooking test. The candidate had to prepare, cook, and eat a meal meeting certain criteria. An independent adult must observe the procedure and taste-test the finished meal. Mrs. Rousseau agreed to be my observer, so I prepared a spot across the road from her backdoor, in front of the long open-front woodshed. My preparation, technique, and the resultant meal must have met with her approval because I did advance to Second Class Scout.

For the most part, however, those of us who were children of the Ranch School employees generally did not associate or socialize with the school's boys or the school staff, except for the few instances I have already mentioned. One social occasion that I remember was an invitation for dinner extended to Dad and me by one of the masters, Mr. Cecil Wirth, and his wife, Virginia. The Wirths lived in a stone apartment built as a west wing onto the Spruce Cottage, the residence for the older, more mature boys. The apartment faced the stone building housing the diesel-generating plant, and was just across the road from the house where my Uncle Floyd and Grandmother Sallie Womelsduff lived. Dad would spend an occasional evening out playing poker with some of the ranchmen. It was my impression at the time that one or two of the masters, and probably several non-staff employees, were included.[2]

Because of my friendship with the two younger Church boys, Mrs. Peggy Church invited me along on several of their outings. Once we went to Santa Fe for lunch with a family member, a brother I believe, and then attended [Gus and Jane Baumann's] puppet show for children. We also went wading, or swimming, at a sandy beach on the Rio Grande just upstream from Miss Warner's house. On another occasion, we went on a picnic where the small stream running down Pajarito Canyon plunges over the basalt cliffs into White Rock Canyon.

During the time between my sixth birthday and the time we all left Los Alamos, I can remember only one of the Ranch School boys who took the initiative and showed the interest to get acquainted with any of the employees other than the few in direct contact with the school, such as at the Trading Post. There may have been others, but the person I am referring to was Ben Raskob, 1942. My Uncle Floyd's shop was just a little ways west of the Spruce Cottage, and Raskob often walked over to the shop to visit with Floyd. I don't remember ever being there when Ben was visiting with Floyd, but Floyd would often mention his visits, and I know that he enjoyed Ben's company and friendship.

After the new stone schoolhouse was constructed, several more stone structures were built, including a replacement for the log icehouse with a new one made out of native stone, the harder grade of volcanic tuff. My Dad and his workmen built some of these buildings from plans drawn by John Gaw Meem, the architect of Fuller Lodge. These included the Arts and Crafts Building, which was designed in a combination of native stone and logs. A stone apartment was added on to the Spruce Cottage for the Wirths. After the old one-cylinder diesel engine and generator had severely burned a back room of my Uncle Floyd's shop, a new stone building for the power plant was constructed. It was large enough to house the old diesel electric unit plus a brand new Fairbanks-Morse four-cylinder diesel engine and generator, and it included room for the large bank of wet-cell batteries, of the type then in use by telephone exchanges. This provided Los Alamos with 110-volt direct current power for all lights and appliances.

Because of the limited electric power available, we did not have porch lights or streetlights, except for possibly two or three around some of the school areas. Our night-light was the moon, our porch lights were the myriad stars overhead. We could see the lights of Santa Fe in the distance, nestled in the foothills of the Sangre de Cristo mountain range. When night fell, most activity moved indoors, or ceased for the day. With no local light pollution at night, one could actually locate the constellations of stars shown in the *Boy Scout Handbook* and in astronomy books.

An indirect benefit of this same limited electric power was a peace and quiet that I suspect many of us envy in today's noisy environment. An occasional vehicle engine, a few children at play, a tractor plowing the fields in spring or snow from the roads in winter, robins singing in springtime, the pealing of the bell on top of the Lodge three times each day—these were the sounds and songs that I grew up with.

The telephone serving Los Alamos Ranch was only a single-wire party line, but a dozen or so phones at Los Alamos were on it, each using a unique code of short or long rings, or a combination of them. The rings were generated by cranking on the hand crank on the side of the wall-mounted phone. The phone was not the place to tell anything that you did not want everyone else to know.

Directly across the dirt road from our house, there was a small grove of young pine trees, probably measuring from three to four inches in diameter at a yard above the ground. It was an ideal place to make roadways for our toy cars and trucks, as we pretended to be in a grove of giant redwood trees on the Pacific Coast. We soon learned which of the trees could be climbed without breaking their limbs—or ours—and by swinging from tree to tree we could traverse the length of the grove without setting foot on the ground. I also learned how to climb some of the large mature trees near our house, and it seemed that I could see the whole town, a true bird's-eye view. Much like a cat, I soon learned that it was often easier to climb up a tree than to get down from it, but at least I never had to holler for help.

During warm weather, the cooks in the school kitchen would occasionally make ice cream. Whenever there was a surplus, Mrs. Sulier, the school nurse and a good friend of my grandmother Sallie, would bring a big bowl of ice cream to Grandma's. She then called us over, and we all enjoyed some of the best-tasting ice cream that I have ever eaten!

It was while doing my chores one day that I learned to appreciate and respect the power in a bolt of lightning. A typical mountain rainstorm was brewing, the sky was darkened by thick rain-bearing clouds, with an occasional flash of lightning off in the distance, followed several seconds later by a sharp clap of thunder, or by a long growling rumble that echoed back and forth across the canyons. I was standing at the kitchen sink doing my dishes and gazing out of the window, just watching the whole show, when lightning struck a large pine tree right where I was looking. It literally exploded the tree, throwing large slabs of shattered wood and branches in all directions. Since then I have seen several other trees struck by lightning, but nothing as awesome or spectacular as this one.

These good years began to draw to a close when World War II began in September 1939. Then, on Sunday, December 7, 1941, as we were sitting at the table eating lunch, we heard the radio announce that the Japanese had bombed our naval base at Pearl Harbor—we were at war! During the next year we did not notice many changes taking place at Los Alamos, school or ranch, even though we were aware of what was happening in the war outside. The winter of 1941–1942 brought quite a bit of snow to our plateau. In addition, early spring rains in 1942 saturated the ground, except in places where it had been packed hard by some lengthy human activity. After a full day of blowing wind on the twenty-third of April, 1942, the twenty-fourth dawned with an odd ominous look in the otherwise clear sky. A stronger than usual wind was coming down off the slopes of the mountains to the west of town, and as it rapidly increased in speed and intensity, our big 150-year-old Ponderosa pine trees began to topple over right in front of our eyes. Their shallow roots in the very wet ground were no match for the force of the wind against their massive limb and needle structure. One after another, in every direction one looked, except for where the earth over their roots was packed hard, trees fell like matchsticks. It was a heartbreaking sight.

One especially large pine was located about fifteen to twenty feet to the northwest of our new grade-school, on the back side near the plot of dahlias planted by Adolfo Montoya. The children did not play back in that area, the ground was soft, and now wet. Around midmorning, with nothing to hold it up, it too was blown over, crashing right across the roof of the schoolhouse! One very strong limb penetrated through the roof, the attic, and the ceiling, stripped of side limbs along the way, and ended its fearsome journey jammed into the wood floor in the middle of the north half of the room. About an hour earlier, soon after school had started for the day, it had become apparent that the storm was likely to do some damage, and all the children were sent home. Luckily, this tree fell *after* the children had left school.

A lumberman from the far side of the Jemez Mountains set up his sawmill near the upper fields, hauled the downed trees, and sawed them into commercial lumber. In just a few months most of the mess was cleaned up in the community. Although most of the roads were soon cleared, many trees across the plateau were left to decay where they lay.[3]

Then things took a decidedly serious turn one year to the day after Pearl Harbor. On the afternoon of December 7, 1942, we were all called to a meeting in the Big House. With very little preamble, Mr. Connell read a letter from the War Department, informing us that Los Alamos Ranch School and all its property was being taken over and we had two months to leave! The school accelerated the instruction program, Christmas vacation was canceled, the school year was completed by late January, and we were ready to depart by early February 1943.

As I look back on it all, it was probably for the best for me personally, as I was not doing well in my studies. Moving to a public school in Santa Fe probably saved both myself and my family embarrassment over my grades. Grandmother Sallie Womelsduff died at her home in Los Alamos on

December 29, 1942, age eighty-one years, and was buried in the Fairview Cemetery in Santa Fe. In early February, we moved to Santa Fe, where I finished the year at Harrington Junior High School. Dad stayed on at Los Alamos for a few weeks to aid in the transition to the Manhattan Engineer District of the U.S. Army. He then took a job with the U.S. Forest Service, working out of Santa Fe until his retirement. He was foreman of a construction crew that built and repaired bridges and roads in the Santa Fe National Forest, mainly in the western part of the Jemez Mountains. He also spent several months in 1951 doing the same type of work in the Coconino National Forest, on the Mogollon Rim south of Winslow, Arizona. He passed away September 1, 1967, at age seventy-three, and is buried beside his wife, Abbie, in Fairview Cemetery, in Santa Fe, New Mexico.

I had one major advantage over the Ranch School boys: I lived at Los Alamos Ranch for thirteen and one-half years, whereas the students spent at most five years there and the majority considerably less. For me, living in a log house and growing up in the clear, high air of the Pajarito Plateau was idyllic. Each of us who were children there may have had different experiences, but I believe that all who grew up at Los Alamos Ranch came away with the same love and appreciation for this unique community. Some other of these special memories include:

- an old ranch truck with a working thermometer in the ornamental radiator cap;
- Ted Church's model airplane;
- Adolfo's beautiful flower garden;
- the only live rattlesnake that I ever saw at Los Alamos, stretched out beside our front porch;
- burning my hand when I climbed up on the treads of the small tractor and grabbed hold of the hot exhaust pipe;
- the absolute blackness of the night, and the infinite number of stars overhead;
- attending the presentations of Gilbert and Sullivan operettas put on by the all-male cast of the Ranch School;
- the sound of the breeze in the big pine trees;
- the colors and patterns of the Navajo rugs in the Trading Post and those so lavishly used to decorate the Lodge;
- the smells of the woods and fields after a rain;
- lying on my back on the grass and deciphering patterns in the cumulus clouds;
- the quiet and peace and sense of security;

- the smells of the different woods as they burned in our campfires or fireplaces;
- the beauty and serenity of the ranch after a snowfall;
- the sound of the bell on Fuller Lodge. . . .

It was a good time and a place to be a boy.

Mountain Rescue

One snowy night in the early fall of 1938 the Womelsduff brothers were called out. Harry Walen recalled the incident many years later.

When I was a single master in the Big House, my bed was at the end of a sleeping porch near the School office, where the forest service phone line was attached. In the early fall we had an unexpected major snowfall. When the phone's ring woke me up late that night I went across the corridor and heard my forest ranger friend Graeme McGowan on the other end of the line. I remembered that a couple of days before he had driven through in a pickup truck with several men who were to do some maintenance work on the remote fire-watch tower at St. Peter's Dome.

"Harry, I hope I didn't wake you up."

"No problem," I replied. "What can I do for you?"

"How much snow have you?," Graeme asked.

"Half a foot."

"Well, we have more than a foot here. We've finished our project and started back in the truck this evening. We had to use the clutch pretty hard trying to buck through the snow—especially the drifts— and it failed. It took a long time to walk back here through the snow. So we have shelter in the tower here but are out of food. Thank God the wire is still up. Can the ranch help us?"

I called A. J., told him the story, and asked whether he would approve waking up the Womelsduffs to see what they could do. He said that since we had the only heavy equipment to get in there, we had no choice other than to help. Connell told me to wake them up, tell them what had happened, and say that he authorized them to go on the rescue if they were willing to do so.

They were grumpy upon awaking, but immediate in their response, knowing we had the equipment. Jim, the foreman, said he and his brother Floyd, the mechanic, would have to put cleats on the

Caterpillar's treads, because the forest roads all slanted slightly outward for draining. Without cleats, the tractor would push itself over the edge. It would take a couple of hours to do this before they could set forth, with Floyd following in the pickup with fuel and food.

When I called Graeme to tell him what was afoot, he was one happy man. He realized that it would be daylight before the Womelsduffs could get there. I said he could call again if he just wanted reassurance. I also called, as I remember, when the brothers actually started on their journey. It's always good to know there is still someone there to say hello!

It took some time to get up there, shortly after dawn, and then Graeme called to let me know that they were returning. We had a royal welcome for forest service men *and* the Womelsduffs when they arrived back at the ranch![4]

Remembering the Ranch

JOHN DAVIS WIRTH

At the age of six I passed abruptly from a safe and supportive childhood on Los Alamos mesa to the disruptions and uncertainties of America at war. We left the ranch in August 1942, my father Cecil W. Wirth gravely ill with the cancer that in less than a year would take his life at New York's Memorial Hospital, while my mother Virginia, younger brother Tim, and I waited it out in Scarsdale, where I entered first grade. Left behind was my collie dog Tor and a way of life that for everyone remaining at the ranch would in a few short months yield completely to the exigencies of total war. My father's colleagues, called masters, around whom my small boy's world had revolved, now wore military uniforms instead of Stetsons and the modified Scout uniform of the Los Alamos master. As well, the roster of former students in the service filled several pages of what turned out to be the last alumni *Bulletin* of the Los Alamos Ranch School.

What's more, we were losing the war. I recall a lonely subway platform in New York one night, three boys with ocarinas playing "Remember Pearl Harbor"; seeing the capsized French liner "Normandy" under tight security while visiting one of the youngest masters, Hup Wallis, on his Royal Navy corvette; lining up for air-raid drills at school; being aware of the torpedoing and sinking of American tankers by Nazi submarines off the Jersey shore; and taking long cross-country trips by train which, as the war progressed, transmogrified into jam-packed troop trains, on one of which the only space available was the ladies' room, mortifying to a boy.

Later, the turning tide of war brought with it deep lessons of American patriotism and capacity. My uncle Gilbert Davis Jr., LARS 1941, and several of his classmates served in the Army Air Corps, the newly prestigious branch of service. Gil flew B-24s over Germany for the Eighth Air Force. James Anderson, LARS 1938, who for three summers running had been a counselor in my father's summer camp, flew a Corsair fighter for the marines in the Pacific. Our closest friends among the masters were now naval officers: Art Chase, Oscar Steege, and Ransom Lynch. Moving to Clifton, Arizona, to live with grandparents in 1943, I swelled with pride when high-ranking officers presented my Grandfather Gilbert with army and navy "E"s for excellence in war production at the copper mine and smelter he managed in Morenci for Phelps Dodge.

That was the year bubble gum reached Clifton, a sensation to us kids, and knickers for boys went out, to our great relief. Near the San Francisco River a booth was set up featuring hideous heads of Hitler, Mussolini, and Tojo. Hit one on the nose and you got a prize. Mother helped the war effort as a nurse's aide. To get that sleek, rolled look, both she and Gil's bride, Jean McFarland, wore "rats" in their hair. Later, having moved to Denver where Virginia began teaching sixth grade at the Graland Country Day School, I saw parked at Lowry Field rank upon rank of bombers returned from the air war in Japan. A Japanese torpedo plane in mint condition sat in one of the hangers, but not for long. We boys were given sledgehammers and told to have at it. For years a piece of the wing flap sat in our Denver basement, an artifact of American triumph. Still attached to this flap was a superbly milled worm drive in blued aluminum, the craftsmanship of which I, a boy thoroughly imbued with a demonic view of the Japanese, nonetheless had the wits to marvel at.

In fact, Los Alamos and the war melted into one set of growing-up experiences, symbolized for several years by the accumulation of boy things, some of which I still have. Jumbled together in my gear was the standard Los Alamos equipment—a scout knife, match-safe (for keeping kitchen matches dry) and whistle, two cook kits embossed with the initials of their former owners, and Cecil's scoutmaster badge—along with identification cards of fighter aircraft, various military patches, and, by 1945, captured German army stuff including badges, belts, a cartridge box, and my prized possession: a bayonet in mint condition. Today, most of it has wandered off, but I still have the cook kits and the bayonet. I see them now as symbols. The well-used cooking gear—which recalls the pride of LARS boys on the all-day Saturday rides, who learned to cook over juniper wood coals without leaving a trace of smoke on their aluminum pots—is a proxy for the orderly world of my earliest growing up at the ranch. The well-oiled blade of my bayonet clicks shut in its metal scabbard whenever I so command, a reminder from the Wehrmacht of why the Ranch School itself was terminated just before my father's death in April 1943.

Fig. 9.1

1941 LARS graduate Lt. Gilbert N. Davis, USAAF, in 1944 with his B-24 Liberator bomber headed for Europe. Wirth private collection.

As well, the Nazi booty in my gear recalls an inadvertent lesson I received from Duff Gordon, a Denver family friend, who gave most of his German stuff to me when he returned from the war in Europe. Ex-Sergeant Gordon wanted to become a professor of English and enrolled in the Ph.D. program at Denver University, where Cecil had graduated. Perhaps he eventually achieved this goal, but for years poor Duff suffered the agonies of thesis block and could not

Fig. 9.2

1938 LARS graduate James R. Anderson Jr., USMCR, and his F4U Corsair
fighter, training in California in 1944. Courtesy of James Anderson.

finish his dissertation. Although Virginia commiserated with Fran, Duff's
wife, and her old childhood friend, I got the impression that Duff's struggle
was something to be pitied and laughed at all at once. Determined not to follow his example, when my turn came at Stanford years later I wrote the dissertation in six months. This effort paid off: the book won a prize and I
received tenure in Stanford's History Department.

But this was not the end of it. In part, my first book dealt with Volta Redonda, the integrated steelworks in Brazil that was built with U.S. government funds in 1942.[1] Brazil's maneuvering between the United States and Germany to secure the necessary technology and funding was, and is, a fascinating subject. Sometime in the early 1970s, after publication, I discussed the book with Lawrence Hitchcock, who was visiting Santa Fe. To my astonishment Hitch lit up and told me how the Inter-American Defense Board, on which he served as secretary general during the Second World War, had been a player in resolving this very issue. Fortunately, my book did mention the Board in passing, but I sensed in this formidable man what so many LARS boys in their day had discovered: Mr. Hitchcock always knew more about more things.

Later, while researching for the book at hand I found out that Hitch and Cecil were the administrative core of LARS in the school's later years under A. J. Connell. Hitch and Cecil had been close colleagues, if not intimate friends. I also learned that Hitch had cast a long, benevolent shadow over my brother Tim's and my college education at Harvard, which was financed in part by the Los Alamos Foundation. As previously discussed, Hitch served on the board of this foundation, whose income came from the government's purchase of Los Alamos and from Mr. Connell's assets. Coming in recognition of Cecil's long service to the school, this funding was a godsend to my schoolteacher mother, who was raising two boys as a single parent on a tight budget. Hitch, who himself had worked his way through Yale with some scholarship support, made sure that Tim and I did the same to prove our mettle. He specified that the funding be enough to be helpful, but not sufficient to get us through. So we worked on bridge-construction crews during summers in the mid-1950s and had student jobs during the academic year at Harvard to supplement those checks that came to us with the LARS logo still on them. But I only learned of this much later, while going through the Los Alamos Foundation papers deposited by Fermor Church in the New Mexico State Archives.

Los Alamos as a living place was gone—the remaining three Wirths left the ranch after Mother returned that August to close up the house before moving us to Scarsdale—but not the sense of place.[2] My next encounter came at age eleven, in summer 1947, when Mother took us to visit Edith Warner at her new house set well back from the Rio Grande—the place and way of life memorialized in Peggy Church's masterpiece, *The House at Otowi Bridge*. "The Hill," as Los Alamos was now called, was still closed to visitors, but Mother thought she might get as far as Camp Hamilton on the lower road up Pueblo Canyon. Alas, she got stuck in a sand pit. Then, having been pulled out and turned around by the MPs, we returned to Edith's, where, in a later visit, Virginia and Tim retrieved some of our things that had been stored there, including the small black rocking chair she had nursed us on. My own boy's bed, made by Cecil who was an excellent woodworker, had migrated off to the pueblo. Later, family ties in Santa Fe and the teaching job at Stanford became the anchors of my life. Yet I never lost the connection with Los Alamos.

Cecil himself remained closely connected with the school until his death on April 7, 1943—supervising from afar Sterling Colgate and Bob Carter (the Spruce Patrol boys who took over his classes), getting in the weekly grades, recruiting faculty and prospective students from the New York area. And, while receiving cancer treatments at Memorial Hospital, he worked as a purchasing agent for Phelps Dodge, where he expedited wartime deliveries of heavy industrial equipment to the mine and smelter being managed by his father-in-law, Gilbert Davis, at Morenci. Visits from Los Alamos folk were frequent, including Hitch who came up from Washington and later on in January sent a long description of the last LARS graduation and the school's closing to Fay Curtis's widow, Daisy, and to Cecil.

Art Chase and his bride, the former Alice Ann Anderson, Jim's sister, visited us in February. But by now Cecil was fading fast. "It's hard to think of Cecil being gone," Art wrote shortly after his best friend's death in April. "We had many letters from him in the last weeks—always calm and hopeful and thoughtful as he'd always been."[3] Of Cecil's death, Art said to me when I visited him in 1991, when after a long career at the Berkshire school he himself was dying of cancer, "it was so sad, so very sad." They started teaching at Los Alamos together in 1929; they ran the camp together; they had been each other's best man.

Cecil's ashes lie at the end of Los Alamos mesa, a place still very beautiful, where on a winter's day the immense vista of the Sangre de Cristo Mountains glowing faintly in the softly setting sun evoke the deep spirituality of this landscape. In Art's words: there "on the top of Otowi hill with its glorious view of the Rio Grande Valley, the warm pueblo country, and the Sangre de Cristos— like Browning's Grammarian he seems to belong up there." This is Cecil's place, where he spent nights alone under the stars, watched sunrises and sunsets. He and Virginia picnicked together there. Nearby is the horse trail he built with the boys down Otowi Hill to the bottom of Los Alamos Canyon. (Today, the Los Alamos Pathways Association, of which I am a member, is reconstructing the old Breakneck Trail.) But generations were here before it was special to my father, and almost three generations have come to admire the vista since his time.[4] Whenever I visit this place, the rude contingencies of life seem smoothed by continuities.

With a woman's strength, Virginia left the ranch and put her brief seven years of married life with Cecil behind her for a new life in Denver. At Graland, a private country day school founded on the Shady Hill model, she began what would turn out to be a thirty-year career teaching sixth and eighth grade. Her special interest was Colorado history. In 1953, she took on three more children when she married John Wiebenson, making us a real "Brady bunch," of whom four of us were teenagers. But she could never fully escape the ranch and the presence of the past, especially as she grew old and the wonder of a first husband forever young grew on her.

Whenever she went to the mountains Virginia wore a Los Alamos hat, much broken in. (For years Hitch wore his Stetson when gardening or camping, and kept three well-oiled saddles from Los Alamos days at his Maryland home near Washington, D.C.) Peggy Pond Church, a fellow faculty wife and Virginia's lifelong friend, captured the loss of husband and of place in an extraordinary poem, written during the war in 1944. Mother showed it to me much later as something I should know.

Our earliest years and first experiences are crucial to the formation of the intellectual and moral self, and by the age of six one's course is pretty well set. The rest of the growing up years is fine-tuning and experience. What follows is an attempt to recapture those early years and the Los Alamos sense of place, to focus the prism of childhood memory with a historian's optic. What did living at the ranch mean to me as a small boy and, in retrospect, how did it matter to all of us who had the good fortune to have been there in the Ranch School years?

My brother Tim and I enjoyed the care and mentoring of a full-time mother, who read to us frequently. There was of course no television, and I did not see a movie until first grade, when the astonishing visual delight of a cartoon in Technicolor burst onto my consciousness for the first time, followed shortly thereafter by "Snow White," the Disney classic. Our father was always on horseback, it seemed, and when he, Ted Mather, Bences, Art Chase, and the boys returned from a long pack-trip I was proud and excited to ride up in the saddle with him those last few hundred feet toward Fuller Lodge and home. When my bones ached from growing pains he was there in the night to hold me in my Dr. Dentons, the one-piece pajamas with a trap door that kids of my generation wore. We went on family picnics in a green Chevrolet Suburban. (Later, in a burst of overreaching, Cecil bought a bright blue Buick with white sidewalls; with no gasoline available, it was garaged in Clifton for the duration of the war.) And every April for his birthday, Mother and I would search for pasque flowers, which come up in the early spring at Los Alamos.

One of the excitements was to visit the Smithwicks at Anchor Ranch, or better yet to venture out to Mrs. Frye's tearoom at Bandelier—she with the frizzy red hair—and still better yet to drive down the mesa to Otowi Crossing, where Edith Warner served her famous chocolate cake. There, her Indian companion, Tilano, would take me under his wing, sometimes walking onto the wobbly

LETTER TO VIRGINIA

DO you remember those days, Virginia,
When we were young and Time was innocent?
The ripe world flowered around us.
Disaster was a seed whose spear had not thrust through
    the quiet earth.
We lay at night embraced in peace by our husbands.
We gave birth to our children.
The days were luminous. The vines were sweet above the porches.
Thunder did not appall us; the mountains hung with rainbows.
At dusk we walked among moonflowers. The children cried at bedtime.
After they slept we sang, we and the young men together
gathered around the piano in the firelight.
How young we were; how certain of the happy ending.
We planted trees and dreamed of the full harvest,
and dreamed of old age under the quiet branches.

But Time split like a dried seed.
The sleeping gods woke; the dead myths came alive;
lightning fell out of heaven and clashed among us.
We were uprooted from peace like trees in a great storm.
WE found life is not what we dream but something that dreams us.
Now if the dreamer tosses in nightmare what shall wake him?
Never again shall he dream those days of wonder.

But I shall remember you forever, Virginia,
the day that we stood together in the garden
and you knew that your love must die.
I shall remember how you stood in the wind like a flag unbeaten,
like the figurehead of a ship that faces the wave's crash,
proud and unvanquished, grown to the stature of woman.
The past fell behind you like a discarded plaything.
You gathered your children's hands and marched toward the future.

*Peggy Pond Church
July 1949
Published in "Ultimatum for man"
out of print)*

Fig. 9.3

"Letter to Virginia," by Peggy Pond Church.
Wirth private collection.

quicksand at the river's edge, but then coming back twinkle-eyed and smiling when I became really alarmed. As he did for many other children, Tilano made me a turkey-feather headdress. The stone axe head he gave me was part of my gear. From Otowi siding, Mother, Peggy Church, her youngest son Hugh, and I took the last run of the Chile Line into Santa Fe. This was in 1941. In a fit of folly, the rails were taken up and shipped to China, where they promptly fell into Japanese hands, meaning that the rail line was not available to support the Manhattan Project in 1943.

Not so much fun was to be dumped in Santa Fe at Mrs. Wiswall's day-care center, while Mother took time off. To a small boy, this seemed most unfair, and the only good memory I have of it is watching what were then called pursuit planes, maneuvering in the skies over Santa Fe. I have only the vaguest memories of the famous puppet shows presented by Gus and Jane Baumann. But an act of kindness at the Ruthlings' ranch in Tesuque impressed me greatly. For their daughter Doodlet's seventeenth-birthday party, a piñata was strung up and when it burst all the other kids scrambled greedily for the candy while three-year-old John stood by helpless, not knowing what to do. Doodlet, the birthday girl, immensely tall with her long black hair, bent down to help me get some, and my heart skipped a beat for this kindly act. One day Hugh Church, some four years older than I, announced that he was going to throw my red wagon off the rim into Los Alamos Canyon. Trusting and gullible, I believed him and worried for days.

I remember the dips and depressions near Pojoaque on the dirt road to Santa Fe. We called them "the whees," for that sinking feeling you had going over the top. "Whee," we shouted, and the parents joined in with peels of laughter. Coming back, the road wound up Culebra Hill and then, past the turnoff to Frijoles, it snaked up the switchbacks on Otowi Hill to reach the rim of Los Alamos mesa, thence to the ranch. Father and Mother occasionally referred to us boys as their "little tweaks." When Cecil and Virginia went out on the town—perhaps to dance at La Fonda, or to visit with their friends the Dendahls and the Kochs, or to attend fiesta parties—my brother and I were left with baby-sitters. These were usually the Montoya sisters: Margaret, Rose and Adelina, who also kept house for us. They remember a dashing young couple, leaving for Santa Fe in a rush of gaiety.

In truth, I wasn't especially aware of Spanish culture; it was part of ranch life, just as the pueblo ruins dotting the mesa were part of the landscape. Some of the songs come back in snatches, as in:

Pobrecito, animalito
tiene hambre, tecolotito, hummm

CHAPTER NINE

Bences holds a special place in my recall, although of course I could have had no idea of his central role in the functioning of the ranch. What I did appreciate was his showman's flair for making the most delicious sopaipillas. There on the mesa's edge he would drop a square of dough into a hotly bubbling kettle of lard and watch me watching until pop! the sopaipilla ballooned up perfectly and he would break out laughing. Bences had a way with children. For his part, Pedro Montoya, the carpenter and painter, put on a show whenever I came by. When Mother said hello to Pedro, he'd say "Paaintingg" to my delight.

Fig. 9.4
Former master Ransom Lynch and John Wirth, 1941.
Wirth private collection.

Being a small boy in the midst of so many big boys was heady, and I was often tempted (and prompted) to show off. The exuberant joy of shirtless young men in shorts stays with me. At Camp May (on Pajarito mountain near the Valle Grande) the older boys let me drain the dregs of their beer cans, the old-fashioned kind with cone necks then still in use. The sharp, bitter taste of Coors seemed to go with the hope of growing up, although I'm sure the boys found this amusing. At Camp Hamilton (today a sawed-off wreck at the bottom of Pueblo Canyon) there were family picnics, some of them probably with the youngest boys who used this log hut for their outings. A social disaster happened to me one day at Ashley Pond when going down the slide: the seat of my swimming trunks gave out. What to do? With all the world watching, I was mortified but nobody seemed to care.

I know now that the boys were much taken with my parents, a newly married couple arriving in 1935, who began producing babies. That is what the boys were really interested in. In fact, as one of the graduates told me later, Cecil and Virginia were "an item," much discussed by the boys. Occasionally there was a foursome of bridge with the Wirths at Spruce Cottage. Another graduate remembers being coaxed out of his painful shyness by Virginia, who taught him to dance. Boys vied to sit at the Wirths' table at Fuller Lodge. Virginia never forgot her own most embarrassing moment when, as a young bride on display during sit-down dinner in the Lodge, she spilled a bowl of melted butter down her front. She also told me later that once she and Cecil made love in a tent at one of the camps. Now, that was naughty, all the more so because women were not allowed to be out with the boys on rides. But by the time I came along Cecil, not A. J. Connell, was running the camp.

Those long, elaborately planned pack-trips were central to my growing up, even though I was not old enough to go on them. I did get to ride in the pickup delivering supplies to various camps in the Valles Caldera. Coming back late one pitch-black evening in the vastness of the Valle Grande, with the truck's headlights picking out the track, I most vividly recall the reassuring, utterly reliable and very American sound of a straight-six Chevy engine pulling us through the night. To a boy, this was a first experience with the sublime. Of course, after my father died and we moved to Denver, I realized that I never would grow up to have my own horse at the ranch, that I never would get to ride out on my dad's pack outfit with Ted and the others. This was a shock. The sense of loss stays with me, the counterpart, perhaps, to that remembered sound of the straight six.

To be sure, having almost died of appendicitis at the age of four I knew that bad things could happen. After the operation at St. Vincent Hospital, A. J. Connell brought me an illustrated book of Bible stories. Mr. Connell's well-

Fig. 9.5

Cecil and Virginia Wirth, late 1930s. Peggy Pond Church Collection.
Courtesy Los Alamos Historical Museum Archives.

meant, if rather formal and distant gesture did not impress me much. The presents that really perked me up were from the parent who sent a week's worth of toys with instructions to open one new package every day. Recovery was long and slow, some of it spent outdoors lying in my brother's big brown wicker pram, which, this being 1940, sported campaign buttons saying "We Want Willkie." With most of the Ranch School in the Republican camp, what was I to do?

Starting with Adolph, our (in retrospect) ill-named German Shepherd who eventually ran off, dogs figured prominently in my life. Protective to a fault, Adolph nipped at everyone who came close to Virginia, John, and Tim. An irate Bences told Cecil and Virginia that Adolph was not to bite his son Severo ever again. Tor, the collie who replaced him, was smart and a delight. However, when Tor was just a puppy I somehow managed to break his leg by shoving him into a sunken birdbath. The leg was duly splinted up, Tor never had a limp, and his trusting nature stayed intact, but I learned a harsh lesson about mistreating animals. Tor stayed behind when we left the ranch. Mother told me that he had joined the army's K-9 corps, which somehow made the loss of my dog (my father, and our whole way of life) easier to understand and to bear.

Just before we left Los Alamos in May of 1942 a tornado blew through the ranch, sending pieces of tin roof slicing through the air and toppling many of the tall ponderosa pines that formed a noble backdrop to the school complex. Nearly 250 trees were uprooted or snapped off on the property. One of these huge trees clipped a gutter on the porch of our house where Tim was sleeping. A few feet closer to that house and a future six-term congressman from Colorado's Second District and later U.S. senator would not have survived. Close calls like this underscore the role of contingency and chance in life. Going on six and with my father gravely ill, I sensed this keenly. Amidst heavy wind and stinging sand we scurried to the Lodge for safety and the reassuring words of Helen Sulier, the school nurse whom I called "the lady in white."

"All goes well here," A. J. reported to Hitchcock, now on active military duty at Fort Sill. "Most of the big pines on the place are now corded up, so that we look like a wood yard, but still we are very fortunate not to have had anyone injured, and I believe the young trees will grow much more rapidly, as they always do after the removal of the older ones."[5] Always the optimist, Connell could not know that less than one year later army bulldozers would transform this landscape into an industrial site with muddy roads.

In my earliest years and until shortly after Tim was born in 1939, Spruce Cottage was our home. This is the faculty house closest to Fuller Lodge (and for many years starting in the 1960s the home of our friends Betty and Jim Lilienthal, who worked at the Lab). Designed by John Gaw Meem, the faculty apartment at Spruce Cottage abutted onto the dormitory for the older boys, who were in the Spruce Patrol. After that we lived in the cottage that Connell had designed and built for his sister May. All I remember of this house was the perfect swing my father made for me. In order to have more family time, Cecil and Virginia began having dinner together in this house.

Our last house, at the northern end of the faculty cottages, had been remodeled by John Meem for Ferm and Peggy Church in the early 1930s. Faith Bemis, soon to be John Meem's wife and much later still my mother-in-law, designed some of the architectural details for their new living room. When the Churches' two oldest boys began boarding at the school, Ferm, Peggy, and Hugh moved to Spruce Cottage and the Wirths moved into the Church house. My room was a small cubbyhole over the front door, almost a secret place.

Faculty mentoring in the dorm is one of the major benefits of a boarding-school experience. To be with a young, growing family on a daily basis makes a strong impression on adolescents. "I have a very clear picture in my mind of your father and mother striding hand in hand on their way to meals in the Lodge," Charles Pearce wrote. "They walked with long strides, arms swinging and obviously happy. . . . Your parents were a most attractive couple, and sitting at their table for meals was eagerly anticipated."[6] Men in their seventies and eighties still tell me how being with the Wirths in Spruce Cottage was a highpoint of the LARS experience.

My parents were born in Colorado, but came from different social backgrounds. Cecil, called Cec by his friends but always Mr. Wirth by the Los Alamos boys, was one of five siblings (four brothers and a sister) abandoned by their father, George Wirth, when his vegetable farm failed in Parker, outside Denver. Grandmother Anna kept the family together, refusing to put the children up for adoption. For a while the family was reduced to living in a tent, in what was then called "Poverty Flats" adjacent to the Denver city dump. The boys supplemented their family's meager larder by shooting rabbits, which Anna made into hasenpfeffer stew. Illinois-born, she had grown up in a German-speaking family from Luxembourg that emigrated from the Franco-Prussian border area to escape conscription into Bismarck's army after the 1871 war. Poorly educated herself, Anna insisted that the children stay in school, and all of them had odd jobs. Cec carried papers and learned to handle horses at the local dairy. Fortune smiled when Anna, a single parent and a woman facing very tough odds, was hired by the owner of Jonas Fur Company, where she then worked for many years. From the taxidermist's she brought home meat for the five kids. For his part, Cec was active in the Boy Scouts and a church youth group in Denver. He learned social skills by caddying at the Denver Country Club and was taken in tow by the owner of Olinger's Mortuary, who gave him a summer job and encouraged him to attend YMCA college in Chicago. A graduate of Denver University, Cecil, alone of the five children, took a college degree. He was the family star.

Cec and his younger brother, Walter, worked summers as counselors for Cheley Colorado Camps outside Grand Lake. Frank Cheley ran a close-knit, successful operation for which he was nationally known, and he had a major influence on Cecil, who worked there for ten years, rising in the camp operation to become associate director in charge of the boys division from 1929 to 1932. The "Chief" (Frank Cheley), who was like a father to Cecil, considered him "very much above the average at every point, a man who is bound to make an outstanding place for himself in the world." It was at Grand Lake, in the summer of 1928, that one of the campers, who was also a student at Los Alamos, told him about the Ranch School and urged Cec to apply for a teaching post.[7]

Given his outdoor skills, scouting background, and ability to work with boys and handle horses, Cecil passed muster with A. J. Connell, and in 1929 he became a master, teaching history and mathematics, one of the few masters without an eastern private-school background and/or Ivy League degree, a big leap for a young man coming out of poverty. With her grit and determination, Anna surely played a role in this American success story. To this day, the Wirth family is known for strong, resourceful women.

Except for a year away, when he took leave from the faculty to work full time for Cheley and then to attend the Harvard Business School in 1933, Cec settled into a career of teaching and mentoring well-to-do young men. Lacking the funds to complete his MBA, he was grateful to A. J. for taking him back; in turn, Wirth's return helped Connell to deal with one of his persistent problems, which was faculty turnover due principally to the low salaries. Cec's duties included leading Scout Troop 22, serving as assistant to the director, and running the summer camp. By 1937, as mentioned, Hitch, Cecil, and A. J. formed the core administrative team. Lucky to have a job during the Depression, my father harbored aspirations to be something other than a schoolmaster, but the closest he came to a business career was during the last months of his life when he worked at Phelps Dodge corporate headquarters in New York. I now know that A. J. Connell had been thinking of Cecil as his successor. "Cecil is the one I would have expected to carry on," he wrote Professor Carson (the father of two summer campers) shortly after LARS shut down. "He had both the desire and the interest as well as the executive ability."[8]

Virginia Davis, the Brownmoor school teacher whom Cecil married in 1935, and who took up housekeeping in the faculty apartment at Spruce Cottage—designed by my future father-in-law to accommodate the new family—came from a different background. Virginia's father, Gilbert, was from old New England stock: his father was a Connecticut Yankee and his mother was a Newhall from Philadelphia; they raised five boys in Arlington Heights, Illinois. Virginia's mother, Hortense, was one of the first graduates of Denver High and took her degree at the State Normal School in Greeley. Gilbert held a series of management jobs in the bleak, remote coal-mining camps of Colorado and Wyoming before advancing up the Phelps Dodge corporate ladder. He and my grandmother Hortense "followed the mines," a classic career pattern in this extractive industry of the Rocky Mountain West. Virginia grew up riding horses and camping and joined the Girl Scouts, but chafed at the rigid hierarchy in these isolated mining camps and disliked having to be the boss's daughter. She escaped this world by taking her senior year at East Denver High, staying with the family of her lifelong pal, Marguerite Quarrels Schenkman. When Gilbert became superintendent of the Stag Canyon mine in Dawson, New Mexico—then a coal town of some five thousand people and one of the state's largest employers—Virginia went to Mount Holyoke, a women's college in Massachusetts so remote from Dawson that one of her classmates asked for "stamps from New Mexico." She had a fling with a Princeton man named Carl, coonskin coat, Stutz Bearcat, and all, but came back west. After taking a masters at the University of New Mexico she started teaching at Brownmoor, the private girls school located just north of Santa Fe on the old Pulitzer estate, now Bishop's Lodge. To be young and single in Santa Fe was very heaven.

Once a year, the Brownmoor girls were invited to a formal dance in Fuller Lodge. The girls wore long dresses, but the boys came in short pants, pressed khaki shirts, and bandanas—the standard uniform, which they also wore when they visited Brownmoor. Cec and Virginia did not meet at one of these closely chaperoned affairs. No, it was Peach Van Stone who arranged the date. (Amusingly enough, Peach's future husband Walter Mayer had pursued Virginia when she was at the University of New Mexico.) Soon Cec was courting her in earnest, borrowing Art Chase's snappy Ford roadster for maximum effect, and receiving tips on how to handle women from the older men like Fermor Church, the science teacher who, as Peggy's husband, was already a family man, and Tommy Waring, who taught foreign languages and was married to the former Anita Rose, A. J.'s favorite among the wives. A self-contained New Englander, Ferm loved opera and had his romantic side. Young bachelors like Cecil and Art Chase enjoyed listening to his extensive collection of classical records at the Churches on Tuesday nights.

With Hitch and Ferm the younger men learned the intricacies of contract bridge, and Cecil may well have participated in the weekly poker games that Hitch, for his part, greatly enjoyed playing with the staff. Occasionally, the faculty read books together and when the New Testament was the subject of discussion Hitch checked translations with his text in the original Greek. Although "the school was totally centered on the kids," Oscar Steege recalled, and "we were all dedicated to the care of these kids," there was time off the ranch for partying and dating in Santa Fe. During Prohibition, the masters laid in a supply of Pojoaque Lightning, which circulated liberally at fiesta parties. In fact, Santa Fe had the reputation as a fun, hard-drinking town, and eligible bachelor masters were part of the scene. Los Alamos was indeed remote, and certain aspects of Connell's program were like a military camp, but A. J., who enjoyed a glass himself, had no objection to high spirits as long as the care and nurturing of the boys came first. This was the world that Virginia married into.

In Dawson, the Wirths and their wedding party were saluted by the coal miners who formed a vast circle around the superintendent's house, singing to the newlyweds and enjoying their holiday while paying homage to the boss. Mother must have been embarrassed by the antique aspects of this show. As

Fig. 9.6

Cecil Wirth at Camp Hamilton with Art Chase's
Ford roadster, 1934. Wirth private collection.

for the best man and the ushers, Art Chase recalled that their white flannels
were made a little worse for changing a tire on the Dawson-Raton road before
the wedding.[9] When it was time for Gilbert's first grandchild to be born, he
insisted that the delivery occur not in Santa Fe's St. Vincent Hospital, which
was closer to the ranch, but in the Phelps Dodge company hospital at Dawson,
where he could control everything except the act of birth itself. This explains
why Dawson is listed as my place of birth and why, when the mine shut in 1954
and Dawson became a ghost town, I came to see it as the perfect starting place
for a historian. By the time my brother was born in 1939, the Davises had
already left for Arizona; thus Tim's birth certificate lists Santa Fe's St. Vincent
as his place of birth. Gilbert was also an expert fisherman. His wool cap was

studded with flies and he could tease the fish to rise when nobody else could get a strike. My grandfather was blessed with infinite patience, teaching Tim and me how to fish. He and Cecil had a good relationship, but not to the extent of testing the nepotism rules at Phelps Dodge to get his son-in-law a position with the corporation.[10] But then in New York, with the wartime shortage of employees, for a few short months Cecil had his wish: serving as a purchasing agent for P.D. Corp., as we called it.

Much to their credit, my maternal grandparents accepted Cecil as their daughter's choice, even though in the style of the times Hortense did wonder if the rather prominent hook in Cec's nose might not reveal "the map of Israel," as the saying then went. It helped that he was very bright, and Virginia herself "was no slouch," Art Chase recalled. Cecil sensed, but was self-confident enough to overcome, the social gap. His truly heroic mother Anna had since married Sam "Pop" Roberts, a crusty veteran of the Spanish American War, who had been keeper of the Bird House at Denver's City Park Zoo. Grandmother Roberts obtained her high-school degree by correspondence course when Tim and I were undergraduates at Harvard. I'm glad to say that we recognized and then said to Grandmother what a splendid achievement this was.

And what of Cecil Wirth, the man? Everything I know directly about my father has been told already, so what follows is an adult's speculation based on the written record, and certain character traits that my brother Tim and I seem to carry in varying degree. As our careers took off, Mother would occasionally admonish us not to forget Cecil's legacy (and parenthetically her own).

Cecil's legacy—a mix of nature and nurture in our case—is highly congruent with the ideals of Los Alamos Ranch School. "Cecil Wirth was the manliest man around the place," one former student recalled, "a role model for many. All we boys were, of course [he added], in love with your beautiful mother."[11] Another student from the school's last years wrote:

> Of the teachers there at the time, Cecil Wirth made by far the greatest impression on me, and I suspect that the same was true of a large majority of the students. Many of the staff were more or less obviously just going through the motions in one element or another of the School's programs (particularly the riding, or the skiing, or the boy scout program that A. J. Connell was so proud of. . . .), but Cecil seemed to enjoy it all. He approached no task with resignation. He was always enthusiastic: he seemed always to be having the full share of fun that the situation afforded. So far as we students could tell, he got the full potential out of everything he touched.

A reasonably good athlete and a fine horseman, Cecil tried hard and swept others along with him.[12] Others of the "lifers" among the masters such as Hitch, Waring, Steege, and Church, and especially Art Chase, had deep impacts on certain students—such is the nature of a highly structured and successful boarding school. In the competition among the faculty for popularity with the students that naturally develops in boarding schools, however, Cecil's qualities of enthusiasm and commitment propelled him to the top.

Yet Cecil was not all that familiar in his dealings with students; friendly enough, he kept a certain distance from them, which enhanced his effectiveness as a mentor. Cecil "was friendly but never close and confiding in the manner of Waring. Over a bridge game he could laugh and joke, but not often during the school day. I think he felt too much closeness would undermine discipline."[13] Masters like Boz Bosworth, who taught math from 1926 to 1930, and Tommy Waring, who taught English, French, and Spanish from 1926 to 1939, were virtually, if not actually, addressed on a first-name basis, but not Cecil. He was close to some of the junior faculty like my godfather Ransom Lynch (math, 1937–1939), yet exercised a certain leadership style with them, as well. His way of running the summer camp was less authoritarian than A. J.'s. Lynch recalls how, on the 1941 summer camp (Cecil's last), "If we overlooked something we would get a suggestion, sometimes gentle, sometimes not, but never offensive."[14]

Cecil was socially at ease and got on well with everyone, including A. J. Connell, despite his daunting personality and occasional clashes with Cecil over policy issues. Hispanics on the ranch remember him as companionable and even-handed. Cecil had strong convictions about the importance of foreign affairs and introduced a weekly discussion group at LARS, but he was not an academic leader of Hitch's stature or ability.[15] Rather, his special contribution was in making the community go, all of it, which is probably the reason why A. J. would have wanted Cecil to succeed him.

In fact, Cec lived and practiced the Boy Scout ideals. Shortly before he died, our father left a letter for his sons to read when they reached age twelve, an important birthday for we could now become Scouts. "I guess it was important to me," he wrote, "because I became a full and complete Boy Scout, a member of Troop 22 of Denver." (By coincidence, he was a scoutmaster of Troop 22 at Los Alamos, which recently celebrated its eightieth anniversary.) He continued:

I think it is very important for a boy to belong to some group [even if there is no Scout Troop near you] and to do his share in making that group a success. A boy of twelve is old enough to know how important cooperation, loyalty, honesty and 'guts' are in helping to make a group a success because these same qualities plus many others are necessary to make your home life happy and successful. I remember somebody told me when I joined Troop 22 that it was just like a bank. I would get as much out of the Troop as I put in. I remember working hard, trying to put in to the Troop just as much as possible and I know I got it all back with interest.[16]

Cecil was unable to finish this letter, but his message resonated with us over the years. I became an Eagle Scout at age fourteen and took a Ph.D. in history from Stanford, making teaching my profession, while Tim received his Ph.D. in education from Stanford and went on to his career in public service.

When I work with the Pathways group on one of the Ranch School trails that Cecil built with the boys, it seems I am not only walking in his footsteps but also I sense in an uncanny and deeply intimate way that this is how I would do it if I were designing old Breakneck or the Camp Hamilton Trail. The stones really speak, and in the deeply spiritual landscape of Los Alamos I know my father again.

Life at the remote hilltop community of Los Alamos was not easy for a young married woman. Cec was away with the boys much of the time, or otherwise engaged in school activities. Virginia and Anita Waring adapted rather well, but Peggy, a strong individualist with a poet's sensibility, bridled at the regimentation and boycotted dinners at the Lodge until Harry Walen brought Elizabeth there as a bride in 1938. Virginia's advice to Betty was realistic: "You'll never have a husband weekends, holidays or vacations. You must plan projects for those times." Betty needed help adjusting and the women rallied around. Harry, who taught English for five years at LARS, wrote to me years later after the 1991 reunion:

> The social structure in our school was similar to that in an Army outpost, where the women tend to become very close friends, for they rapidly learn to depend on one another. Betty remembers your Mother saying to her soon after she arrived as a bride that she would have to put up with a great deal of loneliness, especially during family times. For those times—the weekends, the holidays, the school vacations—were the times for pack trips, long rides, vacation tours to places like Aspen, the Grand Canyon, Carlsbad Caverns.[17]

But what would a small boy with lots of attention from his mother have known of this or cared? My world was neatly captured in a letter Mother wrote Elizabeth Carson when I was almost five. "We have a new collie puppy, aged 3 months, named Tor, who adds to the charm but confusion of the household.

Tim is now dashing about at a great rate [and] John brought in a large fat toad today 'to live in his room. . . . ' Life is very merry, and the ranch is oh, so beautiful. All our rain has made the world almost lush in feeling."[18]

Yet being left alone with small children was probably no easier to take in those preliberation days. "Things are going very well in camp—25 boys, you've probably heard. First pack trip goes out Monday. Cec is taking the whole group at once this year, so I shall be very much the widow. However my own boys keep me too busy to catch an extra breath or be lonesome."[19] And still another letter to Elizabeth revealed that she was at her wit's end what with Johnny teasing Tim and pestering the dog.

To the north and west was canyon land, heavily forested and bordering on wilderness. The sense of being out in nature was overpowering to some of the boys from back east, but for me, exploring more and more out from the house with each passing year, the look of big sky and the sound of wind in the ponderosa pines stirs the deepest memories. I shared secrets with a make-believe playmate named He-He. My best friend was Kim Hunter, the son of Virginia and Vernon Hunter, the well-known Santa Fe artist and head of the WPA artists project. We invented a story together, about a little calf who wandered off from his mother and got lost on a mountain, but then managed to strap branches to his hooves and ski back to safety and his mother in the Valle Grande.[20] No stranger to remote places, Virginia saw parallels with the lifestyle described by Marjorie Kinnan Rawlings in her best-selling novel *The Yearling,* later a popular movie. In fact, her nickname for me was Jodie, the young boy in Rawlings's book, and the way she called us home, something like *whooou, whoou, whoou,* was I think inspired by the movie.

It bears repeating that the power of a boarding-school experience lies in a full round of multiple activities mixed with a large measure of adult mentoring. LARS was no exception, and the mentoring Connell prized were the ties and sometimes close friendships formed between the masters and their students. "Most of the boys seemed to focus on one or another of the Masters," Jay Gilchrist recalled, "some on Hitch, others on Ferm and still others on Tommy, Cecil or Art. Not one of them was less than a total delight as a person, and each was admirable in his own way beyond the usual. In the second place, all of them participated more directly, and immediately, in our instruction, whether that be academic or otherwise in the course of play or ranch duties."[21] Most students and the unmarried masters lived in the Big House, which with its sleeping porches, classrooms, and administrative offices was the academic heart of Los Alamos Ranch School. "Since we either lived with the boys in the dormitories, or spent hours with them during study periods; since we did everything together, from working on the trails to riding or skiing or what have you, we had a very direct, positive relationship." Harry Walen continued: "We lived and learned together, and nothing was more natural than for a boy to request help and to get it in a casual, masculine fashion."[22] The many boys who flourished under this regime had an unforgettable experience; those who bridled and wanted out had plenty to push against.

But aside from raising kids and taking on support roles, there was little, really, for women to do. Mother's gaiety and lack of pretense lifted spirits. She advised the younger masters like Oscar Steege and Ransom Lynch on affairs of the heart. She drew students out in dinner conversation and with Cec ran a relaxed and popular dorm. In winter she and Fred Rousseau were a sight waltzing together on Douglas Pond, where Cec played ice hockey with the boys. "Virginia, Peggy, and Anita brought imagination, friendship, and a bit of laughter to the mesa," Art Chase recalled. "Even Mr. Connell, who had reservations about women in general, had to admit that they were a remarkable trio."[23] Cec asked A. J. several times to give women a larger role, but it never happened. Women were not even allowed on school rides, including the all-day Saturday horseback ride, until Connell finally relented in the school's last year.

Wives bridled at Connell's controlling presence, each in her various ways. Peggy Church, a serious published poet, was put out with the exclusion of women. For her part, Anita Waring kept the peace between Peggy and A. J. Yet Anita and her husband Tom, fed up with Connell's overbearing ways, left the mesa in 1939 to start a day school of their own in Santa Fe. Virginia, a bright spirit, was able to laugh it off . . . most of the time. Given her background in the mining camps she found Connell's paternalism understandable, but still hard to take.

I got wind of this in the summer of 1941. My parents planned to climb the Black Mesa with Oscar Steege, I believe, and asked me if I wanted to come along. Connell heard about it and advised my mother not to take me because at five, I was just too young. Boiling, she asked me if *I* thought *I* could climb Black Mesa. I said yes and I did, although descending the mesa down a rocky trail in the deep twilight was scary and the hike itself did seem awfully long. Sacred to the pueblos, *Tunyo* (the Tewa name) or *Mesa Huerfana* (the Spanish name) stands by itself east of the Rio Grande and just upriver from Otowi Crossing, where Edith and Tilano lived. It became my symbol of challenge and achievement. With this earlier triumph in mind, in 1959 I proposed to a young woman named Nancy Meem on the top of Black Mesa. To my lasting joy, she said yes. Later still, Nancy's organization—called Cornerstones, Community Partnerships—helped the Vigil family to restore their Pajarito chapel, just across the river from Black Mesa. The Vigils had owned several ranches, including the Ramón Vigil Grant, where Ashley Pond established his Pajarito Club in 1915. Generations of Hispanic families, some with homesteads on the Pajarito Plateau and ties to Los Alamos, have worshiped in this church.

Sometime in the 1970s, Peggy gave me an unpublished poem that she still considered rather subversive. And now with the cultural turn against male chauvinism running full force, she thought I would enjoy it, while teasing me besides. But I also sensed that her giving it to me was something of a test.

That she and A. J. did not cotton up to each other was no secret. Perhaps to spite her, Connell named his little terrier Peggy, which the boys, doubtless loving every bit of it, nicknamed Peggy-dog. And when Mother produced a second male baby, she said, "What are you trying to do? Have as many sons as the Churches? Hope you weren't disappointed it didn't turn out a gal. Or was the old school spirit too much for you after all?"[24]

Reflecting on Connell's legacy a few days after his death in February 1944, she was generous to a fault. To her son Ted, she wrote

You can't help knowing that I differed from him in many ways. Yet when most annoyed at some of his oddities—the ones, of course, which most interfered with my comfort and convenience!—I always realized that he was a really great man. He was more of an influence on my life than my own father. . . . I wish I knew of any other school that stood as firmly as Los Alamos for the real decencies of manhood. I hope you are as grateful for your training there as I am.

What did it all mean? She concluded: "I can't help thinking that somehow those of us who care must see that the ideal that Los Alamos stood for does not die. Somehow we must try to build it up again." After all, when her father's first attempt had been flooded out at Mora, he "kept his vision alive for fifteen years until he was able to put it into effect. Perhaps we should look forward with the same faith and determination." The successor, Los Alamos School in Taos founded by Ferm in 1944, did not, alas, survive. However, her valedictory on Los Alamos endures: "We were all extraordinarily blessed to have lived so long in such surroundings. The way of life was good."[25]

Reflecting on the ranch, I realize that this brief era in the history of the Pajarito, even my own years there from 1936 until almost the end in 1942, is soon to enter the deep past. History happens, and then when firsthand memory fades it becomes history without us, to be reconstructed on the basis of old letters, photos, oral histories, and remnants of the built environment. Change over time is the essence of history, but what does it mean when a time and a

SOME LINES SUGGESTEDKFOR A BOARDING SCHOOL PROSPECTUS

Behold the adolescent boy,
the nascent youth, the budding man.
'Tis now he must be disciplined
and governed by a stable plan.
He sprouts like some ungainly weeĦ,
with food and drink he must be plied.
His greatest needs are those that féed
the biological inside.
Oh stuffĺhim well and shelter him;
a strongĺphysique he must attain;
with rest and lots of exercise
build bone and brawn and blood and brain.

And if he steals away to brood
Oh follow him and bring him back.
'Tis veryhuncooperative
and shows a grave, unmanly lack.
His soul must don our uniform.
No difference will be allowed;
no individualistic trait
to mark him out among the crowd.
He must cɒnform in all his ways.
If he does not, beyond a doubt
this mass-productive stream-lined age
will turn on him and cast him out.

And since the feɓale of all sex
it is which causes tears and strifɐ,
We'll solve the problem here and now
by expurgating it from life.
No bitches may disturb the peace
among our canine population.
No restless mare may here abide
to cause our geldings mild vexation.
And if ourselves should choose to wife
why wives may come and they may sit
in little harmless hennish grupps
apart from us and chat and knit.

For man it is must rule the world
but womanis'hness will not let him.
We'll wall the boy away from it
lest it should here intrude and fret hɱɱ.
No thought that smacks of femiñine,
no dark emotionality
shall threaten here ħis manly mein
nor stir his equanimity.
If he will stay awhile with us
we'll make him into something human
that bears no more the horrid trace
of having once been born of woman.

                              March, 1939

Fig. 9.7

"Some Lines Suggested for a Boarding School Prospectus,"
by Peggy Pond Church. Wirth private collection.

place just vanish, as it did for the Wirths during the Second World War? In personal terms, this double loss of father and of place is something I learned to cope with. Things happen; life goes on.

Yet, to me still, the total shift of context is mind-boggling. Consider that, from the perspective of wartime Los Alamos, as a small boy my having used in our various faculty quarters not one but three of the prized tubs in "Bathtub Row" is an incredible achievement. (On the military post these were the only bathtubs.) Consider also that the gun mechanism for Little Boy (the Hiroshima bomb) was designed by Captain Deke Parsons, the naval officer whose family moved into the Church house after we left; the Oppenheimers lived in the cottage designed and built by A. J. Connell for his sister May, later the Wirth's second house; and the mathematical solution for the hydrogen bomb was conceived by Stanislaw Ulam in Spruce Cottage, where my own existence owes everything to a gleam in my father's eye.

Over the years in her correspondence with Virginia, Peggy tried to fathom the meaning of change. "No, I don't think very often of 'our past'—it does all seem part of another world," she wrote in 1950. "I wonder if ever a people has seen their whole world change so fast. The world we grew up in and even the world we lived our young married lives in just doesn't exist anymore. My feeling about Los Alamos isn't personal any more; it's only a symbol of what has happened to our whole generation. But, with you, I often think how blessed we were to have had what we did."

"If you were still my neighbor," she continues, "I'd have run over this afternoon, I think, and shed a few tears over one of those commonplace female crises that are worth more if shared." She then went on to write about the last grown child leaving home, and wondered what would she do with the next forty years of her life.[26]

With a new life in Denver, Virginia was less engaged although she did pass on a good deal of practical camp lore to Roger A. Sanborn and his wife, Laura, when they started what would soon become the highly successful Sanborn Western Camps and Nature Center behind Pikes Peak in Colorado. On an ocean liner to England in 1949, she shared tales of Los Alamos with Klaus Fuchs, not yet unmasked as a Soviet spy. But, for the most part, she put Los Alamos behind her.

As Peggy became less engagé herself about the loss of her Los Alamos place in later years, the presence of the past weighed differently. "When I hear myself talk about things that happened [at Los Alamos] 'fifty years ago' I feel appalled at how one's own lifetime suddenly becomes 'history,'" she wrote in 1978. "It's interesting that we have this particular slice of life in common and to see how in our different ways we have grown through and around it. Stages of life! When we are in the midst of one of them or another how ignorant we are that stage won't go on forever, and after awhile will dwindle almost into non-existence. Like mountains that become molehills! But oddly they are still part of what we are."[27]

Although Virginia did not really think of herself as part of the old guard, she and the others did not have much more time. "The pull of Santa Fe comes over me in spasms of yearning," Virginia replied to a letter from Hitch in 1981. "I guess one never gets over having lived in New Mexico." Then, "I think of you today as I transplant lovely white iris in my tiny garden plot, and remember you lovingly and laboriously transplanting iris all along the paths at Los Alamos."[28] She passed Hitch's letter on to Peggy.

Los Alamos came up again in letters exchanged near the end of their active lives. As Peggy wrote in 1984: "Here's a copy of the poem you wanted. . . . I've read the LETTER [to Virginia] quite often when giving talks or poetry readings about the 'early days at Los Alamos,' and it sometimes makes me cry."[29] This poem, one of her best, is about personal loss, coupled with the loss of

Fig. 9.8

LARS master Jerry Pepper with John Wirth's dog Tor, fall 1942.
Courtesy Los Alamos Historical Museum Archives.

place. To capture a more collective sense of loss, sometimes she shared only the first stanza in her public readings.

The piercing lance of memory opens the way for understanding. It happened to me this way: Leaving my dog Tor behind, I was consoled by the knowledge that Tor was serving his country in the K-9 corps, although I somewhat suspected this story might be Mother's way of making me feel better. Knowing this about Tor, in my imagination he then became another symbol for dealing with discontinuity and dislocation. In due course—fifty-five years later, in fact—I learned from Esilda and Jerry Pepper, the math teacher who followed my

Fig. 9.9

Tor in the K-9 Corps, 1943. Courtesy of Jerry and Esilda Pepper.

CHAPTER NINE

father, what really happened to Tor. It was the Peppers who inherited Tor from me, and they soon bonded with him. All went well until Los Alamos was "terminated (exterminated?)," as Peggy would say. The Peppers stayed on to manage the army's recreation program, including a new golf course, but they had to vacate their school cottage for Robert and Kitty Oppenheimer. Jerry and Esilda found quarters in one of the Sundt's, but Tor could not adjust to apartment living. Accustomed to roaming the mesa at will, and now confined and miserably unhappy, Tor reacted by biting a boy in the building who was teasing him relentlessly. Now, as I remember, this was one smart collie dog and biting that kid was assuredly a rational act. But the animal control people thought otherwise and told the Peppers that Tor had to go, even from his much, much reduced territory. And so he really was enlisted in the K-9 corps. The army trainers sent word of Tor's progress to the Peppers, including photos and a certificate of graduation. Tor saw duty in the South Pacific.

In memory of this good and faithful dog, and in gratitude to the Peppers and to him for his companionship and service to our country, I have enrolled Tor at the new World War II Memorial in Washington, D.C. If the organizers have a category for dogs in the K-9 corps, Tor is on it. But if not, he's listed in with everyone else who served: one great dog.

Conclusion

A Sense of Place

In 1943, the life of Los Alamos Ranch, which was both a community and a school, was over. This Los Alamos is remembered for its impact on the lives of those who lived there—students, faculty, the support staff, and their children—for its contributions to the social history of New Mexico, and for its role in American education. To recuperate this history is to reach beyond nostalgia and regrets to grasp the life and meaning of a good and special place. To do so, however, is also to recognize inescapably that this history is forever associated in the minds of most people with what came next: the Manhattan Project and the Los Alamos National Laboratory (LANL). To be sure, the Ranch School years are real enough in the minds of those who knew this place; and although the place they knew is in a sense long gone, they do not see their lives as some sort of prelude to the bomb. Searching for deeper meanings, the Ranch School years are perhaps better seen through another optic, a longer focus that draws out the rhythms of overlay and juxtaposition that have occurred for centuries on the Pajarito Plateau. Indeed, to follow this pathway is to explore the multiple meanings of place.

Symbolically, the Ranch School years are bracketed by the burials on the mesa of two young masters. Fayette Curtis, the first headmaster, died at the ranch from the debilitating effects of tuberculosis in November 1926. At his request, Fay was buried by the faculty and students on the rim of Pueblo Canyon, in an unmarked grave. A room in Fuller Lodge was named after him. The gravesite of Cecil Wirth (who died of cancer in April 1943) at the end of Los Alamos Mesa is also unmarked. Although military security was already tight at Otowi Hill, A. J. Connell pulled strings so that Cecil's ashes could rest on what was then still Forest Service land. These two young men loved Los Alamos; there, they became accomplished teachers, brought young wives, and lived life to the full. Connell himself departed the ranch in February, never to return; he aged rapidly and died unhappy and discouraged one year later. He had wanted to be buried at Los Alamos, but by 1944, due to security concerns and the change of ownership, it was impossible to comply, so Connell lies in the Albuquerque family plot instead of on the Pajarito Plateau and the Jemez country he loved. As firsthand memory fades, Connell, who shaped a school, a garden spot, and a community into being at Los Alamos, casts no shadow over what was once his unquestioned domain.

On leave from army duty to speak at the last LARS graduation at Fuller Lodge that January, Lawrence S. Hitchcock, the classicist headmaster, took his theme from Pericles's funeral oration to the Athenians. Now that LARS was closed, he said, it would be remembered not for the monuments left behind, but as an exemplar of an educational ideal that inspired its students and would endure. Yet the deeds to come in this place would soon change the world, transforming Los Alamos into what the historian Richard Rhodes has called "one of the world's most significant historical sites."[1] In light of this transcendence, Curtis's scholarly article entitled "The Influence of Weapons on New Mexico History" was prescient.[2]

The first atomic bomb was tested successfully near Alamogordo in July 1945, and this achievement—something utterly new—hastened the end of World War II. Arguably, weapons developed at LANL since then have demonstrably kept the peace between the major powers for more than half a century. Was there anything in the social reality of Los Alamos at war and afterward that related remotely to the Ranch School years evoked by Lawrence Hitchcock?

Consider that different social realities have long been conjoined in the complexities of this place. Los Alamos, the school and ranch, like Los Alamos, the town and national laboratory that supplanted it, were both set in an Indian and Hispanic place. For hundreds of years forebears of the Tewa-speaking pueblo Indians at Santa Clara and San Ildefonso lived on the plateau. Hispanic herdsmen and dry-land subsistence farmers filtered in during the eighteenth century, but their presence in the Jemez was contested by Apaches and Navajo raiders for many years until the American occupation of New Mexico. Signs of these peoples abound: in their ruins, their sacred places, their place-names.

Moreover, each Los Alamos in its way was defined by a chain of connections to the outside world. The school was linked to corporate and professional families, mostly well-to-do Midwesterners from such places as Grosse Point, Chicago, and St. Louis, as well as New Yorkers and a sprinkling of West

Coasters. Their sons went to LARS to develop character and physical strength in a vigorous outdoor program, while learning the academic skills to enter the nation's leading universities. Living in harmony and respect for the other cultures on the Pajarito Plateau, LARS could not be characterized, simply, as an Anglo enclave.

Starting in 1943, the scientists who built the atomic bomb forged powerful bonds between their academic research, government, the military, and the universities. For those mostly very young scientists and engineers who met the extraordinary intellectual challenge of this project, their months at Los Alamos were suffused with excitement under pressure, and then the results were crowned with a sense of mastery and achievement, and for more than a few, foreboding. For recreation in the closely guarded military camp, they hiked and rode horseback on Ranch School trails; skied near Camp May; dined, danced, and held theatricals in Fuller Lodge. The lucky few with priority lived in the masters' cottages, dubbed "Bathtub Row." Built at breakneck speed, the military post with its muddy roads, isolation, and restrictions is not remembered with affection. Yet for these Americans at war, it was now their turn to thrill to the Pajarito's beauty. The high birthrate was another artifact of their creation. And their children recall the special qualities of growing up under unusual conditions in a special place.[3]

The Ranch School was so special it could not be reproduced, as the two failed attempts to do so after the war bore out, and as A. J. Connell himself concluded, even when offered an alternative site for the school to continue at the old Sunmount Sanitorium in Santa Fe. The wartime scientific laboratory was so special that it could be reproduced. What has been called "the spirit of cooperation, commitment, and wholeness that had permeated the wartime laboratories, that of Los Alamos in particular," was recreated after the war at Argonne, Brookhaven, and Livermore. Los Alamos was the primary model for something really new: the clustering of large numbers of creative people to do science and engineering projects in the national interest. Not only did postwar Los Alamos receive the lion's share of federal funds, but also Lab Director Norris Bradbury broadened its charter to include basic, intellectually stimulating research not geared necessarily toward weapons.[4]

Today's Los Alamos resonates to the cultural heartbeat of a largely Anglo, middle-class America, its town looking more like California than New Mexico. However, just as the school in its day was an important source of jobs for Hispanic and Pueblo families, so Los Alamos under government control has acted as a catalyst for change in northern New Mexico by employing thousands of people from surrounding communities.[5] In historical perspective, the earlier hamlet at Los Alamos Ranch was a diverse community; the current city of Los Alamos is seemingly still searching for ways to achieve a more diversified community.

Yet the town's central core of historic school buildings is a reminder of the simpler, more tasteful aesthetic of the Ranch School. The Big House is gone, demolished in 1949 to make way for the town's first shopping center. When the Trading Post was razed two years later, the Santa Fe paper lamented that "another link with the Hill's historic past, one of the original ranch school structures, [has been] broken."[6] However, Fuller Lodge remains the focal point of community life, a source of inspiration and continuity amidst great change. One of America's heritage log buildings, the Lodge has been lovingly preserved. After the war, the first subdivision was laid out on what had been the western fields, donated by Connell to Los Alamos Ranch for one dollar. Houses there are still prized for their original wooden flooring, a first at post-war Los Alamos. Camp May, the school's alpine cabin, crumbled away in the 1970s, although its stone fireplace is preserved in a picnic shelter. Today the picnic area of that name anchors the northwest corner of the ski area. And the log house near the Lodge, which was occupied for many years by Floyd Womelsduff, the ranch mechanic, and his family, may become the gateway interpretative center for visitors on their way to the old Baca Location, now under federal ownership as the Valles Caldera National Preserve. Ironically, if in the 1920s and 1930s Connell and the Forest Service had not mobilized opposition to the proposed Cliff Cities National Park, the history of Los Alamos might have been very different. Recall that it was the availability of Forest Service land, about 90 percent of the projected military reservation, that greatly facilitated the takeover, something that a national park with established public access would surely have precluded. In 2000 the Baca Ranch finally passed into federal ownership, a national treasure for future generations to enjoy, as the Ranch School in its time did.

Another irony is that the idea of selecting Los Alamos for the site to perfect and craft nuclear weapons owes much, perhaps more, to Percival Keith, a Ranch School parent, than it does to Oppenheimer and Groves. As a senior manager at the Kellog Corporation, Keith played a leading role in the Manhattan Project, and it was because of the links LARS had to corporate America that Keith can be seen as the historical agent who fused the two worlds of Los Alamos.

To be sure, the ranch under Connell was like a company town in which the Boss, if not always right in fact, was always in control. He saw Los Alamos as his school, his creation, his ideal, and brooked no interference. Younger men like Art Chase and Cecil Wirth felt that he was not open enough to change, and indeed A. J. sometimes stifled their good ideas just to validate his control.

For example, when Wirth wanted to build a rope tow on the Sawyer Mesa ski hill, "I told him nothing doing for the duration. [The boys] will make better soldiers if they climb up the hill." Mr. Connell "was very much in charge, [and] with all his moods, was something we had to deal with," Oscar Steege recalled. Why did the masters stomach such an autocrat? After 1943 the bureaucratic hand of government was often frustrating, and not just to the most creative scientific minds. When asked today, "Why do you put up with it, when opportunities for creative work beckon elsewhere?" the answer often involves a tradeoff that the masters and their wives would have appreciated. "Because living and working in this beautiful place is most definitely a consideration." Or, in Oscar's words: "despite Connell, we were really thrilled with the place."[7]

Nature, as well as culture, defines the sense of place. Consider that well before the short life of LARS the forests surrounding the ranch were going through the changes that threaten today's Los Alamos with catastrophic fire. The forest that burned in the Cerro Grande fire in 2000 had its origins in the coming of the railroad in the 1880s, which opened the Pajarito Plateau to large-scale sheep grazing and lumbering. Nature's pattern of periodic, low intensity fires was abated by heavy grazing, which, in turn, when the sheep and cattle were taken off in the 1930s, permitted the buildup of underbrush and young trees that fuel today's eruptive crown fires. Concurrently, the policy of fire suppression begun in the 1910s exacerbated this break in the natural cycle of fire and recovery. Today the forest is simply too dense and overgrown, something that the conservation-minded inhabitants of the ranch never thought about. In short, there is now "a tree epidemic" on the Pajarito.[8]

A comparison of aerial photographs of the Pajarito Plateau taken in 1935 and 1981 shows a region heavily impacted by postwar road building. Logging roads snake through the Jemez backcountry once mainly accessible by horse trails.[9] Yet the isolation in Connell's day was already somewhat of an illusion, due to the penetration of automobiles. For two or three generations before that, woodcutters and homesteaders had cut numerous wagon trails through the area. And for hundreds of years before that, the region had been knit together by Indian trails. Nonetheless, old-timers were aghast when the once-daunting switchbacks up Otowi Hill were eliminated at General Groves's directive. "I can't visualize a three lane highway to Los Alamos—and I resent it," a Forest Service officer, now in uniform, wrote in 1944. "Nobody has any right to put a highway up on Pajarito!"[10] For many years after the war the highway was in fact two-lane, but it was paved to accommodate heavy trucks and a much larger flow of people. Five lanes traverse Culebra Hill today, and indeed this place name (like Otowi Hill) has passed out of use.

Or consider the overlay of landscapes, as, for example, the differences in trail maps from Ranch School days and the maps today. Routes on school maps lead outward through Indian and Hispanic lands, through the Baca Location, and on to the San Pedro Peaks, whereas today's trail maps feature day hikes within a much shorter radius of the town. As well, mountain bikes, not horses, are much more likely to transit this landscape today. In his excellent *Los Alamos Trails,* Craig Martin lists the old school trails, but notes that access has now been shut off to some Pueblo lands.[11] The good news is that historic trails that have crossed Los Alamos mesa and the Pajarito for generations and some of their ancestral names are being recuperated by the Los Alamos Pathways Association. Soon an interconnected trail system will be available. Moreover, Los Alamos will once again become a gateway to the former Baca Ranch, which is a natural metaphor for the overlay of cultural landscapes in the Jemez.

This overlay of landscapes is captured beautifully by Don Usner, in *Sabino's Map.* Having grown up in Los Alamos, Usner has family roots in the traditional community of Chimayó, which overlays an earlier Indian landscape with Tewa names. Each working day the Chimayosos race down the road to Española, and on to Los Alamos, where they are part of the large Hispanic workforce from northern New Mexico drawing paychecks from the Los Alamos Laboratory. In *The House at Otowi Bridge: The Story of Edith Warner and Los Alamos,* Peggy Pond Church describes exceptionally well the landscape at San Ildefonso Pueblo. Edith's place was a cultural crossroads well known to LARS and then to the first scientists at Los Alamos.[12] Recently, Santa Clara Pueblo has reclaimed from the Baca Ranch ancestral lands at the headwaters (*P'opii Khanu* in Tewa) of Santa Clara Canyon. In their time, Los Alamos summer campers pitched tents at the Rito del Indio nearby, and took the Skyline Trail to Chicoma, highest point in the Jemez and sacred to the Pueblos.

Starting in 1943, Los Alamos drifted apart from Santa Fe. This was painful, especially since Santa Feans were fond of the Ranch School. It was Connell's experience leading a Scout troop in Santa Fe (and his Forest Service ties) that first recommended him to Ashley Pond. Having designed a house for Pond on Santa Fe's Palace Avenue, the fledgling architect John Gaw Meem gained entrée to Los Alamos and became the Ranch School architect. Attracted to designing what he thought would be a much larger project, the army flying school at Roswell, he turned down the initial war-contract work at Los Alamos and was never to work there again, although in the 1970s he supported petitions to save the Lodge and to retain some of its grounds, at that time being encroached upon for such things as a new post office, roads, and a business center. In 1975 the fledgling Colorado congressman Tim Wirth, Cecil's son, was enlisted by local preservationists to help in the effort to reclaim nine

Navajo rugs taken from Fuller Lodge (now owned and run by the county) to grace the Atomic Energy Commission's new Resource Study Center—but to no avail.[13] For her part, the poet Peggy Church, appalled at the slipping away and mispronunciation of place-names, would begin her Los Alamos poetry readings by asking the audience to repeat after her: "Ōtowi, Ōtowi, Ōtowi." Sufficiently warmed up, her listeners might be less inclined to confuse the pronunciation of this Pajarito place with the capital of Canada.

Socially, the school had been incorporated into Santa Fe. All this changed abruptly with the Manhattan Project, when hundreds, then thousands of newcomers with little or no prior connection to Santa Fe flooded up to what they called "the Hill." A one-industry company town developed and with it a cultural gap that has been slow to close. In 1943, two offices in Santa Fe were worlds apart. In the Bishop Building, Connell and Rousseau worked on closing down the school's accounts. In the historic Sena Plaza, Dorothy McKibbin began offering her celebrated warm welcome to the stream of bewildered newcomers on their way up to Site Y on the mesa. For all Santa Feans knew, Dorothy's office could have been the closet into Narnia.

Lieutenant Colonel Whitney Ashbridge, the second post commander and an early LARS student in 1918–1919, was one of the few remaining links with the ranch during the war years. The Arts and Crafts Building was remodeled to accommodate him and another family. With the significant exception of Bences Gonzales and his family, few of the old Ranch School employees stayed on. Jerry Pepper managed the post-recreation program during the war and he and Bences reconstituted Troop 22, which still uses the LARS logo on its shoulder patch. As mentioned, former master Oscar Steege taught briefly in the high school after the war, as did Joan Rousseau, daughter of the business manager. Both were shocked by the highly degraded central core; having known a different place, they could not go home again. However, Hup Wallis, who taught math and science at LARS from 1938 to 1940, did return to teach in both the high school and the junior high school in the early 1950s before working at Sandia Laboratories in Albuquerque as an engineer.

Richard Womelsduff returned from Santa Fe to work at Los Alamos; later, Dorothy McKibbin told him about a job opening at Sandia Lab, where he worked for many years, some of them reporting to Ted Church, 1943. Architect David Hughes, 1937, returned in the 1950s to work on the Laboratory headquarters building, located across Los Alamos Canyon on what had been Donaciano Gomez's bean ranch—"Shorty's bean ranch" the boys called it, a nearby destination for one of their Thursday afternoon rides. John Reed, who attended LARS in 1932–1933, became president of the Santa Fe Railroad, which, for a time, owned the Zia Company, contractor for postwar Los Alamos. For his part, Sterling Colgate, 1943, relocated permanently in Los Alamos, becoming a senior physicist at LANL, the one who still skis like the wind down trails near old Camp May.

Moreover, the passage of years and the development of new institutions has helped to refound relationships—the Santa Fe Opera, started in 1956 by John O. Crosby (a LARS student in 1940–1941), and the Santa Fe Institute for the study of complex systems, begun in 1988 by George A. Cowan, a prize-winning physicist from LANL. Just as the opera has drawn Los Alamos opera lovers to Santa Fe, so too exposure to some of the brightest scientific minds at the Institute, through lectures and symposia, has attracted Santa Feans. The outpouring of assistance by Santa Feans to Los Alamos families burned out in the Cerro Grande fire is likely to give a strong impetus for closer ties. And as both communities struggle to adapt to nature's limits in terms of water and forests, and as they also grapple with complex growth issues, they share a common interest in preserving and protecting landscapes in the greater community of northern New Mexico.

Fig. 10.1

Charles Ripley and Jim Anderson, camp counselors, 1939.
Courtesy of William Carson.

As of current writing, the national laboratory and Los Alamos have been challenged by fire, security concerns, environmental problems left over from the war and after, and an ambiguous shift in mission partially away from basic research to more emphasis on maintaining the nation's nuclear weapons. That, with few exceptions, the Laboratory has not become the incubator to start-up companies in northern New Mexico is curious and differentiates it from a university like Stanford, which sparked the growth of Silicon Valley. On the other hand, research in such areas as climate change, materials science, and the human genome has produced important contributions to knowledge. For the town of Los Alamos itself, LANL's complex role and uncertain future complicates its search for a more diverse economic base, not to mention a more diverse community.[14]

Our history of the Los Alamos Ranch School portrays a beautiful place, which was of course the physical forerunner to the current place, now much different. Los Alamos Ranch was tastefully designed, whereas (in all candor) the town of Los Alamos itself is neither well designed nor very tasteful. Yet, just as the generations before them, people living on the Pajarito today are inspired by the glorious views and the landscape. Los Alamos Ranch School was, and isn't. Yet the beauty and sense of community at the Ranch still inspire. And, when all is said and done, its legacy is but one thin layer down in the overlapping histories of the Pajarito Plateau.

Appendix

Salute to Lawrence Hitchcock

MAGISTER, LAURENTI HITCHCOCK, OPTIME DOCTISSIMEQUE, HIS
SALUTATIONIBUS NOS, TUI DISCIPULI, TIBI MAXIMAM HONOREM
FACERE VOLUNT. NON EST OMNIBUS HABERE EXEMPLUM ERUDI-
TIONIS PRAECLARAE TE EXCELLENTIS DOCTRINAE CONIUNCTAE
HUMANITATI BENEVOLENTIAEQUE EXIMIAE. NOBIS ADULESCEN-
TIBUS, TE MAGISTRO, FORTUNA FAVIT; TU ORBILIUS NON ERAS, SED
IN REBUS MALIS ADITU FACILI ET IN REBUS SECUNDIS FAUTAR
BENIGNUS. TIBI PRO MERITIS TANTIS GRATIAS MAXIMUA AGIMUS.

Master Lawrence Hitchcock, finest of men and most learned, your students
wish to do you the greatest honor. It is not the lot of everyone to have such an
example of outstanding erudition and remarkable instruction joined with
humanity and remarkable benevolence. Fortune favored us youths under your
instruction; you were no Orbilius but in difficulty easy to approach and in
good fortune a kindly supporter. To you for such services we give you the greatest thanks.[1]

Los Alamos Ranch School Song[2]

Hio, we sing of the mountains
Hio, we sing of the school we love
Far away and high on the mesa's crest
Here's the life that all of us love the best
Los Alamos.

Hio, we sing of the forest green
Hio, we sing of the canyon deep
Blue are skies far over the winding trail
Fleet our steeds that gallop o'er hill and dale
Los Alamos.

Hio, we sing of the sunshine
Hio, we sing of the silver peaks
Flashing bright the trout in the crystal streams
Through the night our flickering campfire gleams
Los Alamos.

Hio, we sing of the happy days
Hio, we sing of the days of joy
Winter days as we skim o'er the ice and snow
Summer days when the balsam breezes blow
Los Alamos.

Hio, we sing of the youth time
Hio, we sing of the open sky
Ever true to Los Alamos we shall be
Pledge anew forever our loyalty
Los Alamos.

Hio, for the sunsets glowing rose
Hio, for the glorious opal dawn
Pueblo land of the caveman vanished long
Mystic land hear the echo of our song
Los Alamos.

Horses in the Ranch School Inventory, 1942[3]

Type	Name	Color	Age
Saddle Mare	Benigna	Chestnut Sorrel	17
Saddle Horse	Laddie	Black	16
Saddle Horse	Rabbit	Bay	12
Saddle Horse	Coal Dust	Black	6
Saddle Horse	Chile	Light Sorrel	17
Saddle Horse	Largo	Blue Roan	11
Saddle Horse	Donaciano	Dark Brown	21
Saddle Horse	Chromo	Dark Bay	9
Saddle Horse	Bunny	Dark Brown	21
Saddle Horse	Navajo	Red and White Pinto	9
Saddle Horse	Cacahuate	Dark Bay	16
Saddle Horse	Hot Shot	Sorrel	20
Saddle Horse	Alfredo	Chestnut Sorrel	11
Saddle Horse	Bob	Iron Gray	10
Saddle Horse	Skeeter	Bay	12
Saddle Horse	Colt	Dark Brown	3
Saddle Horse	Smoky	Gray	18
Saddle Horse	Chico	Sorrel	13
Saddle Horse	Leo	Sorrel	18
Saddle Horse	Senator	Dark Bay	12
Saddle Horse	Billie	Bay	16
Saddle Horse	Jemez	Gray	23
Saddle Mare	Jicarilla	Black	20
Saddle Horse	Rusty	Strawberry Roan	20
Saddle Horse	Tamaqua	Brown & White Paint	8
Saddle Horse	Lucky	Palomino	10
Saddle Horse	Ribbon	Black	11
Saddle Horse	Choriado	Strawberry Roan	17
Saddle Horse	Blanco	Gray	17
Saddle Horse	Armijo	Strawberry Roan	14
Saddle Horse	Nogal	Dark Bay	14
Saddle Horse	Indio	Bay	10
Saddle Horse	Blackbird	Black	18
Saddle Horse	Alazan	Chestnut Sorrel	12
Saddle Horse	Circle	Chestnut Sorrel	21
Saddle Horse	Ashley	Black	21
Saddle Horse	Nig	Black	16
Saddle Horse	Roaney	Strawberry Roan	14
Saddle Horse	Blue Foot	Black	16
Saddle Horse	Pajarito	Bay	13
Saddle Horse	Toney	Chestnut Sorrel	12

Horses in the Ranch School Inventory, 1942 *continued*

Type	*Name*	*Color*	*Age*
Saddle Horse	Cochiti	Bay	13
Saddle Horse	Miguel	Dun	6
Saddle Horse	Pecos	Dark Brown	21
Saddle Horse	Spider	Black	21
Saddle Horse	Obsidian	Black	10
Saddle Horse	Raton	Black	14
Saddle Horse	Black Jack	Black	9
Saddle Horse	Fidel	Buckskin	6
Saddle Horse	Two-Bits	Bay	15
Saddle Horse	Frijoles	Red and White	12
Saddle Horse	Joaquin	Dark Sorrel	6
Saddle Horse	General	Bay	12
Saddle Horse	Dandy	Dark Brown	10
Saddle Horse	Blue	Gray	19
Saddle Horse	Santos	Bay	14
Saddle Horse	Mutt	Dark Brown	10
Work Mare	May	Gray	15
Work Horse	Blue	Dark Gray	20
Work Horse	Queen	Bay	11

Biographies of the Los Alamos Masters

LARS indicates service at Los Alamos; * signifies a core faculty member.[4]

Baker, Cecil Sherman, Jr. (1906–1987): B.A. University of Arizona, 1934, PBK. Attended Princeton, 1929, and Jefferson Medical College, each for a year but withdrew from each because of illness.

U.S. Army, 1942–1943. Teacher, Kingman, Ariz., schools for fifteen years. Wrote articles for *Natural History* and *Frontier Magazine*. Designed and made artificial limbs for the handicapped. Plagued by long-term health problems. His second wife, Louise Maxwell, earned Connell's admiration for being an avid tennis player even though she had only one leg.

LARS: April–June 1942. Taught English and French. Replaced Bernard Rogers, who was drafted.

*Bosworth, Henry Burt "Boz" (1899–1971): B.S. Cornell, 1921; M.F. in Forestry, Cornell, 1922.

U.S. Army, Second Lieutenant, 1918–1919. U.S. Forest Service: Bland and Silver City, N.M., 1922–1925; Assistant Supervisor of the Tropical Region, USFS, in Rio Puedras, 1937–, then Director of the Tropical Region in Puerto Rico, 1950s.

LARS: 1925–1930. Secretary to A. J. Connell for short period in 1925. Taught math 1925–1930. Camp staff, 1925. In charge of Spruce Cottage. His sister Charlotte lived at the Ranch for several months; she and Lawrence Hitchcock were a couple.

Bradner, Leicester "Les" (1899–1988): B.A. 1920; M.A. 1923; Ph.D. 1926, all at Yale.

Instructor of English at Union College, 1924–1925. Instructor; Professor of English at Brown University, 1926–1968. A frequent publisher in his field, especially the Renaissance in England.

LARS: January–June 1921, replacing Henry Ruhl. Taught English and history. Yale college roommate and lifelong friend of Lawrence Hitchcock after whom a son was named.

*Chase, Arthur Carleton "Art" (1908–1991): B.A. Harvard, 1929, cum laude; M.A. Yale, 1938.

Taught at University of Munich, 1932. U.S. Navy, Lt. Commander. Teacher at Berkshire School 1938–1970s; Director of Studies, Assistant Headmaster of the Berkshire School. Town Selectman, Sheffield, Mass..

LARS: 1929–1937. Taught English, Latin, chemistry, math, and history. Summer Camp staff 1930–1932. Supervised the Koshares, student drama group. Associate Camp Director, 1937–1941.

*Church, Fermor Spencer "Ferm" (1900–1975): B.S. Harvard, 1921; graduate studies in geology at Harvard and Stanford.

Harvard unit, Students' Army Training Corps, 1918. Teacher, Cate School, 1943–1944. Founder and Director of the Los Alamos School in Taos, 1944–1945. Teacher, Taos public schools. Staff, Philmont Scout Ranch. Assistant to manager of Kit Carson REA. Field

Engineer, designing power line and substations for rural electric cooperatives in the Southwest. Founding member, New Mexico Citizens for Clean Air and Water.

LARS: 1921–1943. Taught math and science. Registrar, 1933–1935. Acting Headmaster, 1935–1936, 1942–1943. Assistant Headmaster, 1937–1941. Summer Camp staff, 1923–1925, 1927, 1929–1930, 1942. Justice of the Peace, Sandoval County, 1926–1942. Board of the Los Alamos Foundation, 1940–1973. Church married Margaret (Peggy), the eldest daughter of Ashley Pond, founder of the School. Their three sons grew up at Los Alamos: Ted, LARS 1943; Allen, Los Alamos School, 1945; and Hugh. Ferm and Peggy were both active in Gilbert and Sullivan productions at LARS.

Cobb, Richard Neil (1911–1979): B.A. Bowdoin College, 1932; M.A. Harvard, 1933; postgraduate studies Lehigh University 1936–1939, 1954–1955.

Math Instructor, Williston Academy, 1934. Teaching fellow in math and physics, Bowdoin College, 1934–1935; graduate assistant in math, Lehigh University, 1936–1939. Math teacher at Deering High in Portland, Maine, 1939–1945. Instructor, professor, Sinclair professor of math at Worcester Polytechnic Institute, 1946–1976.

LARS: 1935–1936. Taught math.

Connell, Mary K. "May" (1884–1971): Academy of the Sacred Heart (later Manhattanville College), New York City.

Music teacher, Brownmoor School for Girls, Santa Fe, 1930s. Artist, Santa Fe.

LARS: 1930. Taught voice, music appreciation, and art.

*Curtis, Fayette Samuel Jr. "Fay" (1896–1926): B.A. Yale, 1918. Historian and translator.

LARS: 1918–1926. Taught all classes. First Headmaster. Served as Justice of the Peace, Santa Fe and Sandoval Counties, 1918–1926. Editor, *NM Historical Review*. Died of recurrent tuberculosis, leaving his wife of six months, Rosa Margaret "Daisy" Curtis.

Diaz, Manuel C. (?–?): B.A. University of Cincinnati, 1937. M.S. University of Chicago. From Merida, Mexico?

Before coming to Los Alamos had been with Sylvanus Morley at the School of American Research in Yucatan, as his secretary. Teacher, Los Alamos School, Taos, 1945. Taos Summer Camp, 1945.

LARS: 1942–1943. Taught Spanish and biology.

French, Robert H. (1914–2000): B.A. Princeton, 1936. Captain of the baseball team. LL.D. Yale Law School, 1940.

U.S. Army, 82d Airborne Division, 1942–1946, Captain. Legal Department, Celanese Corp, 1947–1949. President, Canada Dry Bottling Company of Dayton and Cincinnati, 1950–1963. Financial services, 1964–1968. Shearson American Express, 1970–1983.

LARS: 1936–1937. Taught math.

Geehern, Richard J. (1921–1997): B.A. Harvard, 1942; graduate work in Education, 1945–1946; Ph.D. in English, University of North Carolina.

U.S. Army Air Corps. Faculty, Lehman College, City University of New York.

LARS: 1942–1943. Taught English and history.

Heald, George Edgar (1904–1977): B.A. Amherst, 1927. Graduate studies at the University of Kansas, where he also taught.

Math teacher, Cushing Academy. Town Alderman, Ashburnham, Mass.. Manager of Naukeage Farm in Ashburnham. Grange official.

LARS: 1930–1931. Taught math and Latin.

*****Hitchcock, Lawrence Sill "Hitch"** (1898–1983): B.A. Yale, 1919, PBK; graduate work in Classics at Yale, 1926, 1935–1936, receiving his M.A. in 1936. Summer study at University of Chicago, 1929, 1937, 1938. American School for Classical Studies in Rome, 1930.

Harvard Unit, U.S. Army Training Corps, 1918; U.S. Army Reserves, 1919–1941. Colonel, U.S. Army: Secretary General, Inter-American Defense Board, 1942–1947. Central Intelligence Agency, 1947–1964: Latin America unit; Administrator, supervised construction of CIA headquarters at Langley. Certificate of Merit with Distinction.

LARS: 1919–1943. Taught all courses but mostly Latin. Headmaster 1927–1943. Treasurer, 1938–1943. Summer Camp staff, 1921–1922, 1926, 1928. Board Member, Los Alamos Foundation, 1940–1973.

Hope, Quentin M. (1923–). B.A. magna cum laude, 1942; M.A., 1946, both at Harvard. Ph.D. Columbia, 1956.

American Field Service during World War II. Teacher, Elisabeth Irwin High School (The Little Red Schoolhouse), 1946–1952. Instructor, Wesleyan University, 1953–1956. Professor of French and Italian, Indiana University, 1956–1988. A frequent publisher in his field.

LARS: August–December, 1942. Taught French and English. Left at end of 1942, replaced by Esilda Pepper.

Jenney, Charles Jr. (1905–1984): B.A. Harvard, 1926. Graduate studies at the University of Toulouse, the American Academy in Rome, and Harvard.

U.S. Navy, Lt. Commander. Classics teacher, Belmont Hill School, 1927–1982. Assistant Headmaster, and interim Headmaster, 1965. Award winning author of Latin textbooks, written with Rogers Scudder, 1929.

LARS: 1926–1927. Taught Latin and history. Summer Camp Staff, 1929.

Kinney, Charles M. (1884–1944): B.A. State College at Amherst. Student of Nadia Boulanger at the American Conservatory in Fontainebleau.

Taught ten years at the Francis Parker School in Chicago, head of the music department. Director of music for ten years at the Lincoln School for Teachers, New York. Director, music program of the Museum of New Mexico, 1937–1943, and Brownmoor School for Girls, Santa Fe.

LARS: 1937–1942. Taught music appreciation, instrumental music, and piano.

Lynch, Ransom VanBrunt (1915–): B.S. magna cum laude, 1937; MAT, 1947, both at Harvard.

U.S. Navy, 1941–1946. Phillips Exeter Academy, instructor in mathematics and Wentworth Professor, 1939–1984; special instructor 1984–1987, 1990. Visiting Professor of Mathematics, University of New Hampshire, 1987–1990. Author of *First Course in Calculus* and coauthor of several mathematics textbooks.

LARS: 1937–1939. Taught math and science. Summer Camp staff, 1941.

Mills, William Elligood, Jr. (1900–1977): A.B. Harvard, 1922, cum laude; graduate studies in history at the Sorbonne; LL.B. Harvard, 1928.

Harvard Unit, Army Training Corps, 1918. Lawyer, partner, Boyd and Holbrook, in New York City. By the 1970s he was a committed conservationist, on the board of environmental organizations.

LARS: 1922–1923. English, French and history. It was Mills who named the old duck pond "Ashley Pond."

Newman, Henry L. "Heb" (1908–1967): LARS Graduate, 1927. B.A. Williams College, 1931.

Teacher, Fountain Valley School, 1934–1966; Assistant Headmaster.

LARS: 1932–1934. Taught math and history. Summer Camp Staff, 1928–1932.

Nicholas, Edward Mithoff Jr. "Caesar" (1907–1996): LARS graduate, 1925. B.A. Princeton, 1929. Graduate studies at Cambridge University.

Ohio real estate interests. Historian and author; rancher in Roswell, N.M.

LARS: September–December 1934. Taught Latin. Having been a boy patient at Sunmount Sanitorium, he was a recovered tubercular while a LARS student from 1921–1925.

Otto, William R. (1904–1946): B.A. Harvard, 1927. BST, Virginia Episcopal Theological Seminary, 1933.

Episcopal priest. Dean of the Cathedral, Phoenix.

LARS: 1927–1929. Taught English.

Page, Warren K. "Lefty" (1910–1977): B.A. Harvard, 1931; star pitcher on the baseball team.

U.S. Navy, aerial gunnery instructor. English teacher, Lawrenceville School, where he coached skeet shooting, 1936–1942. After the war he was for twenty-four years gun editor for *Field and Stream*. Founding president, National Shooting Sports Foundation.

LARS: 1932–1936. Taught English.

Peery, Okel Cleo (1908–1986): B.A. University of New Mexico; M.A., University of Colorado.

Teacher, Hickman County, Tennessee, and Metropolitan public schools in Tennessee.

LARS: 1942–1943. Taught history and Latin.

Pepper, Esilda Beauchamp (1914–): B.A. St Mary's in the Springs (Ohio Dominican College), 1936.

Taught high school in Florida for one year. After leaving Los Alamos, taught fifth grade in Milford, Conn., for twenty-five years.

LARS: for two weeks in 1943, taught French, replacing Quentin Hope. Aside from May Connell, she was the one female instructor in the history of the Ranch School.

Pepper, Jerry R. (1909–2000): B.A. Fordham University; star baseball player.

Director of recreational program for the Los Alamos Manhattan Project, 1943–1945. Before coming to LARS he taught math, science, and French at Milford Academy in Connecticut, and returned to Milford after the war, becoming Headmaster. Later on the staff of Gompers Magnet School, San Diego.

LARS: 1942–1943. Taught math and science, replacing Cecil Wirth.

Petrizzi, Ralph (1915–): B.A. Middlebury College, 1939, and graduate-level courses at Middlebury. Born in Italy of American parents.

One year teaching at the Bainbridge School in New York. Entered military intelligence as a civilian employee, working in censorship and translation in New York. U.S. Army service, then thirty years in the Philippines as a civilian employee for the Air Force at Clark AFB, specializing in employee and career development. Trained singer (tenor).

LARS: 1939–1940. Taught French, Spanish. Gave a concert in Santa Fe with Charles Kinney.

Rogers, Bernard J. (1917–). B.A. Yale, 1939, PBK.

U.S. Army, Signal Corps. Faculty, Barat College of the Sacred Heart, teaching history and literature. Advertising in Chicago, and rehabilitation work at the VA Hospital. Faculty, Henry Ford Community College, teaching history, retired in 1984.

LARS: January–April 1942. Taught English. Replaced John Stegmaier, who was drafted. In turn, he himself was drafted and was replaced by Cecil Baker.

Ruhl, Henry Walker (1894?–1920): B.A. Yale, 1916?

Ruhl was badly wounded and gassed in World War I.

LARS: September–October 1920, when he died of exposure in Water Canyon. Taught English, history. Ruhl married Virginia Davis and they became the first married faculty couple at LARS.

Scudder, Rogers V. (1912–): LARS graduate, 1930. B.A. Harvard, 1934. M.A. University of Wisconsin, where he taught briefly. Diploma in Classical Archaeology from New College, Oxford.

Teacher, Roxbury Latin School, 1934–1935. Teacher, Brooks School, North Andover, Mass., 1936–1966, with two and one-half years in the American Field Service as an ambulance driver for the British 8th Army. Teacher, Groton School, 1968–1975; 1983– teaching archaeology. Director of the Library of the American Academy in Rome, 1975–1983. Taught Latin and Roman topography at St. Stephen's School. Author of Latin I and Latin II textbooks, revised edition with Charles Jenney, and of Latin III and Latin IV.

LARS: 1935–1936. Taught Latin during Hitchcock's leave of absence. Summer Camp staff, 1931.

Sellers, Mark Ashley (1902–1977): A.B. Princeton, 1924; LL.B. University of Texas, 1928; S.J.D. Harvard, 1933.

Lawyer, Abilene, Tex., 1928–1930. Law Professor, Emory University, 1931–1933. Special assistant to U.S. Attorney General, 1933–1935, 1945. Law Professor, University of Georgia, 1935–1938. Attorney, USDA, 1938–1943. Member of various law firms, 1947–1977, including Sellers, Conner and Cuneo in Washington, D.C.

LARS: 1924–1925. Taught English and history. Summer Camp staff, 1925.

Shain, Charles E. (1915–): A.B. Princeton, 1936; M.A. Princeton, 1947; Ph.D. Princeton, 1949. Fellowship at Kings College, Cambridge. Woodrow Wilson Fellow, Princeton, 1946–1947. Scribner Fellow, Princeton, 1947–1948. Fulbright Scholar, University of London, 1952–1953.

Teacher, Milton Academy, 1938–1942. U.S. Army Air Force, Major. Professor of English at Carleton College, 1949–1962. President of Connecticut College for Women, 1962–1974, which during his tenure became co-ed. Honorary degrees from Wesleyan, Princeton, and Emerson College.

LARS: 1936–1937. Taught English.

Slaughter, E. Dick Jr. (1902–1929): LARS postgraduate 1920–1921, after Hotchkiss. One year at Princeton, 1922–1923, withdrew because of illness. B.A. University of Colorado.

Died of tuberculosis in Colorado Springs. His family had a ranch in Roswell and hired Ben White, the former Los Alamos Ranch foreman.

LARS: 1923–1924. Taught history. Summer Camp staff, 1924.

*Steege, Oscar A. (1913–1999): B.A. Yale, 1934. M.A. Columbia University, 1938.

U.S. Navy, Lt. Commander. Teacher, Los Alamos High School, 1946. Teacher, the Waring Ranch School, Pojoaque, N.Mex., 1946–1949. Teacher, then Headmaster, the Mooreland Hill School, in Kensington, Conn..

LARS: 1934–1942. Taught Latin and history. Summer Camp staff, 1939–1940, 1942.

Stegmaier, John (1915–2001): B.A. Harvard, 1937; postgraduate studies, Harvard 1939–1940, and Japanese language and area studies, Yale, 1948–1949.

Teacher, Brewster Academy, 1938–1939. Teacher, Browne and Nichols School, Cambridge, Mass., 1939–1940. U.S. Army service, WWII. U.S. Foreign Service, 1946–1968, his last post being Consul-General in Kobe-Osaka, Japan. President, *Encyclopedia Britannica,* Japan, and President, East-West Associates, Tokyo. Active on the boards of two national mental health organizations.

LARS: 1940–1941. Taught biology and math.

Sword, Charles H. (?–1984): B.A. Michigan University, 1924, with a teaching certificate. Musician, actor.

LARS: 1924–1925. Taught Spanish.

Talbot, Clinton Davis (1904–1983): B.A. Yale, 1925; M.A. Columbia. Teacher at Tabor Academy, in Marion, Mass., 1926–1928. Math teacher and head of the math department at Columbia High School in Maplewood, N.J., retiring in 1968.

    LARS: 1925–1926. Taught French and English.

Todd, Charles H. (1906–): B.A. Yale, 1928, LL.B. University of Washington, 1936.

    Reporter for the *Journal of Commerce*, New York City, early 1930s. Reporter for the *Seattle Times*. Law practice in Seattle until retirement in 1977.

    LARS: 1928–1929. Taught history, English, math.

*Walen, Harry Leonard (1915–): B.A. Harvard, 1937; graduate studies in history at Harvard.

    Teacher, Groton School, 1942–1946. Teacher, Newton High School and Instructor, Newton Jr. College, 1946–1951. Administrator Newton High 1951–1955. Director, secondary school English textbooks for Ginn and Company, 1955–1961. Principal, Needham High School, 1961–1972. Alderman, City of Newton, 1961–1972. Active in YMCA and genealogical societies.

    LARS: 1937–1942. Taught English. Deputy Sheriff, Sandoval County, 1942. Walen married Elizabeth Benson; their son Harry Benson (Ben) was born while they were at Los Alamos.

Wallis, Herbert S. "Hup" (1913–1977): B.S. Harvard, 1936.

    Teacher, New London, Conn., public schools for two years before LARS. World War II service in the Royal Navy, navigator for six years on a corvette. Teacher, Waring Ranch School, Pojoaque, N.Mex., 1946–1949. Math and science teacher, Los Alamos High School and Junior High, 1949–1952. Engineer at Sandia National Laboratory.

    LARS: 1938–1940. Taught math and science.

*Waring, Thomas R. Jr. (1903–1973): B.A. University of the South, 1925. Graduate studies at the Universidad Nacional de México and Toulouse University.

    Founder and Director, Waring School in Santa Fe, 1939–1941; Director, the Waring Ranch School in Pojoaque, N.Mex., 1941–1949. Teacher, Brownmoor School, Scottsdale, Ariz., 1950–1951. Hotel management in Mexico, 1950s. Teacher, Sewanee Military Academy, Tenn., 1960s–early 1970s.

    LARS: 1926–1939. Taught English, Spanish, French. Summer Camp staff, 1930, 1931. Waring married Anita Rose in 1929; their daughter Carolina was born while they were at Los Alamos.

White, Howell North Jr. (1911–1974): A.B. Princeton, 1932.

    Freelance writer. Purchasing agent for the aircraft industry, 1942–1962. A graduate of Hotchkiss, where his father was on the faculty.

    LARS: 1932–1934. Taught Latin and French.

*Wirth, Cecil W. "Cec" (1909–1943): B.A. University of Denver, 1929. Semester at the Harvard Graduate School of Business, 1933, left because of tight finances.

Staff, Cheley Camps, Estes Park, Colo., 1919–1931; Director of the boys' camp; Assistant Director, 1932. Purchasing agent, Phelps Dodge Corporation, 1942.

LARS: 1929–1942. Taught math and history. Secretary, and Assistant to the Director, 1933–1937. Director, Summer Camp 1937–1942. Scoutmaster, Troop 22, and directed the outdoors program. Wirth married Virginia Davis, a teacher at Brownmoor School for Girls in Santa Fe. Their sons John and Timothy were born while they were at Los Alamos.

Wiswall, Wilbur Wellington (1877–1941): Attended the Conservatory of Music, Colorado College, 1897–1901.

Photographer and musician; also playwright and author. He and his wife Etna West were members of the Santa Fe arts scene in the 1930s.

LARS: 1933–1937. Taught instrumental music and piano.

Wright, Alfred J. (1916?–2000): B.A. Case Western Reserve, 1937. M.A. Ohio State, 1938. Ph.D. Columbia University, 1950.

U.S. Army, World War II, cryptographer and translator. Professor of French, Trinity College, 1949–1956, and at Bates College, 1956–1984, where he was chair of the Department of Foreign Languages and Literatures. Published author in his field.

LARS: 1940–1942. Taught French and Spanish.

Notes

Abbreviations

BHL Bentley Historical Library, University of Michigan
FSC Fermor Spencer Church Collection
LAHM Los Alamos Historical Museum Archives
MNM Museum of New Mexico
NMSRCA New Mexico State Records Center and Archives
PPC Peggy Pond Church Collection
RDC Roy D. Chapin Collection
SFNM Santa Fe New Mexican newspaper
UNM University of New Mexico

The book's epigraph is from a letter of July 31, 1975, by Edward T. Hall to Margaret Wohlberg, which may be found at LAHM, in clipping file R24D. Hall, a leading social anthropologist, attended both the school and the summer camp.

Preface

1. Related to John Wirth by Ransom VanBrunt Lynch, a former master at both LARS and Phillips Exeter Academy (and Wirth's godfather). Oppenheimer visited Exeter in February 1955.
2. Linda was a day student at St. Agnes, an Episcopal school in Alexandria, Va., which has since merged with St. Stephens School. Williston merged with the Northampton School for Girls; it is now the Williston-Northampton School.

Prologue

1. While this account is overall an accurate description of Lancellot Pelly's early life, the details were compiled from letters in a number of student files from the school's first decade as well as from Pelly's own open file; all in FSC, NMSRCA.

2. The Rose family set aside a room in their house for Connell's use when he was in Santa Fe. In later years, Connell kept a room at Ashley Pond's home on Palace Avenue.

3. The Buckman Road can still be seen where it emerges from White Rock Canyon just north of the present-day town of White Rock. From that point State Highway 4 follows approximately the same route Lance traveled north to Los Alamos Canyon, just before today's junction with State Highway 502 coming from the Rio Grande to Los Alamos.

4. This side canyon track was called the Short-cut Trail; it went up what is now called DP Canyon.

5. Peggy Pond Church. "Talk at Authors' Luncheon," manuscript dated April 10, 1970, in Box 29, PPC, LAHM.

6. The wolves that inhabited the Jemez when Lance arrived were exterminated by the 1930s. Elk had been eliminated in New Mexico shortly before the school's founding; they were reintroduced in the Jemez in the late 1940s.

7. For background, see Christopher Wilson, *The Myth of Santa Fe: Creating a Modern Regional Tradition* (Albuquerque: University of New Mexico Press, 1997); Hal Rothman, *On Rims and Ridges: The Los Alamos Area since 1880* (Lincoln: University of Nebraska Press, 1992); and Don D. Fowler, *A Laboratory for Anthropology: Science and Romanticism in the American West, 1846–1930* (Albuquerque: University of New Mexico Press, 2000).

8. The name given by the owners, Judge A. J. Abbott and his wife, to their ranch was Ten Alders, but a printing error led to its being called the Ten Elders Ranch. The Abbotts referred to it by its original name.

9. *SFNM,* June 19 and December 29, 1916.

10. For insight into how New Mexico's roads affected the quality and delivery of medical care, see Meldrum K. Wylder, *Rio Grande Medicine Man* (Santa Fe, N.Mex.: Rydal Press, 1958); and Jake W. Spidle, Jr., *Doctors of Medicine in New Mexico: A History of Health and Medical Practice, 1886–1986* (Albuquerque: University of New Mexico Press, 1986).

11. In 1920 an existing road following a more northerly route from Santa Fe was graveled between that city and Pojoaque Pueblo, and in 1922 a new road section was built from Pojoaque west to the railroad's Otowi Crossing on the Rio Grande. In 1924 a highway bridge was built over the river at Otowi Crossing connecting to the Culebra Hill Road. This is the route the present-day highway follows from Santa Fe to Los Alamos. Between 1922 and 1924, when there was no highway bridge at Otowi Crossing, travelers could choose to follow a road north along the east side of the Rio Grande to cross at a river ford at San Ildefonso or on the bridge at Española. Some brave travelers familiar with the Denver & Rio Grande schedule chose to cross the river at Otowi on the railroad bridge. Portions of the Otowi Hill road can be seen from present-day State Route 502 as it climbs out of Pueblo Canyon onto the Los Alamos mesa.

Chapter 1

1. The title is from Samuel F. Bemis, "A School With Nature as a Textbook," an article on Pond's new school published simultaneously in the *Boston Transcript* and the *SFNM,* March 22, 1917. Bemis was the school's first secretary-treasurer.

2. Obituary for Ashley Pond Sr., *Detroit News,* January 13, 1910; Virginia W. V. Shaw, "Mr. Ashley Pond Loved His Profession," August 1 and August 8, 1937, copy of two-part article in unattributed source. Information on the Huron Mountain Club, which still exists, is found in Bayard H. Christy, *The History of the Club* (privately printed, no date). All in box 30, folder 14, PPC, LAHM. Today, the Huron Mountain Club lands provide a large undisturbed tract of rare old-growth maple-hemlock forest.

3. Christopher F. Armstrong, "On the Making of Good Men: Character-Building in the New England Boarding Schools," in *The High Status Track: Studies of Elite Schools and Stratification,* ed. Paul William Kingston and Lionel S. Lewis (Albany: State University of New York Press, 1990), pp. 3–19. Also, see James McLachlan, *American Boarding Schools: A Historical Study* (New York: Charles Scribner's Sons, 1970).

4. Yale records show that Pond was a student from 1891 to 1893 and 1893 to 1896 and that he did not graduate. In the first Ranch School brochure, Pond stated that he was "a Yale man." In subsequent school literature, after Pond was no longer directly involved in the school, he is shown as "Yale 96-S." See Ranch School booklets in PPC, LAHM, and in FSC, NMSRCA.

5. *Las Vegas Daily Optic,* November 6, 1903, and September 30, 1904; *Detroit News,* January 13, 1910.

6. Francis Wilson, Eulogy for Ashley Pond Jr., June 28, 1933. Typed manuscript in box 30, folder 14, PPC, LAHM.

7. *Detroit Free Press,* January 16, 1910.

8. The Ramón Vigil Land Grant was awarded by Spain in 1742 to Pedro Sanchez. In the Treaty of Guadalupe Hidalgo (1848), the United States agreed to honor land grants awarded by the Spanish and Mexican governments. There is an extensive literature focused on Spanish land-grant history and current issues.

9. See Rothman, *On Rims and Ridges,* for a detailed account of use of the Ramón Vigil Grant lands.

10. Information on the Pajarito Club is contained in copious notes taken by Peggy Pond Church from her father's correspondence with his Detroit partners, in the RDC, in the Michigan Historical Collections, BHL. Peggy Church's Pajarito Club notes are in Box 21, folder 12, PPC, LAHM.

11. *SFNM,* March 17 and 24, 1914; Ashley Pond Jr., letter to Roy Chapin, April 10, 1914, copy in PPC, LAHM, original in RDC, BHL.

12. Peggy Pond Church, letter to George Fitzpatrick, March 28, 1978 in Box 29, folder 5, in PPC, LAHM.

13. Ashley Pond Jr., telegram to Paul Gray, May 1, 1914; letter, Roy Chapin to Paul Gray, May 4, 1914. Copies of both in Box 21, folder 12, in PPC, LAHM, originals in RDC, BHL.

14. *SFNM,* April 14, 1914; Ashley Pond Jr., letter to Roy Chapin, June 5, 1914, copy in Box 21, folder 12 in PPC, LAHM, original in RDC, BHL.

15. Alan W. Johnson, e-mail to Linda Aldrich, December 10, 2000.

16. Colonel Francis W. Parker was an early educational reformer and advocate of Progressive education.

17. Ethel Mintzer Lichtman, *The Francis Parker School Heritage* (San Diego: Francis Parker School, 1985), pp. 1–25.

18. Katherine Brook was the daughter of George Cross, an editor of the *Santa Fe New Mexican.* She married Frank Brown, owner of the Capitol Pharmacy on the Santa Fe Plaza, who died in 1910, leaving her with an infant son. She married Harold Brook in April 1914.

19. Frederic W. Dennis, Joy Realty Company, letter to Roy Chapin, April 20, 1916, copy in Box 21, folder 12, PPC, LAHM, original in RDC, BHL.

20. Ashley Pond Jr., letter to Luman W. Goodenough, June 26, 1916, in Box 21, folder 12, PPC, LAHM, original in RDC, BHL; *SFNM,* September 9, 1916.

21. Francis C. Wilson, letter to Harold H. Brook, December 15, 1916, copy in clipping file R22A, LAHM.

22. *SFNM,* May 9, 1917. Also, see photo narrative in clipping file HS42L, LAHM.

23. Peggy Pond Church, letter to Dorothy Pond Benedict, January 9, 1979, in Box 21, folder 12, PPC, LAHM; *SFNM*, October 4, 1916; D. W. James, letter to Roy Chapin, December 25, 1916, copy in Box 21, folder 12, PPC, LAHM, original in RDC, BHL.

24. LARS headmaster Lawrence Hitchcock described Fuller as having "a slowed though in no way deranged mental process and one conspicuously dragging leg. His speech would generally be perfectly normal but boisterous and ejaculatory when excited. [He was] far from being a keeper case . . . [and] very fond of riding and outdoor activities in general . . . [but] uneasy in purely social situations." See notes from Hitchcock, letter of March 18, 1976, in Peggy Church's index card notes, LAHM-M1991-31-1-1.

25. *Michigan Tradesman,* November 14, 1928; *The Grand Rapids Spectator,* February 23, 1929; obituary, Mrs. P. C. Fuller, March 13, 1890, unidentified newspaper, in Grand Rapids Public Library Scrapbook MKG9 R415 v. 16.

26. *SFNM*, February 16, 1917.

27. Mrs. F. W. Waknitz, letter to Linda Aldrich, August 5, 1999; telephone conversations between John Curtis and Aldrich, April 30 and May 4, 2000; Aldrich, interview with John Curtis, October 16, 2000; records description for Catholic Club of the City of New York Collection, in American Irish Historical Society, New York City.

28. Although complete employment records for Louis Comfort Tiffany's studios no longer exist, many at Los Alamos recalled Connell's statements that he worked for Tiffany.

29. In 1912 Walter and Emma moved to Albuquerque, where he later served on the first Albuquerque City Council. In 1914 Walter formed the Bond-Connell Wool Company with prominent northern New Mexico businessman Frank Bond. See Ellis Arthur-Davis, ed., *The Historical Encyclopedia of New Mexico,* vol. 1 (Albuquerque: The New Mexico Historical Association, 1945), p. 1000; and Ralph Emerson Twitchell, ed., *The Leading Facts of New Mexican History, vol. 3* (Cedar Rapids, Iowa: The Torch Press, 1917), p. 35. Also, see Frank H. Grubbs, "Frank Bond: Gentleman Sheepherder of Northern New Mexico: 1883–1915," *New Mexico Historical Review* 36, no. 4 (1961).

30. Hugh McLeod, "Catholicism and the New York Irish," in *Disciplines of Faith: Studies in Religion, Politics and Patriarchy,* ed. Jim Obelkevich et al. (New York, 1987), p. 347. A. J. Connell, letter to Mrs. Bernard Pelly, April 9, 1919, in open Lancellot Pelly file, FSC, NMSRCA.

31. Leon Kneipp, quoted in Paul H. Roberts, *Hoof Prints on Forest Ranges: The Early Years of the National Forest Range Administration* (San Antonio, Tex.: The Naylor Company, 1963), p. 4.

32. Roberts, *Hoof Prints on Forest Ranges,* p. 4.

33. In this respect, Connell was not unlike the Groton School's Endicott Peabody, whose brief time in Tombstone, Arizona, gave him a certain cachet with his students.

34. Quoted in Edwin A. Tucker and George Fitzgerald, *Men Who Matched the Mountains: The Forest Service in the Southwest* (Washington, D.C.: USDA Forest Service, Southwest Region, 1972), p. 38.

35. Stephen J. Pyne, *Year of the Fires: The Story of the Great Fires of 1910* (New York: Viking Penguin, 2001), pp. 1–4; Roberts, *Hoof Prints on Forest Ranges,* p. 67.

36. Tucker and Fitzgerald, *Men Who Matched the Mountains,* p. 36.

37. Official Forest Service records for A. J. Connell are incomplete and do not agree with contemporaneous accounts of his Forest Service dates, assignments, and activities as published in the newspapers of Silver City and Santa Fe. We have assumed that the newspapers are correct in reporting Connell's presence at and involvement in places and events.

38. Silver City newspapers noted, in January 1911, that local Chinese were following the recent edict of the Chinese emperor and cutting off their queues; in June of 1913, gypsies were accused of swindling several Silver City citizens.

39. *Silver City Enterprise,* March 8, 1912; *Silver City Independent,* July 2, September 17, October 8, November 19, 1912, and February 25, 1913.

40. H. Allen Anderson, *The Chief: Ernest Thompson Seton and the Changing West* (College Station: Texas A & M Press, 1986), p. 131.

41. Robert G. Athearn, *The Mythic West in Twentieth-Century America* (Lawrence: University of Kansas Press, 1986); Washington Irving, *A Tour of the Prairies,* ed. John Francis McDermott (Norman: University of Oklahoma Press, 1956), as quoted in Roderick Nash, *Wilderness and the American Mind,* 3d ed. (New Haven, Conn.: Yale University Press, 1982), p. 73.

42. "The Bad Boy Proposition," *SFNM,* January 22, 1922.

43. David I. Macleod, *Building Character in the American Boy: The Boy Scouts, YMCA, and Their Forerunners, 1870–1920* (Madison: University of Wisconsin Press, 1983), pp. xv–13. See also his "Act Your Age: Adolescence and the Rise of the Boy Scouts of America," *Journal of Social History* 16, no. 2 (winter 1982): 2–20.

44. William D. Murray, *The History of the Boy Scouts of America* (New York: The Boy Scouts of America, 1937), p. 217.

45. In April 1915 the Jemez and Pecos (northeast of Santa Fe) Forest Reserves were combined and renamed the Santa Fe National Forest.

46. "Model Log Cabin Built Entirely by Boy Scouts," *SFNM,* February 12, 1917.

47. Ibid.

48. *SFNM,* April 30, 1917.

49. Aileen Baehrens O'Bryan, "Seven Gardens," autobiography in manuscript form, pp. 202–3. Exhausted by the relentless work and bridling at "their masculine absorption in the launching of the school," she left after a few months. See also Peggy Church, letter to Lawrence S. Hitchcock, March 3, 1979, in Box 29, PPC, LAHM.

50. A. J. Connell, letter to Elisabeth Pelly, April 19, 1919, in Lancellot Pelly open file, and Connell, letter to Fayette Curtis, June 30, 1919, in Box 1, folder 2; both in FSC, NMSRCA.

51. Mrs. Guy Turley's outdoor school is mentioned in *SFNM,* June 17, 1915, and May 29 and June 1, 1916.

52. See Porter E. Sargent, *A Handbook of American Private Schools* (Boston: Porter Sargent, 1916, and following).

53. Bemis's account of his time in New Mexico is contained in his memoir, pp. 211–50, in the Bemis Collection, GN 74, Box 49, folder 643, Yale University Library Archives. His book *Pinckney's Treaty* won the Pulitzer Prize for history in 1927. In 1950 he again won the Pulitzer for the biography *John Quincy Adams and the Foundations of American Foreign Policy.*

54. Pond served on the Santa Fe City Council several times, was selected to serve as Don Diego at the 1927 Santa Fe Fiesta, and founded the city's Volunteer Fire Department, for which he maintained a lifelong passion. He was famous in Santa Fe for having a fire pole in his bedroom so when an alarm sounded he could whip down the pole and be first to arrive on the fire scene. Hazel Pond's organization of Santa Fe's first Girl Scout troop in 1917 is mentioned in "Girl Scouting in New Mexico to Celebrate 75 Years," *Albuquerque Journal North,* March 11, 1987.

55. The handwritten note from Roosevelt to Pond, dated August 13, 1916, is on display in the Los Alamos Historical Museum. Theodore Roosevelt states that he "never endorse[s] a school . . . unless I know it and can speak from personal knowledge." Apparently this was not the case with others; Yale Professor Irving Fisher endorsed the planned school based on Edgar Hewitt's good opinion of it. See Fisher's letter to Hewitt, September 12, 1916, in Hewitt Papers, Box 5, folder 3, Fray Angélico Chavez History Library, MNM.

56. At about this same time, Nusbaum provided "advice and assistance" in the design and construction of another building on the plateau, the summer home and Indian crafts school of Rose Dougan and Vera Von Blumenthal, located near the Tsankawi ruins on leased Forest Service land. See Clipping file on Rose Dougan at the Fray Angélico Chavez History Library, MNM.

57. Boy Scout records for Santa Fe and Los Alamos no longer exist for this period. An informal history of Los Alamos Scouting states that the school troop was registered in October of 1917 and that Fayette Curtis, a master who did not arrive until the fall of 1918, was the first scoutmaster. It is likely that, given the few boys at Los Alamos, they were initially members of Connell's Santa Fe troop, which he continued to lead until October 1918. See Peggy Church notes in LAHM clipping file R22B.

Chapter 2

1. Frederick S. Allis, Jr., *Youth From Every Quarter: A Bicentennial History of Phillips Academy, Andover* (Hanover, N.H.: University Press of New England, 1979), p. 47, as quoted in Armstrong, "On the Making of Good Men," p. 9.

2. Information in this chapter on LARS employees, facilities and equipment, and finances comes primarily from the school's annual reports and audits in FCC, NMSRCA.

3. The school's mail originally came via train to the Buckman Station on the D&RG. Around 1921, when the town of Buckman ceased to exist, the railroad stop was moved a short distance north to the Otowi Crossing, where the D&RG crossed the river, and Otowi became the school's mailing address. The school picked up the mail two or three times a week, daily in later years. In 1941, when the D&RG tracks were abandoned, the mail was delivered directly to the school, and the mailing address became Los Alamos.

4. Arthur Chase, "Conflagration on Bathtub Row," manuscript written July 1990, in clipping file R24A, LAHM.

5. L. S. Hitchcock, letter to Margaret Wohlberg, November 26, 1975, in clipping file R23D, LAHM.

6. Treasurer's Report for 1931, in Box 2, folder 26, in FSC, NMSRCA. In 1941 Connell deeded land he owned at El Vado, New Mexico, to the Los Alamos Foundation. Minutes of Board of Trustees of the Los Alamos Foundation, October 15, 1941, in FSC, NMSRCA.

7. Bond first leased, then in 1919 bought, the Baca Location Grant (now the Valles Caldera National Preserve), allowing the Ranch School to graze its cattle and sheep and conduct its summer camp there. Bond bought the Vigil Grant from Pond's Detroit partners in 1918 and sold it to the Soil Conservation Service in the late 1930s.

8. This chimney stands behind the present-day Los Alamos Historical Museum, the former Ranch School guesthouse and infirmary. A homestead cabin now located near Fuller Lodge was not part of Brook's homestead. Built by the Romero family, homesteaders on the plateau, it was moved in recent years to its present site from its original location southeast of the school. After the fires of May 2000, the Romero cabin is the only remaining homestead cabin on the Pajarito Plateau.

9. Ranch School publications are largely undated, although some can be dated with accuracy if they contain calendars for the year. Some have handwritten notations, presumably by Fermor Church, indicating approximate dates. FSC, NMSRCA, PPC, and the Ranch School clipping files at LAHM have copies and a few originals of school brochures and catalogs. Neither archive holds a complete set.

10. See Sargent, *Handbook*.

11. Annual reports and audits in FSC, NMSRCA. The exception to this was Fermor Church,

the only faculty member to build his own house. However, the Churches sold their home to the school in later years, in return for the education of their sons at the Ranch School.

12. Sybil Ellinwood, "East Meets West in the Field of Education," *The Journal of Arizona History* 15, no. 3 (1974): 269–96.
13. Numerous letters and one-page reminiscences of student life by former LARS students are in the Ranch School clipping files. Longer manuscripts by former students Mack Wallace and Earl Kieselhorst, and collections of letters written while at LARS by Jay Rice and Douglass Campbell, are invaluable. All are found at LAHM.
14. Brochure for Los Alamos Ranch with handwritten notation "before September 1919," in Box 1, folder 13, in FSC, NMSRCA.
15. Connell letter to parent in student files, NMSRCA. Unattributed quotes hereafter are from closed student files in FSC at NMSRCA.
16. David McCullough, *Mornings on Horseback* (New York: Simon and Schuster, 1981), p. 90.
17. George F. Rehberger, *Lippincott's Quick Reference Book for Medicine and Surgery,* 2d ed. (Philadelphia: J. B. Lippincott Co., 1921), no pagination.
18. Henry Hyde Salter, *On Asthma: Its Pathology and Treatment* (Philadelphia: Blanchard and Lea, 1864), quoted in McCullough, *Mornings on Horseback,* p. 93.
19. I am indebted to Dr. Ben Neal of Los Alamos and the late Dr. Harold Wilson for my understanding of why boys at Los Alamos may have responded so well to Connell's regime. Any errors in interpretation are mine alone. My telephone conversations with them took place on April 27 and May 4, 2000.
20. Ranch schools had varying purposes, witness the short-lived Rocky Mountain Ranch School in Silver City, whose focus was on boys with emotional or mental disorders. Physical health, achieved through time spent outdoors, was considered an integral part of its mental health program.
21. Paul Starr, *The Social Transformation of American Medicine* (New York: Basic Books, 1982), p. 140; Frank Reeve, *History of New Mexico,* 3 vols. (New York: Lewis Historical Publishing Company, 1961), 2:284.
22. Rehberger, *Lippincott's Quick Reference Book.*
23. John Wirth, interview with Rogers Scudder, October 11, 1999, at Groton School.
24. Student files reveal only one exception to Connell's policy—a boy whose family were vegetarians was allowed to refuse meat. Even when a doctor requested that a boy not have milk, Connell agreed only to seeing that he would drink less milk.
25. Sweets were allowed, with each boy having a carefully controlled weekly allotment of candy from the Trading Post, and desserts were served with meals. A detailed chuck list for one of the summer camps reveals the variety of foodstuffs that Connell believed necessary for a proper diet, among them: beef, mutton, tongue, and sardines; potatoes, beets, kohlrabi, turnips, chard, and spinach; apples, oranges, and dried and canned fruits of all varieties, including figs. School recipes included not only favorites like chicken pie and macaroni and cheese, but also a boiled scraped liver sandwich and a banana, peanut, and carrot salad.
26. Thomas E. Cone Jr., *History of American Pediatrics* (Boston: Little Brown, 1979}, pp. 161–62.
27. Jan Jarboe Russell, *Lady Bird: A Biography of Mrs. Johnson* (New York: Scribner, 1999), pp. 45–46.
28. Robert L. Church and Michael W. Sedlak, *Education in the United States: An Interpretive History* (New York: Free Press, 1976), p. 379.
29. Alistair Horne, *A Bundle from Britain* (London: Macmillan, 1993), pp. 202–3.

30. A. J. Connell, letter to Elisabeth Pelly, April 21, 1922, open Pelly file, FSC, NMSRCA.
31. LARS *Alumni Bulletin,* spring 1941, in clipping file R26, LAHM.
32. A. J. Connell, letter to Elisabeth Pelly, April 19, 1919, open Pelly file, FSC, NMSRCA.
33. Lawrence A. Cremin, *The Transformation of the School: Progressivism in American Education, 1876–1957* (New York: Random House, 1961), pp. 18, 100–102.
34. Jay Rice, letter to parents in Rice Collection, n.d., Box 25, LAHM.
35. Earl H. Kieselhorst, "Atoms of Reminiscence: Before the Atomic Bomb," pp. 1, 8. Manuscript in clipping files R24B, LAHM.
36. Ibid.
37. Douglass Campbell, letter to his mother, March 19, 1933, in Campbell Collection, LAHM.
38. John McDonough, as quoted by Lore Watt in untitled six-page manuscript, p. 3, submitted to the *Albuquerque Journal,* October 5, 1978. In clipping file R24A, LAHM.
39. LARS brochure, n.d., but after 1928, probably early 1930s.
40. LARS *Alumni Bulletin,* spring 1936, winter 1937, spring 1940; all in LAHM.
41. Kieselhorst, "Atoms of Reminiscence," p. 5.
42. Outline of talk given by Dechert in 1990, in clipping file R24B, LAHM.
43. Mack F. Wallace, "The Los Alamos Years: 1934–1936," p. 4. Manuscript in clipping file R24B, LAHM.
44. Jeremy Taylor, e-mail communication to Linda Aldrich, October 27, 1999.
45. *SFNM,* June 25 and 27, 1917. Troop 22 continues to exist in Los Alamos, with only a brief hiatus during World War II, and uses the Ranch School logo. Information herein on Boy Scouting at LARS is derived largely from contemporaneous sources, particularly student files at NMSRCA, from the Ranch School clipping files and Campbell and Rice collections at LAHM, and from later recollections of those involved.
46. Edward T. Hall, *An Anthropology of Everyday Life: An Autobiography* (New York: Doubleday, 1992), p. 31.
47. Howard Meyer, letters to Cleo Byers, May 17 and June 7, 1970, in clipping files R24A, LAHM.
48. Douglass Campbell's letters to his family contain several invaluable references to Scouting at LARS. See Campbell Collection, Box 18, LAHM. Connell lists his service on the National Boy Scout Council in Michel D. Abousleman, ed. and comp., *Who's Who in New Mexico: Biographical Sketches of Contemporary New Mexicans,* vol. 1 (Albuquerque, N.Mex.: Abousleman Company, 1937), p. 51.
49. Apparently no records of this survive in the Boy Scout National Archives. A typed two-page informal history of Troop 22 compiled by Albro Rile in the 1970s and based on interviews with Bences Gonzales, among others, states that Connell provided suggestions to Scout executives for ways to successfully engage older boys in Scouting programs. This history was provided by Bill Erickson of the Los Alamos Boy Scouts.
50. Connell, letter to Elisabeth Pelly, April 9, 1919, open Pelly file, FSC, NMSRCA.
51. Ernest Thompson Seton, "The 1927 Indian Trip," journal of trip to New Mexico, at Seton Museum, Philmont Scout Ranch, Cimarron, N.Mex. See August 30–September 1.
52. Macleod, *Building Character,* p. 5. Macleod details Progressive-era concerns about boys and adolescents and institutional responses to these concerns. Another view is presented in Michael Rosenthal, *The Character Factory: Baden-Powell and the Origins of the Boy Scout Movement* (New York: Pantheon Books, 1986). Also see Murray, *History,* especially for what the Boy Scouts considered their mission.
53. For instance, the Evans School in Arizona maintained an informal atmosphere, rather loose classroom standards, and gave students almost unlimited and unsupervised freedom to roam on horseback. California's Thacher School fell somewhere between Los

Alamos and the Evans School, with an informal atmosphere and conventional, well-taught academics. Deep Springs in California was—and is—a Progressive school challenging minds and bodies in a rigorous, demanding, and unconventional manner.

54. Both Cremin, *Transformation of the School;* and Patricia Albjerg Graham, *Progressive Education: From Arcady to Academe* (New York: Teacher College Press, Columbia University, 1967), provide perceptive analyses of progressive education. See also Fred M. Hechinger and Grace Hechinger, *Growing Up in America* (New York: McGraw Hill, 1975); and Harold Rugg and Ann Shumaker, *The Child-Centered School: An Appraisal of the New Education* (Yonkers: World Book Co., 1928).

Chapter 3

1. A. J. Connell, letter to Yale, June 26, 1918. Copy in clipping files R22B, LAHM.
2. Curtis's illness is not specified in the incomplete copies of this correspondence, but his death certificate states that he first had tuberculosis in the spring of 1918. Yet the school brochure for that fall stated that "Los Alamos is in no sense a sanatorium. We take no boys whose health or condition would in any way be a menace to others or a source of unreasonable care and anxiety to the staff."
3. Curtis's records at the Taft School apparently no longer survive; his presence there is documented only in the list of graduates and in the yearbooks. Obituary, *SFNM*, November 4, 1926.
4. Connell considered the year 1917–1918 to be the first official year of the school; he makes reference to this in alumni bulletins of 1934–1935 and 1942–1943. Some have argued that because there was no academic program until 1918, that year should be considered the first year of the Ranch School. From the beginning Pond considered it a school, and in Connell's view the academics were always secondary to the health and character-building program.
5. In 1938 the grading periods changed to seven and then to six periods, while the length of the school year remained the same.
6. Lawrence Hitchcock, "Autobiography, August 1981," unpublished manuscript, p. 37.
7. Lawrence Hitchcock, letter to his mother, October 19, 1919, in Hitchcock, "Young Man at Los Alamos, 1919–1922," unpublished manuscript.
8. Earl Kieselhorst, letter to Hitchcock, September 14, 1970, in Hitchcock Collection 84.832, LAHM.
9. The Borrowdale Collection of weapons, which Curtis catalogued, was given to the Museum of New Mexico by W. M. Borrowdale of Magdalena in 1917. Curtis's original, unpublished translation of Villagrá is found in Miguel Encinas, Alfred Rodriquez, and Joseph P. Sanchez, eds., *Historia de la Nueva Mexico, 1610,* [by] Gaspar Perez de Villagrá (Albuquerque: University of New Mexico Press, 1992). As the editors state, on p. xix: "An earlier, unpublished English translation of Villagrá's *Historia* was completed in the 1920s, in verse, by Fayette S. Curtis, Jr. . . . An expert on Spanish colonial weaponry in the Southwest, Curtis appears to have initiated his extraordinary translation as early as 1923, completing a first draft four years later. . . . The present edition in English is a revised and corrected version of Curtis's translation."
10. "Los Alamos Instructor Dies of Exhaustion on Hunting Excursion," *SFNM,* November 1, 1920.
11. These three were Warren K. "Lefty" Page (English), Oscar A. Steege (History and Latin), and Harry L. Walen (English).

12. Los Alamos brochure with handwritten notation "printed before Sept. '21" in Box 1, folder 13, in FSC, NMSRCA.

13. Connell's policy was to never stay in any boy's home, student or potential recruit, so as to avoid any hint of favoritism or obligation. He traveled by train or, on occasion, ocean liner through the Panama Canal and always stayed in very good hotels.

14. Hometowns of only about half of the students are recorded, but certain geographic patterns nevertheless seem clear.

15. L. S. Hitchcock, "Los Alamos Notes, 1922 Summer Camp," unpublished manuscript, p. 1; 1921 Audit, in Box 2, folder 34, in FSC, NMSRCA.

16. The two older Church boys, Ted and Allen, both attended LARS, and Ted was in the last graduating class. Allen attended and graduated from his father's short-lived venture, the Los Alamos School at Taos. Both schools were gone by the time the youngest son, Hugh, graduated from secondary school.

17. Douglass Campbell, letters to his parents, April 12 and 17, 1935, in Campbell Collection, LAHM.

18. Lance was never truly healthy after he left LARS. His older brother Thomas, whom the Pellys briefly considered sending to Los Alamos, became a U.S. Representative from the state of Washington, serving in Congress from 1953 to 1973.

19. Quote from unidentified student letter to Peggy Pond Church, in manuscript of talk by Church to the Santa Fe Women's Club, November 30, 1976. Copy in Box 29, folder 10, in PPC, LAHM.

20. Peggy's comments are in a letter she wrote to Fern Lyon, February 22, 1984, in clipping files R24A, LAHM. Vidal's comments are in Joseph Dispenza, "Vidal Delivers Sharp Wit, Recollections of New Mexico," *Albuquerque Journal North,* July 17, 1993.

21. In contrast, Billy's older brother, Mortimer, enjoyed Los Alamos and for a later college architectural studies' project designed a school based on LARS.

22. Lore Watt, six-page untitled manuscript, submitted to *Albuquerque Journal,* October 5, 1978, in clipping file R24A, LAHM.

23. At most eastern boarding schools this role was filled by the wife of the headmaster, or if the head was a bachelor, by his mother or sister.

24. Dr. James Rolls served as the first LARS doctor; in later years Dr. Robert Brown held the position.

25. There are gaps in school records showing who filled the matron and nurse positions in several years. Connell's sister, May, was at Los Alamos for at least a brief time in 1926–1927, perhaps continuously from that time until 1931, and she may have on occasion served as hostess, although there is no record of that.

26. Doris Barker, three-page manuscript, September 1977, in clipping files R24A, LAHM; Jeremy Taylor, e-mail communication to Linda Aldrich, October 27, 1999.

27. John Curtis, in telephone interviews with Linda Aldrich, April 30 and May 4, 2000, and in personal interview on October 16, 2000. May Connell's house at Los Alamos became home to various faculty over the years and during World War II to Kitty and Robert Oppenheimer.

28. Beasley worked for Connell again in 1929–1930, and served as the LARS representative in the Chicago area.

29. Arthur Chase, letter to Maxine Joppa, May 2, 1975, in clipping files R24G, LAHM.

30. The others were Andrew White, son of George White, the dairyman; Ashley Pond III, son of founder Ashley Pond Jr.; Ted and Allen Church, sons of Fermor Church; Rubel Montoya, son of Adolfo Montoya, the head gardener; Richard Womelsduff, son of Jim Womelsduff, Ranch foreman.

31. Parkhurst was from New York and came to Santa Fe around 1910 to work with an archaeological expedition. Self-taught, he received further training from archaeologist Jesse Nusbaum and established a photography studio in Santa Fe in 1915. See the Parkhurst Photo Collection at the Fray Angélico Chavez Library, MNM.

32. Thanks to the efforts of Fuller, Parkhurst, and Gilpin, and to the prints of countless amateurs, LARS is documented photographically in depth and detail. The LARS photographs at LAHM are the primary repository outside of the Parkhurst Collection at the MNM and the Gilpin Collection at the Amon Carter Museum in Dallas.

33. Doris Barker, September 1977, in clipping files R24A, LAHM.

34. Hitchcock, "Young Man at Los Alamos," pp. 4, 6–7, 9–13, and "Autobiography."

35. Connell was a member of the school's advisory council, along with Dr. Frank Mera, director of Sunmount Sanitorium, and Isabel Eckles, president of the National Council of Administrative Women in Education and an acquaintance of Connell's from his days in Silver City. See letter of Jean Forsythe Rieder to Miss Mercer Kendig, July 3, 1931, in Box 129, folder 1731, in Francis Wilson Papers, NMSRCA.

36. Linda Aldrich, interview with Peggy Pond Church on August 14, 1984, in Santa Fe. Peggy Church gave a number of talks over the years about her life on the Pajarito Plateau and at LARS. Texts of some are in PPC and the RS clipping files at LAHM.

37. Peggy Church became a prolific and much-loved poet, publishing many books of poetry and a biography/memoir of her friend Edith Warner, *The House at Otowi Bridge.*

38. Arthur Chase, letter to Maxine Joppa, March 7, 1975, and letter to Hedy Dunn, November 13, 1986; both in clipping file R24A, LAHM. Hitchcock, letter to his mother, February 15, 1922, in "Young Man at Los Alamos"; Harry L. Walen, letter to John Wirth, September 7, 2000.

39. Fermor and Peggy Pond Church, "Los Alamos Ranch School: A Scattered Profile," pp. 13–14, a twenty-six-page manuscript in Box 21, folder 3, in PPC, LAHM. This manuscript is a preliminary draft for the book by Fermor and Peggy Church, *When Los Alamos Was A Ranch School.*

40. Peggy Pond Church, "Letter" read to Los Alamos Garden Club, December 1982. In clipping file R24I; manuscript of talk by Peggy Pond Church to AAUW, October 22, 1983. Both are in LAHM.

41. Russell, *Lady Bird*, p. 53. The Taylor brothers' younger sister, Claudia, was shipped off to family in Alabama when her mother died. The Ranch School and the Santa Fe area worked its magic on Antonio, who returned as a young man and made Santa Fe his lifetime home, for many years running the Old Mexico Shop in downtown Santa Fe. Claudia later became the focus of national interest as Lady Bird, wife of President Lyndon Johnson.

42. Jay Gilchrist, letter to Ann Miller, March 31, 1975, in clipping file R24B, LAHM.

43. Both graduates planned entrance at Yale, although Rose, in fact, ended at Colorado College. At least seven LARS graduates went on to Colorado College, with which Los Alamos had an early connection in the historian Samuel F. Bemis, a faculty member at the college for a few years. At least fifteen LARS graduates attended Yale.

44. *SFNM*, June 4, 1921.

45. *SFNM*, June 16, 1926.

46. Tsianana was a mezzo-soprano of Cherokee-Creek parentage, who toured the country with composer-pianist Charles Wakefield Cadman, who wrote an opera for her that was performed at the Metropolitan Opera House. She entertained American troops in Europe during World War I and continued touring the United States, singing alone or with symphony orchestras, for many years. She was a featured singer at the Santa Fe

Fiesta in its early years. In her Los Alamos concert, she was accompanied by Oskenonton, a tenor of the Mohawk Nation. See Fred Hamilton Rindge, "She Always Sings in Buckskin," in *Holland's Magazine,* September 1926, in clipping files at Fray Angélico Chavez History Library.

47. The talk Curtis was preparing was later the basis for a paper entitled "Spanish Arms and Armor in the Southwest," published posthumously in the *New Mexico Historical Review* 2, no. 2 (April 1927): 107–33.

48. Descriptions of Curtis's death and funeral are in Hitchcock, "Autobiography," p. 42, and in his obituary and following article, *SFNM,* November 4 and 15, 1926. A somewhat different version is given in the transcript of an interview of Pedro Gonzales by Margaret Wohlberg, 1970, in clipping file R23E, LAHM. Also, see the tribute to Curtis in *New Mexico Historical Review* (January 1927). Curtis's publications are listed in Lyle Saunders, *A Guide to Materials Bearing on Cultural Relations in New Mexico* (Albuquerque: University of New Mexico Press, 1994). Among them is "El Conejo," a play written for the Santa Fe Community Theatre, staged on May 13, 1919, with set design by Gustave Baumann. See *El Palacio* 6, 195–203. Curtis's translation of Villagrá's epic poem was not published in his lifetime.

49. Daisy Curtis stayed in Santa Fe for the remainder of her life and was listed as an artist, as was May Connell, in city directories through 1960. To avoid confusion with another artistic Santa Fe woman by the name of Natalie Curtis, who also used the nickname Daisy, Fay's widow listed herself as Rosa M. Curtis.

Chapter 4

1. Fermor S. Church and Peggy Pond Church, *When Los Alamos Was a Ranch School: Historical Profile,* 2d ed. (Los Alamos, N.Mex.: Los Alamos Historical Society, 1998), p. 23.

2. Oscar Steege, comments to John Wirth on April 9, 1999. Oscar was a longtime master, serving from 1934 to 1942, and returning after the war to teach briefly at Los Alamos High School in 1946, before teaching at the Waring Ranch School until it closed in 1949.

3. Lawrence Hitchcock, letter to Bernon Woodle from Otowi, N.Mex., January 26, 1936, in Peggy Pond Church papers, LAHM.

4. Baird was one of four in the last graduation held in January 1943. Telephone comments from Collier Baird to John Wirth.

5. Steege, comments to Wirth, April 9, 1999.

6. *SFNM,* November 1, 1920; Lawrence Hitchcock, citing a letter to his mother, November 8, 1920, in "Young Man at Los Alamos."

7. Chase, "Conflagration on Bathtub Row," July 1990, in clipping file R24A, LAHM.

8. Art Chase, letter to G. Glyphs [*Graphic Glyphs,* an early newsletter of the Los Alamos Historical Society], from Berkshire School, May 2, 1974, in clipping file R24G, LAHM. Ransom Lynch, personal information to John Wirth.

9. Gilbert N. Davis and Harry Walen, personal information to John Wirth.

10. John S. Reed, letter to John Wirth from Lake Forest, IL, November 2, 1999.

11. Harry Walen, letter to John Wirth from Rockport, Mass., April 12, 2001.

12. Page, who taught English from 1932 to 1936, went on to be the gun editor at *Field and Stream* magazine. Anecdotes from Jim Anderson and Charles Ripley.

13. At least seven Hotchkiss students transferred to LARS, four of whom then returned to graduate at Hotchkiss. Rather than graduate from LARS, several boys chose to finish up at other eastern boarding schools, but the relationship with Hotchkiss was special.

14. Van Santvoord's long reign from 1926 to 1955 was profiled most recently in Ernest

Kolowrat's *Hotchkiss: A Chronicle of an American School* (New York: New Amsterdam Books; 1992). Apparently, no correspondence between the two headmasters has survived.

15. Jay G. Rice, 1930, letter to his family [1928?], in Rice Collection, Box 25, folder 9, LAHM.
16. Reed, letter to Wirth, November 2, 1999.
17. Hall, *Anthropology of Everyday Life*, p. 27.
18. Steege, comments to Wirth, April 9, 1999.
19. Arthur Chase, letter to Maxine Joppa from Sheffield, Mass., March 7, 1975, in File R24A, LAHM.
20. Steege, comments to Wirth, April 9, 1999.
21. "Notes of A. J. Connell, working with Charles Kinney on a song in prospect, never finished," undated, folder 51, FSC, NMSRCA.
22. Card courtesy of Joan Rousseau Wright. See p. G25. Inside, a poem by Peggy Pond Church reads: "Starlight sparkles and little fires glow; Over the white and silent snow; And a christmas wish that is old and true; Shines from our mesa land for you."
23. Peggy Pond Church, letter to Bainbridge Bunting from Santa Fe, November 8, 1980, relaying information from Lawrence Hitchcock, in PPC, LAHM.
24. John Gaw Meem, letter to Carol Ann Mullaney, president of the Los Alamos Arts Council, from Santa Fe, September 17, 1972, in John Gaw Meem archive, Job File 47, Box 4, UNM Southwestern Studies Center.
25. John Gaw Meem, letter to Peggy Corbett from Santa Fe, October 7, 1974, Box 4, UNM Southwestern Studies Center.
26. The file for job 196 in the Meem collection is extensive. The quote is from John Meem's letter to Col. John Hudson Poole, husband of Caroline Boeing Poole, from Santa Fe, August 12, 1932, Box 2, UNM Southwestern Studies Center.

    John Meem also became the school architect for the Fountain Valley School in Colorado, and designed the Sandia School for Girls in Albuquerque. After the war, his office remodeled a property in Pojoaque to house the Waring Ranch School. As well, Meem served on the board of the short-lived Los Alamos School in Taos, and sketched a main building that was never built.
27. Arthur Chase, letter to Maxine Joppa from Sheffield, Mass., March 7, 1975, File R24A, LAHM. An early victim of the Depression, this girls' school was supplanted by Brownmoor School, which started in Santa Fe and soon moved to the old Pulitzer estate at Bishop's Lodge in 1931.
28. A principal source for Lawrence Hitchcock's life is his "Autobiography."
29. Recollection of LARS matron Doris M. Barker, Albuquerque, September 1977, in clipping file R24A, LAHM.
30. Robert M. Wood, letter to Maxine Joppa from Atlanta, Ga., April 19, 1974, in clipping file R24G.5, LAHM.
31. Lawrence Hitchcock, "Autobiography," pp. 42–48.
32. Cecil Wirth, letter to Virginia Wirth from Otowi, ca. June 20, 1936, Wirth personal papers.
33. Information from Barbara Hitchcock; Lawrence Hitchcock, letter to the Trustees of the Los Alamos Foundation, from Washington, D.C., July 22, 1945, in clipping file R24M, LAHM.
34. Sue McIntosh Lloyd, *The Putney School: A Progressive Experiment* (New Haven, Conn.: Yale University Press, 1987), chapter 8, "Strike."
35. John Wirth, interview with Ted Church, December 2, 1999; Los Alamos Alumni Association, *Spring Bulletin,* 1936, and *Winter Bulletin,* 1937. Graeme McGowan of the U.S. Forest Service laid out the trail (which still exists at the extreme western end of the modern ski area) and was hired to give ski lessons.

36. For an astute evaluation of the issues, see Nicholas Lemann, *The Big Test: The Secret History of the American Meritocracy* (New York: Farrar, Straus and Giroux, 1999).

37. McLachlan, *American Boarding Schools,* p. 265.

38. Amanda Katie Geer, "The Progressive Origins of the Putney School, Examined through the Life of Its Founder, Carmelita Hinton," senior thesis printed at Putney, Vt., in 1982.

39. See Robert B. Aird, *Deep Springs: Its Founder, History, and Philosophy, with Personal Reflections* (Dyer, Nev.: Deep Springs College, 1997).

40. Robert D. Stuart, Jr., letter to John Wirth from Lake Forest, Ill., July 17, 2000.

41. McLachlan, *American Boarding Schools,* p. 256.

42. Robert D. Stuart, letter to Wirth from Lake Forest, Ill., August 1, 2000.

43. SFNM, June 1927; Hitchcock, letter to a parent on January 13, 1934, in which he also said: "Not only does our care over the physical development bring about that physical strength without which, of course, there could be no accomplishment in studies, but the limitation of the time and importance of the classroom work to its proper proportion of time seems actually to bring about a more concentrated effort in the limits set for that work."

44. A. J. Connell, letter to Lawrence Hitchcock from Los Alamos, September 21, 1942, Hitchcock Papers, Box 25, folder 2, LAHM.

45. Arthur Chase, letter to Maxine Joppa, undated but written in 1974, clipping file R24, LAHM.

46. Peggy Pond Church, letter to Harry Walen from Carpenteria, Calif., February 12, 1944, courtesy of Harry Walen.

47. John Wirth, interview with Rogers Scudder at Groton, October 27, 1999.

48. A. J. Connell, letter to Lawrence Hitchcock from Los Alamos, February 20, 1942, Hitchcock Papers, Box 35, folder 2, LAHM.

49. Harry Walen, "Interview with AJC June, 1942," memo in his possession. Another factor in the move to Groton during these uncertain early months of the war was the opportunity to be closer to their parents.

50. The reference is to Sally Hemmings, the mulatta slave mistress who may well have been Jefferson's wife's half sister, with whom he fathered several children.

51. 1970 Los Alamos Ranch School Reunion file, LAHM.

52. William S. Burroughs, *Naked Lunch* (New York: Doubleday, 1992); and Gore Vidal, *Palimpsest: A Memoir* (New York: Penguin Books, 1996). Los Alamos anecdotes involving these two writers are related in Ted Morgan's *Literary Outlaw: The Life and Times of William S. Burroughs* (New York: Henry Holt and Company, 1988); and Fred Kaplan's *Gore Vidal, A Biography* (New York: Doubleday, 1999).

    First published in 1959, Burroughs's Beat Generation classic is a freewheeling celebration of the drug culture, which also parodies Connell and Hitchcock. However, Rogers Scudder, who knew Burroughs in St. Louis and later at LARS, and roomed with him at Harvard, thought his alienation from Los Alamos was crafted well after he left. In a letter to John Wirth, November 30, 1999, Scudder wrote that it seemed "odd that Burroughs regarded Los Alamos in later life as he records, for he seemed rather fond of it as we recalled it in our years at Harvard." In fact, Burroughs returned to LARS after his Harvard graduation.

    One reviewer noted of Gore Vidal's *Palimpsest* that it "contains enough errors and inconsistencies to make us question just how precise Vidal's memory is . . ." (Harry Kloman, review of *Palimpsest* in the *Pittsburg Post-Gazette,* October 29, 1995, on-line version *http://www.pitt.edu/~kloman/palimpsestf.html*). Not unexpectedly for such a brilliant nonconformist, Vidal "always hated the place [LARS]," Peggy Church wrote Fern Lyon, on February 22, 1984 (letter in clipping file R24A, LAHM), and was happy to leave after one year there. In fact, Vidal acknowledges "my problems staying in school" and never attended college. (Karen Durbin, "A Family's Legacy: Pain and Humor (and a Movie)," *New York Times*, September 15, 2002, p. AR17)

53. Rogers Scudder, interview with Wirth, October 27, 1999.

54. William C. Baird (1936), letter to Linda Aldrich, January 27, 2000; Peter Dechert, "Personal Responsibility," *The Los Alamos Ranch School and Summer Camp, Book of Rosters* (Santa Fe, N.Mex.: Los Alamos Ranch School Reunion Committee, 1991), p. 57.

55. This is Hitchcock's term. Lawrence Hitchcock, letter to Carmelita Hinton, director of the Putney School, from Rockville, Md., February 16, 1954, in Church Collection, Box 5, File 104, NMSRCA. In July 1945, Mrs. Hinton and her daughter Jean were guests at Oppenheimer's ranch in Pecos. At that time her other daughter Joan was a physicist with the Manhattan Project.

Chapter 5

1. While maps refer to this stream as Rito de los Indios, camp and school usage was invariably Rito del Indio. Valle San Antonio is part of the Valles Caldera complex, an extinct volcano encompassed by the (then) privately owned Baca Ranch. Campsites in the Valle Grande, the Valle Toledo, and at Los Posos were also in the Baca Ranch.

2. Especially fine are the slides taken by counselor Charles Ripley in 1939 and camper Bill Carson from 1939 to 1942, and the 16mm movie by counselor James Anderson taken in 1938. Cecil Wirth's 8mm promotional film is also in color. Scenes from Anderson's movie, including a shot of Cecil, and another of summer camp boys swimming nude in the Rio Grande, are featured in the video shown today to visitors at the Bradbury Science Museum in Los Alamos.

3. FSC, Box 3, folder 52, NMSRCA.

4. Albert J. Connell, early school booklet, in PPC, LAHM.

5. Rothman, *On Rims and Ridges,* chapter 7 and pp. 159–62.

6. Lawrence S. Hitchcock, "Los Alamos Ranch Summer Camp, 1922. Report to the Director," FSC, Box 3, folder 52, p. 16, NMSRCA.

7. In 1922 this trail network brought a later plateau resident for his first exploration of the Valle Grande country. As a sickly teen, Robert Oppenheimer (a graduate of the Ethical Culture School in New York City) spent a summer in northern New Mexico. Among the areas he explored with various guides were the Pajarito Plateau and the Valle Grande. Like so many, Oppenheimer returned from his summer in the high desert and mountains of New Mexico with renewed vigor and health.

8. Antonio Taylor, letter to his father from Los Alamos, September 15, 1919. Taylor became Lyndon Johnson's brother-in-law and for many years ran The Old Mexico Shop in Santa Fe.

9. Lawrence S. Hitchcock, "Los Alamos Notes, 1922 Summer Camp," written in 1980 from family letters and his 1922 camp diary, p. 14, Hitchcock Collection, LAHM.

10. Unless otherwise noted, all Connell quotes hereafter are taken from the abundant LARS student record files in FSC, NMSRCA. The recollection is by Jim Anderson, in a letter to John Wirth, January 22, 2000.

11. 1924 camp file, FSC, Box 3, folder 52, NMSRCA.

12. Bill Carson, letters home for July 13 and July 20, 1942, in LAHM.

13. Fermor S. Church, letter of recommendation in LARS student record files, FSC, NMSRCA.

14. Wirth replaced the camp's three-patrol scheme with a more flexible grouping—the older boys were Montaneros, the younger were Villeros.

15. Hitchcock, "Los Alamos Notes," p. 14.
16. Hitchcock, "Autobiography," p. 48.
17. Fermor S. Church, "Summer Camp Season of 1930, A Report to the Director," TCS Bulletin no. 2 (July 7, 1930), FSC, Box 3, folder 55, NMSRCA.
18. Hitchcock, "Autobiography," p. 49.
19. David Hughes, letter to his father from Los Alamos, May 30, 1937, courtesy of David Hughes.
20. Church and Church, *When Los Alamos Was a Ranch School,* p. 21.
21. Cecil W. Wirth, "Los Alamos Camp, 1942, Twenty-First Season," promotional brochure, Wirth personal papers.
22. Peggy Pond Church, "Los Alamos Ranch School (A Scattered Profile)," manuscript, Box 21, folder 3, PPC, LAHM, pp. 17–18.
23. Hitchcock, "Los Alamos Notes, 1922 Summer Camp," p. 20. The eastern reach of the Highline—the Skyline—was still marked by the Forest Service as late as 1973, when Virginia, John, son Peter, and the Churches climbed to the summit of Chicoma, but it is now abandoned although still passable overall. The western reach, descending from the San Pedro Peaks Wilderness in the direction of Coyote, is still called the Highline Trail on the USGS topographic map. Yet even this remnant of the once-important Highline seems to have lost its name, being now called by the Coyote Ranger Station an extension of the Las Vacas pack trail.
24. Ibid., p. 21.
25. Ibid., pp. 20–21, 24.
26. Hitchcock, "Los Alamos Notes, 1922 Summer Camp," Bulletin 14 (August 8, 1922), in FSC, NMSRCA.
27. Ibid., pp. 13–14.
28. Fermor S. Church, "Los Alamos Ranch Summer Camp: Report, Summer of 1927," Box 3, folder 3, p. 10, FSC, NMSRCA.
29. Hitchcock, "Autobiography," p. 49.
30. Hitchcock, "Young Man at Los Alamos," January 9, 1922.
31. Hitchcock, "Autobiography," p. 41.
32. "Brilliant 14th Commencement," *SFNM,* June 15, 1935. Francis R. Rousseau, questionnaire for 1973 LARS Reunion, in clipping file R24B, LAHM.
33. Among students who earned the twenty-one merit badges needed to became Eagle Scouts, Rousseau stands out for achieving bronze and silver palms for a total of thirty-five merit badges, and then for becoming the nation's first Mountain Scout. William C. Baird, 1936, also became a Mountain Scout. Alan H. Meyer, 1940, recalls that "some few did take scouting seriously." Joe Ryan and Kent Hutchinson were Eagle Scouts, and perhaps one other boy in his time. Alan Meyer, letter to John Wirth from Dallas, November 5, 1999.
34. Church and Church, *When Los Alamos Was a Ranch School,* pp. 19–21.
35. Bruce Carson, letter, July 28, 1941, LAHM.
36. William Norton Baird, "Memories of Los Alamos," p. 2, LAHM.
37. James W. Powell, letter to Linda Aldrich from Kansas City, Mo., July 2, 1985, passing on this story from his cousin, in clipping file R24G.5, LAHM.
38. Cecil W. Wirth, "Los Alamos Camp, 1939," brochure, LAHM.
39. This was true at least in 1937, the camp's first year of operation. By 1939 everybody packed horses.
40. Los Alamos Alumni Association, *Bulletin,* winter 1937, LAHM.
41. Professor William Carson diary for August 30, 1939, courtesy of Bill Carson. Los Alamos made a big production of the mint julep; Hitch, for example, always served them "just-so" in frosted glasses.

42. Los Alamos Alumni *Bulletin,* summer 1941, p. 3, LAHM.

43. Bill Carson, Letter of July 13, 1942, in LAHM.

44. Maurice Lonsway, 1942, was senior counselor; Ben Raskob, 1942, and Ted Church, 1943, helped as well.

45. Oscar A. Steege, "Los Alamos Ranch School—Reflections," March 2, 1999, p. 2, in Wirth personal papers.

46. William Carson, letter, September 1, 1941, in LAHM.

47. Charles Jenney taught Latin and History during the 1926–1927 academic year, and assisted with the camp in 1929. Jenney, letter to Margaret Wohlberg from Lincoln Center, Mass., August 22, 1977, in clipping file R24A, LAHM.

48. Baird, "Memories."

Chapter 6

1. For example, the navy's takeover of the Mount Vernon Seminary, a girl's school in Washington, D.C. "The high-handed seizure of the Mount Vernon campus came at a time of maximum military hubris. What the armed services wanted they took," writes David Brinkley, in *Washington Goes to War* (New York: Knopf, 1988), p. 117. In Albuquerque the Sandia School for Girls was taken by the Army Air Corps; the main school building, designed by John Gaw Meem, became the officers club at Kirtland Air Force Base.

2. An early official source is Vincent C. Jones, *Manhattan: The Army and the Atomic Bomb,* in the series *United States Army in World War II* (Washington, D.C.: Center for Military History, 1985), especially pp. 82–88, 328–31. A site in Utah on Mormon farmland was rejected on grounds of cost and, likely, because these farmers had the political clout to resist. Jemez Springs, the first New Mexico site selected by Col. John H. Dudley, was rejected by Oppenheimer and Groves in favor of Los Alamos. (In addition to its physical limitations, Jemez Springs was close to Jemez Pueblo, whose title was safeguarded under the Treaty of Guadalupe Hidalgo, and which could have stirred up awkward questions from the formidable Harold Ickes, Secretary of the Interior.) Dudley's account, "Ranch School to Secret City," is in *Reminiscences of Los Alamos, 1943–1945,* ed. Lawrence Badash, Joseph O. Hirschfelder, and Herbert P. Broida (Dordrecht, Holland: D. Reidel, 1980), pp. 1–11. See also LANL's account: "Oppenheimer's Better Idea: Ranch School becomes the Arsenal of Democracy," at the website: www.lanl.gov/worldview/welcome/history/07_school.arsenal.html. Also, see Robert W. Seidel, *Los Alamos and the Development of the Atomic Bomb* (Los Alamos, N.Mex.: Otowi Crossing Press, 1995), pp. 20 ff.

3. When cancer struck Cecil Wirth in April, Ferm asked Dr. Lawrence if the Radiation Lab had possibly developed a suitable therapy.

4. "In the spring [Keith] had recommended Los Alamos to the OSRD Planning Board [which turned him down] and when Col. James C. Marshall formed the Manhattan District that summer he had recommended Los Alamos to Col. Marshall." Eugene Sundt, letter to Lawrence Hitchcock, May 7, 1970, in Hitchcock Collection, Box 25, folder 6, LAHM.

5. Keith was first introduced to Connell by Harold Osborn, an executive of the Continental Oil Co. whose son Greg was going to Los Alamos. A major contributor to the success of the Manhattan Project for his design work at Oak Ridge, where as president of Kellex Corporation he supervised design and development of the huge gaseous diffusion plant, Keith was president of Hydrocarbon Research from 1943 to 1963. He died in 1976.

6. Eugene Sundt, interview with P. C. Keith in Tucson, April 10, 1970, transcribed in the

Duffy Paxton manuscript "Job 444; The First Year of Zia," p. 219, in Sundt Collection, Box 36, Folder 1, LAHM. "All I know, Mr. Sundt, is that of the people on the Planning Board, and of all the people connected with the project, I was the only one as far as I know, who kept suggesting that something should be done out in New Mexico. . . . I know that [sometime that fall] beyond any doubt that I discussed in detail with Groves Los Alamos . . . [and] the use of the school as a laboratory" (p. 230). Also, see the reference in LANL, "Oppenheimer's Better Idea"; and Seidel, *Los Alamos*, p. 21.

7. A. J. Connell, letter to Lawrence Hitchcock, September 21, 1942, Hitchcock Collection, Box 25, folder 2, LAHM. Harry Walen, letter to Connell, July 1942; Cecil Wirth, letter to his brother Walter, July 23, 1942, both in Wirth personal papers.

8. Fermor Church in Harvard Class of 1921, *Twenty Fifth Anniversary Report* (Cambridge, Mass.: Harvard University, 1946), p. 114. Church, letter to Eugene Sundt, March 21, 1970, in FSC, Box 1, folder 4, NMSRCA.

9. Peggy Pond Church, letter to her mother from Los Alamos, November 23, 1942, in PPC, Box 21, folder 7, LAHM.

10. Fermor Church, letter to Eugene Sundt, March 21, 1970, in FSC, Box 1, folder 4, NMSRCA.

11. Jones, *Manhattan*, p. 84. Stephane Groueff, *Manhattan Project: The Untold Story of the Making of the Atomic Bomb* (New York: Bantam Books, 1967), p. 72. Richard Rhodes, *The Making of the Atomic Bomb* (New York: Simon and Schuster, 1986), p. 451. Williamson Murray and Allan R. Millet, *A War to be Won: Fighting the Second World War* (Cambridge, Mass.: The Belknap Press, 2000), p. 518.

12. "Bences Gonzales Recalls 62 Years of Hill Development," in *Community Affairs News* (January 1959), p. 5. According to Bences, Lt. Col. Whitney Ashbridge, an early LARS student and soon to be the second post commander, was a member of this group.

13. "Zia Project Notes on Dr. Carl Anderson, March 14, 1970," in FSC, Box 1, folder 4, NMSRCA. Connell's secretary, Perry Merrill, recalled Anderson's January 1942 visit and ride with Hitchcock. See also in same source Eugene Sundt, letter to Fermor Church, April 16, 1970, which summarizes and quotes directly from Church's letter to Hitchcock of November 20, 1942, and Hitchcock's reply of the twenty-sixth—neither of which survive in the original.

14. Memo, "Final Disposition of Lands Acquired by War Department [Los Alamos Demolition Range]," E. G. Miller, Assistant Regional Forester, Santa Fe National Forest, Albuquerque, February 7, 1944, Box 31, folder 11, LAHM. Lt. General Leslie R. Groves, *Now It Can Be Told: The Story of the Manhattan Project* (New York: Harpers, 1962), p. 67.

15. Hitchcock, who was consulted throughout the negotiations, considered the final settlement a fair price, given the uncertainties of valuing the school property during wartime. Hitchcock, letter to Fred Rousseau, June 5, 1943, in Hitchcock Collection, LAHM.

16. Los Alamos Alumni *Bulletin*, spring 1943. A. J. Connell, letter to William Carson, April 10, 1943. As E. G. Miller, the Assistant Regional Forester, reported to the Forest Supervisor of Santa Fe National Forest, in a Memo dated February 8, 1944: "I recall hearing Mr. Connell say that he hoped eventually to acquire the lands that the War Department had taken over from him." Box 31, folder 11, LAHM.

17. Dudley, "Ranch School to Secret City," p. 3.

18. Phone conversation with Van Dorn Hooker (Meem's successor as UNM architect) on September 10, 2000. Kruger, a self-styled "architect-engineer" (more businessman than designer), oversaw the reconfiguration of Ranch School buildings: adding two wings onto Fuller Lodge and turning Spruce Cottage and the Arts and Crafts Building into residences. Kruger also drew plans for the laboratory buildings along military specifications

and made construction plans for the famous Sundt duplexes. In 1947 his firm designed the master plan for the town of Los Alamos, working on a cost plus basis. Meanwhile, the Roswell flight school designed by Meem—which might have become the future Air Force Academy—was never built, and lacking Kruger's political contacts (specifically close ties to Senator Clinton Anderson) he received no work at the new Los Alamos.

19. Lawrence Hitchcock, letter to General R. E. Wood from Washington, D.C., May 15, 1944, in PPC, Box 6, folder 31, LAHM.

20. *The Waring Ranch School*, brochure, courtesy of Carolina Waring Stewart. Waring founded a day school for younger boys, first operated out of the Rose family home in Santa Fe. In 1941 it moved to Pojoaque. After Los Alamos closed, it added horses to its program and opened to boys ages twelve to eighteen.

21. Lawrence Hitchcock, letter to A. J. Connell from Washington, D.C., August 1, 1943, in Hitchcock Collection, Box 25, folder 2, LAHM.

22. Fred Rousseau, letter to Lawrence Hitchcock from Santa Fe, January 24, 1944, in Hitchcock Collection, Box 25, folder 2, LAHM.

23. Information from Barbara Hitchcock. Lawrence Hitchcock, letter to his Aunt Beb from Washington, D.C., February 14, 1943, in Hitchcock Collection, Box 25, folder 2, LAHM.

24. Fermor Church, letters to Hitchcock from Los Alamos, December 7 and 8, 1942, in Hitchcock Collection, Box 25, folder 2, LAHM.

25. Lawrence Hitchcock, quoting Ferm Church in letter to the Trustees of the Los Alamos Foundation from Washington, D.C., July 22, 1945, in clipping file R24M, LAHM.

26. However, even in 1919 to reach the Pecos high country they had to ride past encroaching private cabins and ranches being built on leased national forest land, a land-use process of which Connell disapproved.

27. In another of the multiple connections that linked Los Alamos to Santa Fe, Aileen O'Bryan, who had decorated the Big House when LARS first opened in 1917, was interior decorator for the Santa Fe Inn when it opened in 1939.

28. At the last meeting of the Board of Trustees of the Los Alamos Foundation, on February 28, 1973, the board signed over its residual assets of approximately fifty-one thousand dollars to the foundation endowment fund of St. John's College. "Gift Agreement" in FSC, Box 4, folder 98, NMSRCA.

29. Fermor Church, letter to Lawrence Hitchcock from Santa Fe, May 22, 1943, in Hitchcock Collection, LAHM.

30. Howard Meyer, letter to the Los Alamos Historical Society from Tulsa, May 17, 1970; in clipping file R24A, LAHM. Peggy Church, letter to Ted from Carpenteria, Calif., February 12, 1944, courtesy of Sharon Snyder.

31. Hitchcock, letter to Virginia [Wirth] Wiebenson from Rockville, Md., September 17, 1981, in Hitchcock Collection, Box 29, folder 16, LAHM.

32. A. J. Connell, letter to Lt. Colonel J. M. Harman, Corps of Engineers, January 26, 1943, in FSC, Box 1, folder 11, NMSRCA.

33. The sense that students had of being in a special place was by design reinforced in the rural ambiance of other schools of the day, among them Groton, Putney, and Deep Springs.

34. Sterling Colgate, "LARS: Isolation vs. Intellectual Intensity," talk given at Los Alamos on June 12, 1988; notes by Linda Aldrich.

35. Boy Scouts of America, *Adventuring for Senior Scouts* (New York: Boy Scouts of America, 1942), p. 465.

36. Christina Hoff Somers, "The War against Boys," *The Atlantic Monthly* 285, no. 5 (May 2000), on-line version.

37. David Brooks, "The Organization Kid," *The Atlantic Monthly* 287, no. 4 (April 2001), p. 54.

38. "It is reverence that must be taught, day and night, if boys are not to be apes," a master relates in Louis Auchincloss, *The Rector of Justin* (Boston: Houghton Mifflin Company, 1964), p. 291.

39. Auchincloss, *Rector of Justin*, chapter 22.

40. John Katzman, founder and CEO of *The Princeton Review,* says that "the SAT's day is long past, [being] a vestige of another era, a crummy test of testmanship that should be discarded at the first possible moment. It provides no data to colleges that can't simply be gleaned from the race, gender, and socioeconomic class of applicants." Source is on line, from the *Chronicle of Higher Education.* Also, see Diana Jean Schemo, "Head of U. of California Seeks to End SAT Use in Admissions," *The New York Times* (February 17, 2001), pp. A1, A11.

41. L. L. Nunn, the founder, "wrote of the Deep Springs experience of isolation, liberal arts education, and student management of the ranch and college: each student comes 'not for conventional scholastic training; not for ranch life; not to become proficient in commercial or professional pursuits for personal gain. You come to prepare for a life of service.'" Quoted by Stephen Trimble in "A Wilderness with Cows," p. 128, in *The Geography of Childhood: Why Children Need Wild Places,* by Gary Paul Nabhan and Stephen Trimble, (Boston: Beacon Press, 1994). See also L. Jackson Newell, "Deep Springs: Loyalty to a Fault?" in *Maverick Colleges: Ten Notable Experiments in American Education,* ed. L. Jackson Newell and Katherine C. Reynolds, no date: http://www.gse.utah.edu/EdAdm/Galvin/Maverick.html.

42. "Rancho Valmora, a non-profit educational and social learning environment for adolescents," brochure.

Chapter 7

1. Based primarily on oral testimony, this chapter also draws on the author's extensive experience working with Hispanic sources and the history of northern New Mexico.

2. Theresa Strottman, interview with Ray and Severo Gonzales, Los Alamos Inn, March 24, 1998, in LAHM-M2001-72-1-2, p. 15.

3. Ibid., p. 15.

4. A. Samuel Adelo, "Emilio Naranjo: Bondadoso Lider Politico del Norte," *La Herencia* 29 (2001) p. 16.

5. Ray and Severo Gonzales interview, March 24, 1998, p. 7.

6. Ibid., p. 12.

7. Ibid., p. 10.

8. Interview by Theresa Strottman and Yvonne Delamater with Ray and Severo Gonzales at Los Alamos Historical Museum Archives, September 20, 1991, in LAHM-M2001-72-1-1, p. 37.

9. Ibid., p. 37.

10. Ray and Severo Gonzales, interview, March 24, 1998, p. 12.

11. Ray and Severo Gonzales, interview, September 20, 1991, p. 43.

12. Ibid., p. 44.

13. Ibid., pp. 44–45.

14. Ray and Severo Gonzales, interview, March 24, 1998, p. 24.

15. Ibid., p. 9.

16. Ibid., p. 8.

17. Ibid., p. 9.
18. Interview by Theresa Strottman and John Wirth with Margaret Montoya Caperton at her Española family home, July 30, 1999, in LAHM-M2001-72-1-3, p. 4.
19. Ibid., p. 2.
20. Ibid., pp. 4, 10.
21. Ibid., p. 11.
22. Ibid., p. 10.
23. Ibid., p. 1.
24. Theresa Strottman, telephone conversation with Rubel Montoya, March 8, 2000.
25. Margaret Montoya Caperton, interview, July 30, 1999, p. 19.
26. Ibid., p. 13.
27. Ibid., p. 14.
28. Ibid., p. 2.
29. Ibid., p. 6.
30. Ibid., p. 20.
31. Ibid., p. 8.
32. Ibid., pp. 5–6.
33. Raymond Bences Gonzales, "A Boy on the Hill," unpublished memoir, LAHM, n.d.
34. Theresa Strottman telephone conversation with Adelina Montoya Montaño, March 8, 2000.
35. Margaret Montoya Caperton, interview, July 30, 1999, p. 15.
36. Ibid., p. 9.
37. Ibid., pp. 11, 19.
38. Ibid., pp. 8. 19.
39. John Wirth, interview with Helen Sulier Robertson in Albuquerque, November 23, 1999.
40. John Wirth, interview with Joan Rousseau Wright, in Albuquerque, November 16, 1999.
41. Gonzales, "A Boy on the Hill"; Strottman, phone conversation with Rubel Montoya, March 8, 2000; Caperton interview, n. 18, p. 11.
42. Joan Rousseau Wright interview, n. 40.
43. Margaret Montoya Caperton, interview, July 30, 1999, pp. 13–14.
44. Ray and Severo Gonzales, interview, September 20, 1991, p. 38.
    Whitney Ashbridge, who attended LARS in 1918–1919, was the second post commander of Los Alamos.
45. Other employees who stayed on and worked for the Manhattan Project were Gilberto Solis, the second cook; Lee Gomez; Basil Helm; Ruben Quintana; and Pablo Herrera, the night watchman.
46. Wirth, conversation with Rubel Montoya at the 1997 reunion.
47. This account is based on conversations with participants, and a close reading of the Foundation's records in the State Archives. In 1973, all remaining assets of the Los Alamos Foundation were transferred to the St. John's College endowment fund.
48. Rothman, *On Rims and Ridges,* p. 179.
49. Miller, memo, February 8, 1944, chapter 6, n. 14.

Chapter 8

1. Vehicles negotiating the remote, unfenced roads leading to the ranch were at risk. Cecil Wirth's van struck a horse one dark evening on the way back from Santa Fe, and later his new Buick, driven by two of the Spruce boys, suffered a similar fate.

2. Among the men who played poker in the workers' clubhouse, Lawrence Hitchcock, Bences Gonzales, and the Womelsduff brothers were regulars. Anyone could play. "It was a way of keeping in touch with the entire male population." Harry L. Walen, letter to John Wirth, September 10, 2000.

3. In early 1943, this deadfall was used again to make lumber for some of the first buildings at Site Y.

4. Harry Walen, letter to John Wirth, September 7, 2000.

Chapter 9

1. This was *The Politics of Brazilian Development, 1930–1954* (Stanford, Calif.: Stanford University Press, 1970).

2. Cecil left the Ranch in late May for treatment in New York, where Virginia soon joined him after leaving my brother and me with our Davis grandparents in Clifton.

3. Arthur C. Chase, letter to his sister Elizabeth, April 1943, courtesy of Janet Chase Soldati.

4. Ibid. This place, with its many switchbacks up to the top of Los Alamos mesa, used to be called Otowi Hill in school days. Today, it is dubbed "Meditation Point" by current residents. In 1932, Breakneck was renamed Lower Los Alamos Mesa Trail, probably to reassure anxious mothers; now the old name has come back.

5. A. J. Connell, letter to Lawrence Hitchcock from Los Alamos, May 27, 1942, in Hitchcock Collection, Box 29, folder 16, LAHM.

6. Charles S. Pearce Jr., 1938, letter to John Wirth from Corsicana, Tex., May 6, 1997.

7. F. H. Cheley, letter of recommendation to Harvard Business School, November 30, 1932. Also, H. M. Winter, 1929, letter to John D. Wirth from Charlemont, Mass., May 1, 1997. "When I knew him at Estes Park," Winter writes, "your father was one of my earliest and strongest 'role models,' and I recall clearly many episodes when, as counselor and friend, he steered me from folly to reason, and from fear to courage. I welcome this chance, after all these years, to express my admiration and affection for that *good* man!"

8. A. J. Connell, letter to William Carson, Santa Fe, April 10, 1943, courtesy of his son Bill Carson. Not that Connell had reconciled himself to letting go. A. J., now past his prime, had blocked several of Cecil's good ideas for improving the school and fulminated that Cecil, "who had come out of nowhere," was ungrateful. Still enjoying the trappings of power in those last difficult months, he told Harry Walen that Cecil "was feeling his oats too much" and probably would have left. "As long as I am alive, this is my school, and I will run it the way I want." Harry Walen, "Interview with AJC, June, 1942," dated March 19, 1944, courtesy of Harry Walen.

9. Arthur C. Chase, letter to Senator Timothy E. Wirth from Sheffield, Mass., January 11, 1987, courtesy of Tim Wirth.

10. Gilbert C. Davis, letter to Cecil Wirth from Morenci, Ariz., October 27, 1940.

11. Joseph Whitehill, letter to Senator Timothy Wirth from Tulsa, June 9, 1992, courtesy of Tim Wirth.

12. Peter Dechert, 1941, letter to John Gaw Meem from Santa Fe, August 30, 1971.

13. Pearce, letter, May 6, 1997.

14. Ransom V. Lynch, letter to John Wirth from Exeter, N.H., October 19, 1999.

15. In *Time* magazine's current-affairs contest, he won the Los Alamos faculty prize for 1938 and 1939.

16. Cecil W. Wirth, letter to John and Tim Wirth from Memorial Hospital, N.Y., April 1, 1943.

17. Elisabeth Walen, "Memories of Los Alamos Ranch School from a Faculty Wife," manu-

script, September, 2000, p. 2; Harry L. Walen, letter to John Wirth from Rockport, Mass., August 16, 1991.

18. Virginia D. Wirth, letter to Elizabeth Carson from Otowi, N.Mex., May 28, 1941, courtesy of Bill Carson.

19. Virginia D. Wirth to Elizabeth Carson, July 13, 1941, courtesy of Bill Carson.

20. Kim Hunter, *The Little Cow in the Valle Grande,* illustrated by Mary Sundstrom (Mission Viejo, Calif.: Acrobytes Software, 1995).

21. Jay Gilchrist, 1932, "A. J. Connell," profile submitted to the Los Alamos Historical Society, December 8, 1977, clipping file R24A, LAHM.

22. Harry L. Walen, letter to Margaret Wohlberg from Newton Highlands, Mass., September 11, 1975, clipping file R24D, LAHM.

23. Chase, letter to Senator Tim Wirth, January 11, 1987.

24. Peggy Pond Church, letter to Virginia Wirth from Otowi, N.Mex., September 1939.

25. Peggy Pond Church, letter to Ted Church from Carpenteria, Calif., February 12, 1944, courtesy of Sharon Snyder.

26. Peggy Pond Church, letter to Virginia Wirth from Ranchos de Taos, September 11, 1950.

27. Peggy Pond Church, letter to Virginia D. Wiebenson from Santa Fe, January 25, 1978.

28. Virginia D. Wiebenson, letter to Lawrence Hitchcock from Denver, August 14, 1981, in Hitchcock Collection, Box 25, Folder 6, LAHM.

29. Peggy Pond Church, letter to Virginia D. Wiebenson from Santa Fe, November 28, 1984.

Chapter 10

1. Richard Rhodes, "Vital Connections: Santa Fe, Los Alamos and the World," address delivered at Santa Fe, March 23, 2001, reprinted in the *Los Alamos Monitor* (March 24, 2001), p. A11.

2. F. S. Curtis, "The Influence of Weapons on New Mexico History," *New Mexico Historical Review* 1, no. 3 (July 1926): 324–34.

3. The literature is vast, and Rhodes's *Making of the Atomic Bomb* is certainly the place to start. See also Mary Palevsky, *Atomic Fragments: A Daughter's Questions* (Berkeley, Calif.: University of California Press, 2000); and Katrina R. Mason, *Children of Los Alamos: An Oral History of the Town Where the Atomic Age Began* (New York: Twayne Publishers, 1995). Living conditions in wartime Los Alamos are profiled on pages 11–18 of [LANL Public Relations Office] *Los Alamos, Beginning of an Era 1943–1945,* reprinted by the Los Alamos Historical Society, 1999 edition.

4. S. S. Schweber, *In the Shadow of the Bomb: Bethe, Oppenheimer, and the Moral Responsibility of the Scientist* (Princeton, N.J.: Princeton University Press, 2000), p. 16. Richard G. Hewlett and Jack M. Holl, *Atoms for Peace and War, 1953–1961* (Berkeley, Calif.: University of California Press, 1989), pp. 253–56.

5. Craig Daniel Allen, "Changes on the Landscape of the Jemez Mountains, New Mexico," Ph.D. diss., University of California, Berkeley, 1989, p. 18.

6. Notice published in *The New Mexican,* April 13, 1951, cited in the April 13, 2001, *SFNM,* p. A7.

7. A. J. Connell, letter to Hitchcock, February 20, 1942, Hitchcock Collection, Box 25, folder 2, LAHM; Wirth, phone conversation with Oscar Steege, May 5, 1997.

8. See William deBuys, "Los Alamos Fire Offers a Lesson in Humility," *High Country News* vol. 32, no. 13 (July 3, 2000), pp. 16–17. For the full argument by a landscape ecologist, consult Craig Allen's dissertation, "Changes on the Landscape of the Jemez Mountains."

9. Allen, "Changes on the Landscape of the Jemez Mountains," pp. 217 ff. "Paved roads had not yet reached the Jemez Mountains in 1935, but by 1981 449.61 km of paved roads

had been built. The paved road network reflects the intensive development activities associated with LANL and the town sites of Los Alamos and White Rock to the north of Bandelier National Monument, and the town of Cochiti Lake to the south" (p. 224).

10. Graeme McGowan, letter to Harry Walen from Fort Leonard Wood, January 28, 1944, courtesy of Harry Walen.

11. Craig Martin, *Los Alamos Trails: Hiking, Biking and Cross-Country Skiing* (Los Alamos, N.Mex.: All Seasons Publishing, 1999). Also, see Andrea Kron, "Hiking Trails and Jeep Roads of Los Alamos County, Bandelier National Monument and Vicinity" (Los Alamos, N.Mex.: Otowi Station, 1993).

12. Don J. Usner, *Sabino's Map: Life in Chimayó's Old Plaza* (Albuquerque: University of New Mexico Press, 1995). *The House at Otowi Bridge,* also a UNM Press book, was first published in 1959 and is still in print.

13. "These historic rugs and this historical building have enhanced each other for nearly fifty years," the petition stated. "In substance, it is public sentiment that the rugs are intrinsic to the building and the history of our unique community. They should be returned to grace the walls of Fuller Lodge once again." Maxine Joppa et al., "Background of the Navajo Rug Controversy," ca. April 3, 1975, in Hitchcock Collection, Box 25, Folder 6, LAHM.

14. For example, Vernon Loeb, "Dark Cloud Hangs Over Los Alamos," *The Washington Post* (August 27, 2000), p. A01.

Appendix

1. Latin salutation and translation by Rogers Scudder, LARS graduate 1929, and master 1935–1936. The salute was read by Arthur Chase at the first LARS reunion, which was held at the Yale Club in New York City on September 17, 1970, to honor "the school's beloved headmaster." Orbilius was Horace's stern, harsh teacher.

2. Adapted from Navajo peyote song—*Hio, Hio, Witsy-Nah-Yo*—six beats, the first beat with an accent.

3. In U.S. District Court, Civil Action No. 528, served upon "A. J. Connell, President and Statutory Agent for Los Alamos Ranch School, Inc.," June 18, 1943. Courtesy of Jean Seth.

4. Compiled by Linda Aldrich, Sharon Snyder, and John Wirth. This roster is striking both for the high quality of teachers—"a very good stable," as Harry Walen commented—and also for the large number of one-year men or short-termers who were lured by the chance for adventure in the West, but were not overly encouraged to stay on because of low salaries, the isolation, and other opportunities. Overall, the portrait is one of a serious academic program, run on a shoestring and anchored on a small core faculty.

Selected Bibliography

Libraries and Archives

Boy Scouts of America: National Archives, Irving, Texas; Seton Museum Archives, Philmont Scout Ranch, New Mexico.

Brown University Archives.

Clark University Library, Archives.

Cornell University, Krock Library, Rare and Manuscript Collections.

Francis Parker School, San Diego.

Harvard University Archives.

Hotchkiss School Alumni Office.

Irish American Historical Society, New York City.

Los Alamos Historical Museum Archives [LAHM]. Douglass Campbell Collection; Peggy Pond Church Collection [PPC]; Lawrence S. Hitchcock Collection; Los Alamos Ranch School Clipping and Miscellaneous Files; Los Alamos Ranch School Photo Collections; Jay Rice Collection; Eugene Sundt Collection.

Museum of New Mexico: Fray Angélico Chavez Library; Photography Archive.

New Mexico Medical History Program and Health Science Center Archives, University of New Mexico, Albuquerque.

New Mexico State Records Center and Archives [NMSRCA]: Fermor S. Church Collection [FSC]; John Gaw Meem Photo Archive.

Taft School Archives.

United States National Archives: Papers of General Leslie R. Groves, RG 200; Records of the Office of the Commanding General, Manhattan Project, RG 77.

University of Michigan, Roy B. Chapin Collection [RBC], Michigan Historical Collections, Bentley Historical Library.

University of New Mexico, Southwestern Studies Center [UNM]: Peggy Pond Church Collection; John Gaw Meem Archive.

Yale University Library, Manuscripts and Archives. Samuel Flagg Bemis Papers.

Unpublished Manuscripts and Papers

Aldrich, Linda H. Correspondence with respect to LARS.

Allen, Craig Daniel. "Changes on the Landscape of the Jemez Mountains, New Mexico." Ph.D. Dissertation, University of California, Berkeley, 1989.

Baird, William Norton. "Memories of Los Alamos." LAHM, 1999.

Church, Peggy Pond. "Los Alamos Ranch School (A Scattered Profile." PPC, LAHM.

Dechert, Peter. "Book of Rosters: The Los Alamos Ranch School and Summer Camp." Santa Fe, The Los Alamos Ranch School 1991 Reunion Committee, 1991.

Dechert, Peter. School Rosters and short sketches, on disk.

Geer, Amanda Katie. "The Progressive Origins of the Putney School, Examined Through the Life of its Founder, Carmelita Hinton." Senior thesis printed at Putney, Vt., 1982.

Gonzales, Raymond Bences. "A Boy on the Hill." LAHM, n.d.

Hitchcock, Lawrence Sill. "Autobiography, August, 1981." Courtesy of Barbara Hitchcock.

———. "Los Alamos Notes, 1922 Summer Camp." Hitchcock Collection, LAHM.

———. Los Alamos Ranch Summer Camp, 1922. Report to the Director. FSC, NMSRCA.

———. "Young Man at Los Alamos, 1919–1922." Courtesy of Barbara Hitchcock.

Kieselhorst, Earl. "Atoms of Reminiscence: Before the Atomic Bomb." LAHM.

Stewart, Carolina Waring. Personal collections.

Walen, Harry. Personal letters and collections.

Wallace, Mack. "The Los Alamos Years: 1934–36." LAHM, n.d.

Wirth, John D. Correspondence and personal papers with respect to LARS.

Newspapers

Santa Fe New Mexican [*SFNM*]
The Silver City Enterprise
The Silver City Independent

Interviews

Anderson, James R. Jr., 1938

Baird, Collier W., 1943

Caperton, Margaret Montoya

Carson, William C.

Chase, Arthur (master)

Church, Peggy Pond

Church, Theodore S., 1943

Curtis, John

Davis, Gilbert N., 1941

Dechert, Peter, 1941

Gallegos, Eugene

Gonzales, Raymond

Gonzales, Severo

Hinton, Betty Huning

Hitchcock, Barbara

Hooker, Van Dorn

Hughes, David H. Jr., 1937

Johnson, Alan W.

Lynch, Ransom VanBrunt (master)

Meem, Barbara Townsend
Montaño, Adelina Montoya
Montoya, Rubel
Moore, Robert E.
Palmer, Ellen Curtis
Raskob, Benjamin G., 1942
Ripley, Charles Percell, 1938
Robertson, Helen Sulier
Scudder, Rogers V. Jr., 1930 (master)
Shain, Charles E. (master)
Steege, Oscar A. (master)
Stewart, Carolina Waring
Walen, Elizabeth
Walen, Harry L. (master)
Wallace, Jean
Wirth, Timothy E.
Wright, Joan Rousseau

Published Books and Articles

Aird, Robert B. *Deep Springs: Its Founder, History and Philosophy, with Personal Reflections.* Dyer, Nev.: Deep Springs, 1997.

Anderson, Carl David. *The Discovery of Anti-matter: The Autobiography of Carl David Anderson, the Youngest Man to Win the Nobel Prize.* Edited by Richard J. Weiss. Singapore: World Scientific, 1999.

Armitage, Shelley, contributing editor. *Bones Incandescent: The Pajarito Journals of Peggy Pond Church.* Lubbock: Texas Tech University Press, 2001.

Armstrong, Christopher F. "On the Making of Good Men: Character-Building in the New England Boarding Schools." In *The High Status Track: Studies of Elite Schools and Stratification.* Edited by Paul William Kingston and Lionel S. Lewis. Albany: State University Press of New York, 1990.

Athearn, Robert G. *The Mythic West in Twentieth-Century America.* Lawrence: University of Kansas Press, 1986.

Auchincloss, Louis. *The Rector of Justin.* Boston: Houghton Mifflin Company, 1964.

Baylor, Ronald H., and Timothy J. Meagher, eds. *The New York Irish.* Baltimore: Johns Hopkins University Press, 1996.

Boy Scouts of America. *Adventuring for Senior Scouts.* New York: Boy Scouts of America, 1938–1942 editions.

Brinkley, David. *Washington Goes to War.* New York: Knopf, 1988.

Brooks, David. "The Organization Kid." *The Atlantic Monthly* 287, no. 4 (April 2001).

Burroughs, William S. *Naked Lunch.* New York: Doubleday, 1992.

Butts, R. Freeman, and Lawrence A. Cremin. *A History of Education in American Culture.* New York: Holt, Rinehart and Winston, 1953.

Carnes, Patrick. *Out of the Shadows: Understanding Sexual Addiction.* Minneapolis, Minn.: CompCare Publishers, 1983.

Chauncey, George. *Gay New York: Gender, Urban Culture and the Making of the Gay Male World, 1890–1940.* New York: Harper, Collins, 1994.

Church, Fermor S., and Peggy Pond Church. *When Los Alamos Was a Ranch School.* 2d ed. Los Alamos, N.Mex.: Los Alamos Historical Society, 1998.

Church, Peggy Pond. *The House at Otowi Bridge: The Story of Edith Warner and Los Alamos.* Albuquerque: University of New Mexico Press, 1959.

———. *Ultimatum for Man.* Stanford, Calif.: The Greenwood Press, 1946.

Cone, Thomas E. Jr. *History of American Pediatrics.* Boston: Little, Brown, 1979.

Cremin, Lawrence A. *The Transformation of the School: Progressivism in American Education, 1876–1957.* New York: Random House, 1961.

Curtis, Fayette Samuel. Original translation of Gaspar Perez de Villagrá, *Historia de la Nueva México, 1610.* Annotated and updated by Miguel Encinias, Alfred Rodríguez, and Joseph P. Sanchez. Albuquerque: University of New Mexico Press, 1992.

———. "The Influence of Weapons on New Mexico History," *New Mexico Historical Review* 1, no. 3 (July, 1926).

———. "Spanish Arms and Armor in the Southwest," *New Mexico Historical Review* 2, no. 2 (April, 1927).

deBuys, William. *Enchantment and Exploitation: The Life and Hard Times of a New Mexico Mountain Range.* Albuquerque: University of New Mexico Press, 1985.

———. "Los Alamos Fire Offers a Lesson in Humility," *High Country News* 32, no. 13 (July 3, 2000).

Dolan, Jay P. *The Immigrant Church: New York's Irish and German Catholics, 1815–1865.* Baltimore: Johns Hopkins Press, 1988.

Dudley, John H. "Ranch School to Secret City." In *Reminiscences of Los Alamos, 1943–45.* By Lawrence Badash et al. Dordrecht, Holland: D. Reidel, 1980.

Ebright, Malcolm. *Land Grants and Lawsuits in Northern New Mexico.* Albuquerque: University of New Mexico Press, 1994.

Ellinwood, Sybil. "East Meets West in the Field of Education." *The Journal of Arizona History* 15, no. 3 (1974).

Fowler, Don D. *A Laboratory for Anthropology: Science and Romanticism in the American Southwest, 1846–1930.* Albuquerque: University of New Mexico Press, 2000.

Goodchild, Peter. *J. Robert Oppenheimer: Shatterer of Worlds.* Boston: Houghton Mifflin, 1981.

Graham, Patricia Albjerg. *Progressive Education: From Arcady to Academe.* New York: Teachers College Press, Columbia University, 1967.

Greenfield, Myrtle. *A History of Public Health in New Mexico.* Albuquerque: University of New Mexico Press, 1962.

Groueff, Stephane. *Manhattan Project: The Untold Story of The Making of the Atomic Bomb.* New York: Bantam Books, 1967.

Groves, Leslie R. *Now It Can Be Told: The Story of the Manhattan Project.* New York: Harpers, 1962.

Hall, Edward T. *An Anthropology of Everyday Life: An Autobiography.* New York: Doubleday, 1992.

Harrison, Laura Soulliere. *Architecture in the Parks: National Historic Landmark Theme Study.* Washington, D.C.: U.S. Government Printing Office, November 1986.

Hein, David. "The High Church Origins of the American Boarding School." *Journal of Ecclesiastical History* 42 (October 1991).

Hewlett, Richard G., and Jack M. Holl. *Atoms for Peace and War, 1953–1961.* Berkeley: University of California Press, 1989.

Horne, Alistair. *A Bundle from Britain.* London: Macmillan, 1993.

Johnson, William Templeton. "Where Lessons Come from Real Things." *The California Outlook: A Progressive Weekly* 17, no. 19 (November 7, 1914).

Jones, Vincent C. *Manhattan: The Army and the Atomic Bomb.* In the series *United States Army in World War II.* Washington, D.C.: Center for Military History, 1985.

Kaplan, Fred. *Gore Vidal: A Biography.* New York: Doubleday, 1999.

Kolowrat, Ernest. *Hotchkiss: A Chronicle of an American School.* New York: New Amsterdam Books, 1992.

Lemann, Nicholas. *The Big Test: The Secret History of the American Meritocracy.* New York: Farrar, Straus and Giroux, 1999.

Lichtman, Ethel Mintzer. *The Francis Parker School Heritage.* San Diego: Francis W. Parker School, 1985.

Lloyd, Susan McIntosh. *The Putney School, A Progressive Experiment.* New Haven, Conn.: Yale University Press, 1987.

Macleod, David I. "Act Your Age: Boyhood, Adolescence and the Rise of the Boy Scouts of America." *Journal of Social History* 16, no. 2 (winter 1982).

———. *Building Character in the American Boy: The Boy Scouts, YMCA, and Their Forerunners, 1870–1920.* Madison: University of Wisconsin Press, 1983.

Makepeace, LeRoy McKim. *Sherman Thacher and His School.* New Haven, Conn.: Yale University Press, 1941.

Martin, Craig. *Los Alamos Trails: Hiking, Biking and Cross-Country Skiing.* Los Alamos, N.Mex.: All Seasons Publishing, 1999.

Mason, Katrina A. *Children of Los Alamos: An Oral History Of the Town Where the Atomic Age Began.* New York: Twayne Publishers, 1995.

McCleod, Hugh. "Catholicism and the New York Irish." In Jim Obelkevich et al., *Disciplines of Faith: Studies in Religion, Politics and Patriarchy.* London: Routledge and Kegan Paul, 1987.

McCullough, David. *Mornings on Horseback.* New York: Simon and Schuster, 1981.

McLachlan, James. *American Boarding Schools: A Historical Study.* New York: Charles Scribner's Sons, 1970.

McPhee, John. *The Headmaster: Frank L. Boyden of Deerfield.* New York: Farrar, Straus and Giroux, 1966.

Morgan, Ted. *Literary Outlaw: The Life and Times of William S. Burroughs.* New York: Henry Holt and Company, 1988.

Murray, W. D. *The History of the Boy Scouts of America.* New York: The Boy Scouts of America, 1937.

Nash, Gerald D. *The American West in the Twentieth Century.* Albuquerque: University of New Mexico Press, 1977.

Nash, Roderick. *Wilderness and the American Mind.* 3d ed. New Haven, Conn.: Yale University Press, 1982.

Newell, L. Jackson. "Deep Springs: Loyalty to a Fault?" In *Maverick Colleges: Ten Notable Experiments in American Education.* Edited by L. Jackson Newell and Katherine C. Reynolds. No date: http://www.gse.utah.edu/EdAdm/Galvin/Maverick.html.

Palevsky, Mary. *Atomic Fragments: A Daughter's Questions.* Berkeley: University of California Press, 2000.

Parry, Martin L. *A Way of Life: The Story of John Burroughs School, 1923–1973.* St. Louis: The John Burroughs School, July 1973.

Pearce, Charles S. *Los Alamos Before the Bomb.* 2d ed. New York: Vantage Press, 1990.

Peterson, Martin E. "William Templeton Johnson, San Diego Architect," *The Journal of San Diego History* 16, no. 4 (fall 1971).

Prescott, Heather Munro. *A Doctor of Their Own: The History of Adolescent Medicine.* Cambridge, Mass.: Harvard University Press, 1998.

Rehberger, George F., ed. *Lippincott's Quick Reference Book for Medicine and Surgery.* 2d ed. Philadelphia: J. B. Lippincott Company, 1921.

Rhodes, Richard. *The Making of the Atomic Bomb.* New York: Simon and Schuster, 1986.

Roberts, Paul H. *Hoof Prints on Forest Ranges: The Early Years of the National Forest Range Administration.* San Antonio, Tex.: The Naylor Company, 1963.

Rosenthal, Michael. *The Character Factory: Baden-Powell and the Origins of the Boy Scout Movement.* New York: Pantheon Books, 1986.

Rothman, Hal K. *On Rims and Ridges: The Los Alamos Area since 1880.* Lincoln: University of Nebraska Press, 1992.

Russell, Jan Jarboe. *Lady Bird: A Biography of Mrs. Johnson.* New York: Scribner, 1999.

Sargent, Porter E. *A Handbook of American Private Schools: An Annual Survey.* Boston: Porter Sargent, 1916 and following.

Schweber, S. S. *In the Shadow of the Bomb: Bethe, Oppenheimer, and the Moral Responsibility of the Scientist.* Princeton, N.J.: Princeton University Press, 2000.

Seidel, Robert W. *Los Alamos and the Development of the Atomic Bomb.* Los Alamos, N.Mex.: Otowi Crossing Press, 1995.

Sommers, Christina Hoff. "The War against Boys." *The Atlantic Monthly* (May 2000).

Spidle, Jake W., Jr. *Doctors of Medicine in New Mexico: A History of Health and Medical Practice, 1886–1986.* Albuquerque: University of New Mexico Press, 1986.

Starr, Paul. *The Social Transformation of American Medicine.* New York: Basic Books, 1982.

Tucker, Edwin A., and George Fitzpatrick. *Men Who Matched the Mountains: The Forest Service in the Southwest.* Washington, D.C.: USDA Forest Service Southwestern Region, 1971.

Usner, Don J. *Sabino's Map: Life in Chimayó's Old Plaza.* Albuquerque: University of New Mexico Press, 1995.

Vidal, Gore. *Palimpsest: A Memoir.* New York: Penguin Books, 1996.

Wertenbaker, Lael Tucker. *The Hotchkiss School: A Portrait.* Lakeville, Conn.: The Hotchkiss School, 1966.

Wilson, Chris. *The Myth of Santa Fe: Creating a Modern Regional Tradition.* Albuquerque: University of New Mexico Press, 1997.

Index

finances, gifts to LARS from students' parents, 38, 41, 45, 60, 97, 113; LAR Camp, 146–47; LARS, 41–45, 95–97, 114–16, 156, 164. *See also* Fuller, Edward P.; Fuller, Philo Carroll; Los Alamos Foundation

fires, 39, 198, 205, 216, 254, 257; fire safety, 39, 103, 216

foremen, 28, 37, 199–200

Forest Service, U.S., 18–19, 22–24, 27, 41, 58, 130, 159, 199, 219–21, 251, 253; expectation federal government would return land after World War II, 196; forest fires, 254–55, 257

Francis W. Parker School, San Diego, 16, 29, 128. *See also* Johnson, Clara; Johnson, William Templeton

French, Robert H., *75*, 264

Frye, Evelyn C., 228

Fuller, Edward P., 18, 58, *74*, 86, 96, 143

Fuller Lodge, *G23*, *G25*, 39, *58*, 111–12, *112*, 214, 219–20, 252

Fuller, Philo Carroll, 18

gardens, vegetable and flower, 182, *182*, 201, 210

Garza, Alejandro, *208*

Geehern, Richard J., 265

Gilbert and Sullivan operettas, 62, 87, 219

Gilchrist, James M., 93, 147, 242

Gilchrist, Robert, 147

Gilpin, Laura, *75*, 87, *112*

Girl Scouts, Santa Fe, 89, 132

Gomez, Marcos, 195

Gonzales, Alejandro, 200

Gonzales, Amador, *G31*, 37, 186, 207

Gonzales, Benceslado (Bences), *G15*; closing of LARS, 192; LAR Camp, 129, 150; LAR Camp cook, *G31*, 139–40, 179–80; LARS employee, 175–79; Manhattan Project, 166, 193, 256; public service and politics, 178; recruitment of Hispanic employees, 176–77, 180–82; relationship with Cecil Wirth's family, 231; relationships with students and campers, 37, 181; Trading Post, 200

Gonzales, Ernestina Romero, 176, 189

Gonzales, Fermin, 192, 200

Gonzales, Isabel, 200

Gonzales, Jose, 200

Gonzales, Josie, *188*, 191, 193, 200

Gonzales, Patricio, 200

Gonzales, Pedro, 191, 193, 200

Gonzales, Ray, 166, 173, 176, *185*, 186–87, 189–90, 192–93, 200

Gonzales, Severo, 166, 173, 176, 178, *185*, 186–87, 190, 192, 193, 200, *208*

graduation, awards, 94; ceremony, 94; requirements, 62, 64, 94–95

Gray, David, 14

Gray, Paul, 14

Groton School, 119–20, 122–23, 169–70

Groves, Leslie, General, 157, 160, 253

guns, 58; gun safety, 104

Hall, Edward T., *xiv*, 109

Hall, Fred, *136*

Harman, John M., Colonel, 158

Haskell, Herman, *46*

Heald, George E., 265

health, 8, 24, 29–31, 48–52, 113. *See also* asthma; meals, tuberculosis

Highline Trail (Skyline Trail), *G28*, 143, 151

Hinton, Carmelita, 119, 169–70. *See also* Putney School

Hispanic culture, 173, 176, 230–31, 251; attachment to land, 196–97; Christmas customs, 191–92; discipline of children, 190–91

history class, *105*

Hitchcock, Barbara Singley, 166

Hitchcock, Charles, 166

Hitchcock, Josephine, 166

Hitchcock, Lawrence S., 265, *G8*, *G9*, *72*, *74*, *75*, *112*, *117*; administration of academic program, 99; CIA career after World War II, 166; closing of LARS, 158–59, 161, 164, 251; early life, 113–14; financial aptitude, 97, 99; friendship with George Van Santvoord, Hotchkiss headmaster, 107–8; LAR Camp, 142–43, 145; LARS headmaster, 81, 98, 184, 240, 242; LARS master, 71; leisure activities, 87–88; military service during World War II, 158–59, 162–63, 166, 227, 234; partnership with A. J. Connell, 133; pension, 165; personal style, 114–15; plan for administrative changes at LARS, 115–16; post World War II life, 226; safety, 104; tribute from former students, 259

holidays, 89–90, 213–14

homesteaders, 16, 38, 130, 158–59, 174; expectation federal government would return land after World War II, 196; Hispanic, 173, 176, 182, 195, 196

Hope, Quentin M., 265

Horgan, Hap, 143

horses, 30, 43, 57, 62–63, 128–29, 138, 139, 142, 152, 167, 207, 261–62

Hotchkiss School, 80, 107–8, 121, 170–71

house parties, 89

Hughes, David H., 140, 153, 167, 256

Hughes, Lafayette M., 97, 116

Hunter, Kim, 242

Hunter, Vernon, 242

hunting, 58, *60*, 179, 182, 183; accidents, 75, 103

Hurley, Wilson P., 77

Huron Mountain Club, 11–12, 14

ice hockey, 60

ice-skating, *188*, 213–14, 243

icehouse, 205

Jemez Mountains, 6, 8, 27, 41, 63, *128*. *See also* LAR Camp

Jenney, Charles, Jr., 154, 265

Johnson, Clara, 16

Johnson, William Templeton, 16

Joy, Henry, 13–15

outdoor program, 11, 35, 56–68, 170
Outwater, Eric, 184

pack trips, *G26*, 43, 130, *138*, 140–41, 166, 179, 187, 232, 242; routes, 142–43, 151–52; training boys to pack mules, 139. *See also* LAR Camp
Page, Warren K., 266
Pajarito Club, *15*; management, 14–17
Pajarito Land Corporation, 14
Pajarito Plateau, *G2*, 5, 7–8, 10, 68, 92
Parkhurst, T. Harmon, *G1*, *G23*, *G24*, *42*, *72*, 86, *106*, *136*, *138*, 141, *144*, *149*
patrols, 45, 63–65. *See also* Boy Scouts
patrón system, 175–81. *See also* Connell, Albert J., *patrón* to the Hispanic community
Peabody, Endicott. *See* Groton School
Pearce, Charles S., *G18*
Pecos Region. *See* Sangre de Cristo Mountains
Peery, Okel C., 266
Pelly, Lancellot Ingelsby, 3, *9*, 28, *46*, 81
pensions, faculty and staff, 165, 194
Pepper, Esilda B., 85, 164, 166, 248, 267
Pepper, Jerry R., 165, 166, 193, *247*, 248, 256, 267
Petrizzi, Ralph, 267
Phelps Dodge Corporation, 227, 239
photographers, 86–87
physical fitness, 48
Pond, Allen, 31–32
Pond, Ashley, III, 29, 45, *46*, 78
Pond, Ashley, Jr., *G4*, 11–18, *15*, 30–33, 88, 96, 170; health-seeker, 12; LARS, Founder, 5, 11
Pond, Ashley, Sr., 11, 13
Pond, Hazel Hallet, 12, 84
Pond, Margaret. *See also* Church, Peggy Pond
power plant, 201, 216
Progressive education, 25, 29, 33, 53, 68, 78, 115, 119–20, 168, 170; attitude of cooperation and service, 54. *See also* LARS; Progressive values; Putney School
Progressive philosophy, 22
Pueblo Indian culture, 173, 251; dances, 192, 195
Putney School, *ix*, 115, 120, 163. *See also* Hinton, Carmelita

racial discrimination, 186–87
railroads, 37, 40, 93, 175, 211, 230; tourism, 9–10
Ramon Land and Lumber Company, 13
Ramon Vigil Grant, 13, 41
ranch schools, 30, 48, 50, 100
ranch work, 36, 57, 142
Rancho Valmora, 170
Ranger, Genevieve, 84
ranking within LARS, 64–65, 133–34, 150–51. *See also* patrols; Boy Scouts
Raskob, Ben, 216
recreation, 46–48, 61–62, 86, 97–98; facilities, 40, *188*
recreation for faculty and staff, 86–90; alcohol, 88; dances, 87; sports, 91; spring break school trips, 89–90; trips to Santa Fe, 87–89
Reed, John S., 104, 109, 256

Regnery, William, *60*
Rennehan, Neal, 143
Reynolds, Francis, 86
Rice, Jay G., 56, 109
Ripley, Charles P., *G18*, *G27*, *G28*, *G29*, 140, *257*, 257
Rito de los Indios, 141, *144*, 151
roads, *G2*, *G3*, 38, 131, 175, 230, 254; tourism, 9–10
Rogers, Bernard J., 267
Rose, William, Jr., 5, *9*, 29, *46*, 94, 140, 143
Rousseau, Edna, *G18*, 37, 86, 186, 193, 206–9, 215
Rousseau, Francis, *G24*, 103, 165
Rousseau, Joan, 165, 190
Rousseau, L. A. (Fred), *G18*, 153, 160, 163, 165, 193, 206, 243; LARS business manager, 86, 97
Ruhl, Henry W., 75, 103, 267
Ruhl, Virginia D., 84
ruins, 174, 203
Rutledge, Thomas G., *90*

safety. *See* Connell, Albert J., safety record
San Ildefonso Pueblo, 94, 131, 173, 192, 196, 203, 251, 255
sanatoriums, 8, 24, 30, 31, 113. *See also* health
Sandia National Laboratories, 165, 207, 211, 256
Sangre De Cristo Mountains, 6, 132, 150, 155, 163, 227, *G1*
Santa Fe, 8, 89, 132, 193, 200, 255–56
Santa Fe Fiesta, *G16*, 89
Santa Fe Inn, 162–63
Santa Fe Opera, 257. *See also* Crosby, John O.
Santa Fe Preparatory School, 163
Santa Fe School for Girls, 89
scholarships, 45
Scudder, Rogers V., 76, 110, 122, 140, 154, 267
secretaries, 86
secure environment for children, 174, 209
Sellars, Mark A., 268
sense of place, 81, 154, 173–74, 176, 181, 195–97, 219, 226, 228, 250–58
Seton, Ernest Thompson, 25, 67
Shain, Charles E., *75*, 268
sheep, grazing, 174, 254
Sheffield, Lucille, 85
Sheffield, Wallace, 85
Silver City, N.M., 21, 24
skiing, 60–61, *118*, 118–19, 163
Slaughter, E. Dick, Jr., 76, 268
Spanish language, 189
Spanish terms glossary, 197
sports, *G1*, 47, 59, 59–61, 187, 190, 209
Spruce Cottage, 32, 39, 91, 96–97, 112, 234–35
St. John's College, 163, 165
St. Paul's School, 12
Steege, Oscar A., 268, *G8*, 75, 87, *105*; family life, 194; LAR Camp, 142, 154; LARS master, 76, 110, 237, 240, 254, 263; military service during World War II, 223; post World War II life, 166, 256; relationship with Cecil Wirth's family, 243; Waring School, 161
Stegmaier, John, 268